We

BOOK 1

Walter Anderson and Elizabeth McGuire

XULON PRESS

Xulon Press
2301 Lucien Way #415
Maitland, FL 32751
407.339.4217
www.xulonpress.com

Unless otherwise indicated, Scripture quotations taken from the King James Version (KJV)–*public domain.*

ISBN-13: 978-1-6628-2054-0

Prologue

We, are, ready.

We left Earth. The ones we left behind called it the Rapture. We call it Evolving. We are many. We are waiting. We are ready.

It is as if a dark stage awaits you while you wait in the wings. Cutting through the darkness center stage, one lone spot light beckons from directly overhead. On your left is a vastness filled with a murmuring audience that cannot be seen through the dark. Though apprehensive, you will yourself to move across the dark stage and step into the light.

The noise dies down to a silence so complete you can hear your own heartbeat. The light is warm and comforting. Looking down at yourself you raise your arms out at your side basking in the peaceful bliss of the light.

Then, like magic, the things that were a part of you come streaming out like the radiant beams of a star going nova. Experiences that shaped who you are push back against the darkness as the spotlight dims. There is a collective gasp from the audience and the music begins, soft at first, barely discernable; raising in volume. From nothing TO A FORCE all around you; and you realize the music has always been there; you just couldn't, wouldn't hear it. It is beauty incarnate, it is you. It is life

Welcome home. We are ready.

By Walter G. Anderson

Chapter One

April 21, 2003

Dear Bud Plant people;

I'm a Sacramento and Fair Oaks, California raised waste of human life living in a Texas prison. I was brought before Judge "Buh-Buh good ole boy" and sentenced to 25 years for being a tree hugging hippy from California, something to do with blasphemy to a Stonewall Jackson statue sitting in the town square of "Armpit Texas". Actually I was convicted of attempted murder against an individual trying to molest my nine year old daughter (true story, but not mine). Lack of funds for a shyster landed me in this Texas prison hoping and praying for a little action in the Appeal Courts.

Anyways I got a hold of your catalogue (or a piece of it) and I'm writing in hopes of convincing you to throw an old (41 year-old) fan of fantasy art an act of random kindness. I am truly in a financial bind here and probably will never be able to scrape up enough money to buy the books I have drooled over in your catalogue; books from Frank Frazetta. When I was younger I was, and still am, a fan of his art. I couldn't ask anyone I know for funds to pay for this one fancy I have. I lost my family because of this, what they say I did make me feel as useful as tits on a bull. Texas doesn't pay their convicts to work and I ain't pretty enough to get a hustle going. In short...got any books on fantasy art or old calendars that you can't sell due to damage? Anything the dog might have peed on? I don't know what I can say to convince you of my utter hopefulness at a little human kindness. Even if you send me some art books or one book or a calendar from 1989, I can go away in these pictures and escape the sorry hand life's tossed me. Help me out and I'll pray to God you all do well and live to be a million years old! I'll sing you a song; tell ya a joke or a story. I won't crap on the floor anymore. I'll quit cussing, spitting and putting my elbows on the table. I'll create a shrine of your address. I swear I'll never tell and never ask again unless I sell my kidneys. Geez, what can I say, PALEEZE, for the love of God! Did I mention I have cancer? Yup I'm gonna die! What do ya say? Today's my birthday. My dog died! Well that's all I got. I hope to hear from you.

Sincerely,
Walt

PS: Anything sent can come straight to the address on the envelope. Thanx. Ya know I never got no Christmas present. Did I mention we was homeboys? We went to different schools together. At the same time!

****

April 22, 2003

Dear Bud Plant;

Yesterday I wrote and sent a letter in hopes of appealing to your sense of human kindness (charity) and kicking me some fantasy art books that maybe aren't marketable due to rat damage. Not that ya'll have rats. Hell I got cockroaches in my cell…well one. He's pretty big, his name is Spike. Spikes in for child support neglect. He's got 94,396 kids, so far.

I've got some ideas. Maybe we can do some tradin? I've got some old comic books that are in great shape. I have no idea what they're worth but I'd be willing to trade them for some Frank Frazetta art books or a book? I've got a couple of Batman's from 1982 #515 and #516 in great shape. I've got one July 1987 Silver Surfer, where he finally breaks through the Earth's atmosphere and with the help of the fantastic four he goes and makes amends with Galactus, also in perfect condition. A 1977 #66 Feb. Spiderman and a 1982 Spiderman w/X-Men the Punisher, first issue of an unlimited series vol #11 July 1987. Geese what do ya want? I have no idea what they're worth, but the guy what gave them to me took really good care of them and so have I. Wanna trade? Spike says I'm crazy for doing it but I want some stuff like Frank F., Mike Hoffman or Roca stuff looks good too. I have a friend who will trade a 1978 Fantastic Art of Boris Vallejo. Boris's stuff looks too posed, whereas ole Frankaroonie puts in drama and action. Jeeze who am I telling? You've got all the good stuff.

I work on a 200 foot power antennae cleaning off the bird doo so the wardens wife can watch "As the Stomach Turns" everyday. Bird-doo fades the reception. Anyways since I got hit by lightening I can understand Spike. I've got a deal to sell my internal organs but until I do that I'm broker than Evil Kneivel's spine. But I most certainly will trade these comic books. Did I mention I'm probably dying? Yeah I got gohna-herpa-syphil-aids. That's a little bit of everything. The good part is I can only get it once. I should be dead now but Spike's been to medical school so he helps me out. But Spike also lies a lot.

Well Bud Plant, until I sell my kidneys I'm racking my pea-brain trying to think of a way… hell I can't even afford lines on my paper. The State of Texas foots the bill for three letters a week. In closing, let me condense this letter to some selfless groveling. Did I mention I'd convert to any religion, even though I'm already a Christian? I'd even eat a bug, (not Spike tho.) swear to an alibi in court or wrestle a wino for his bottle. Can I please talk you into sending me some art? I really will swap the afore mentioned comic books. I'll tell people I know ya and vouch for your character. I'm not sure if that's good or bad. I'll root for your favorite football team. What can I say? Have you got an ugly sister? I'll marry her! Swear to Buddha.

Thanx a lot for your time and considering my request. If you want the comics, my kidneys, spleen, liver, one eye or the other or any gut ya might need, I'm in the mood to nagociate (sorry, spelling).

Sincerely,
Walter G. Anderson

PS: PALEEZE! In case you're interested, I'm Viking stock. I was born in Oakland though don't hold that against me. Raised in Sacramento though don't hold that against me as well. What's your favorite bank? Mine too! Wow, how about baseball? Me too! What a coincidence, we might be related. Did I mention I'll never ask again and never tell anyone except the God of your choice? *(Note: It was this letter I replied to and signed my name.)*

****

May 10, 2003

Dear Bud Plant and Liz;

Yesterday was a very eventful day for yours truly. First I got your catalogue. Thank you very much! Spike got to show me who Brom is and a couple of others. Today I got your note. I knew you didn't have any free Frazetta books; I didn't take any business courses when I was in school, but giving away your product isn't good business.

I was trying to appeal to y'alls (Texan for "you all's). I sense your thinking, "Gee this guy's pathetic." As I've stated before, I have no income or way to afford your products. *(Note: In this space of the letter he drew a picture of a smiley face.)*

First I'm sitting in my cell drooling over your awesome catalogue when Spike brings home his new girlfriend. I'm kicked back, book propped upon my chest, when I feel Spike climb up on my belly with his new friend. I lift up the catalogue to see her. She's got eight hairy legs and has eight eyes. Yup, she's a spider. Now I'm 6' 4", 240 pound big ole Viking type macho-man who'd rather poke my eye out than deal with spiders. So I rolled off my bunk and before my feet hit the floor they were doing the track-star thing. Only trouble with that is my cell is 5' x 9', not too much room to run, but I did. I woke up in the infirmary with the prison doc preparing to amputate my leg. "Hey" I said as he checked my toe tag. I high-tailed it out of there. I try not to go to sick call. The doctors name is...umm, Kevorkian or something like that. Any way it got me out of work.

Then at mail call they gave me your note Liz. At first I thought it was a mistake because no one writes me. I recognize your hand writing from the reply you sent before. Looking at your catalogue I see Luis Royo in here. I'm 41 years old and other than Olivia, Boris and Frazetta I'm ignorant. *(Note: Yeah, one of his nicknames is "Idiot Savant")* I had no idea there was that many fantasy artists on the circuit. I studied art in American River College for a couple of semesters. But it was artists of old, Paul Rubins, Rembrandt, Michelangelo etc, etc. I know what you're thinking;

I should have studied spelling huh? Well some are good at math and some are good at spelling. I can tell ya what one and one is...eleven! Anyways, if you're offering to turn me on to Luis Royo, I'm gonna be as grateful as if you'd, well given me an art book.

I used to have money but the last of it went to an appellate lawyer. I was still optimistic that I'd get some action. They really did give me 25 years and as rotten as everything is, I have faith I'm gonna rise above this. They say, "All men fall. The great ones get back up." I look at the bright side if I'm able. Spike says, "Hi".

Look, I truly appreciate your attention and truly believe in Karma. Even though I'm a Christian too, I'm hoping God grades on the curve. I've never bullied anyone. I swerve to miss squirrels when I drive; I pick up hitch hikers, help old people and enjoy doing it. I even gave a wayward cockroach a home when no one else would. So maybe I got good karma saved. I'm thinking being y'alls stepchild in this matter even just once will get you some good karma too. Wait a minute, now the flip side of that is, I may draw some very grateful pictures and write you some crazy humorous letters now and again just to hopefully brighten someone's day. I'm like that if you haven't noticed. No strings attached and if I sell my guts, I'm gonna spend it with y'all. I've already got you a cash paying client. His name is Fred Berry and he lives three cells down. You should be processing his order soon. Thanx again home-boys and home-gals. Anybody got any requests for drawings? I'll try anything.

Sincerely,
Walter Anderson

PS: Know what a Yellow Rose means? Me neither. It's amazing how I can draw like that and write this sloppy huh? Well some have it and then there are the rest of us. *(Note: He drew a beautiful yellow rose for us, which I still have)*

****

May 11, 2003

Dear Bud Plant/Liz;

Today is Mothers Day and I was sitting here thinking to myself. I said, "Self", sometimes I ignore me. I may be crazy. I don't know. I ain't gonna see Dr. Kevorkian to find out. Anyways I said, "Self?" "What?" I said to myself, "why not show your good manners and culture by doing that LeBrun drawing for Liz". "Why?" said I, "well for one, she was insane enough to actually sign her name on the note she wrote to me and for another, I didn't see any old artists in that catalogue except Norman Rockwell who's awesome too". Anyways, someone got left out for Mothers Day, if so; they can have this picture if Liz don't want it. *(Note: I've kept most if not all his pictures)*

It's from a painting done in 1789 by a woman named Elizabeth-Louise Vigee-Lebrun, she was also a Liz. My pen just blew a gasket on her left eye and I wanted to throw a fit. I was told by an art instructor once that I "could be an artist if I only apply myself, BUT I'm my own worse critic." I'm half color blind, cool huh? I come to a flaw in the picture I'm doing and lose interest, hence the left eye. Well anyways, Happy Mothers Day. This concludes my stamp supply for this week.

Yeah I know life's rough. Speaking of rough, I was working on the 200 ft tower scraping away when a Texas sized gust of wind caught me. Y'all might have heard we've been having tornado problems lately, anyways, off the tower I went. On my way to the ground I thought to myself, "self", well I didn't get an answer cause myself was busy filling my pants with the very substance I was supposed to be scraping off the tower. Just then I crashed through the roof of the house below back first. I didn't wanna look, can you blame me? And into the attic I went. Though I noticed a full length mirror and figured if I was going to die I'd check my hair. It was a little wind blown but fine. Anyway, I continued on thru the attic floor and into the living room below. I came to a full stop atop the now flattened coffee table beside the couch and the warden's hefty wife. I'm not a man who appreciates Anorexia or model-thin women. I'm a big guy, not fat. Well I got one love handle, but I have worked my life in construction and concrete so I'm healthy and like healthy women, "Rubenesk" not muscular, never mind. There I was with my left leg broke, three broke ribs on my left side, a broke collar bone and a broke left arm. The wind knocked from my lungs and she says, "You're not on a break convict, git out of here!", and I got!

So after arguing with Dr. Kevorkian about needing amputation he gave me two chewable children's aspirin and put me in a cast from the neck to the ankle, mostly on the left side. Well the first thing Spike did was have his new girlfriend, Sherry Spider, spin a hammock from my left arm cast to my rib cast. She is now stretched out there snoozing. Man I hope those two don't reproduce. I fell asleep at noon today and woke up with my eyes webbed shut. I hate when she does that. I thought I was blind…again.

Well listen y'all, I'm gonna sign off. I hope someone got a lift out of this letter and picture. If any of this gets old let me know and I'll pester someone else, okay?

In closing, let me say one of my fondest memories came from a Blue Grass Festival in Grass Valley. Do they still do that up there? My favorite saying reserved for those deserving, "May you live as long as you want and never want as long as you live".

Peace,
Walt

PS: Please don't panic, I truly am harmless and mean it about when you've had enough, just say so. *(Note: I'm so very glad I saw / read more of what he said in his letters.)*

PPS: Spike said to ask you if you can flit open any book that published Frank Frazetta's art books or open any book of Frazetta's and see who published it and let me know so I can…he won't say, I'll get back to ya, bye.

****

June 29, 2003

Hey Liz;

Did ja miss me? Its 347 degrees down here in the South. Humidity is up 226, so the heat index is about 573. We're all dead down here. Boy it feels like I'm dying. I hung myself by my foot. I ain't crazy or nothing! Because of the heat, I haven't seen Spike in a week. I think I know where he is but I ain't getting involved in his domestic disputes. Besides Sherry keeps the mosquitoes down. I thought the mosquitoes were little humming birds at first. But then one started drilling on my neck. They say everything's big in Texas, well maybe...

So Liz, yer a Limey huh? Well that's great! I wanna say, "Blimey" but I'm not sure it's appropriate. We have a saying in the U.S., me being a member of the male chauvinist pig union; I have to put it in code, "R-U-4-B-U-N-8." Now that ought to get your knickers in a twist? Turn the page for blatant act of groveling.

Thank you so much for the Frank Cho. I had never read or seen any of his stuff before. I have a friend, Fred Berry, your number one customer right now, who reminds me of the pig in that comic strip. Well he and Spike are two of a kind.

I think I'm shrinking. Umm let me rephrase that. I'm getting smaller...tee hee. This heat is melting away myself. I'm down from 250 lbs to 248 lbs and from 6'4" to 5' 16".

Hey, one of your homeboys is on the radio, Ringo Starr. What part of England are ye from? I went to Germany in 1972, that's the extent of my European travels.

Learn me Liz. Did y'all get the pictures I drew for ya'll? Want me to draw ya some more? I'm just learning ya know. I'm sending another piece of paper since all you have is that small yeller sticky stuff. *(Note: Up until then I was sending notes back on large Post-It notes)* I was pleasantly surprised to get the Cho and your...ummm note. I truly am harmless and if nothing else, entertaining.

My lawyer said I should go back to court this year.

Did I ever tell you why I learned to draw? I did? Okay then let me tell you a story to brighten your day before I go.

Once upon a time, all stories should begin like that, there was a dog named Hank, stop me if you've heard this before. His master liked to hunt and one day took him to Africa on safari. Well Hank was a real smart dog but he got lost and became worried. He looked around and saw elephants, giraffes, monkeys and a snake bigger than any he'd seen on his usual hunting trips.

Just then Hank saw a leopard and freaked out because he knew that the leopard had seen him too and there was no where to hide. "What am I gonna do, what am I gonna do?" Hank thought in panic. Just then he got an idea. He saw a pile of bone's and squatted down with his back to the approaching cat. Hank started chewing on the bones. With the leopard getting ready for a dog sandwich and preparing to pounce, Hank poked his head up and says, "Boy that sure was a good leopard, I wish I had another to eat". The leopard snuck away, and glad to do so.

Well, a monkey in the nearby tree saw the whole thing and caught up with the leopard. "What are you doing you stupid leopard?" He said to the big cat and then told the leopard how the dog tricked him. "Well!" says the leopard, "we'll see about that! Get on!" he tells the monkey and stomps off to get the dog. Well Hank see's them coming and figures out what happened. "Oh damn, what am I going to do now?" he says, looking around and seeing no escape. He gets another idea and squats down over the bones again as the angry leopard and monkey approach. Hank poked his head up again and says, "Where's that stupid monkey? I sent him after another leopard an hour ago!"...needless to say the leopard had monkey that day.

Well Liz, thanks again for thinking about me, I truly appreciate it. You let me know about the drawings and if you need more paper. Is that a hint or what? Tell me about England. What's a Piccadilly? I truly hope Blimey ain't an insult I don't know about...Thanx again.

Peace, hope to hear from ya,

Walt.

PS: This letter is written by Walter Anderson, directed by Walter Anderson, produced by Walter Anderson and edited by God. Ya know what they say in Russia? Bye ski!

****

October 16, 2003

Dear Liz and Co;

Oh thank you, thank you, and thank you for writing! I thought you'd forgotten me and got yourself hooked up to another fallen Angel. (That's me, the fallen Angel part)

Spike was mad. His spider girlfriend, Sherry, ran off so he naturally tried convincing me I was as worthless as he was. He has the morals of a...well, a cockroach! When he gets back from Mexico, (he's visiting relatives), I'm gonna tell him so.

Anyway these two lil comic books are cool as crud! I've never heard of either one of em but now I own proof they exist. So how have you been? Might I say that the ladies, all of em, in Bud Plant's customer service area are the prettiest bunch-o-ladies I have ever seen, and I ain't even seen ya! If I were Nigel Rathbone I'd say you were rather smashing!

I wrote to a law professor. He sent me a dictionary. As soon as I find out where to stick the batteries I'll start her up and spell something for ya. That always impresses the ladies. That and a good head-o-hair. I got hair! Even though the Texans won't let me grow it. Unfortunately for who knows why. I don't cultivate the stuff on my chest. No hairy chest. I've been writing in my print hand lately and the cursive stuff, pretty as it is, ain't working like I want it to. Can you tell? Well it's awfully nice of you not to mention it. That's a plus for you not being vocal in the written relationship. I can never complain about you complaining.

Anyways, since Spike left for the winter I've been writing legal folks and it turns out the State of Texas is not allowed to do the things they did to prosecute me in my trial…go figure! So there's a pretty good chance I may get some real action at getting out. Cool huh? Well I thought so too. Also, there's a rumor that y'all are gonna stock a soft bound addition of Icon by ole Frankie! I'm gonna pray for a defect, a strategically placed squirt of bird poo, mice chewing a corner, (but having the good taste not to chew more-n-that).

Did I tell you lovely ladies how magnificent you look today? Why Liz, are you losing weight? A photographer for the next swim suit addition of Sports Illustrated could do well to see you ladies, (how am I doing?) I'd ask how a book like that cost, but Larry Hagman backed out of negotiations on my liver. I would sell some pretty choice guts to get an Icon book. Problem is, I got no buyers. And sayyyy...anyone there need a kidney?? What about a goiter? I don't even know what one of those is but I'm sure I got one. I might have two. Wait a minute; let me check my handy-dandy dictionary because I may have two of em but not willing to part with them. Anything external is non-negotiable. I plan to use some of those things. A toe! How about a toe? Well get back to me on that.

I was going to draw ya something but no one there ever said they even liked my meager drawing ability. How's that for a pathetic plea for attention? You know there are no strings attached. If you want, maybe a rose or a unicorn or a fly, I would draw ya one or two just for the asking. No strings other than the writing me and saying, "yo Einstein, how about drawing me a finger or something" I don't get much mail, so it would be a surprise.

I wonder why this Dawn artist only does half her mug. Ya know Liz; you never explained what a Piccadilly was. Is it anything like a Jabberwocky? Why are those black hats on the Royal Guards so big? What do they have under there? Do you speak with an accent? I do, well I can, wanna hear it? Okay, which one? What's the difference between Rugby and Football? (American football). Cool how an English Bobby ain't got any Sue on his name like over here in Texas. A lot of these Texicans have two first names, Bobby Sue, Billy Bob, Thelma Lou etc. Aren't you glad you weren't named Thelma Lou? Man it could have been bad for me too, Clem or Cletus Roy Bob Clanton, how about that? Not many English names like that huh?

This morning I woke up in prison. Tonight I sleep between the pages of these lil illustrated magazines you sent me and I am truly grateful. Your random act of kindness makes me a little skeptical of mankind and I also am grateful for that. Thank you for being a part of that. I hope to hear from you again, soon. I'll write again, soon, till then I remain in your debt.

Respectfully,
Walt

PS: "Benevolence," I found a word in my handy dandy dictionary, by for now, me.

November 11, 2003

Dear Liz and Company;

Well howdy ya'll. I was reading a true-account of the Alamo last night and discovered several things. One being the words "holy shit" as uttered by William Travis when he saw all the Mexicans wanting a piece-o-him. That fight was 184 to 5000. Travis had the 184. Travis didn't do too well. Oh well...Santa Anna wasn't very neighborly. I wonder if Santa Anna in Calif. was named after that cockroach.

Speaking of cock roaches, Spike showed up a week ago wearing a sombrero and singing La Bomba with a flea. The flea didn't stay but Spike did. I told him about Sherry taken up residence in the port-side of my locker. Being drunk and all he went over and started yelling at her only to find out it was her exoskeleton. Seems spiders shed their out...well, stuff when they out grow it. Sherry had been gone quite some time. I am such a coward when it comes to spiders, I just left her alone. Spikes getting another tattoo down at Rednecks cell. Something to do with a bowl-o-beans and a '57 Chevy. Nothing like stereotyping.

Anyways I just thought I'd drop you guys a line and see if I got any-o-my new friends there at Bud Plant wanna drawing for Christmas. I was gonna do Thanksgiving only Texas does not serve turkey for Thanksgiving meal. They serve Armadillo meat tacos. It's a toss up on what type of meat it is but we're damn sure it ain't no flying kind of meat or anything to gobble down...that's a pun...oh you got it! Try this one, there once was a man from Nantucket, no wait, that's a limerick...never mind.

I have a Norman Rockwell type drawing on double rag board that's quite impressive that I'd be willing to part with, drawn with this very pen, only stipulation is the first really cool Christmas card that hits my hands gets it. Yup, ya gotta express an interest or I send it to nurse Ratchet at the hospital where Rachel resides. She only writes to give quarterly reports. All attempts at communication outside the techno-crap have been thwarted by Dr Evil himself. Yup, thee Dr Evil.

Anyways I just wanted to keep in touch. Liz, I saw your picture in the catalog. Do you always smile so? Someone said that English women were bland and unresponsive to humor. You don't appear to be anything of the sort. Anyways, you all looked rather sporting I'd say.

Well I'm gonna go for now. I truly hope all is well at Bud Plant and everyone's happy. I try to be and do okay. I don't have a home for a very detailed and nice drawing, anyone wanna see it? No strings attached. Hang it in your office. Tell Mr. Bud Plant Hi and all-o-you in the service department, take care

Respectfully and Sincerely,
Walter

PS: They changed the structure of my return address, check it out! Liz, I have the Norman Rockwell drawing, it's one of my favorites.

****

Thanksgiving Evening 2003

Dear Customer Service Bud Plant;

Well it's a little hard to see today thanks for my ace duce cockroach, Spike. But I wanted to write anyways. Ya see, since my tower accident I've been off work. They removed my body cast a week ago and put me to work in the kitchen for about two days. Now I'm a pretty big man, or was. I worked out all the time and believed if it could be caught I could eat it! In fact, that's how I made it through childhood. There wasn't a stray animal in my neighborhood. Only opportunities for lunch! Okay, so I was trying to eat my weight in groceries when the kitchen captain caught me and fired me.

Yesterday was my first day back on the tower. It seems the last guy was hospitalized due to hypothermia. He saw a little sign I made last year half way up the tower reminding me not to touch the bare metal with my tongue during cold weather. Well being a Texan it took them one day to notice he wasn't in his cell at count time and one more to talk him into pulling his tongue free. It wasn't pretty. But it gave the local media something to do. They covered the story and gave out free stuff to all the ladies. A real event for these parts. Anyway I'm back on the tower. Heck I didn't wanna pluck 500 Armadillos for Thanksgiving any way.

My cell block is about 100 yards down a central hallway with guards placed about every 20 yards to shake down and hassle any suspicious looking convicts. I was strolling down about half way to my "boot leather dinner surprise" and could smell the chow hall when all of a sudden I heard what sounded like a fog horn and a semi truck horn going off two feet from my head. I instinctively started to duck as my eyeballs rattled in their sockets, when I noticed something dark slide down my shoulder and into my pocket. "What the fu..." I started to say, then the hallway suddenly tilted and I heard 200 phones ringing. A knot was developing upon my head. I turned and saw what I thought were three huge women, of the Negro persuasion, all of them bigger than me and drawing back their arms looking at me. "Hey, someone get the phone" I said and then, BAM! I was knocked back against the brick wall of the hallway. "Aunty Em?" I mumbled sliding down the wall only to be yanked up by my shirt front. "A bug?" they yelled in my face, "wha??..." I started to say and then was shaken like a vodka martini and thrown to the floor. "A big ole nasty bug was attacking that inmate!" they yelled, stomping on me. "There it is!" and out of the corner of my eye I saw Spike make a break for the hole in the wall. "AAAAK!" the three large women screamed as I saw in slow motion, them leap up in the air bending their knees, aiming their size 14 or better, Jack boots for my chest. That's when all three women became one, again. I was seeing triple from the head thumping. "Mommy" I said and don't remember anything after that. But I remember telling Spike just before chow he couldn't ride on my shoulder, as he does sometimes in the yard, down the hallway. But he took advantage of my numb shoulder and bad vision in my left eye. He was perched there when the guard in the hallway (kin to Reggie White of the Green Bay Packers) must have freaked out. Spikes a water roach (cockroach) about 3 ½" long. He happened to be wearing his Batman cape I gave him for his birthday and must have looked like something strange to this guard.

Well, I received a write up for assaulting the guard; she broke a nail pounding on the back of my head when I conked out. She claimed it was CPR but my face print is still in the concrete where this happened. Spikes at my friend Redneck's cell until I cool off and get Thanksgiving dinner through a straw...heavy sigh. Other than that things are peachy. I got another chest cast and don't have to climb the tower to knock the bird doo down until it comes off. That's a plus because it's two degrees down here in the South.

Thanks for writing Liz. I'm gonna put a drawing together on paper to go with this letter. I hope you like it. It will be for y'all office board. I got a letter from my appellate lawyer. He sent me his dry cleaning receipt. I'm at a loss. I hope some legal form didn't go to the Chinese Laundromat that needs my signature in x amount of time.

Say did anyone catch the new Matrix movies? That Revolutions and the new one. 11.05. If so are they any good? Well I'll write more when I get your picture done. Keep your fingers crossed for my safety and well being, I need it!

Soooooooo, in starting this I've done two things. I've pushed the level of my abilities and almost guaranteed that it won't accompany this letter. However, shortly after receiving this you will get another letter, all the service dept., with my best work in it and that will be y'all's Christmas card. Maybe Spike will write a little something. How can I stay mad at my lil friend? All he left home with was his Batman cape. He left his favorite t-shirt, which says, "Genius" on it. I don't have the heart to tell him. Anyway, he and Redneck can't stand each other more than two days so...ya'll be good.

Peace,
Walt

****

Chapter Two

January 2004

Dear Liz, Customer Service and Friends;

I would like to share something with ya; maybe, we can both or all get something out of this. I have a G.E.D. education so bare with the spelling and grammar mistakes...heavy sigh!

Rachel

On June 9th 2001 I was arrested for kidnapping a taxi driver in a small Texas town. After two trials I was convicted, illegally, and sentenced to 25 years in a Texas prison. I'm <u>still fighting</u> in the Federal Courts for my release.

In 2003 I was in the Ellis Unit in Huntsville, Texas. I lived on the old death row wing in medium custody; A term that is misleading. It is a maximum security setting but "medium" in the sense that our privileges are limited to four hours a day outside our cell, not counting the field work. The equivalent of a Southern Chain Gang. "Medium custody" is a form of punishment, usually for bad behavior, but in Texas prisons this status can be given just for pissing off the wrong boss.

Friendships develop under adverse conditions, and I had a friend I knew as "Redneck." He lived two cells down from me and we hung out together, worked out together, went to chow together and sometimes played dominoes together. Redneck was my "road dog." Our common ground for becoming friends in the first place was we were both from other states, he from Montana and I was from California. Neither one of us was a fan of the Lone Star Republic. I didn't receive money from the outside world, and there is no job in a Texas prison that pays, so I drew cards and envelopes to get the things I needed. Redneck was a customer. Although with Redneck, I also included a story with his cards.

You see, Redneck had a daughter, Rachel, who lived in a nursing home due to a traumatic event that affected both their lives. Rachel was raped and brutalized at a young age. Her daddy, Redneck, took vengeance upon her attacker and ended up in a Texas prison. Once a week I drew a card and wrote a story that went with it. Redneck would mail it to the nursing home never receiving a reply, but he told me that a nurse there always read the story to Rachel and set the picture I had drawn in a little frame beside her bed.

One day Redneck didn't come out for chow or recreation. When I went by his cell he was curled up under the covers. I didn't say anything to disturb him, as some days are like that in prison. I asked his celli what the deal was but he didn't know anything. The next day was the same thing only this time his celli said that his daughter, Rachel, had passed away. As far as I knew, Redneck had no other people on the outside that he could draw comfort from in his hour of need. I had no idea how to console a friend with a loss of this magnitude, but he was my friend and I cared, so I wrote the following.

A boy, maybe eight years old, enters the back door of a Southern Texas nursing home, quietly closing the door behind him. He was immediately taken by the strong odors of people in various stages of forgotten life. Old age had a scent about it that mixed with despair, lingers about the heart of all the visitors not soon to be forgotten. Cries could be heard, dishes clinking and doors closing. Somewhere a TV drones on un-attended.

The boy makes his way to room six. Entering he see's an old man facing the wall counting on his fingers and talking to someone only he can see. The boy is thankful that he doesn't have to disturb him yet. Quietly he leaves and is taken by surprise by an old woman seated in a wheel-chair. Grasping at his arm she says, "David! it's so good to see you", looking at her smiling face he feels compassion. "Hello Mrs. Davis, it's so nice to see you too" he said with a warm smile. "You're not David," she says, pulling her bony hands away as if burned. "No" he says gently, "but I am a friend" "Where's David?" she asks, lower lip quivering. Her son had died many years before and the boy did not want to remind her of a past she had forgotten. "He's here" said the boy placing her hand over her heart. The scene hangs suspended for a moment and a serene look comes over the women's face as the boy draws away and makes his way down the hall, looking back once to see Mrs. Davis smiling with her hands still held to her chest.

The boy starts past a room and see's another woman lying alone in her bed, eyes stare vacantly through the ceiling, hearing nothing, paralyzed by a fear laid at her feet years ago. A situation given to a child that a grown person would struggle to remain sane over. The boy approaches the bed noticing she is lying in her own waste, oblivious to everything relevant in this life. He reaches his hand up and touches her forehead, pushing a stray strand of hair out of her face. "Soon Rachel, very soon now" he whispers and he left the room walking back into the hallway.

He stops as he sees a dime lying directly in his path; just then a nurse rounds the corner, not seeing the boy. "Well" she says, bending to pickup the dime, "Must be my lucky day". The boy smiles as he watches her straighten up.

Miss Day is a caring devoted nurse of many years; the boy had a great deal of respect for her. She spies her charge and moves to intercept a fearful old man trying to avoid her. "Please don't hurt me" he says turning away from her. "No one is going to hurt you Mr. Jones, it's just time for your medications" she says gently, laying a caring hand on his shaking arm. "You know" she continues, stroking his arm, "your youth pills". Miss Day had such a way with the residents. The boy visited nursing homes often over the years and he was always satisfied with the conditions here.

14

It was true that not all homes were run with staff as caring as Miss Day and that the conditions of those homes were deplorable. Ironically though the visits to those homes were always easier for him. "See, that didn't hurt, did it?" Miss Day said cheerfully. The boy smiles as he watches Mr. Jones follow Miss Day down the hall. The boy moves on.

Perched on top of a chair, his long white hair uncombed, an old man crowed like a rooster. The boy stopped to watch and listen. To some this would be disturbing, but the boy watched in amusement. He understood the mystery of the mind and its beauty; to him he saw the celebration of life. The man crows for the youthful days that were spent in an adventure called life. The magic called time that carries us into tomorrow where we should all crow atop of a chair for the gifts that were bestowed us in our youth.

"Where are all the paintings?" an older woman asks from behind. The boy turns around to see Mrs. Cain and the bewildered look upon her face that must have been stunning in her youth. Mrs. Cain had been an art dealer in her younger days and could talk for hours about great artists like Gogan, Monet, Van Gough, and could describe the smallest detail on the beauty that others miss. "The paintings are here", says the boy, touching the top of her head, "look, can you see them?" and he pulls a yellow rose away handing it to her. "Oh," she whispers as her eyes light up, "it's so beautiful" she says taking the rose and smelling its fragrance. She closes her eyes and drifts away while humming a forgotten tune. The boy watches her go and turns to the old man still crowing and says, "thank you Mr. Williams". Mr. Williams waves and continues his celebration of life as the child starts going back the way he came.

Quietly he enters the room where the women lays staring at the ceiling. "Rachel!" he says, taking her hand. She shudders at his gentile touch. "Let's go home now" he whispers, stroking her forehead. She turns to look and he smiles at her. "Its time" he says and she smiles while sitting up. Rachel notices a picture drawn for her by her father who is far away. She reaches out and touches it in its frame. "Its alright, you'll see him again" he says as he helps her to stand. Rachel smiles at him as they leave the room.

It is but a moment before Miss Day enters to see a peaceful look on Rachel's face. Slowly she approaches the bed and feels for a pulse that isn't there. "Oh Rachel" she whispers. Looking around she notices an empty picture frame beside the bed and wonders...In the distance the rear door to the Southern Texas nursing home closes for another day.

Years have passed and as is with many prison friendships they fade into the years that, in the end, become one's life. I haven't seen my friend Redneck since he left in 2005 to return to Montana and I remain to continue my battle with the Feds. I like to think that fate dropped me into his path to soften the blow of something that could not be avoided. I will always remember him gripping my hand in both of his as he eyes teared up on the day he left. "Thank you." He said and tried to say more, but nothing else needed to be said. We both knew what he was talking about, and he was welcome.

Next letter I won't be so damn depressed and I'll make ya laugh. I've got too much time on my hands. Hope all's well with you guys, I like to think things are better but it's hard. Take care and tell me a joke or something.

Sincerely,
Walt

****

March 2004

Dear Liz and Bud Plant;

I'm writing to find out what I have to do to get a copy of "Sotheby's American Painting, Drawing and Sculptors?" It's advertised in the winter catalogue 2003-04 Incredible Catalogue.

I gotta do something or lose my mind here. It was something all together when I had Rachel to think about, God knows she's probably better off with her "race on life" behind her. However, I gotta occupy my mind and maybe the paintings in that book, if you guys still have it, can inspire something. I have a couple of illustration boards, three new pens and a bag of coffee to get me going. I have no material to work with. My birthday is the 16th of this month so maybe I can talk my sister, (who doesn't like me...she has no sense of humor. Can you imagine growing up with no sense of humor with a little brother like me? Poor girl!) Maybe I can ask her to spring for that book. I'd seen a Sotheby's European painting book and was surprised at the diverse array of painting they displayed. So, maybe the American one? I dunno.

I'll keep this short and hope all is well there with you guys. Take care and all that. Perhaps I'll send ya'll another drawing if this pans out, huh?

Okay, Peace,
Walter

PS: This is my new address. Walter Anderson #1092654, Ellis I Unit, 1697 FM 980, Huntsville, Tx 77343

****

April 2004

To da goils at da Bud Plant Soivice Dept. Liz, Paula, Diane S., Diana, Diane R. and of course Alberta; *(Note: He drew two small hearts)*

Before we get started heah, I wanna make a lil speech. Ahem...A wish for you! Today I wish you a day of ordinary miracles. A fresh pot of coffee you didn't make yourself, an unexpected phone call from a treasured friend and green stop lights all day. I wish you a day of little things to rejoice in like the fastest line at the grocery store, your favorite sing along song on the radio when you're alone and no one else can hear you. Your keys in the first place you look. I wish you a day of happiness and perfection. Little bite sized pieces of perfection that give you the funny feeling that the

Lord is smiling on you, holding you gently in his hands because you're special and rare. I wish you a day of peace and joy so profound that it strains your memory for years to come.

They say it takes a minute to find a special person, an hour to appreciate them, a day to love them but a lifetime to forget them. Thanks for the birthday card ladies. I'll not forget ya.

Not much to report in this letter. Oh yeah a guy came by looking for organ donors and I sold my kidneys. He said you only need two and since I've got four, I sold the two which weren't working. I also sold my spleen, gall-bladder, pancreas (whatever that is. If I don't know, I don't need it) and some spinal fluid. These will un-load the strain on my Internal Revenue Service).

So I ordered two books from ya'll! Yep I'm a paying customer now. Well as soon as they cut the check. I raided Shaw's (another inmate customer) spring catalogue and used his order form with my name. As soon a Huntsville cuts the check, badda-boom, badda-bing. That's Italian for badda-boom, badda-bing we're in business. I read somewhere that when Adam and Eve were being created, God held up a bag saying, "okay, I've got two special abilities, one for each of you. "Let's see" he said reaching into the bag and pulling out something, "okay, who wants to pee standing up"? "Ooh, ooh me, me!" says Adam and God gave man the ability to pee standing up. "Now let's see, what's left?" he says pulling out multiple organisms and giving it to the women. I read that somewhere. I suppose there's a moral to that somewhere.

Anyway I have to stay in this part of the prison until next month. I was kinda bad. Not evil, just having a bad day. I live with a crack-head and am not comfortable at all. When I'm not comfortable I find it hard to be creative and draw too.

I love this Art Nuevo (I can't spell Nouveau) book. I was not aware of "Mucha" or this type of art. I read it and am anxious to try my hand at it. I will send you examples of my attempts as they emerge. My art history book didn't even cover this dude.

Anyway, Mothers Day is around the corner. I'll have something on that board of yours for sure. Anybody see that Passion of Christ film? I don't see much movie stuff but I did start a crucifixion picture that's almost finished. I'll send it next letter.

I was mainly writing to tell you thanks. I'm pulling out of my nose dive. I'll send you some groovy stuff soon. Let me close by telling you a story.

This 87 year old man went to the doctor for a prostrate check up. The doctor said, "alright Ed, I want you to take this jar home and bring me back a semen sample in the morning. It's important!" He handed Ed the jar as he left. Ed came in, embarrassed and asked the nurse to see the doctor. The doctor ushered him into the exam room and closed the door. "Well, how did you do?" the doctor asked. "Well" said Ed, "I went home and tried my left hand till my arthritis gave out. Then I tried my right hand until I got blisters. So I called my wife in to help. She tried both hands, then she tried her mouth, with her teeth in, and teeth out but that didn't work, so we called Edna from next door" "My God man, you asked the neighbor for help?" said the exasperated doctor. "Yep, we did, and we still couldn't get the lid off this jar".

You guys didn't think I was gonna be rude did ya? Okay I'll get some art work in the mail to you gals soon. Thanks again. Spike says, "El high".

Peace, respectfully,
Walt

****

August 2004

Dear Liz, and Company,

I wrote to the Fortune 500 Club and they referred me to the miss-Fortune 150 club who got tired of me pestering them, as I've been told I have a habit of doing. They sent a representative who took a special interest in my legal case. It seems I've got some leeway in the legal circles. I have been extremely busy trying to get my "no-karma-having-butt out of prison". I'm sorry it's taken me so long to get a note to ya'll. You know I'm always thinking about how wonderful my friends at Bud Plant are to me.

I'm back on the tower. I have a co-worker named Benny-Billy-Joe-Bob-David or some other. You can never have too many first names in the South. Anyway he's very religious. I know this because when I explained what it is we do, he hit his knees and started calling on Saint's I've never heard of. Seems a safety organization got involved and we now are equipped with a genuine imitation parachute guaranteed to deploy somewhere before hitting the ground. I keep mine in my pocket because ya never know.

I started three other letters to y'all and one rather large Christmas drawing. A very tastefully drawn Santa (Norman Rockwell style). Spike's pushing a blue pill over to me now, I don't like the looks of this.

Anyway, I'm gonna cut this short and make sure it get's mailed. I truly appreciate the books and will follow this with another letter. The drawing will take some time. Y 'all are in my prayers and I'm still above ground. That's a good thing.

Peace,
Walt and spike

(Note: I have the Santa drawing. It hangs in my living room 24/7)

****

November 2004

Dear Liz and Company;

My friends, well Christmas came early fer y'all. Merry Christmas and may you all get what ya want.

The drawings are thus. The Angel is from a 2004 Angel calendar which I believe y'all sold to someone here, Fred Berry, around 2004 (I know, I know, I'm a genius) Did ya miss me? Yeah me too. This particular picture (reclining Christ) appeared in the Sotheby's European Art Auction, May 22, 1994 that you guys sold for 27 billion bucks, I kid you not! Well I might exaggerate a little, ya just never know about me. I don't usually draw this type of drawing; it's serious and totally alien to me. As was the Christ picture which was fully intended to y'all. *(Note: The "Reclining Christ" is still at Bud Plant. However he drew another one for me a year later, which I still have, framed.)* I know I told you I was drawing Santa, well alert the press, I lied! Ya never know what to expect when ya get something out of me and in a predictable world ain't that kinda nice?

It seems like, from where I am; that no ones very nice anymore. Maybe because this year started off badly. But it was nice of you to send me a Birthday card and the Art books, "Far Side" and "Mucha" The Mucha book taught me something. I loaned it out and "they" left with it. I made a vow to NEVER loan nothing again. Then I broke that vow as most of the books I have were "donated" to me and I'm thankful. Besides not everybody is as deceitful as that @#!?! Individual. If no one shared, I wouldn't have had it in the first place, which was nice.

I stand a pretty good chance of not growing old in here thanks to some pretty imaginative letters and some nice folks that also never gave up. Ain't that nice? I'll keep you posted. I'm bogged down in legal crap where ya gotta use the dikshunary all the time. Dot all yer tees and cross yer eyes, well you know. It may take another year but that's better than 25.

I appreciate y'all and wanted you to know sometimes its folks like you all there at Bud Plant's that makes the difference in living and merely existing. For that I thank you. I am a Christian and Spike is too, although he's a Cath...say are any of you...? Never mind. I think Spike's learning to actually read. He's on my shoulder as I write and commenting on what I write. With accuracy!

So anyways I thought the reclining Christ picture might make someone happy. I hope you like it. Merry Christmas from me and Spike.

I hope all is well out there and everyone's well. I hope Christmas, Thanksgiving and every other day goes better than you expect. May Peace be yours this Holiday Season.

Sincerely and Respectfully,
Walt

PS: If anyone has a suggestion for another drawing, and I get time (duh!) let me know.

****

Chapter Three

January 26, 2005

Dear Liz and Girls;

Hi ya toots. Yes I did receive the books you sent for Christmas and I thank you. I guess I can "assume" you did not receive the card and short letter I wrote you. Oh well I guess it could be worse.

I can't spare the time to sit and write an in-depth letter due to my present legal maters. I have six months to draft and get before the 6th District Court of Appeals before Feb. 1st. However, I will as soon as I can.

I'm so glad you liked the drawings, which was my ultimate goal. My only complaint that no one said in the card. "Hey, we like it." I gotta tell you I thought ya'll were anti-Jesus (I know better) or anti-cupid, but I guess (after thinking about it) you did express appreciation by the lovely card and books. Duh! Geese, I can't even milk a compliment right. I think I've been stuck in these legal books too long. They say British comedy is dry (no offense Liz) you should see these legal books.

For the record I have a portrait of Benny Hill tattooed on my back and I'm a big fan of several sitcoms that I watched on public TV stations in Calif. e.g.; Fawlty Towers, Waiting to Die (good one) etc. etc. We have TV's in our day rooms that we can watch during the day. All stations run re-run after re-run of Walker Texas Ranger or sports.

Well I guess we lost a letter in the mail, it was bound to happen. I was not familiar with the artist you sent and was intrigued. I shared the Mutt's book and many of these deprived convicts were thankful for your kindness as was yours truly. Thank you guys, very much. I keep all the cards and letters you send me. *(Note: Over the years he tried to keep them all but its hard when you don't stay in one place, plus, space is an issue)*

I've got Valentine's Day coming up. Does everyone have a Valentine? Didn't I make this offer last year? Liz, I know you're married so you're excluded, but we can still be friends. Hey let's all be friends. Why am I all of a sudden feeling the need to hug Yoko Ono? Anyway, anyone left out on Valentine's can drop a hint and I'll pretend I'm Tom Selleck or Tom Cruz and send a Valentines card. Maybe I'll do a group thing, ya never know with me. Relax ladies, to you who don't know me, not only am I harmless, I'm locked up tighter than Get Smart's hideout, but I'm working on that.

Listen, I'm embarking on a legal maneuver that could get my sentence knocked down from 3,568 years to 356 years. If any of you have an extra prayer, throw one out there for me will you please? I have included all of you in mine but I've got time on my hands that you don't.

Liz, you are my hero (no kidding)

Respectfully,
Walter

****

Fathers Day June 2005

Hi Liz;

How are things in Grass Valley? It's hot here. I got your letter the first week of the month or there about. We were locked down for our annual search, bummer, it's over now but it still sucks around here.

My shyster lawyer wrote back rather quickly when I questioned his loyalties or moral ethics. I'm not sure how rude I seemed. All I did was point out the facts as I see em. I wrote back and smoothed it all out. I do need him. But five months of ignoring me doesn't instill my confidence in him. My "other" lawyer, the one who represented me initially, isn't practicing law in Texas or anywhere, anymore *(Note: Yes he is, Texas gave him back his license after they slapped his hand)* and it seems our Mr. Haynes took offence when I told him he wasn't any better than him. It must have hit a nerve. I couldn't help having a little fun with him when I returned his letter telling me how "he was doing everything he could and if I didn't like it, I could hire someone else, otherwise we're stuck with each other." I started my letter acting extreeeemly irritated by his letter. Just as I was getting warmed up I told him I was kidding and proceeded to write three pages explaining my situation and where he might find the trial transcripts. He said my friend Carolyn called. I got a card from her but not much of a letter.

I went to church today. I usually go on Sundays because it's air conditioned but that's not why I go. It's nice to be yelled at on Sunday mornings. Our Baptist Chaplin get's worked up and delivers a fine fire and brimstone sermon. He will check your trust account for ya and that's easier than going through the nine kinds of hassle waiting in the store line just to check ones trust account.

I ain't sweating you over the fan $$. You'll get to it when you get to it. And, if you never do, I'll probably die or melt. Today is the first day of summer and its 101 degrees with a heat index of 164 degrees. It cools off to 80 degrees at night though. That's nuts!! You mentioned in your letter that I never asked for $$ before. You know why don't you? Six years and I never have. Maybe it ain't the money I was after but friendship. Unfortunately I can't get a fan off the streets or black market. I can but I would lose it the first time an officer shook my cell down and it ain't no fun when you have no way to get cool, or cooler. We've been over this. I'm not gonna say no more about it except, you may be my last and only hope. Heavy sigh. I did not want to do another summer here.

The bus barn where I work is hot. The chow hall is hot. Welding in this heat stinks but I can stop and get under a big fan, drink cool water and rest. In the chow hall it's about 20 degrees hotter than in the cell blocks and in the evening it's obnoxiously hot...all I've done is complain huh? Sorry!

Say, I read a book over the lock down...well actually two books in a series that made me think of you. It was book #3 and #4 of a four book series by Larry McMurtry. (He wrote Lonesome Dove) The series is called "The Berry Bender Narratives". The first book is called "Sin Killer' I didn't get to read that or #2 "Wandering Hill" but I read the 3rd and 4th books. It's a story of a Lord from England coming to America in the 1830's. He brought his family, mostly young daughters and his servants, and hooked up with a guide named Kit Carson. Mr. McMurtry wrote some authentic American, early American, hero's like Kit Carson, Captain Clark of Lewis and Clark, etc, etc. But the books authentic depiction of the Old West and mannerisms of English aristocrats or the more fortunate of English culture was entertaining and I thought you might like something like that. However one must beware as Mr. McMurtry's tragic events in his books are just that, tragic and sometimes heart wrenching. The American Indians were very cruel to their captives sometimes. It seems like the natives were either peaceful or not peaceful, to the extreme. Anyway, someday I'll read books #1 and #2. I don't read a lot of Westerns but McMurtry's "Berry Bender Narratives" series I am recommending. The last book I recommended to you by Tim Dorsey didn't go over too good with you, but this is something different. The English have come over for a visit and stay.

Please do me a favor, if and when you send the $, please write and tell me. I ain't gonna mention it again because I don't like to ask you. I hate this place. I'll write more later. Spike's wanting to say Hi, so...Hi! Take care,

Your friend,
Walt.

****

July 28, 2005

Dear Liz and Company;

You Are Not gonna believe what happened to me!!!!

First, let me apologize for not responding to your inquiries. Okay ready?? I'm so sorry. I'm scum, and for the love of God I couldn't help it! Please, please forgive me. There was a flood! Something happened! It wasn't my fault!

There I was clinging to the TV tower on a January morning. I had a helper but got in trouble when I talked him into touching the tip of his tongue to the cold metal at the top. We had to get a crane in to get him down. Actually once up there he stayed for 2 days, until the news helicopter spotted him and called the Governor. Big head lines and the warden was mad. You know how crap rolls down hill. And we know who's at the bottom of the heap around here. Anyway getting him down wasn't hard once we stripped an extension cord off the end wires and touched it to the tower, he came down pretty quickly. Now I don't have a helper.

I was abducted by the U.S. Marshals and whisked away to court to hear a Federal Writ-of habe-as-corpus (which I won,) and sent back to the county that convicted me where they redid part of my trial called sentencing. Now instead of 7465 years I only have 725. I will be eligible for parole in 2375, actually 2013. The lawyer said I may go back again due to more sentencing errors. This is why it's taken me so long to get back in touch with you…Did ja miss me?

I'm actually choked up here. I may need the Aunt Polly maneuver (that's not like the Heimlich maneuver). The Aunt Polly is where you get slapped up one side the head for acting like an idiot. Y'all being women, you can probably do the Aunt Polly at will. They say women are born with the ability to do this naturally, is that true? Anyone got an Aunt Polly? I had one.

Anyway, when a prisoner is in transit he can't take anything but legal stuff (work) and a Bible. Since it was a given that I'd be coming back my mail was held for me. I got the book by Nelson for my Birthday. I'm touched and thank you sincerely for being so thoughtful, Liz, Alberta, Diane and Diana, you're my hero's. I also had a Birthday card from a Christian lady, Carolyn, that writes sometimes, bless her heart, she must have umpteen-million prison pen-pals because this time I was "Pete" and this was my 27th birthday.

I would have written you lovely ladies sooner but I had to get an entry in to the Fortune Society's Annual Art Contest for prisoners. I learned about it last year but it was too late to enter. The idea is not to win, with so many entries that's not really feezable. All entries go online in December to be auctioned off to the highest bidder. That's when one gets rewarded based on their own merits. I believe the public can go online and look up Fortunesociety.org and see the entries and vote to see all the talent "doing time" somewhere. My piece won't be hard to find.

I have a grown son, who had a son last November, so that makes me a Grandpa. He doesn't write often but he did let me know about the baby. The baby's name is Adolph Melville Anderson (tee hee), actually it's Eli. Maybe one day I'll have to chance to tell him "Spike" stories. By the grace of God I will get out of here one day. In the meantime, I cannot let them get me down.

Anyway I'll write again soon and thanks again for the book. I'm shooting word off to Spike on the "yoink machine" to let him know ya'll say hi. Take care and let me know if you'd like another picture and what of? How about Joan of Arc? I've been wanting to do that for awhile.

Per Liz, I have that picture I'm planning to place an order before December so please keep me on the winter catalog list. Thanks again for being my friends.

Peace,
Walt

PS: Do you have any freebie Batman stuff? I have a hankering to do a Batman board for a 6 year old lil dude who's having a bout with some unpronounceable disease, his dad is a friend here… long story.

****

August 8, 2005

Dear Liz and Co;

Well I got me a little rude awakening the other day. First of all it seems Sherry (Spike's spider girlfriend) has grown and made an appearance. She straddled my celli's (Ronnald) face while he slept. He sleeps on the bottom bunk. Our bunks are sheet steel with a pad they call a mattress, but are no thicker than a used quilt. Anyway, Sherry was straddling Ronnald's face doing push ups when he woke up and saw the world through the hairy legs of a large spider. He screamed, jumped up knocking himself out on the top bunk. We had the discussion of waking each other up and he said not to wake him up for any reason unless he said so prior to going to sleep. He didn't say, "If there's a spider from hell straddling my face you can wake me up." So I sat on the toilet and drank my morning coffee.

I said Hi to Sherry who wanted to know where Spike was. She didn't believe me when I told her he left on the Standing Hampton (the name of the Space V.W. that came to get us at one time) Anyway I wasn't there when Ronnald came too.

I got called down to the desk where the higher ranks of the Texas Dept. of Corrections Officers hang out. One of my old celli's came out of nowhere, grabbing my shirt and repeating, "Can you see me? Can you see me? You can't can you? Then ran off, giggling. I wonder what's up with that.

Things are pretty much the same around here. It's hot and humid. At least I'm not in a cast or anything. I'm beginning to think I'm not so lucky, well not always. I woke up this morning with my eyelids webbed shut. This isn't the first time. Sherry parked in the corner of the cell above my bunk; Ronnald won't go near her. Can't blame him really. I'm going to get a Spiderman comic book and try to entice Sherry that way she won't buy the Alien story. I'll get hold of Spike and let him know, Houston, we have a problem.

I put this letter down for a while and low and behold I got your post card wanting to know what's happening because you hadn't heard from me for awhile. Great minds think alike. You know I was probably mailing the last letter as you were, I think. I don't know. Too many shots to the head.

Well Lady's if I don't get this out right now I'll have to wait til Monday, that's three days away. I'll put something together this week. I start a new job on Monday painting the water tower.

I hope all's well with you, everyone is healthy and every one of you loves well too.

Take care, Peace,
Walt

PS: Say, I got a question on that Ken Kelly guy. Is he a lot like Frazetta? Because they bill him as such. Is he anywhere near good as his Uncle? Just wondering, you know I'm a big Frazetta fan...

****

August 2005

Greeting and Salutations;

This letter is short and sweet. I've decided what to draw for ya'll. Something you won't find in your place of business. It's something tasteful (as I'm always tasteful…no pun intended) I've managed to set up an appointment with the organ merchant to sell a few internal organs so I can buy the stamps to mail the art board, also pens. I don't believe I need my spleen. I don't even know what it's supposed to do. My gizzard was removed last time and I haven't missed it at all. So what's a pancreas? Maybe I can do without that as well. Unless you gals have a suggestion, I'm going ahead with my original plan.

How's everyone? Well I hope! I'm doing okay here. I'm glad Sherry's busy elsewhere, Ronnald is really glad. I haven't told him she's on a different planet with Spike, but this way he's quiet.

Ya'll be good, God Bless and Peace,
Walt.

****

September 19, 2005

Dear Liz and Customer Service Gals;

Howdy ya'll. Guess who's sitting next to me as I write this? Ronnald McDonald. He busted his butt last week for chasing a chicken who was crossing the road, why? Who knows, but this here's Colonel Sander's country and the only one who can legally chase chickens around here is the Colonel. Anyway, according to Ronnald the Colonel used to choke his chickens but the SPCA got on to him and the cheap old dude got him an axe.

So, how is everyone? Liz you wrote, are you back yet? *(Note: I was on vacation in England.)* Don't fret about Spike, he'll be back, guaranteed. How do I know? Well Sherry's now on Planet Argo and if I know our five legged friend, it won't take long.

I'm trying to talk Ronnald into volunteering for the chow hall. He's doing his mime routine though. Maybe I'll take him to work with me one day that should change his mind. You know that face paint is permanent. Even though he said he was born that way. I'm trying to talk him into taking his Mac Nuggets out and lift some weights. He's pretty skinny but we'll see if we can put some weight on him and maybe invent a new burger or something.

I've finally acquired a board and have started work on it. It will be ya'll's Christmas present. I'm about to start the Christmas rush and it's really the only time of year I can make some scratch. *(Note: He draws cards for inmates to send home.)* Wanna hear what I'm drawing? Well it's a full 20x15 illustration board. Liz said to let my lil ole imagination fly, so I thought, Cool!

When you get your Christmas board I won't be able to put more than a page of stamps on it, and in case I forget to mention it, please let me know when it arrives. Probably next week. Maybe I'll just wait to mail this and slip it in. I'll worry about it until I know it's there.

I've already got the Oscar Mayer Wiener started on the tower. I'm gonna put 19 gun turrets on it with machine gun ports and 119 genuine midgets (dressed up like clowns in honor of...well you know, running around with water balloons doing battle with Batman and Robin. But you don't know its Batman and Robin unless you check out his Batman belt buckle. Spike would love it, and we all know he's got good taste.

Gotta go, we're having pig stuff for dinner. Not sure exactly but a guys gotta eat. Always remember when life hands you lemons make lemonade, but when life hands you crap...just leave it!

Take care, peace,
Walt

October 24, 2005

Baseball, Go Astro's, yeee haw!!!!

Greeting Liz and Co;

Howdy ya'll. Guess who dropped in on me and ole Ronnald? Yep Spike almighty himself. Actually I knew it wouldn't be long before he showed up. Sherry didn't come with him. I don't have all the facts on that but I'm thinking Spike's A.W.O.L. He says Planet Argo has a season that doesn't agree with him. I think they call it Spider Season. Anyway Ronald and Spike are out of the cell right now. Oddly enough they get along well now.

I barked at Ronnald the other day for using my comb, he denied it vehemently. I might be responsible for that due to my "deny everything" lessons, but the bright orange hair (he's Ronnald McDonald) in the broken teeth of my comb is evidence to the opposite. Oh well, what ya gonna do?

I've got five boards to draw and am writing ya'll instead. I don't gotta do them all right now but I got my Christmas rush as I knew I would. It's okay for me. I'm hoping ya'll haven't sent your winter catalogs out yet, if so I didn't get one. There are a couple of things I've got my eye on and have made deals to pay for them.

I'm worried that partial nudity might cause problems even though the mailroom says it's on a one to one basis. I have art books (art history) that depicts nudity in historical situations or books by artists that have nude painting, like Frazetta's "Testament", which I own, and "Living Legend", which I also have. Both of those have nudity. I'd like other books, like the Ken Kelly one or Icon and am hoping they don't get turned away.

The rule, according to the mail room lady is, No pornography. Yet you've had catalogs turned away because of casual nudity on the cover of an art book. Have you ever thought of contacting (eh-hem) these people to get something in writing narrowing the guidelines down to something you can work with? Business wise to have orders turned down over an artist's rendition of Venus

Demilo makes no sense when it has nothing to do with explicit nudity that falls in the pornography category or whatever. I hope this information helps.

The mailroom people said, "It's on a one to one basis", I don't know what that means myself. I've never been into pornography but I own Boris Vallejo's 1st art book in America (1978 Ballantine) and it has nude women in it. I consider this art and believe it or not Paul Rubens also has nude women in his book, of which I also have from 1967 or was it 1679? Hmmmm maybe it was even earlier than that.

I think Jimmy Carter was President back then. "Welcome Back Carter" that is, or was that "Welcome Back Cotter?" I also have Norman Rockwell's pictures for The American People and Gardner's Art through the Ages (big book). It starts in Egypt 24,000 years before Christ and ends with some ya who who draws 20th Century Contemporary Art that looks like a mess on canvas. I used to have a Mucha Art Nuevo which you guys sent me, but someone made off with it. I guess they felt they needed it more than me. That's the chance you take when you loan things out.

Ronnald isn't into art very much; he's more of a Calvin and Hobbs and The Far Side kind of guy, who I really like. I let him read the one you guys sent and caught him weeping, don't know why, Ole Ron's a little off-beat. At least he likes Elvis. He doesn't like chicken. And he's made himself a Brigadier General (he outranks Col. Sanders) Ronnald starts therapy next week. I've got Ronny (he hates that name) on a weight program. Yoke him up some. He says he wants to dye his hair blonde like mine, only mines natural. Orange really is his color though, his natural color.

Spike's back to his usual tricks. He's taken bets on the World Serious and has set up Saturday night poker games in the pipe chase. His relatives are coming here from Mexico for Thanksgiving but they'll still be here for Christmas. I'll let you know how that goes. Until then, take care and Peace,

Walt, Spike and Ronnald (Ronny).

****

December 2005

Dear Liz and Co;

Hi ladies and dudes. I'm drawing one Christmas card this year and you're getting it. Please let me know it arrived! Ya don't gotta do it right away, just mention it one day in passing. I hope you like it.

Did I ever tell ya about my sisters? I have four sisters, all of em bigger than me. I know, I know, it's usually the other way around. I have two sisters older and two younger. My oldest sister, Kelly Bob is 6' 7" tall and weighs in at 480lbs. She used to fell trees for the Forestry dept in Ukiah. Now I think she runs a day care center for Iranians, I don' know for sure. My next oldest sister, Kim Bob is closer to 7' tall and a lean 340lbs. She used to be heavier but started jogging. I think I started her on that. One Christmas we were all sitting in our living room in Kelseyville Calif. (by Lakeport). Kim Bob leaned over to dislodge a human tooth from her steel toe boot and I made the mistake of taking a bite from her doughnut she was holding. She took a swing at me, which I ducked from, and punched a hole through the wall where my head was, the chase was on. I broke two chairs, one end table and dove through a closed window to get away from that women. And she was only a girl then. Anyway, that was a Christmas to remember. My youngest sister, Konny Bob was up all night waiting for Santa. She and my other younger sister, Katy Bob, had worked over the mailman earlier that day thinking he was Santa. They ambushed him from behind a bush and broke four ribs, his arm and swiped his mailbag, thinking it held all the presents. Their pictures still hang in the post office.

Spike's got about two million brothers and sisters, uncles and aunts, not to mention grandparents, so this is why he usually winters in Mexico just so he doesn't have to buy presents. However, this year they're all be here.

Well, Happy Christmas, I hope it's a truly wonderful one for all of you. Take care and I'll drop you a line when the book comes. Liz, I got your postcard, thanks.

Peace from your friends,
Walt, Spike and Ronnald

******

Chapter Four

To Liz and Co;

Howdy girls, it's me!!! They confiscated the Spectrum book, (Please see the enclosed rejection slip). The book arrived in December sometime. Anyways I took a chance and instead of doing the smart thing and allowing Liz to remove the pages with the offending, life threatening, rude paraphernalia that Texas has decided I can't see. I took a chance and thought I'd challenge their reasoning. After all it's the pornography they're targeting. Okay so I ain't the brightest light bulb in the drawer, but there comes a time when ya gotta make a stand. When the chips are down and the cards are dealt why ya just gotta play the hand yer dealt and hope for the best. I'm trying out my Jimmy Stewart speech, how am I doing?

I've been up on the tower for 45 days, refusing to come down till they give me the book. I was hammering on the tower disrupting the warden's wife's soap operas. I know she's a big fan of the "Hung and the Breast less" and "As the Stomach Turns" so why didn't she move?

I got the book. They gave it to me the other day saying it qualifies as art and I get to have it. I was supposed to sell a board I drew for Fortune Society, but it didn't do as well as I'd hoped. Anyway, I have three different things going on now and maybe I can make an order this year.

Spikes in Mexico and Sherry's in the corner knitting new 812 baby spider booties. Ole Ronald's getting a new tattoo by the biker down the run. Me? Why I'm marveling at the new book, thank you, thank you ladies. How wonderful it would have been to have a mom with a sense of humor like the one in the pictures. We should all take advantage of life's little moments.

Peace, respectfully,
Walt

****

May 18, 2006

Dear Liz and Co.;

Greetings from Texas! Well we all got fired from our paint job due to a little misunderstanding mentioned in my last card. We won't mention it again due to the rating of this letter.

Spring has sprung around here, I'll bet its pretty there. I've been to Grass Valley, went there in 1979 with a bunch of tree huggin hippy's from Humboldt County in a Chartreuse Micro bus. They all had Jerry Garcia tee shirts on and of course, beards. I was only 18, I didn't have a beard. We went to a Blue Grass Festival where I had a bowl of nuclear chili. I've never been the same. I should have known though because of the three pots of boiling, bubbling beans that didn't have a fire under it. I'm ever the adventurer though.

Anyways the only thing that's bloomin here in armpit Texas are the idiots I'm surrounded by. I contacted my lawyers (Dewy, Screwem and Howe) and am waiting to hear back. I'm suing the District Attorney of Fannin County for being an idiot. I've got good grounds and my lawyers (Wally, Clee-otis and Clem, their first names) are confident we are gonna win SOMETHING! Well as long as I get a third of that something, that's cool, I guess.

Well I'm gonna close for now. Peanut Butter sandwiches for dinner, with raisens..Yum! At least I hope they're raisins. Spike say's Hi and hopes everyone got what they wanted for Christmas...I don't know, I just translate. We've been writing like this for years now, do you know it? I'm well; I'll write more later, I gotta finish my fishing picture this week...the one with Lucy in it. *(Note: Lucy is a Praying Mantis in another of his story's)* Y'all take care.

Respectfully,
Walt.

****

May 25, 2006

Hey Liz and Company;

Three years ago I wrote you at the customer service dept. Let's celebrate! *(Note: Actually it was April 2003, but what the hey.)* I was going through my old letters; most of them aren't anything to write home about. This one was after I threatened to stop bothering you, remember? Well, anyway before we get started I gotta do a disclaimer. Somewhere in this letter I'm gonna cuss. Now we're all adults and I can't achieve total description without using the word "shit", so if yer squeamish you've been warned.

As you know I'm back on the tower and was up there with Spike this morning. He was talking about Nixon again; Spike goes on about how Nixon was a lost boy in Peter Pan and won't admit he's wrong. Spike's been booted out of the pipe chase poker games because of his cheating habits.

We were up on the tower thinking about Planet Argo when I pointed out a flock of humming birds. Spike said they weren't humming birds and that we should RUN! "Where?" I asked, we were 200ft off the ground. Besides what could they be that we should run? "Well, they're mosquitoes" said Spike. "No way" I said. I looked closer and could hear them buzzing. My next move was to fill my pants with shit while Spike and I started a fireman's slide down the tower. The Texas Safety Commission made Ellis Unit equipped me with safety equipment, e.g.: a parachute, which I let go trying to punch a mosquito as it came in. I gotta tell ya its drilling equipment was enough to scare even the toughest of hides. Spike activated his wings and I pulled the emergency ripcord. The chute opened and ripped all my clothes off. I went south and my clothes floated east with the breeze. I was headed for the roof of the warden's house...again. I noticed the swarm forming a dive pattern as if they were a wing of the R.A.F. or a WWII combat plane on attack. I had just enough time to see that I was going straight through where I went through before.

As I crashed through I noticed the same mirror was still set up in the attic. I also noticed, to my horror, that I had my Calvin and Hobbs underwear on. My mind didn't have long to dwell on that as I went through the floor and onto the coffee table where the warden's wife had her Havana cigar burning in an ashtray where I landed. I came off the floor and rolled as I saw a line of mosquitoes veer off from me and stick in the warden's wife as if someone were tossing darts into a beanbag chair. My underroos were smoking and I made tracks out of the warden's house, when I heard her bellow, "you again!!!" I broke nothing this time, I couldn't believe it. The last time I was in a body cast for six months.

I walked up to the East gate and the cop there knew me. He opened it without a second look. "Your butts smoking" he said dead pan. I looked and sure enough it was smoldering. I slapped it out, trying to be nonchalant about walking around in Calvin and Hobbs boxers in a Texas penitentiary.

I really didn't need the bikers to see me because I was supposed to be tough. I gotta reputation here. No sign of the mosquitoes...yet. Spike met up with me outside the bathhouse. They were showering the medium custody so I was able to slip in unnoticed getting new clothes and underwear. The prison air raid siren went off and everyone thought, Hurricane! (Katrina went through here) Anyway, me and Spike knew different and when the gun towers started shooting everyone else did too.

We got back to the cell and immediately knew Sherry (Spike's girlfriend spider) had been eating flies, they give her gas. She blamed it on Ronnald, who wasn't there at the time. Anyway it could be worse.

We have mystery-meat for dinner, so there's that. I'm still working on my fishing board with Lucky the one legged dog.

Well I'm gonna close. I hope all's well there. I was looking through my letters and noticed it was our anniversary for writing so I hope you liked it. I'm still here and you're still there. Thanx for encouraging my imagination. There was one time it wasn't fun but that just goes to show ya. Take care and be good

Respectfully,
Walt.

****

August 2006
(Note: There's no date so I don't know if it's before 9/12 or after, oh, forgive his "English")

Wool Howdy Thar Liz and Co;

Spike ain't heah right now dew tew his having pulled an Elvis. As one would say, left the building. I am experiencing a bit of the "Southern flew" they say it affects ones speech, but I do declare it ain't done nothing to mine.

The picture of y'all's cacti was well received and afta lookin up the Cactus dilecti in yonder "Book o de Plants" I have come to the conclusion that, that book ain't worth "sheee-it" you will pardon mah grammah. At first it looked as if you were saying y'all's plant weighed 701 pounds, I was quite flabber gastid. I bragged to several of my fellow...eh hem...colleagues, for lack of a better word. They in turn pointed out that you wrote 70 lbs. Imagine thar suprize when I adamantly argued that the abbreviation for pounds was "BS" not "lbs" which I knew to be the case as well. That's the moment I realized I had the "Southern flew" Arguing when y'all knows y'all's wrong. And ones grammah gets colorful as well.

Case in point; I was detained. I say, in the chain room the other morning, when two correctional officers (Southern Correctional Officers) were arguing that Florida was closer to Texas than the moon. Absurd to say the least. They took their grievance to a Sergeant who settled the argument by asking. "Well can you see Florida?" "No" they said. "Can you see the moon?" At which point they looked out a nearby window and low and behold there was the moon! "Well, there ya have it" and he walked away. It's hard to argue with logic like that huh? It's also hard to believe these "Southern Gentlemen" lost the Civil War huh?

You mentioned a friendly phone call in y'all's letter. I do have a cell phone. I tried callin y'all to be right neighborly just last night. First I lift the lid on my cell phone, than I drain all the water out of it and then I scream loud as I can. Y'all must not have bin home. In order to have an opportunity to use a REAL phone, there are requirements one must meet. First, one must have been just out of surgery (not as uncommon as one might believe) Second, one must have a note from Robert E. by God Lee saying that Jefferson Davis authorized it. (A note from John Wayne won't do. Him being a Yankee and all) and third, the final requirement, one must have absolutely no reason, what-so-ever in which a phone call is necessary. So what can y'all do? NUTHIN. And that's what ya get if'n ya try to get a phone call. What's e-mail? *(Note: On 11/21/2014 Walter called me for the first time and to date, 2016, has been calling four or more times a week)*

Ronnald has no concept of WWII Nazi's. They kicked him out for being **too** opinionated. Can you imagine that? The prison Nazi's are only Nazi's because they can't spell Aryan Brotherhood and besides most of them are Mexican. It's a mixed up world we or "I" live in.

I'm glad y'all's heat wave has passed. I'm also glad ya wrote, thank you. My civil suit is goin poorly and I needed a lift, which I always get when you write. I am fighting two different legal battles and am late for the Law Library so I'm gonna cut this short. Someone stole the lines off my paper, but then what do ya expect when yer in a Texas penitentiary surrounded by Mexican Nazi's?

I'll write more later, y'all take care. God Bless y'all.

Respectfully,
Walt.

****

September 12, 2006

Dear Liz and Co;

I got your little card last night. They weren't sure of my number matching the one on the envelope. I'm glad they checked and didn't return it. Anyway I meant to write before this but I've been busy trying to access the courts for some more "sparring"

The doctor (Kevorkian) here at the prison has diagnosed me with some incurable disease. "Ghona-Herpa-Sypha-Litus" or something like that. "Is it contagious?" I asked him, "No" he says, "then, how the hell did I catch it?" I mean if something ain't contagious and you didn't have it before…Anyway, not to worry. I ain't. Spike's mixin me up some concoction that's supposed to fix it. He's been drinking it for six months and it grew him his leg back, so…yeah I know if I start growing another leg I'm going bug hunting.

The enclosed card is an original and I thought y'all would appreciate it. I haven't been doing much of anything except legal stuff. I'm in the Federal Courts now with my law suit. I'm appealing to the 5th Circuit Court for some kind-a-mercy order that you can file if yer dyin. I ain't dyin but according to the doctor it **could** kill me in about 60 years if I ain't careful. If I live to be 60 years old at all I'll feel ahead of the game and ya won't hear me complain as I mount the stairway to my final destination. I'm hoping for an escalator to be honest. At any rate it gives me an opening to file in the courts.

If you think your letters from me are creative imagine a Federal judge getting hold of a brief Spike and I have written on the validity of my conviction. I got a letter back from the Court of Criminal Appeals with one word on it, "What?" Well they had six question marks on *their* word. That's impressive when you take into consideration that the Texas Court of Criminal Appeals only reads 6% of the cases before them.

I'm trying to convince Ronnald he's invisible. It was so much fun the last time I did that, I figured why not? I think between him and Spike they got rid of Sherry. She's been gone for awhile.

Someone put a plastic spider in her web and thought I wouldn't notice. Well I didn't for awhile. I don't get shook down because of Sherry's (cell search) presence. The cops haven't noticed she's gone though. Both Ronnald and Spike claim to know nothing.

I think Texas has lightened up on art books. As long as it isn't sexually explicit and the nudity is a painting or drawing they'll let it through. Go ahead and send it as is. I took a clipping from the catalog to the mail-room and the lady read the write-up from yer catalog and said it should be okay, so...maybe they remember the last episode with the Spectrum book, remember that?

I will sit down and write or draw something for y'all soon. I have a four hour session at the clinic today so I gotta go. Tomorrow is law library and I can't miss that. They're zapping me with a cosmic ray that's supposed to cure what ails me. I ain't gonna worry unless my hair and teeth fall out. So I'm here, keeping my...umm...pecker up, as they say in "Blighty"

Your friend,
Walt and Spike.

****

November 2006

Dear Liz and Co;

Surprise!! Merry Christmas too. Now before you start with the "is he crazy?" Which by now the answer to that should be obvious? Let me explain why I drew this particular picture. *(Note: A beautiful drawing of a reclining Jesus)* #1; it ain't exactly original but the original is so old, 1501, that no one's gonna throw my stupid butt in prison, besides, I'm already here, for copyright infringement. Besides I made enough subtle changes that it actually looks or is a better picture. #2; it is a task finding a picture that I like that ain't in your vast warehouse and I'm betting it ain't, so I wanted something that ya'll haven't seen before and #3; while one might blanch at the picture of a dead Jesus, let's face it if he hadn't done what he did we wouldn't be celebrating his birth 2007 years later. Even if you're not a Christian you should be able to appreciate the concept. Spike told me I should put that last part in there. Me and Spike are Christians, just for the record. We may not practice as devotedly as some, but we don't claim to be perfect. Enough said about Theology. Read what is said on the back. "We look forward to the time when the power of love will replace the love of power. Only then will our World know the blessings of peace", William E. Gladstone. Oh yeah, that Gladstone guy was the Prime Minister of England in the 19th Century. And since this picture was specifically for an English bird, cool huh!

Due to the direct attention this person has shown, it's only fair she should end up with it to do with as she pleases. So if you run into anyone who says "Blimey" or calls ya'll "Guv-nor" (you probably don't do that any more huh?) okay, anyone named Liz. Now if anybody else wants something like this all they gotta do is write and say so. I hope it's accepted in the spirit in which it's given, I also hope you like it Liz, please drop me a line telling me it arrived safely. I'm gonna worry until you do. The original artist was Andrea Mantegna, Italian I believe, in 1501. The original wasn't in black and white and as I said, different in a few ways. Mostly the same though.

I gotta go. Take care, drop me a line and let me know you got this. And, Merry Christmas to all of ya. Your friend.

Peace,
Walt and Spike

PS: Ronald says Hi. He's grumpy this time of year but when is he ain't though.

****

December 2006

To the Service Dept. at Bud Plant;

I say hi to all you lovely customer service ladies, I got your Christmas card and am honored to get it and place a name with a face. A special "thank you" to Liz. If it weren't for you I'd a lost my mi...wait! I can do better. I suppose the Queen knows you're missing? You of obvious...no that's no good either! How wonderful life is, (even from my perspective) knowing there are people like yourself in it to show us how to lighten up and go with what it has to offer. I believe you are an example in human kindness and (though a bit gullible) a champion of things of the heart. How I wish things where different and I could have known you, because even though our encounters are brief (letters) it's you who makes all this possible. Thank you Liz, my friend.

Anyways on to other things. You ladies must really be special to take up a whole friggin page just to say hello to me. This is a keeper. Spike's setting up "Monte Carlo" night for the June Bugs, they haven't arrived yet. I keep telling him, Mayfly's, Mayfly's but he's been in Texas longer than I have.

Have you ever wondered how someone's life of crime starts? Well mine started down on "J" Street in Sacramento, California. I was 19 (I ain't telling ya what year then you'd know I'm 42 so don't try tricken me) I weren't much of a drinker, never have been but growing up next to Humboldt County in the 60's and 70's I learned there are other ways to inebriate one's self. Me and my best bud Ricky were on our way back home from buying two sacks of Ho Ho's, potato chips, popsicles, candy, dips and whatever else filtered through our Marijuana haze on a Sunday afternoon. I was working steady, so was Ricky. We were in my 1966 Chevy Caprice with the track tape playing Black Sabbath. (The tape dragged and Sabbath was the only tape you couldn't tell was distorted) We just shared the last joint and were talking about the Forman's fat butt falling off a roof we were working on Friday, laughing with not a care in the world. "Oh crap there's a cop!" says Ricky pointing off to the left. "Don't point!" I said looking where he was pointing. Sure enough there sat a Sacramento Police officer molesting a box of doughnuts. "Okay, okay" I say, "is everything cool?" "Yeah, we got no more pot"; "did you ever pay that ticket?" Ricky, my then trusty side kick asks. Everyone needs a side kick don't cha think? "Yeah I did" I say realizing I had nothing to worry about, even if he did pull me over...which he didn't. Suddenly, "Watch the light!" Ricky yells and I break hard stopping almost through the cross walk. "Idiot!" Ricky says and I start laughing as I'm backing up where I ain't in the crosswalk. Just then two or maybe it was three Nuns' dressed in their habits; slowly walk in front of the car. I remember the song "Dominique" as they slowly walk across the road. "You coulda got us pulled over" Ricky says. "What's so funny?" he asks, "you" I say still laughing. Ricky starts laughing, "You're the idiot for riding with me" I say almost out of control from laughing. You know once you get the giggles its gotta run its course. "Hey look" he says through his laughs, "the cops behind us" he, he, he, "so what! We ain't doin nothing" I say, still laughing. "Watch this Mister officer Sir" acting like I'm racing. This brings another bout of laughter. "Hey Walt, did you get the body out of the trunk? Ricky says laughing. "You mean your Mama?" I say banging on the steering wheel, laughing harder. Just then a Corvette pulls up along side us with a blonde from Hell in it. (Translated, one fine woman) Instantly we're both composed, trying to be cool. The lights still red. Yeah everything happens in slow motion when you're stoned. "Look she's checking us out" says Ricky, I turn and sure enough she's looking at the little 396 V8 ornament on the side of my chariot of fire. I give it a little rev. "Be cool stupid! There's a cop behind us" Ricky says. "Geese give it a rest Einstein, we're sitting still" Just then she looks over, smiles and gives her vette a rev. "See ding bat, she thinks I'm cool" I say, sitting a little taller in the seat. The cop behind us doesn't even seem interested. Just then the light turns green and the vette shoots out in front, I step on the gas and shoot back words slamming into the grill of the cop car. I had forgotten to put the gear shift back into drive after backing up from the cross walk. "What the fu..." thinks me. Ricky has done the Lumbadda off the dash into the seat and back into the dashboard. (Duh, no seatbelt) I had my seatbelt on but I still knotted my forehead on the steering wheel. I spent the rest of the day spending a weeks pay to get my bumper pulled out, a tow and eventually, a fine from a judge who, thank God, had a sense of humor. Anyways, maybe not such a criminal act after all.

I'm just sharing a little cheer and by the way, that's a true story. I got a drawing going from that Sotheby's book you sent. It's a Norman Rockwell "The Buddy Ride" I'm gonna send it to my lawyer for the ride he's giving me. Just kidding, I ain't fond of lawyers enough to send them anything.

Y'all take care. I'll write again soon.

Peace, respectfully,
Walt

****

December 28, 2006

Dear Liz and Co;

I sent the photo of me that was taken accidently when someone came to see someone else, Liz you said I "looked nice," you obviously have a good eye for handsome fellas. Okay, you didn't say I was handsome, so shoot me why don't cha!

I just got back from the hospital, again. I was there over Christmas and they found out what's ailing me, I'm fixed now. I mean literally, I was having radiation treatment on my thumb (I had thumb cancer, it's very bad in the south, hitchhikers get it a lot...) Anyways the tech. finished one of the treatments, spun the radiation shooter thingy and walked out with me still tied to the table. His apron caught the "on" switch and when the radiation shooter thingy stopped spinning it was pointed directly at my testicles. Yeah I'm lucky like that. Well being a convict (a very big, very loud, at that point, convict) I can't just roam the hallways of a public hospital. I was literally tied to the table with my family jewels starting to cook. You wouldn't believe the range ones voice has in a situation like that. Celine Dion woulda been proud. Anyway, Dr. Kevorkian came by and turned off the machine. He said the glowing sensation would pass. It hasn't yet but it's real handy in the middle of the night when ya gotta go and ya don't wanna turn on the light and wake your celli. Ronnald's still here and he's a crazy ole clown when he doesn't get his 8 hours.

I got yanked outa here shortly after I started y'all's board. I hafta do something different now, and I will! Y'all just be patient, I'll find the picture I was gonna work off of and show you why I gotta start over...Christmas is past.

Legal mail built up but your card was the best in all that junk. I did get a nasty note from the Amish Community telling me I'm evil and must be destroyed. They don't really mean it, they like hearing from me even though they don't answer all of my letters, but hey, neither do you! *(Note: I've answered every letter he's written that I've received since 2003.)* Spike started me writing them and started a Theological discussion about the demise of the Quakers and Adolph Hitler. I ain't going into it but ya just hadda be there.

Spike didn't go with me to the hospital and I haven't seen Sherry since I've been back. Her web's gone and Ronnald or Spike ain't talking. I suspect something funny here. Spike has an orange clown wig now, if he only knew how silly he looked in it, I guess he got it for Christmas.

Did you get what you asked for, for Christmas? I got my eye lids taped open, strapped to a bed and forced to watch a James Bond marathon. Can you imagine? I got a half a can of cheese whiz, the tongue from a shoe, one piece of Hubba Bubba Bubble gum (only chewed once) I traded that to Spike for one Butterfly wing...I may have traded "up" on that deal. Anyways, other than those and my new crotch night light your card was the most memorable. (It's the little things in life)

Well last Christmas I drew one card and it was for you, remember? Even though I wasn't here at Christmas I suppose I'll do one for this year too. I'll include it in this or this in that or...well you know what I mean. You should have already seen it; I ain't even drawn it, yet. How does that work? Spike has his Quantum Physics book out and we'll get back at ya.

Ronnald says if you drink French fry grease you can time travel. I think if you attempt that the only time travel relevant is the time it takes to hustle yer butt to the bathroom, probably coming out both ends. Okay, I know! Sorry.

Ya know ya gotta love me, I have a 5 legged cockroach (water roach) for a pet. He has an orange haired clown for a pet, who's better off? He (Spike) used to tell me his leg magically grew back to get me to take a concoction brewed in the pipe chase behind the wall inside the prison cell block. Actually the little bugger was wearing a prosthetic leg. He meant well I suppose. I was ill at the time and he was worried. Everyone needs someone to worry over em. *(Note: This was when I began to realize that "maybe" he had a real health issue. Turned out, yes he does)*

I hope y'all have that and Christmas was as magical as it should be. In that may you be blessed. I gotta go draw a card now. Then I'm gonna start the board I wanted to send for Christmas. Anyway I'll let you go now and do what ever it is you do when y'all ain't entertaining a crazy ole convict.

Peace and Prosperity for the New Year.

Yer friend,
Walt and Spike

****

Chapter Five

Somewhere in the neighborhood of today, spring 2007

Hey Liz and Co.;

I got your letter concerning the Directors Review Committee, fair enough! I'll handle this. Send the Spectrum book as is. I'm going to the mail room today with my handy dandy Winter 2005-2006 Bud's Incredible Catalog complete with a description of Spectrum, and I'm gonna ask "Hey! What the @#*!!" only it will come out more like "A hem...excuse me kind mail room lady, can I have this?" and then show Miss Mail Room lady all mighty the description and even tell her "there might be brief nudity to convey the artists interpretation and the integrity of the piece. Certainly nothing of the sexual explicate nature" Only she may not be able to comprehend the words I can say but cannot spell...hmmm, why is that? *(Note: He doesn't know I'm using spell check, sometimes.)* Spike says it's because I'm an idiot...oh, not me, her. Yeah that make's sense. I won't mail this if she says "Duh...what?" "NO!" I have nothing but respect for these...folks. I have seen several Spectrum Books and would absolutely feel blessed from my head to my toes to receive it. Groovy!

Ole Ronnald's on his bunk doing his toe nail cutting. Spikes here, he was supposed to be in Mexico by now but I think he missed me while being away on Planet Argo. Sherry's still missing in action and Johnny Walker (Spike's personal Seagull pilot) hasn't shown up anyway.

Ronnald got a job in the kitchen and works from 10 pm till 6 am. (We go to breakfast at 3:30 am here, true) I don't do breakfast at 3:30 am. Spike wants to go to the mail room with me. He thinks I need legal representation, why not? So if your reading this, "please send the book and thank you" I got a five legged water roach getting excited here. He wants me to tell Alberta how pretty she is in her photo from the magazine. In fact he says all of you customer service loidy's are "the best" but we won't tell Sherry he feels that way. Maybe Sherry has found her place on Planet Argo, I doubt it though. I'll close for now and go talk to the powers that be. Y'all take care, ya heah!

The next day

Well me and Spike set off for the mailroom. He had his Batman cowl and cape on and I had my jail house lawyer's handbook under my arm with my handy dandy Incredible Catalog (page 119 marked)

Now, normally to get off the cell block I have to have a pass but I don't. I'm winging it. I have Spike on my shoulder tucked under my 1970's size collar and just about to lay down my best convict razzle dazzle line to the wing officer when he opens the gate to poke his head out. Something's happening in the quarter of a mile long hallway. Just then a raw half a chicken hit's him full in the face knocking his head into the open crash gate and cartoon birds circle his head as he slides to the floor. Spike and I poke our head out in time to see, Ronnald? Yup ole Ron's got what looks like an ore from a canoe and he's running back the other way…??? A couple of officer's from the goon squad are hot on his trail. Except for the chicken's in the hall way and the officer, I see no problem getting out of the cell block now. Stepping over the officer I start toward the mail room. I can just see Ronnald cutting the corner for Chow hall "A". I think he has a paddle for stirring big kettles in the kitchen. Anyways I got to the hallway where the officer's are and no one's there. Now usually there's someone to ask "wha-da-ya-want!" I know the way to the mailroom. So I go to the stairway and then up to the second floor. "Wha-da-ya-think?" I ask my co-pilot Spike. He thinks it's strange too. I go up to the counter and ring the bell. A Miss La-hoy-a-keesh-awn comes in and says, "wha-da-ya-want?" I tell her I'm here to enquire about a publication and the probability of its being accepted into the institution due to…she stopped me there and asked that I speak English. "I wanna know can I have this?" I say pointing at the Spectrum II write up in my handy dandy… well you know. She points to a conference room, "Ask Miss English!" she says. I go to the open door she pointed at and look inside. "Excuse me" I say, "wha-da-ya-want!" comes back from a crotchety old bag who's scowling down her nose at me from behind a conference table. This table is huge! It could seat 30 to 40 easily. There are maybe fifteen people seated at various points but the noise I heard came from the head of the table on the other side of the room. "Well, don't just stand there stupid, wha-da-ya-want?" she says. I come into the room, "I wanted to know if I will be able to receive this book from…" "Here, let me see" she says, stretching her hand for the catalog. I'm standing with my right shoulder to the wall, the table is on my left and beyond that is a wall with eight large windows that look out over the prison fences and what's beyond. I point out the Spectrum II book to her and as she's going over the synopsis in the catalog I hear, "what in the name of…" Well, past experiences tell me to look for Spike but this person is looking out the window. I follow her gaze and low and behold I see Sherry riding Johnny Walker headed right for the window. Just then Miss English and Spike see what's coming. "Blimey!" Miss English says and Spike takes flight. I reach for Spike, knowing he won't get far with his cape on (he get's tangled up in his wings, don't cha know) sure enough he falls into the mess of hair of one of the linebacker size women sitting around the table. She screams and our attention is drawn away from the spider who's riding a Seagull. This scream has rattled the eyeballs of everyone in the room. This lady is up and flailing wildly with meaty arms. Spike narrowly misses being smashed but she catches the guy beside her, and at first I think she's knocked his head off but it's only his hair piece. "A Bug!" someone yells and breaks a chair, slamming it into the hair piece. "Spike!" I yell and dive for what I thought was him. The chair rises again and came down across my shoulders knocking me to the floor where I see I'm holding the hair piece. "Thunk!" I hear and look over to see Johnny Walker sliding down the glass. He missed the open window by half an inch, but Sherry didn't! She came in and did an eight point landing on Miss English's face, who promptly fainted. (Lucky for her) The chair wielding mail person took a swing at Sherry who did a spider man move and vacated Miss English's face, just in time. I rolled out of the way of moving feet. I went under the table where I thought I'd be safe. Spike was already there, asking, "What kept you?" It was then that we noticed a base ball size cotton ball under the table and as people were scrambling hither and yon in the room I picked up a pencil and gave it (the cotton ball) a lil poke. The fabric of the cotton ball parted and out crawled tiny spiders. I broke to the left and Spike broke to the right. As I rolled out from under the table something dropped onto my chest. At first I thought, Spider! But saw it was the hair piece. "Whew" I thought as a table leg size piece of lumber came crashing down on my hands and chest. "Kill it!" says a lady wielding this piece of lumber and she swings again. I rolled back under the table. Six webs catch me in the face and I roll back out the other side. "Momma!" I said, getting to my feet. Two huge women with blunt objects are coming my way (?) Oh my God, I'm still holding the hair piece! I toss it onto the table and break for the door. I almost make it when something drops down in front of me. I see Spider and veer to the left taking the wall full in the face. I'm not clear what happened after that. I managed to make it to the stairs and Spike caught up with me there. He says I was jabbering nonsense about baseball season being over. There was more chaos in the hallway. Three goon squad officers shot past us going toward the mailroom. We reach the main hallway and there's Ronnald throwing raw chickens up in the air and swatting them with his paddle. He line drives one into an on coming officer and is then tackled, cuffed and dragged off screaming something about eColi. I don't think we're having chicken tomorrow after all. But ya never know around here. The Warden shows up and yells at me to go to work. "Yer bleeding" he says and then show's he cares. "Go see Nurse Ratchet after work" He says Hi to Spike and heads toward the mailroom. I go back to cell block "7" and am just in time to see that officer wheeled away by the medical people. I went to take a nap and Spike went looking for Johnny Walker. He told me he might catch a flight out after all.

So I have the cell to myself for a day or two...well almost, Sherry's back in the corner, Ronnald's missing in action (lockup for three days) and I believe Spike went south for a while. I left my books in the mailroom but hey it's the mailroom, they can mail them to me.

Did you know that Ronnald's dad has a famous song named after him, or is it about him? You guessed it; Old Mac Donald is Ron's dad! He had a farm ya know. Anyways take it easy.

Peace,
Walt & Co.

PS: Yes I got your note saying you got the drawing, it was a nice note to let me know you got it.

****

May 2, 2007

Dear Liz and Co;

I got your letter the other day and immediately felt like...umm that I should have written prior to this. I had done a board of this very picture (see enclosed card) and was trying to get it out before shakedown / lockdown (one in the same) some idiot offered me $50.00 for it so I sold it. $50.00 is a lot of money for me. I'd tell ya I was ashamed but (over a cup of coffee) I honestly can't say that. I felt flattered actually, and since we went on lockdown right directly afterwards I haven't got any boards yet. The store has been out of them. It's a crap shoot going to the commissary around here. Anyway for the better part of this year we've been locked down due to shortage of staff or whatever excuse the Warden hands down to us bottom feeders. So Spike guilted me into at least drawing this card. Since Mother's Day is almost here maybe someone there can use it. Liz you say you have grandkids so...I gotta figure...see; this is where I get into trouble all the time. The "figuring" thing. I hope you like the picture. *(Note: I've not thrown away or misplaced "any" card or picture he's ever sent, but I don't know which one this was. He wasn't good at putting dates on them so I probably still have it.)*

Ronnald has had a French fry grease accident and lost all the hair on the left side of his head. Me and Spike tried to get him to just cut the right side of his hair to match the left till it grew out but that's one stubborn clown!! He did the "comb over" bit, can you believe it? It's hard to take him serious these days with that doo.

Spike's already back from his trip and stay's around the cell a lot. Sherry ain't been seen or heard from in a while. I keep her web up though, cause the moment I take it down...It's been pretty peaceful around here. Hell, we've been stuck in the cell! At least baseball seasons in, well it started last month. The only game we can get on the radio is Houston Astros (they stink!) but why would a Texas radio station play the Cleveland Indians? Ronnald likes the Greenbay Packers. I tried to tell him they don't play baseball but you can't tell him nothing some times. I'm thinking about doing the "invisible treatment" to him. Maybe I will. But actually with him working in the chow hall I eat better than most. So, to ensure I'm not "pullin" orange hairs out of my peanut butter sandwiches...ewww.

I could answer your letter. This is the longest letter I've got from yawl. It's a nice friendly letter too Liz, thanx. Yes I am allowed hard cover books and the nudity isn't that big a deal if it's art. I doubt those graphic novels would make it in, but I did get the Spectrum and would have got the Amizona but they denied it because it was altered. (No good deed ever goes unpunished) *(Note: I probably "inked out" bare breasts or somewhere else)* Trying to reason with these people over that kind of stuff, it ain't happening. Anyway, hard covers are okay. I do like most art too. Scott Gustafson did that fairytale book and he's got some art in this Spectrum II book. His detail is awesome. Stuff like that I love. Gary Larson is always good, great even. Comedy is always welcome. Calvin and Hobbs, or _any_ art. I'm an art freak. I love nice pictures. You ask why am I in Texas.

Well in reality or my opinion? Because if you want my opinion, let's say Texas was a mule...and that mule was facing north and you were looking at the south end...catch my drift? Actually geographically speaking we're South East Texas, close to Houston. We got some of Katrina when she blew through here. It knocked out the power, and blew down some things. You know Hurricanes do that sometimes. Spike got scared but he survived.

When you take a photo of your Lilac save me a copy as I don't know what one looks like. Are they pretty? Stupid question!

I haven't written many stories lately, to send out to publishers. I was pestering an art professor at Cornell University a while back. He sent me a huge art history book and told me until I read it he wasn't gonna respond to my silly antics anymore. Since then I've been reading about art history. Cool huh? Anyway until I got your letter I've been unconcerned with mail call. I ain't expecting nothing so why bother? Is that pathetic or what? Geese, I started this letter wondering what I was gonna say, and now I'm already into three pages. Thanx again Liz.

I ain't been in a cast for awhile. All my internal organs have grown back. I think being locked down keeps me out of trouble, I guess. I'm a winter person too Liz. The summer heat down here get's an extra boost of humidity that's "not" always nice. Boy if they ever let me out of here I'm heading north till I get called a Chinook!! (Legally of course) I have two suits in the Federal Courts still so we'll see. Lately it's been raining getting ready to heat up and sweat! At least with the cold you can put something on.

Do your plants speak with an English accent? I mean the seeds you bought back from England? Another stupid question huh. I still expect Spikes doughnut seed to grow, it hasn't as of yet. What kind of music does your little radio play? My radio plays Classical, Country and Classic Rock. The Country is Classic too. I play Classical while I draw. We got a Sam Huston University radio station that don't talk, just plays some pretty cool classical stuff.

Okay I'm gonna close now. I'll work on another "adventures of" story for the archives. Oh that reminds me, a student at Cornell University caught a whiff of my "silly antics" and suggested I send her a couple of "Spike story's" She said she'd type em up, correct the grammar (that hurt!) and submit em to her creative writing teacher. I haven't done it but maybe...well gotta go now. We get showers today so I can drop this on my way. Y'all take care; let me know you got the card. Believe it or not it took a lot longer to draw than it looks. I hope you like it. Spike says Hi, Ronnald smiled and posed...you don't wanna know, trust me. And I remain your faithful friend and God Bless you.

Walt.

****

June 3, 2007

Liz and Co;

Howdy ladies and if there be a gentleman among ya, lucky you! From my point of view anyway. Me and Spike are hangin out. (Literally, I'm on my upside down diet again) Ronnalds back in solitary. We don't know why really. Me and Spike were arguing about why he has to be called a "water" roach instead of a cockroach when a "new boot" officer (a new officer) came and wanted to search the cell. So I put my shoes on and me and Spike came out. Well, as you know Sherry's been on some kind of vacation, again (she hasn't been home very long) but chooses this moment to make her return and she's put on weight too! Most of the officers avoid this cell, probably because of Ronnalds Booger collection, which is gross. I know but what else can it be? Anyway I was standing outside the cell while a Jr. Cadet was going through all mine and Spike's stuff. Ronnald's stuff was there too but he hadn't got that far, yet. All of a sudden the officer came barreling out of the cell screaming with Sherry stuck to his face. "OMG" I said, not recognizing Sherry at first. She's put on a lot of weight. She looks good on the officer's "mug" though. Spike tells me it's Sherry, (that's how I knew,) well this very excited cop turns and starts down the tier acting so unprofessional. He runs into the wall and knocks himself out. I run over to see if Sherry's okay. She is and I'm taking her back to the cell when up the stairs came a whole herd of cops. I live on the third tier and I'm the only one up here in the hallway...well, except Officer Beaver Cleaver who's out like a light. The herd of cops stop next to their fallen comrade and check him out to see if he's alive. Then out come the sticks, the mace and anything else they have and the chase is on. Immediately Sherry shoots a web and vacates. Spike dives into my shirt pocket while I do an about face and take off running down the tier. At the end there are no stairs. The only stairs are back the other way and that way is blocked at the moment by five angry TDC officers who "assume" I did something bad, why? Because I ran. I climbed over the rail and try doing a Spiderman thing down the opposite wall which is three stories of open windows. I should be able to climb down if I were Spiderman, except I ain't Spiderman. Well, I hit every open window on the way down landing on my back looking up three stories at five cops looking over the rail. I waste no time getting up. I start crawling toward the yard door, which is open for the hourly yard call. I make it out before it closes and lose myself in the crowd. They make us wear white (like chefs) so it's easy to blend in. Spike's glad Sherry's back and I am glad to get out of another wall to wall therapy session. When we got back to the cell, Ronnald was gone and it looked like a struggle had taken place. Sherry said they didn't say nothing just came in and got him after he came back from work. He'll be back. There's no word on the officer that shook the cell down while we were out in the yard.

In the news today I read they'd released Dr. Kevorkian the other day. There's hope for us all now!! What I mean is if he can get out...not the other thing.

Well Liz, I was thinking about you up there in Grass Valley. How's yer flower garden? Have you ever grown a Venus Fly Trap? I hope all's well and you got my last card. Did ja? It's getting hot and humid here. Do they still have the Grass Valley Bluegrass Festival each year? *(Note: He's been there too long. I've told him several times that yes we still have the Bluegrass Festival every year.)* Well I gotta go and hang back upside down, y'all take care.

Walt and Spike

****

June 13, 2007

Dear Liz and Co.;

I have conversed with my ace duce partner Spike and he asked why I don't tell story's anymore. So I told him a story. It wasn't a long one, just a story that made him smile. So Sherry wanted a story and I told her Charlotte's Web. She liked it. Then Ronnald wanted one so I told him about Peter Pan, which instigated an argument between Spike and me about who the lost boys really were. Spike won. So Richard Millhouse Nixon was second in command in the lost boy's troop which, according to Spike, inspired him to run for President thus becoming the closest thing to a water-roach becoming President, ever! Now who can argue with that? Ronnald liked his story none the less. And now I'm gonna spin you a yarn. Nothing depressing but as in all true stories it's out of tragedies that most good drama's occur. Take for example Peter Pan. If there was no conflict between Capt. Hook and Ole Pete, the lost boys biggest accomplishment would be who could fart the loudest in which case Tinker Bell would have passed through the wrong cloud one day and, well, perhaps tragedies cannot be avoided after all.

This story, as all good stories are better when read with an English accent. Liz reads everything with an English accent probably because she likes it. She don't even know she's doing it. We do though. So, we'll use foreign words from her country like, "Beastly" and "Blimey" and so on and so forth. I am, if nothing else, a considerate story teller, don't cha think?

(Note: This story is my favourite from Walter. It's called Giraffalo.) **Here goes.** Once upon a time in a land called "The Serengeti" on a continent called Africa a herd of water buffalo were grazing on grass in the heat that was the normal climate of that place. A female water buffalo, who's name is Hazel, was extremely distressed over her calf that was born only moments before. "Come Hazel, he's not moving" said Hazel's friend Maggie. "No" said Hazel nosing the still born calf that lay lifeless in the grass. "He just needs more time." She said.

A feeling of unrest had been growing through the herd and slowly the herd had been moving away from the area. "Come on ole girl, something's amiss." Maggie said. "No! I can't leave him," said Hazel. "I won't leave him." And Maggie believed her.

Just then, south of the herd, a pride of lions made their move to stampede the herd, to weed out the old and very young. The ones who couldn't keep up. It's nature's way of keeping a species strong. The herd bolted. Hazel and Maggie were pushed along forcing Hazel to come to terms with her loss. This was Hazel's first calf and she knew no other feeling to compare to the devastation she felt over loosing her first and as yet, only baby. Maggie was the friend Hazel needed, yet an exhausting stampede in a random direction seemed to be more effective.

"We must go back Maggie," Hazel said while looking at the huge dust cloud left in the wake of the herd. "We cannot Hazel, your baby is gone and there were lions. How could we survive?" She was trying to reason with Hazel, but Hazel would not be reasoned with. "I'll find him," Hazel said, and she started braying for her calf. Maggie followed silently.

Day's followed and Maggie noticed Hazel looking behind every bush in the thickest grass. She sniffed other calf's until she was satisfied this was not her baby. Maggie endured. The lead bull was concerned but knew enough not to say anything. Time heals all wounds. It was several days later that the herd was strung out over several miles. Hazel was tired. Maggie and the lead bull kept watch and waited.

The heat kept shimmering on the horizon. "Blimey it's hot," said the lead bull. "Aye it is that!" said Maggie while watching Hazel. "What's she looking at," said Maggie. The lead bull, who's name was Spike, (that of course ain't his real name, but you can figure it out.) followed Hazel's gaze. Two young male lion's were stalking a giraffe that looked as if she were bracing for a fight. "Uh oh," said Spike and as they watched, Hazel started moving in the direction of the giraffe. Slowly at first. Then the giraffe charged the lion's as they split up, one going left, the other going right. This latter one was not fortunate enough to avoid a huge foot stomping on his tail and as he turned, in a flash a huge giraffe head hooked him with the two stubs of horn and launched the lion twenty feet in the air while twisting and turning to maintain his balance. The other lion leapt up and sank his teeth and claws into the neck of the giraffe. Spike and Maggie were lost in observing this struggle for life. The giraffe bucked and stomped trying to lose the lion on her neck. She was moving toward the lion who had taken the fall. The other lion raked his paws ever deeper into the giraffe's neck and dropped to the ground, avoiding the giraffe's stomping feet. "Let's help her," said Maggie to Spike. "It's not our way" he said. "Come on, for Hazel." She said, indicating Hazel, alone, was moving slowly toward a distant clump of grass. Spike pawed the ground and put his head down. Several other bulls noticed and closed in to join Spike and Maggie who were moving toward the giraffe.

The two lions had moved off to wait for the inevitable. The giraffe was standing defiantly, her legs sprawled and trembling. It was clear by the amount of blood coming from her wounds that she wouldn't last long. As Maggie approached, the giraffe looked over at the approaching buffalo and her front legs gave out. The lions started to move in as ten big buffalo males took up a position in front of the giraffe. "It is our way!" roared a frustrated lion. "You can wait," said Spike, lowering his massive head and horns to punctuate what he said. The giraffe looked back over her shoulder and collapsed to the ground. "Rest my Lady," said Maggie as soothingly as she could. She knew these were the final moments of the valiant animal's life.

"I have a…" started the giraffe. "A what?" asked Maggie? "I have a baby in the grass." She said breathless. Maggie looked up and saw what had attracted Hazel. "Oh my!" she said under her breath. "Promise me…promise me he'll be okay," said the giraffe. Maggie turned back and said, "I promise your baby will be taken care of as if you were there." The giraffe looked at Maggie. "Your baby will know no grief as sure as I'm standing here. As she stared in the direction of her foal, through fading eyes she said, "Will he know love?" Maggie looked at her and said, "He will my Lady, he will. You rest now." And rest she did

Further out Hazel approached a bundle of legs, neck and two huge eyes. She sniffed and nuzzled the little fella. "Are you my momma?" said the little guy. Hazel looked over to the finished drama and back down to the foal. "Yes, I am your momma. We must go now, can you stand?" She said pushing him with her nose to help him stand. Hazel led the little fella off in the direction of the herd and away from the previous scene.

Spike, Maggie and the rest of the herd met her later. "I told you I'd find him!" she said. "Yes you did." Spike answered. Maggie asked, "What's his name?" while giving him a sniff. "I'm Giraffalo!" the little fella said, while skipping along beside him mom. And the herd moved on across the pains of the Serengeti.*(Note: Walter re-did it years later, adding on a second story of "Giraffalo" grown up and leading the herd out and away from a huge fire.)*

The End

June 26, 2007

Liz;

Hi, I don't have much time to write right now. I'm dealing with a Federal Magistrate who's trying to understand my way of thinking. Silly mortal!! I wanted to get this in the mail last week but got a recommendation from the Magistrate Judge that I had 10 days to respond so...

Spike and Ronnald say Hi and life here is still the same. I hope everyone there is fine and dandy. Gotta go, take care.

All my best,
Walt

****

July 9, 2007

Liz;

Hi, I finally have a chance to sit down and write. First I received the books, thank you so much! I read the Gold Cities books right away, thank you I loved it. *(Note: I sent history books on Grass Valley and Nevada City)*

I got a letter from Cornel University in New York, they want me to write some of my unique experiences down and a student would edit them. They would appear in a news paper the college puts out. It got me to thinking...No really! You can kick this around with some of the people who have read our correspondences and see what they think. I read where J.K. Rawlings, the writer who did Harry Potter, started taking down notes on napkins and finally put it all together while she was a waitress, and then sent it to a publisher. The rest is history. Stephen King taught school, lived in a trailer with "Carrie" written and taking up space in his closet until his wife finally sent it to a publisher and Bam! (I always wanted to do that, I watched Batman as a kid) Zowie!!! Okay I'll quit. Anyway, Dean Koontz was skeptical till his ole lady threatened to kill him, now look at him. What about Arnold Zelwigger (?) that guy has written three novels that are the best crime drama's ever written, bar none! What? You've never heard of Arnold Zelwigger? That's because he never published them and rats are making nests from the manuscripts in his garage somewhere in Newark, New Jersey, while he eats Aleppo on a fixed income. Okay, his wife or ole lady didn't push him. I made that up but why not compile all that stuff, change it to English (punctuate it), write an entro, make my title "my lunatic friend from across the country", send it to an English publisher and see what happens. The worst thing is you'd be out the time it took to retype all that, postage and...what else? That's it! Even if it wasn't big enough they'd tell you "hey yer on to something" or "don't quit your day job" You could write a disclaimer and blame anything that went wrong on me. Yeah, what can they do, put me in prison? Do you know how many times someone's said, "Hey stupid, why don't you write that crap and publish it?" I'm never motivated enough but you said you saved all them letters? If they like it and actually publish it there are a few things it would have in its favor, #1: It's original, new, clean, never even remotely been approached in literature before. #2: It's got some funny parts and one sad part which we won't go into just now. Even that was creative though. Ronnald might be a problem, actually not really since I would take any literary infringements. As far as McDonald's whining about copy rights. We could split the proceeds, anyway you want, see it's even in writing. (Spike said to say that) Any art work done would not be included. I don't do much original art work anymore. I have done some but it takes a lot out of me and what would I do with it anyway? You want I should do an original drawing for you? *(Note: He now draws a lot and 99% comes to me, I'm including a lot with this book. Walter Gerald Anderson, this is your life since April 21, 2003.)*

Say, are the mines still open up there? I mean could you stroll down one and see who lives down there? *(Note: Yes you can stroll around some but no one lives down a mine shaft)*

Did you get the Giraffalo picture? *(Note: Yes)* I suppose he crossed paths with your books. You know if you did this and it paid off, you wouldn't have to train no one no more. You could go online and get yourself a '57 Chevy...Orange with white interior, is that what you said you'd like, someday? Yeah I pay attention. Along with dice hanging from the rear view mirror. Dare to dream Liz, I do nearly every day and won't give up. Anyways, think about it and let me know. I think it's a good idea.

I've been fighting in the courts again. I've got filing fees from hell and nothing to show for it but I keep chuggin at em. They're gonna get tired of me I hope they don't shoot me. Geese, I never thought of that...it would be just like those cheap bastard, I don't think they'd spring for the bullet.

I gotta respond to the "pink" tee shirt. The shirt I'm wearing in the photo, the one you said looks pink is actually a heavy white canvas shirt that I wore to a visit one day. I got called to a visit by mistake, (another Anderson) and they had me stop to take a picture before going out to the visiting room. Can you imagine the surprise on the "other" Anderson when I showed up? They let me keep the photo. I had it copied and you got one. Pretty cool huh? Oh yeah, the Giraffalo picture is original. No, I can't vote. *(Note: One of my questions to him)* Am I really wearing a pink shirt? You'd think someone around here would a told me! Not everyone is color blind like me. *(Note: The photo makes the shirt look light pink)* I gotta go find me a five legged cockroach and talk to him. Y'all be good, thanx again for the books.

Peace,
Walt

****

July 16, 2007

Dear Liz and Co;

Howdy y'all. I got your yellow paper letter last night and thought I'd sit down and write back while there's peace. Ronnald has rescued Spike from Sherry. She had him hog tied in the corer of the cell, Spike; she had Spike hog tied in her nasty web. It's really hot down here, Ronnald and Spike are in the day room trying to coax sparrows (out of the shade) into the direct sun light and see if they burst into flame. Cruel I know but yer talking about the ethics of a clown and a cockroach. How's the weather there?

We're supposed to catch the tail end of Erin (Hurricane Erin) this evening or tonight. When Hurricane Katrina came through here and knocked out the power it was still very hot and muggy. The humidity is what really get's me down, I'd take the heat but without humidity. The weather man talks about 96% humidity and I'm thinking 96? Four more degrees humidity and we're under water ain't we? For the love of Pete! Wha-d-ya-gonna do then Einstein? Fortunately that hasn't happened, yet.

How's yer flowers? Ya know you mentioned those awesome old cars coming into Grass Valley and yeah they're really cool, *(Note: Grass Valley has a very large "old cars" show every year. Roads are closed downtown just to park the cars.)* But I favor those 40 foot long land yachts. My last car (by choice) was a 1972 Oldsmobile Delta Royal 88. You could seat eight people in it. Four in front, four in the back with both sets of in laws in the trunk. Comfortably cruise at 100 miles an hour across the desert. Well, maybe not the desert, the in laws might get a little hot back there. It would screw up their card game or whatever they were doing. That car had a priceless drive train with a 350 Rocket engine and 19 carburetors on top. It passed everything but a gas station, which wouldn't be very practical right now. I like big cars. *(Note: He's 6'3", 200+ lbs; he'd look funny in a compact car)* Ronnald has a picture of a mini, what is it with clowns and small cars? He says he'll get me one when he get's out. He's up for parole this year too so you never know.

Sherry's back and notices Spike's missing. Geese she's getting big. Say, do you know why moths have dust on their wings? It keeps them out of spider webs. Sherry learned me that so called fact. Go figure! I'm gonna write a song called, "me and my bug" it will be sung to the tune of "Yellow

Rose of Texas", I hope every Texan south of the Canadian River takes offense...well, <u>after</u> I'm gone maybe. I'll make y'all a copy when it's done.

Let's see what your letter says. You're talking about your mood. I'll bet it's nothing compared to Ronnald's. Geese, that's one high maintenance clown. He saw a commercial on TV where they're using a statue of Ronald McDonald and saying McDonald's get's its beef from New Zealand or somewhere. He was hard to live with for a while. Spike asked him why they were buying New Zealand beef instead of USA beef, and then he reminds us of the hoof and mouth thing going around. That's why the meat comes from New Zealand. Just between us, I think our Ronnalds a few French fries short of a happy meal. Someone should spike his milkshake with Prozac. So, if you're ever pissed off and wanna vent to someone who probably ain't got a clue as to who might be the object of your wrath, you go ahead. I'll co-sign all of it and no one will ever hear it back from me. That's what friends are for.

Yeah, Cornell University hasn't written back since I sent em a story on how I got busted down here in Texas. I wrote them a made up one that was okay. I didn't copy it down but do remember it and will send it right behind this letter. I gotta get more stamps, but will do this over the weekend. I have some cards done for stamps and this will all take place this...um.. weekend. Am I repeating myself? Spike says I do that sometimes. He says it's probably old age. I'm 40 friggin 5, not 85! Did I mention Cornell ain't wrote yet? Oh yeah, well you know. Actually when I sent them that story I requested books from a "Books through Bars Project" these aren't art books but novels or text books on math or sociology. I requested novels, mainly fantasy type, like David Gemmell (one of your homeboys Liz,) he's an excellent story teller too. Anyway they sent me two novels by a guy named George R.R. Martin. Books #1 and #2 in a series. I've read them both before, but! I that's okay because these two books are absolutely the best fantasy I've ever read. One is called "A Game of Thrones" and #2 is called "A Clash of Kings". In case there are any fantasy readers out there, I'd highly recommend them both. Y'all probably don't read much huh? *(Note: He's being facetious; I work in a mail order book co. duh!)* I've read this Grass Valley Gold Mine book three times and still drag it out to look at the pictures.

Alright who farted? Excuse me, the wind just shifted and we have cattle and pigs out here. This prison is a huge agricultural bonanza and when the wind shifts (no pun intended) it's a reminder of the many animals that also share the prison. I've used that as a pickup line before. (It was not meant to be crude. Sometimes things like that just slip out) It's not very effective unless you're trying to go home alone, then it pretty much works out every time. Okay, enough about that.

Okay what else? Oh the publishers! Yeah, say, Spike is excited! He says it was destiny you having a brother in the business and all. He asked if your brother is a Limey too. I, being sarcastic, said, "No, he's French!" Then the little bugger wanted to fight. Do the English take offense being called a Limey? If so I'm sorry. U.S. Yanks don't find "Yankee" offensive, well I take that back. These "Johnny Rebs" do. I've been called worse. For the record Spike and I say it with the utmost amount of respect. Oh yeah, the publishers, my mind wanders so easily. You asked about a format..umm. Okay. Yeah! A format. That would be good. Actually I know exactly what you're talking about... umm, what are you talking about? Whatever you think is best, I thought maybe start from the beginning. *(Note: I'm typing one of his stories for him so he can send it to a magazine.)* You do what you think is best because you're obviously the brains of this outfit. I can't even spell words like colour or rumour or Westminster Abbey. And you are correct, we may not get anywhere at all with this, but then again we might.

I've told the "Giraffalo" story to Ronnald and Sherry; both think I should do another chapter. I should have added something but like an idiot, I never copied any thing. But, you saved everything? Liz you're a genius! A bloody genius? Gee-nee-us, that's the spelling thing you mentioned? Well we all have our rolls in life. Thank God for people like you Liz.

Peace! I hope all is well there and everyone hits the stinkin lottery! Spike's mouth is webbed shut so he's just mumbling. I gotta go. I'll work on my arrest story this weekend. It's far more entertaining than the real one, at least for us. Yeah, I'd love to see a Franklin Booth book, you know I love books. Take care.

Respectfully,
Walt.

PS: Your letters are easy to read. No I don't get money so I know what you're talking about. Just don't change nothin.

****

August 19, 2007

Liz and Co;

Hi you guys! Er gal's…or guys and gal's, you know what I mean. How's everyone today? Well I hope. Did anyone hit the lottery? Me neither. It's really hot here. You probably think it's hot there, you don't know hot until you've experienced this hot. I know some people who live in Phoenix Arizona think its hot there and it probably is but it's a "dry" heat. Whatever, it's bloody hot.

Ronnald woke up yesterday and banged his head on the top bunk (my bunk) which woke me up. He started yelling "I'm blind, I'm blind". He stood up and walked into the wall. I noticed he had his eye lids webbed together, I told him that. He turned around and ran into the bars that are at the front of our cell. "Hey carrot top" I said, "Sherry webbed your eyes shut!" That's when I noticed his ear holes were webbed over too. So I got off the bed and stopped psycho clown before he did any more damage, to himself. Spike was watching all this from his hammock in the corner. Spike has apparently made up with Sherry. He's kicked back in the corner lying on his back being fed something by Sherry. (I don't want to know) What he did to smooth things over with the only female of our humble dwelling, I don't wanna know what he's eating.

I'm supposed to tell ya the story I told Cornell University. You may have to be warned, everything I'm about to write ain't exactly true.

Well, it was close to the turn of the 21st century. I was a younger man, as we all were…well, eh hem, some of you weren't men at all and that's okay. In fact this is helpful when you think about God's last "personal" instructions to us mortals. I think it was "live long and prosper" No wait! That was Spock. "Go forth and multiply!" I'm better at math than spelling. Especially that kind of math. Spike is even better! His "Go forth and multiply" routine is legendary. I think they call it "infestation" but that's another matter altogether. Okay, I digress. I was residing in Sacramento California, Fair Oaks to be exact. Why anyone would leave the rivers of Northern California for Texas is beyond me. I had a sister living down here who asked me to come and visit. So I loaded up my 1972 Olds and started south. I've done some stupid things in my past, No really! But this maneuver was gonna end up topping the list. (In my opinion) Although there was a time, well never mind. Being a native Californian I never experienced anything outside the norm until I hit Highway 40 heading east out of Los Angeles. The Hare Krishna banging cymbals next to the psychogenic hookah smoking long haired hippy freaks partying along the side of the road being the norm that is. I came over the hill just before Bakersfield and ran out of gas. It happens when you're car uses a bilge pump for its engines gas intake. Anyway, it's a good thing I was over the hump and coasted 4000 pounds of Detroit iron 20 some miles with nothing but the radio working (A rarity, it seems the radio only worked when it wanted to) Like I said nothing outside of the norm. I coasted into the nearest gas station; I came down I-5 to the 440, looped around on the 210 and got off on the Santa Monica Freeway to the 190. I took a shortcut on Artesia Blvd. and wound up headed east on 40, which runs to the Eastern Seaboard. So far so good. I'm a simple man when it comes to taking the easy way. As I put California in my rear view mirror and passed into Arizona the sun was going down. I drove on into the night, stopping in Phoenix for a meal and a nap. As I left and continued I saw several people with the "Y2K Doomsday" message roaming around unchecked. Outside of that and the fare at a Mom and Pop Eatery (deep fried bugs dipped in honey and cat meat burrito's) the burrito wasn't bad. Anyways outside of that, Arizona passed and New Mexico was upon me. I stopped for gas in the middle of the New Mexico desert where a convenience store sold fireworks. The fireworks store could pass for an arms dealer in the underworld. I never saw so many different varieties and sizes of firecrackers in my life. You got 250 free Black Cat firecrackers with every fill up of gas. In fact I heard the guy behind the counter say, "look Ma, we can close early. We got us a live one!" Then to me he said, "What'll have son?" "I'm gonna filler up" I said and he smiled showing both of his teeth. I couldn't help but smile too. I also couldn't help checking out the fireworks. This was 30,000 square feet of firecrackers, Bottle rockets, Sky rockets, Anti-tank rockets, Bombs, Sparklers, Roman candles etc, etc. I spent $63.00 on gas and $256.00 on fireworks. The prize piece being a 37 pound rocket on a baseball bat painted red and white like a Barber Pole. $45.00 bucks it cost me and when I let it off, it shot up into the sky and kept going. It could have blown a chunk out of the Moon for all I know. I never seen it explode or come down. Anyway I blew most of em off in the New Mexico desert that night. I slept in the backseat of my car, comfortably too. About 2:30 am the radio came on blaring Wolfman Jack. It hadda been a re-broadcast because Wolfman Jack ain't been on the air for years. I heard, after banging on the dash, "Houston, we have a problem!" "This is Mission Control, what seems to be the problem Discover?" "Ah, someone just took a shot at us!" and the radio turned off. I went back to sleep thinking it took a special sort of idiot to take a shot at the Space Shuttle. The next morning as I passed into what's called the Panhandle of Texas I noticed a place selling purple snow cones on the side of the road. I went past thinking "A purple snow cone sounds kinda good" I hooked a right turn on "I" 35 and headed down into Texas. I drove for an hour or so and came across the Canadian River. "Canadian? What's it doing down here?" then I saw it, kinda muddy and you couldn't see the bottom. There were some scrub bushes growing along the bank, I didn't take a second look. I wonder how much the Canadian's got for it. The roadside view wasn't much to look at, mostly desert and flat with tumble weeds. It very hot and desolate. Mountains (Mesa's) with their tops cut off. (I wonder what happened to the tops) A lot of sky, and then I saw a rest stop with an almost full parking lot gathered around a big giant Cowboy hat that sold Armadillo burgers and purple snow cones. That sounds good. I pulled into the lot next to a Charter Bus. As soon as I pulled up, sixteen Japanese tourists started taking pictures. I climbed out and waved, smiling like I was Elvis. What else could I do, I gotta be friendly! "Oooh you beeg Joe, you got beeg Amewican caw" (car) one said looking up at me. I stand about 6' 3" so compared to him...anyway I said, "yep, jus call me Hoss!" and hey, he did. "Come on Hoss, I buy you snow cone" He rattled something in a foreign language to his friends. I think it was French, how would I know? So we all, me and my new little friends, went to the Big Hat and got a purple snow cone. Someone by the road started making a fuss and everyone grabbed their cameras and rushed to the road. By the time I got there they were all slapping a new roll of film in their cameras. "What is it?" I asked. Hop Sing said, "Snakes!" and after taking a closer look I saw that it was two or three snakes rolling around in the middle of the road. "You know what kind snake?" Hop Sing asked. I thought about telling them the truth and saying, "No" but where's the fun in that? "Yep" I said and as the group of French talking Japanese tourists looked at me I said, "why them's the mating rituals of the South Sascutuan Emerald Belly Side Winding Suicide Snake" Hop Sing translated to his fellow tourists which prompted another photo session. Everyone watched the snakes in silence for a moment, and then someone asked Hop Sing a question. Who in turn asked me? "He wanna know why they called "suicide snake?" Just then a State Trooper shot by us doing about 130 miles an hour. Making goo-lash out of the snakes. Everyone said, "Ooooooh. I watched him go, while eating my purple snow cone. Then I was staring at this small river of red making its way to the mess in the middle of the road. "What that Hoss?" asked my lil friend. "Looks like ants" I said amid multiple shutter clicks. "Ooooh look it dong chow ping pong gooling lang" he said to everybody. "Them's fire ants" someone drawled and a lady in Cowboy boots, Wrangler jeans and a top tied just under her *massive*...umm... ahh...well, boobs! You should have heard the cameras going off then. "Ping goo lang goo lang!" Hop Sing said, "I hear ya little buddy" I said as she came over. "Look, they're just about done. 'Swhy all the Hornie toads are disappearing. Them damn fire ants!" she said and looking back down at the road we seen that she was right. Those little monsters had all but picked the bones clean. "Names Lurlene" she said, stickin out her hand to shake. I shook too. You bet I did. In fact I shook her hand hard enough to ummm...cause her...eh hem...to giggle. Yeah that's it! "Y'all better git outa the road afore the cop git's back" she said, and we did. "Yer purple snow cones melted" she said and I noticed I had a purple hand holding an empty snow cone cup. I drank the juice and looked her square in the eye and crumpled up the paper cup. She giggled. More camera action. "Loy chung bing bang walla walla bing bang" says Hop Sing as we watch her sashay away. "Uh, yeah, that's what I thought too. Say, I gotta git, it was nice chatting with ya" and I got into my boat and headed off down the road. I drove for a while, not seeing many people at all and after a while the radio came on, which was nice. After a while that purple snow cone started making a bid for an exit and I didn't see any sign of where I could find a bathroom. So I pull off and saw a cactus that needed watering. (I am a humanitarian) I climb out and shut the door, look south…nothing. Shimmering road, straight and long, no cars. Look north…more of the same, heat, road, nothing! I walk around the car and walk about three feet to the cactus. Keeping in mind there's nothing over knee high anywhere! The cactus is only visible because there's not anything bigger than a small bush. "Zip down" go my Levis and, "zoom, zoom, zoom" three cars shoot by, "Zip up", what tha?…I think, turning and watching them go into the distance. "Zoom"! Another passes, then… nothing. I look down and up the road. Nothin. "Zip down", "zoom, zoom, and zoom" you'd think it was rush hour in downtown Los Angeles. "Zip up" nothing! Where the hell am I, the Twilight Zone? (My final clue) I walk our about 40 feet and take care of business. Coming back I see a State Trooper parked behind my car. His boot was up on the bumper eyeing my California License plate. I walk up and he asked me," This here your car boy?" I look around as far as the eye can see, and, nothing. "Umm, no officer, I don't know where that car came from" He made a noise sucking his teeth on the toothpick stickin out the side of his mouth, pushed his County Mounty Trooper hat back a little and said, "y'all ain't from around heah are ya?" Seeing how my audience wasn't as receptive as I thought, I thought I'd push my luck. "Why? What makes you think that?" I asked. He took his foot off my bumper, squared off with me and put his hand on the butt of his hand cannon strapped to his hip. "We don't need no smart alec remarks from no tree huggin hippy from California! Now, I asked you a question" I said, "actually Tex, you asked me two and to answer your first, yes this is my car and no I ain't from 'round hear'" I said this smiling, I had a nice smile too. I could see it in his mirrored sunglasses. Probably standard issue to troopers. He sucked his teeth. "Yew pissin on my cactus boy?" he asked. "Well, I hadda go; I don't think I hurt nuthin. It's a long way between gas stations" I stammered. I was getting an odd feeling in my internal revenue service. "You know this is where the Battle of the Sacred Comanche and the Banditos from Mexico took place?" he asked, eying me. "Yer joking right? There's a camera somewhere and you're putting me on right?" He answered by drawing his 700 Caliber shootin iron and said, "Put your hands on the car and spread them legs!" He said this while turning me with one hand and sticking that gun in my face. My hands automatically went to the roof of my car where it sounded like it would if you put your hands on a hot griddle at a burger joint. "Ow!" I said, jerking my hands back. Then someone, I won't say who! Hit me in the head with his cannon and I came too somewhere else, with cartoon birds circling my melon! I was charged with indecent exposure, endangering sacred plants, attempted murder, murder, assault with a deadly weapon, speeding, no speeding, not having a plastic Jesus in my car and shooting Kennedy. (Everyone get's that charge, why take any chances?) The jail was full of Japanese tourists too, that's another story. Geese this story kinda ran away huh?

My fingers are numb, but here's the story. Maybe a little more elaborate but it ain't bad is it? Spike liked it and it turns out the little Japanese guy I called 'Hop Sing' his real name is Ronald, can you guess why? My pet clown is one moody dude, but he feeds me, so...

I gotta go. Hope you like the story. Hope it ain't too much or too long, and I hope it cools off around here soon! Y'all take care, ya heah?

Peace and God Bless.
Walt, Spike, Ronnald and Sherry

****

October 18, 2007

Dear Liz and Co.;

First off please forgive my silence. I'm dealing with the U.S. Judicial system and that takes all of my concentration.

I got all the pictures you sent, except for the one with the "Boss Lady" Alberta in it. Yeah the one where she's walking down the stairs. Well I got it but Spike has it now. Long story. Anyway, y'all are beautiful. Is that really Peggy Sue? 'Cause they got this place called Lubbock, Texas that is Peggy Sue country. That's what they call it anyway.

Okay, I'll quit. Its early here and the coffee waters heating up. I'll be right back. (Nectar of the God's!) Cheery-o! Do they really say Cheerio in England? And while we're on the subject, what's a loo? Do I have one, do I need one? Is it different than a "toodle loo?"

Let me answer your letter. I absolutely dig all the photos you sent. Especially the Queen of the Night flower. That is very impressive if all of what you wrote about them is true and I have no reason to believe otherwise. How did you know they would bloom right then? Simply awesome Liz. Those should be on the cover of a plant magazine or some such thing. Do they smell? Is it a nice smell? *(Note: I'm telling him about my "Queen of the Night" blooming cactus)*

Liz, the typing project is one for your leisure. We ain't under no deadline my new very good best friend. This is one of those things that will get done when it gets done. Do you think this last story should go in it? I guess we've been writing for a while now huh. Anyway let me know what you think. *(Note: I've put all of his stories in that I think would be interesting to other readers. I personally like or love all of them because I know him and why he writes them, but to others who don't know him some of the stories could be boring or let's face it, stupid.)*

About how many books to send. There is no limit on how many books you can send at one time. And nudity in art, if it's artistic and not explicate, its okay. I got that Spectrum book approved on that basis. I am a slut for art. And I know who Arthur Rackham is can you believe it? He was featured in an old auction book I had. Franklin Booth is new to me and you know that I know who Frank Cho is. Send what you can, it'll be like Christmas and yes I am spoiled. Blessed is a good description too.

I told Spike about Virginia City (California) and Bonanza, he's never seen it. They show Walker Texas Ranger four times a day on this TV outside of our cell, but no Bonanza. You mention Cartwright and no one knows who you're talking about. I bet ole Hoss could whup Chuck Norris' butt.

Anyway thanks for your letter and pictures, I ain't sending them back. I may get a photo album and put them in there. (*Note: He did and has done.*)

We're getting ready for the fall shake down. What a drag. Oh well, what the hell. Haggis for supper, that's cool. Y'all take care. Spike and Ronnald send their best.

Rotts a Ruck.
God Bless, yer Friend,
Walt

****

Chapter Six

January 2008

Hi Liz and Co.:

Sorry it's taken me so long to get back to y'all. I've been in trouble. Spike's in Mexico. That's a good place for him.

I got the books you sent and am curious whether you sent them and then got the board or got the board as you were sending them. Great minds think alike and I would have been impressed if we, you and I, had sent them in the blind so ta speak, I mean I knew you were sending that stuff because you told me. Anyway I'm glad you girls like the picture. I absolutely "love" the books, especially the Franklin Booth one. I am truly thankful for y'all.

Did I mention I got in trouble? Ronnald says Spike left after I got tossed in the solitaire. I had to wear a Rabbit suit too. That or freeze my, ummm toes off, yeah toes, that sounds better than balls. Not that I'd ever talk like that to such refined ladies such as yourselves. Hey, I'm from California, gimme a break.

Anyway, Spike was trying to come up with a way to make a little money and he suggested we sell smart pills to the cops. (This is an old trick; the smart pills are actually rabbit poop.) Well the stinkin warden happened to walk up as I was making a sale and wanted to know what was going on. One officer told him they were buying smart pills so he, the warden, wanted to try one. He popped one in his mouth and started chewing it, "This taste like shit." He said. "See, they're working already!" Well that didn't go over too well with the warden. Needless to say I didn't make much money. I actually did have a couple of repeat customers though.

I hope this year is the best for all of you. Thanks again for the books and well wishes. I will write soon. Ronald says Hi and Happy New Year.

Take care, yer friend
Walt.

****

January 8, 2008

Dear Liz;

Hi my friend, how are things up in the mountains? Are you still snowed in? We got one day of snow down here last month. Well, so much for global warming huh.

Thanks for the pictures in your last letter. Speaking of which, you said you were returning a little picture of Santa I sent two years ago. You said at that time that I was going to draw it, and maybe I did and sent it to someone else. I sent you a board in November with this on it, didn't I? I think you said, after receiving it, you were going to put it on your front door. Liz I'm worried!! Spike's been warning me I've been losing my mind. I don't see how that's possible but you never know. I got busy in the Christmas season and wanted to get that done and out to you first so. I know I got a letter around here from November where you received it, didn't you? *(Note: I do have it and it's beautiful)*

I'm sorry your job has kicked you to the curb (prison slang). I can relate. It's okay though I ain't going nowhere, you're stuck with me and Spike. *(Note: "They" didn't "kick me to the curb" I hurt my back so I quit because I didn't know if or when I'd be back.)*

Speaking of Spike he says, "Happy New Year." If you want, he'll get on his seagull and fly up to Grass Valley or send a message to his kin there to have them park their multi-legged-icky- butts where you used to work until they submit to our demands. We need demands. He's all worked up now. He's got his General Patton pith helmet on and is in the middle of a long speech. I can't translate because of the profanity. I may not hear from you again but I'll still be your friend. I'll still write ya, draw ya pictures and tell silly stories. I'm actually overdue for a good old fashioned story of the Adventures of Walt and Spike the Wonder Roach.

Let's see what else did you say in your letter? Your temp is thirty degrees; you couldn't get out before 10 am because of ice, the happenings of Daisy and Dobby *(Note: My dogs.)* the calendar. Oh yeah I wrote and told you I got it, thanks, Love It!!

There's an English lady singing on the radio, "It's a Strange World we live in Master Jack" don't know who she is, Petula Clark, Lulu? I like the song, do you remember it?

Where were we, or yeah, George Bush for a pardon? I ain't important enough, besides I'm a foreigner from California. I have found new evidence and have put motions into the State Court for a new trial. Hey if you want to call them and ask what's going on I'll give you their phone number. I think the last court clerk was fired over jerking me around. I'm not sure, but I'm getting some prompt service from the new clerk, her name is Nancy. Let me know if you want to get more involved and I'll give you the phone number. *(Note: Up until this time I've been typing some of his legal motions and returning them to him. Now I start calling places and writing my own letters to senators and others about his innocence.)*

I sent two motions in. One to the Judge; he got a personal letter with the motion for a new trial. If you call ya might get to talk to "Jim Almighty". But he's probably relying on clerk Nancy to screen out the calls that have merit.

Here's a legal term that applies to my case, it's called "Brady Violation." "Brady" was a guy who won a decision in the United States Supreme Court that is a milestone case in the legal arena. Theoretically, if you can prove a Brady-Violation then a reversal is mandatory. I can and did prove it with the new evidence I sent with the motion for a new trial. You can see this new evidence on your very own handy dandy computer by going to the "Texas Department of Public Safety" www.bonhampd.com. I think that's the site. They will display registered sex offenders in Texas. The man who accused me of the crime I didn't commit is a registered sex offender and lied on the stand with the knowledge of the Assistant D.A. That is a violation of my rights (Constitutional) to a fair trial and a Brady violation. A reversal or at least a new trial. That's all I ask, a fair shake.

I'm taking Spike with me if I get a new trial. Between the both of us we can beat the bastards. We're gonna start a law firm called "Dewy, Screwum and Howe". No wait, that's the law firm that got me where I am today. Okay, enough of that. If you call them and get any news you can pass it along to me and Spike. Spike says he's seen every episode of Perry Mason so I'm in good hands.

Back to your letter. No I didn't hear from my sister after that one letter. She didn't send $$ and I didn't get a Christmas card from her. I sent her one though. Spike thinks she was drunk when she originally wrote. But that doesn't make sense. My sister doesn't drink and besides, her writing was too neat. Not like mine. Spike sits on my writing hand when "we" write, that's why it looks like an idiot wrote in the middle of a violent earthquake. Snot my fault.

No you can't send stamps in your envelope into the prison. And the only way to send $$ is by a postal order. That way you have to have a special form to fill out to do it and only "if" I send it so, I've never asked you for money Liz and don't intend to. I don't get money so in a sense I don't really miss it. Yeah they have a prison store and being able to purchase those things would be nice but I'd rather have a friend who I can write to, get letter from and know our friendship ain't based on money. I don't have many friends so cherish the ones I have. How long have we been writing? *(Note: For the record since 4/21/2003).* Besides the prices for things here are...I think I have a price list around here, somewhere, I'll find it and show ya.

Yes, inmates make the sandwiches that they sell. It's usually fried egg with a meat patty and cheese on toast. The main-line food is mass produced and usually some noodle casserole that's cooked in a huge vat. The food they sell comes from the officers' dining room. It's way different. I ain't really starving. It's easier to sell a good sandwich than a bad one so the extra effort is added. I'm glad you can relate to the sensitive taste buds thing. I ain't kidding about them putting peppers in everything. Sometimes the meal, to me, isn't edible. I also like fish and chips or fries. Long John Silver's is probably a poor substitute but to me it's good fish and fries. You would probably have to get them to wrap it in newspaper to have authentic fish and chips, maybe different fish also.

I ain't ever been to an IMAX Theater, is it a kind of theater with a huge screen? I can only speculate.

I'm gonna go. Take care and write when you can. Let me know what Bonham said if you call them. I've got two motions in there so they should be fairly quick with it. At least compared to the Federal Courts.

Bye for now, I can't very well say "keep your pecker up" to you, being you're a girl. What's a guy say to a girl?

Toodles,
Walt and Spike

January 27, 2008

Dear Liz, Alberta, Diane, Peggy and Cassandra and anyone else I missed.

Y'all are my hero's. *(Note: Even though I'm not there he still writes to me at Bud's address.)*

Well, it's been a pretty eventful week here at the big house. Last week they, the administration, tried giving me a smoke stack cleaning job and moving me to the black lung unit. I have medical restrictions that forbid them giving me certain jobs and inhaling soot is one of em. "No soot inhaling," it says. But they had me moved and I'm already on a different count so I hadda pack up all my stuff and make my way down the big hallway to cell block H-17. I believe I was here when we first started writing. It's the old Death Row wing. Anyway aside from being haunted the cells are bigger. It's not so bad.

Spike is back from Mexico. I was worried about Ronnald though. Spike didn't want to tell Sherry. She wasn't in her web. I told him it wasn't a good idea to not tell her he was back, she'd find out anyway. He decided to take his chances. What a fool! Some bugs you just can't talk to.

I went to pack all my crap and moved into H-wing, 17 block, cell 3, row 3 cell. "Honey, I'm Home!" Geese I hate moving. My new celli has a pentagram tattooed on his forehead with three sixes. Oh boy!

"I see you're religious" I say. He stares, I stare. A little guy that was there when I was there before named "Hot Rod" came up behind me and slapped me on the back. "Walt!" he says, scaring the crap out of me. "Hot Rod, what's the matter with you!" I stepped into the cell and Spike jumps off my shoulder and onto my bunk. "Spike!" says Hot Rod and it's like old home week. "What's the matter with Manson over there?" I asked Hot Rod. "Oh he's been like that for the last three days. He ain't moved a muscle." Sure enough, he hadn't moved at all, he was just staring at me. I just happened to be in his line of sight when I came in. "I ain't staying long, I'm gonna get this straightened out in the morning." I tell him while storing my stuff under my bunk. In these cells there's two bottom bunks. The cell is twice as wide too, so that's a plus. Hot Rod and Spike go down the tier to see the fellas and I head to the day room to touch base with some old friends I haven't seen for quite a while. Later that night I woke up to my new celli yellin about some incoherent thing. Then he lay down and went to sleep. I said a silent prayer to God. I told him I wern't happy here and could he get me back to my old cell? If he did that for me I'll go to church from now on, even though I was going to church on a regula schedule. The next day I went to see the very person responsible for my move and explained my predicament. It was a woman and she said, "Okay I'll fix it today" Boy was I surprised, I expected nine miles of flack and was speechless. "Cool," says I and went back to tell Spike the good news. He and a guy named "Goldie" were organizing a race between Redneck's Lizard and Hot Rod's Rat. (Some people you can tell have no class by their pets) Anyway, they had the whole wing in an uproar. A few of the guards were in on it and even Captain Happy (my old celli) seemed pretty animated. I was still packed and sure enough after the race (No one knew who won because both Rat and Lizard started fighting half-way through and then they escaped under the door that lead to the yard, we aint' seen them since.) I was notified by one excited clown that I'm on the move sheet for C-7. He even helped me carry my stuff back to the cell block. Cool huh?

Well it would be nice if this story ended there, but it didn't. Sunday morning I dug up my Bible and yoinked up ole Spike and we set off to church. Ronnald declined to go, saying, the Chaplin didn't like his cooking so he don't like his preachin. Groovy!

I stuck on my best smile and straightened my halo and me and Spike fell in line to get off the cell block. Some folks were surprised. You don't make a bargain with God and not follow through, no matter how bad things are they can always get worse.

Spike was in my pocket and I had my Bible or what I thought was my Bible, tucked under my arm. Someone (no names mentioned) had changed covers with my Bible and a huge Batman graphic novel. So when the guard letting us in the chapel patted me down and fanned out my Bible we were both surprised by the cartoon like pictures that graced the pages.

"How'd that get there?" I say. The guard just looked at me and handed the book back. I stepped through the chapel doors and everything went silent. I walked past the Chaplin's office and stopped. Before me stood about 150 convicts idling in the isle. Past them was the alter and a huge stained glass window with all kinds of pretty colors. Everyone turned and looked back at me. Spike sensed something and poked his head and antenna over the edge of my pocket. The Chaplin came out of the office and said, "What's going on out here?" I turned and looked at him. His eyes got real big looking over my shoulder. I instinctively ducked and rolled out of the way as a huge bolt of lightening shot past and nailed a convict in the shoulder. Someone said, "Holy Crap!" I looked towards the Alter. The stained glass window had parted and a big eye was looking in. "Run stupid!" says Spike, "good idea," says I. I jumped up and shot across the isle by a big bookcase. This bookcase is 12 feet high and has about a thousand and 60 books in it. I ended up in front of it.

Another bright light flashed with a huge bang. I ducked, it missed me again. I poked my head up and got hit with books raining down as the bookcase was teetering forward. Spike jumped out of my pocket and wisely got away from me. I jumped forward under a table as the bookcase slammed into it, spilling books all around. Yelling and shouting inmates were panicking and running every which way. Some were seated in the pews not daring to move. I leaped out from under the table and jumped two pews; landing in the lap of a dude they call "Big Show." This guy is 6' 10" and weighs about 400 pounds. I smiled up as he was scowling down. I said "Hi", he didn't say nothing. Over "Big Shows" head I noticed a big hand reaching down. "Get off me," said "Big Show" as he pushed me off his lap and on to the floor. As I hit the floor I saw this huge hand close over "Big

Show" and lift him as easy as King Kong lifted little Fay Ray. He screamed like a girl. (No offense) I scrambled up and bolted out into the isle. This was full of fools confessing things that shouldn't be said out loud. I dodged, ducked, zigged and zagged while looking back to see "Big Show" tossed into the Baptismal tank filled with 400 gallons of water, which came out as "Big Show" was tossed in. This put out all the candles and we were all "washed in the blood" (so to speak) I was 20 feet from the door and made a break for it. The crowd parted like the Red Sea. As I was leaping over the Chaplin I caught a blast right between the shoulder blades. I went skipping across the floor out the door and off down the hallway on my face and chest. I was followed by a small wave of water and who do you think was riding that little wave like Jeff from "fast Times at Ridge Mont High?" Spike! "Surf's up dude!" he said riding by my face on a communion wafer.

I rolled over to put my smoldering back on the cool floor. I looked back at the Chapel door in time to see my Bible-Batman book come flying out; it caught me in my forehead. The Chapel doors closed with a bang.

I got up and staggered down the hallway, scooped up Spike and went back to my cell. Ronnald was getting ready for work. "How was the sermon?" he asked. Spike told him how moved we were as he climbed into his spider web hammock. I needed a nap. Next week I'm gonna try the Catholic service maybe that will be better. I hear there's a Mormon one also. It's good to cover all the bases.

I checked my back after my nap and discovered a Celtic cross burned right between my collarbones. God doesn't want me to forget. *(Note: Walter has a beautiful Celtic cross tattooed on his back)*

How are things at Bud's warehouse? Are y'all cold? Snow everywhere? I wish I was there. Maybe if I can ever get out of here y'all can put in a good word and me and Spike can get a job scraping off the roof or collecting pinecones. Spike wants to take a metal detector down into one of those mines, probably not an original idea but what the hey? I won't go in with him in case of cave in's, I ain't tempting the Big "G" again.

Well I gotta go. You all take care and be good! For heavens sake get right with God if you ain't already. I hope I am.

Take care, your friend,
Walt and Spike

****

February 2008

Dear Liz;

Hi friend. I finally got Bud's new catalogue. The mailroom kept it checking for inappropriate material. I guess they have actually relaxed their scrutinizing thing because it hasn't taken as long to get it as the last time.

Spike's trying to get me to draw a Valentine's card for Alberta (from him of course.) So I'll have to dig up some paper or card material, I hope he picks out an appropriate picture for me to draw.

I feel I must do one for him; it doesn't do to piss off your lil buddy, not when he has over 4000 kin running around the pipe chase. Not to mention Sherry, even though they don't always get along, she'd side with Spike if it came down to it.

I told you a long time ago that you could ask me anything and I'd answer best I could so you asked about the kidnapping charge. I thought I'd told you the story but here goes.

On June 9th 2001 I was arrested for the kidnapping. Actually it was two counts of robbery, one burglary and one for kidnapping. An eye witness cleared me of the burglary. Nothing was stolen from the taxi driver. (Who accused me of the kidnapping) In fact I gave him $205.00. $200.00 for a broken down car he was selling and $5.00 for the cab ride. So no robbery. That left kidnapping. Even the sheriff couldn't believe and neither could anyone else. Small town politics. "Y'all must a pissed someone off boy!" was all the explanation I got. Anyway I'm thinking if I had stayed out there I would be in more trouble or dead. Self destruction was what I was into. So if you wanna know the whole story of the night I was arrested I have no problem telling you. I'll have to fill you in on some background about the Councilman who I "supposedly" screwed. I used to work for this City Councilman and him being firmly planted in small town politics, he had more pull than I did. As I said it's a long story. He was a "Boss Hog" character. Did you ever see that show "Dukes of Hazard?" well that's him. Only in the South could this have happened. You can actually look up what I'm in here for on the internet, all you need is my TDCJ # which you have. *(Note: I know the name of this "person," and I'd love to see his name in print for obvious reasons. He did eventually tell me exactly what happened, it's printed later in the book.)* Maybe I was supposed to come here. The law says it's illegal for them to obtain a conviction the way they did it so I'll probably get out one day. But in the meantime it's on me to make sense of it all. For a while I was very angry. I didn't hurt anyone but I didn't want anyone close to me either. The assault took place in the first part of 2000. It took me around 18 months to alienate the rest of my family.

So, how is everyone? Have you noticed that the last three times we've written we've sent our letters at the same time? So maybe I'll have something on the way this time.

We all really like it when you send pictures and computer funnies. Ronnald and I have split the ones of your garden Liz. We don't have no plant life here. The ones of you and your co-workers are also really cool. Any time you wanna put a face on y'all I'm all for it. I'm sorry I don't have any of me and Spike. Ronnald says his pictures are syndicated, I don't know what that means but he's pretty proud of it. Smug bastard!

Oh yeah I have a favor to ask. A possible favor. My sister says she's gonna send me $50.00 for my 26th-no, 38th-no, 41st-no, *Okay*!!! My 46th birthday next month. I want to send her this order form with a couple of books picked out. I know you ain't sending anymore orders to Texas prisons and I don't blame ya, but if this happens and I can get my sister to agree and if you agree to send em and for some reason they refuse me and return them, will you hang onto them for me? I'll pick them up after I'm released. The ones I've picked out look really cool like "The Victorians," and "British Paintings," There's no nudity, it's all art. I'd love to get the "Spectrum 2" book but it's too pricey. Or how about the "Art Nouveau" book and of course the "Ladies of Vallejo." I could go on but that's enough for now. Just let me know. Besides my sister's told me before she was sending money but didn't. *(Note: We at Bud Plant stopped sending books to Texas prisons because if they were refused they were always returned damaged. And regarding keeping the books for Walter. I have an entire shelf of my bookcase with his books waiting for him to pickup.)*

After that episode in the Chapel I tried to go see the Swami Roach (Spike's God and who he bow's down to.) but he ain't there no more. Well he ain't there "right now." They have a rabbit there now, some fertility thing. I don't know but it ain't anything I wanna get involved in right now. I'd better not let Ronnald know the rabbits there or we'll be eating stew. Rabbit stew! Hmmm, that's beats Haggis though.

I'm gonna go now. I don't reveal "me" too often, so take it easy, I'm only little! Life ain't always fun or fair. Maybe it's our individual trials that dictate what comes next? Or that make's us who we become? All I know is it's the ride we're on so all we can do is hang on and make sure to keep your hands and feet inside the car. No spitting or vulgar language, unless you have to. If you can't behave yourselves maybe you get sent back to start again, who knows? We'll all find out eventually.

Howdy to everyone from the Big House in Texas. Peace, love and Davy Jones! Long live the Monkees and God Bless y'all.

Your friend,
Walt.

PS: Yeah the Beatles were okay too, sorta. (tee hee)

April 9, 2008

Dear Liz and Co.;

It is "way" overdue that I write, and receiving your letter last night reminded me that I need to remedy that. So, howdy y'all.

Liz that was a very nice letter you wrote, thanks. I was feeling a wee bit under the weather. I have hay fever. It happens every spring.

That letter you received from one of your customers, Virgie Gifford, was very thoughtful. Do you think Virgie is his real name? I'm not surprised at the sentiment and know firsthand how wonderful the customer service department is at Bud's. Ronnald got a hold of Virgie's letter and almost blew a gasket. He said, "If I were writing about how wonderful y'all were, I would do better, but wouldn't want y'all to get big heads." Then I said, "If y'all were paid based upon your performance, you'd be making 10 million dollars an hour." I only know that Virgie spoke for all of you when that letter was penned." Wait, is Virgie a woman? *(Note: Virgie is short for Virginia. And yes she and husband Keith were old customers. They wrote a wonderful complimentary letter to Bud about all in customer service.)* I hope you don't need that letter back. *(Note: I believe I sent a copy, Bud had the original.)*

My birthday card was and is beautiful! I truly thank you. My bug thanks you and Ronnald thanks you even though he doesn't know when his birthday is, so I share it with him. He smuggled back a couple of hubcap sized cup cakes from the kitchen and we had a party. There were no candles just road flares.

My sister hasn't written back since Jan or Feb. I drew four boards and sent them to her. She wanted them for a festival that happens in Moab (Utah) where she lives. She said she'd sell em for me. I don't know why she hasn't written but this isn't the first time she's done this, but not after coercing me to draw four pictures. Oh well.

Hey, that "Hazel" idea is a good one. I always thought of that story as Chapter one of "Giraffalo." I worry that I wrote it too quickly and should clean it up some. If you want to you could re-type it and send me a copy because I never saved myself a copy. Yeah, I'm an idiot. I could draw another Giraffe to go with it. Wha da ya think? Maybe even expand it some. *(Note: The original title of "Giraffalo" was "Hazel" (which is Giraffalo's buffalo mother. I didn't think it was a good title so suggested changing it.)* Sometimes when I write, I have the story line and idea but tend to go too fast and leave out things that would make the story better.

I did give your phone number to my sister. I ain't worried about her telling you personal things about me when I was a little terror. Thanks for telling me when your birthday is.

The story title thingy is up to you. I will tell you that it is an original thought and completely a product of my own imagination, so it you think sprucing it up some would help, then you go ahead and send me a copy of what we have. Then I'll go back over it, fix it, include what you suggested and do a mini Giraffalo picture.

I'm re-reading your letter. You're going to Nevada Texas! Where's that? "Why" you say, "it's in Texas!" Geese, I walked into that. Just be careful about taking the gun on the plane plan. I ain't telling ya not to, I'm just sayin be careful, that's all. *(Note: I told him I was going to ask if I could take my father's rifle, empty, on the plane or in the luggage for my brother in Texas. And no, they wouldn't allow it.)*

Yes you've told me about your houseguests. I feel for ya sister. July ain't far away, tough love. Even birds boot their young out of the nest after a while. Does em good too, unless they do it too soon, then they're back to regroup. *(Note: I gave my grandson's, all three of them, a year to "find themselves get jobs and an apartment" We had a 4th of July leaving party when they moved out.)*

Can I vote? Who for? Well I guess "if" I could vote it would be for Robin Williams. He had a hell of a plan. If not him then probably Hilary. Why not? I'd like a President with boobs. Not that she'd be the best. Okay, the verdict is in, I'm a pig. But the jury came in on that a long time ago.

I knew you were or are an alien. Can't you get your citizenship or don't want to? Arnold did. Why don't you write to him and include Virgie's letter, hell, put one of mine in there too. I could write you a recommendation. Have all of customer service sign it and make it a petition. Your guv is a "manly" man so don't blanch at the Testosterone that would have to be there.

I'm gonna do that "gonna go" thing. Thanx again for the birthday card, and that's for all of you. Sorry I didn't get back sooner. Let me know what you decide on the story and I'll have Giraffalo drawn by the time you respond.

Peace, love and Davie Jones,

Walt, Spike and Ronnald

****

April 11, 2008

Dear Liz and Co.:

Howdy y'all! I'm writing again because I had a revelation! Well, actually I had a concussion. I ain't kidding neither. Here's what happened. I was asleep in my bunk. Ronnald was snoring, badly. I wear two ear-plugs in each ear. I sleep on the top bunk and have to keep in mind that I cannot sit straight up in my bed because of low clearance. Well, I forgot. Anyways I was sleepin and had an idea and sat straight up knocking my stupid ass back out and woke up with Spike pulling my nose hairs out. I ain't caught him yet but when I do...Anyway, I was thinking about our little Giraffalo. What if your brother Jon knew how to contact Disney? Think about our little guy animated. You have chapter one. The next part of the story is Giraffalo being incorporated into the herd of Water Buffalo and learning that he's different. Of course getting teased for it but developing a rapport with the lead bull who teaches him about trust and instincts. Meanwhile he makes friend with Gregory groundhog, (Wilfred Brimley would be a good voice.) and a Ringtail Miercat who's a bit nuts but loyal. (We could name him Spike.) Toss in a young zebra who introduces Giraffalo to the most adorable girl giraffe and run some romance, comic relief and Bam!! (Love!) And then, Danger! The entire herd is threatened and Giraffalo saves em all. Wha da ya think? How could he do that? Well my first idea was he's secretly Batman and...yeah, see that won't work. But I thought all about it this morning and it all came together. It's a good thing I didn't get amnesia by bashing my brains out when I thought of it.

Let's skip ahead from when he asked Hazel if she were his mom. It's been a couple of weeks and Giraffalo is running his long legs here and there, stretching them out when he comes sliding up to Bruno, the lead bull, bouncing off of him. *(Note: Walter changed the lead bull's name from "Spike" to "Bruno")* Actually Bruno put himself in the path of Giraffalo, "Where ya off to in such a hurry son? Bruno said. Giraffalo is lanky and is intimidated by the huge muscular bull. "You've nothing to fear from me son," he says softly and Giraffalo sees the eyes inside this massive bull's head and knows this to be true. "I'm playin sir," he says hopping around. "Do you know why I stopped you?" asked Bruno. "Nope, I don't, not really. Why is it because I'm little?" Bruno laughs. "My mom says I'm too little to do stuff but I'm not!" says Giraffalo. "Ronnald the old bull says I'm not even big enough to be a good pest," Bruno laughs harder. Giraffalo stares back at the laughing Bruno. "I'm not laughing at you little one. I know Ronnald and he was my lead bull when I was your age." Giraffalo smiles, "I'm Giraffalo." He says stretching his little nose up to Bruno's. "I know" says Bruno and they exchange their breaths which is the animal way to get to know someone. "Well met little Giraffalo, I'm Bruno." Giraffalo steps back because he'd heard of Bruno. "Are...are you my lead bull?" he says. "I am son and I stopped you because there's danger over there in the direction you were going." Giraffalo looks and says, "I don't see nothin." "Use your instincts Giraffalo"

68

Bruno says. "I have 'stinks?" he said. Bruno smiles. "Everyone has instincts," he said. "It's a feeling son, you have it in your heart, and what does your heart tell you? Come" he says walking toward the long grass where Giraffalo was heading. Giraffalo dashes ahead, "slowly now…easy…"says Bruno moving into Giraffalo's path. Little Giraffalo stretched his neck forward; "Can you feel it?" Bruno whispers. "Yes I can" Giraffalo says, "What does you heart tell you son?" Bruno asks, and Giraffalo backs up a step knowing something was not right. Just then a snake the size of Giraffalo's neck slithers forward to be stopped by a large hoof. "This is danger." Bruno said.

Giraffalo stood looking, scared and shaking. The snake continued to slither out and coil around the hoof of Bruno. Bruno watched as the snake formed a large knot around Bruno leg, he stepped back, turned and with his back hooves kicked the snake back into the grass. It's okay now son, but you must be careful. "Yes Sir." Said a shaking Giraffalo. "You were very brave" said Bruno leading Giraffalo back to the herd. "I was?" he asked. "Yes, you didn't run and that's a good sign of courage." "Why?" asked the little Giraffe. "Because sometimes when there's danger, if everyone sticks together and trusts the leader we can overcome the danger as a herd. The herd is bigger than one." As they walked back Giraffalo pondered this. "What's trust Sir?" Bruno stopped, "Trust is when you don't know something and someone you know tells you it's good or bad, like eating berries. If someone tells you the red ones will make you sick, then you trust that person and you don't have to find out yourself by eating them. "Ohhh," he says. "So, how do "you" know who to trust?" asked Giraffalo thinking back to the trick played on him by the other young bulls. "What does you heart tell you?" Bruno replied as he walked away leaving Giraffalo to think about it.

Okay all that's groovy. Then we skip ahead to when Giraffalo's a bigger animal and the herds in danger. We can replay all that and switch rolls. I think the herds trapped with their backs against a cliff and the Serengeti is on fire on three sides moving towards them. I haven't decided whether it was caused by poachers or a natural phenomenon but they got caught against the cliff with the fire closing in. Maybe like this.

The flames from the dry grass and brush were high. The smoke pushed against the cliff by the up-draft. It was obvious by the herds tightly packed ranks that panic was only moments away. "What are we gonna do now?" asks a desperate Ronnald standing protectively by Hazel. "Where's Giraffalo?" she asked. All she could see of him were his legs as he pushes his way through the coughing mass of bovine flesh. "Mom!" he says, dipping his head under the layer of smoke. "Mom! Where's Bruno?" he says. Ronnald answers, "Where the smoke is thickest boy! That bull is always where it's thickest." Giraffalo coughs, "stay with Mom Ronnald and when we move, move fast, okay?" he said. "Ronnald! Promise me, whatever happens you move these cows out fast!" Ronnald stops coughing and looks at the Giraffe, "move? We can't move boy, we're trapped here!" Giraffalo yells above the braying of the herd, "We have a chance if we move as a herd, promise me!" he says pressing his head against the older bulls head. "**Promise!!**" Okay, I promise. And then Giraffalo is gone. As he's leaving he stretches his neck to see where the most danger appears to be and decides it's opposite the cliff. He wades towards the oncoming wall of flame and yells, "Bruno!" and then pokes his head below the smoke, "Bruno!!" he yells and then he see's him with his back to the herd facing the fire as if he could defeat it with his will. The sight of this magnificent bull willing to fight a fight he cannot win. For the love of the herd made the young giraffe proud to be a part of all this.

"Bruno!" he yelled coming up beside the bull. "Giraffalo!" said Bruno not taking his eyes from the approaching fire. "Bruno! I think we can get out," yelled Giraffalo. "How," said Bruno with desperation on his face. "We have to run into the flames as a herd!" he said. Bruno stared not comprehending what he heard. "Run into the flames? Are you crazy? We can't boy, we'd all burn." Said the bull. "We can make it if we all run to the North side," Giraffalo said. "The fire's thinner over there." Bruno turned back. "I can see over all this smoke. We can make it if we all move as one!" said Giraffalo. "Trust me! They'll follow you but only if we go now!" said the desperate giraffe. "What does you heart tell you?" he said. Bruno looked at the giraffe and then looked north, seeing no difference. "What does your heart say Bruno?" he asked again. Then, "Lead us son," said Bruno making the decision. He filled his lungs with smoky air and gave his "charge" bellow that shook the ground. The herd heard it and responded as if it were a life line, which it was, and as one they all moved north-word behind four spotted legs that disappeared into the smoke. *(Note: Wow, I got caught up in that while typing it.)*

See that's pretty rough but it's the idea that put this knot on my head. What do you think? I think the little girl giraffe could be named "Honey" and if we pitched it to Disney we should suggest they use that name and incorporate the song, "Sugar, Sugar" into the movie. That song was the biggest one hit wonder in the entire history of one hit wonders and could be another smash hit if they used it right. *(Note: I wrote to Pixel and described "Giraffalo" to them. They said they don't take stories from the outside public. So, where do they get their stories from anyway?)*

Some of you younger ladies and men wouldn't know that song. Boot it up, listen to it. It's corny but cute.

So…that's my idea, stupid huh. Ya know if you want you could get me the address for Disney Studios and *I'll* pester em. I think they'll take advantage of me; I'm only little ya know. Some feedback on this would be groovy. God, I gotta get out of here! *(Note: I sent him an address for Disney. He wrote but didn't get a response. It's their loss.)*

Well I'm gonna go. Y'all take care. Hey, how about Pixel Studios? I've kept no copy of the first part, so maybe you should send me what we got to start. I already said all this in my last letter huh. Stuff doesn't happen much around here so I forget what I've already said sometimes. Now I really gotta go my hand has cramped up. I could come up with names for characters like, "Liz", "Cassandra", "Alberta", "Peggy Sue", "Diane", even "Bud", etc, etc. That would be cool huh. Which animal would you like to be named after, how about the bird on Hazel's nose? Hey, wait a minute, don't the English refer their woman as "birds?" You know like we called them "chicks" back in the day? Well I think Liz is the bird!

Okay, see ya. El pringals pendejo or yoe keto taco bell. That means "see ya later" in Spanish. I'm taking lessons.

Walt, Spike and Ronnald.

****

June 11, 2008

Hi Liz:

I hope this makes it to ya. If not it's your fault. Even if it ain't it is. I'm tired of everything being my fault.

So it took a numb leg and an overdose of "As the Stomach Turns" to get a long letter from you or was it "The Hung and the Breastless?" Yeah, I'm an idiot but then you know that huh.

From the photo you sent you don't look your age. You're always smiling in your pictures. Hmmmm, perhaps that's a clue to your youthful look, *(Note: I woke up one morning and coughed putting my back in a spasm and a numb leg caused by a pinched nerve and put me down for several weeks.)*

I am beside myself lately. Ronnald made parole. That's wonderful for him but he's gone. We are locked down and have been since last Friday. We're living on peanut-butter sandwiches and hard boiled eggs. Spike and Sherry are plotting against my new celli. One came yesterday but left shortly after discovering Sherry. She's getting pretty big and hairy. I gotta admit she'd make me literally crap my knickers if I weren't prepared first.

I have a couple of pages of Peter Pan and Tinker Spike that were written when I wrote the other part. I didn't have enough stamps to send the whole thing. You don't have to type them Liz. I'd love to write "Giraffalo" but I think I'm a fool if I don't. But I don't think now is the right time.

I have been sparring with the States Attorney General and believe the U.S. Federal Magistrate is about to rule on my Federal writ of habeas corpus. Hopefully in my favor. The law says he should but I don't have faith in the law.

Ronnald says I can get a job at any McDonald's upon his recommendation and left an address, unfortunately I think he headed to the Colonels house. He left his shoe for Spike. It's been kinda nice living without a celli, present company exempt, for the past few days.

It's hot and humid down here. Hey! That Alphonse Mucha card is great. Do you remember the Mucha book you sent a couple of years ago? Well some asshole liked it better than me and left with it after I loaned it to him and I miss it. I don't think he planned to leave with it, Texas moves people around unexpectedly. But the fact remains that Checklesavakian artist has an eye for detail. Forgive me if a Checklesavakian see's this spelling.

I hope I'm not here for Christmas but if I am I'll do ya a Fairy board. If I'm gone I'll call ya and wish everyone a Merry Christmas. I do have the Bud Plant customer service number.

The "Giraffalo" story was a rough draft so don't worry about typing it. I was just shooting an idea by ya.

How are you feeling? I'm gland to hear Cassandra's coming back to work. I hope Peggy finds everything she desires in Colorado. She and Cassandra sure are pretty. Heavy sigh!

Dr. Phil? Spike like's him too. He calls him Baldilocks. Spike always quotes Dr. Phil when he's yelling at Sherry. Of course Sherry doesn't care. She's pissed that Hilary's out of the race.

Yes I have two pictures of your "Queen of the Night" flower. No you never told me of your grandfather Walter Waters Willoughby except for now. Willoughby? How bloody English! Actually that's cool. My name is of course Norwegian. The equivalent of Smith and Jones over there. Bet I could write soap opera stories. Then maybe they'd have a good time.

Do you remember Dark Shadows? I do. That was kind-a a soap opera wasn't it? That was a long time ago. You're talking about your cat, they're cool. I used to be ugly to cats until I owned one. We named it Tarzan. I lived in Fair Oaks Calif. Near Sacramento. Speaking of Sacramento, I read that the queers get to marry in California, is that true? Great! I guess if you're queer. That's probably politically incorrect. I don't have a problem with anyone regardless of their race or sexual preference.

I was raised by an alcoholic mother who had a mean streak towards men. I had two younger sisters and two older. Only one was by the same father as me. I was a wild child and when caught I'd get spanked. I have no qualms against my mom. She did the best she could with what she had. I was fortunate enough to have made my peace with her before she died.

I hope you're feeling better Liz. Yeah it would be better or easier if I could just call or you could call. You can't and I can't so…Have you thought of getting a PO Box? *(Note: I was having all mail from Walter sent to my job place because family members didn't want me to write to him even though my feelings for him were strictly friendship.)* I'm sure your co-workers miss ya. All of you are in my meager prayers. Ronnald sends his best. Well, gotta go, they're serving chow next door and I need to mail this. I hope one stamp does it.

Peace, love and Richard Nixon.
Walt, Spike and Ronnald.

June 15, 2008

Hi Liz;

Hi to you and yours.

Y'all are gonna get some cell time soon. "Cell time" is a term used to describe the time one person gets to himself when his celli leaves. My cell is probably smaller than yer bathroom. For two men to share a space this small it get's kinda cramped. Anyway Independence Day is almost here. Spike says to be careful and relish your time alone.

I got your letter and the card the other day. I like the picture of the church. I'm partial to pen and ink drawings. *(Note: I sent a pen and ink drawing of St. Mary's church in my village of Kintbury in England.)* It's probably because I'm color blind. Oh sorry, "colour" blind.

I read a lot and like it when I'm alone. Ye can always tell the Limey authors by words like colour, Haggis, Blood pudding. That don't even sound good, is it? *(Note: I said, "Only if you like cooked blood mixed with other ingredients")*

Yes I have your phone number and will call "*when*" I'm released. The wheels of justice *do not* move quickly. But they are moving none the less, except I can't see them moving in my direction.

I am absolutely flattered that you'd make such a fuss over our friendship. I don't make many friends and that's because of this place, mostly. But when I do I tend to be extremely bias. I'm thankful to have a friend, you Liz are no exception. So, okay "friend" one day I'll own a computer and we can email each other and talk on the phone. If I ever get to Europe, which is one of my dreams, you can tell me where to not go. I seem to have trouble with going where I shouldn't be.

I intend to pursue some sort of writing when I get out. I know I can draw the pictures that go along with the stories. If I get an acquittal, which is what I'm after, the people who put me here will have to pony up some $$ for the seven years, and counting, I've been here. The money I'm hoping I'll get from the State of Texas and the assholes who put me here will help to keep me until I can get established somewhere. I have a few good ideas for some story's and illustrations.

I have sent you two full 20 x 15" boards, right? Or was it three? The "Cobbler," "Reclining Jesus," and a "Santa?" I don't remember if I sent the Santa with the boy on his knee or not. *(Note: I have all three of those, all framed and hanging on my walls.)* The reason I'm asking is, I'm in the process of making a deal with a guy whose cousin has a friend who knows a dude whose uncle's wife's kid is in the market for a portrait of his dog. Now the dog, if it is in fact a dog, looks like a cross between a rat, a cat and an Aardvark. An experiment gone terribly wrong. It looks like a Lap-rat. Its name is Winston. (Of all things and no he ain't English; at least I don't think he is anyway.) Anyway I told him to buy the boards and give em to me. I'll do the picture for 15 stamps and the extra board. The illustration boards come out of the commissary in packs of two and I only need one for the dog. I was thinking of doing a cowboy picture for someone. Do you have any cowboy art? I was just thinkin about it. Spike wants me to do Mary Poppins but that doesn't even sound right.

Well Liz I'm gonna go for now. I gotta go do my duty on the tower…that doesn't sound right neither. I'm getting a new celli soon, I'll tell you about him in my next letter. Y'all take care and keep in touch. Sherry sends her best and so does Spike.

Audy ose (that's Mexican for Austa La Veesta)
Walt

****

June 23, 2008

Hi Liz;

So I'm sitting here talking to Spike but he ain't listening. I look over and he's reading or writing something. "What cha got there lil fella?" I say. He says it's his letter to Liz. "Let me see that." sez I. And he makes a break for the pipe chase. (We have a hole behind the porcelain sink in the cell that leads to the pipes behind the cell. It goes from one end of the cell block to the other.) Anyway I just get to him before he disappears with *his* letter. "Wow" say I, "this looks just like *my* handwriting." "But it ain't," says Spike, "Because if it *was* then that would mean your silly ass didn't send the first page of your letter to Liz." "Good point" I say: I could not have been so stupid as to have done that! So I tell him, "You misspelled "colour," and he says, "How would you know." Hmmm…, "another good point." Then I tell him I'm writing you again. "Would ya like me to send this?" He said. Well he did so here ya are. See how exactly it resembles page one of the letter I sent the other day? I know, that's friken amazing! *(Note: Yes* he *did send a letter or a page like that; I just thought he'd forgotten to put the entire letter in the envelope.)* Anyway I'm saving on stamps; I mean they are the currency here. I'd rather draw big board for more stamps than cards for just one or two. The cards are usually done for special occasions, birthdays, holidays etc. Anyways I ain't complaining just the opposite, I'm blessed that I can do that and they're liked. "It's the little things!" If I ever do my memoirs that's what I'll name it. Of course Spike and Sherry will be in there. Ronnald's gone and won't ever write, he mostly mimes anyway. *(Note: Well I'll be damned, this book is his memoir. Who woulda thought?)*

I miss Ronnald already. My new celli is Capt. Happy. He got his eyes webbed shut the other day. I doubt he noticed. He's got a daily appointment with the pill window. That's where the infirmary dispenses psych drugs to those who need it. Capt. Happy needs his Thorazeen. I guess at some point in his life someone talked him into tattooing a pentagram on his forehead. I'm not kidding. I told Spike it was his zodiac sign. Sherry knows what it is and doesn't like him. I told her she shouldn't judge a book by its cover. She reminded me that books often have covers that coincide with what's inside the book. That's true, what could I say? Anyway Capt. Happy doesn't talk much. He just sits and stares at the spot on the wall he circled shortly after he got here. I'm gonna ask him one day what that's all about. But not today.

I'm trying to get him to church today. It's Sunday. We'll see how that goes.

Well Liz I'm gonna go for now. This letter Spike wrote should get to you soon as possible for obvious reasons. I got a dog to draw.

Take care, your friend,
Walt and Spike

****

July 19, 2008

Liz;

Hi friend.

You said in your letter, "The only thing I knew about America was what we saw in the films and cowboys and Indians." *(Note: Me as a child and my family emigrated to the U.S. in 1958.)* The card you sent was from a film, "Back in the day." Tell me what it's from and win a prize. And yes I read a lot. I've just read a book, #four in a series, that's by far the best fantasy I've ever read. Actually it's more of a medieval tale. George R. R. Martin's "A Song of Ice and Fire." Book #five has not come out yet. Anyway, yeah you'd think my spelling would be better. Sometimes I'll write a letter and spell the same word differently. You probably already know this huh? Spike says it's because I was dropped upon me bleeding noggin as a wee lad. With my upbringing I suppose that could be true. I seem to have reverted back to English, Blimey!

What's a "circa?" I know or have figured out that it's a reference to a date, dating back too? Like I'm circa 1962? I tell ya learning another language is hard sometimes. What can ya do? Ya buy em books, send em to school and what do they do? Eat the damn books! Actually that was my school's motto. That and "eat shit." You must remember I went to the school of hard knocks. Yeah you told me you retired and your "back" issue's had something to do with that. But it's nice you can sometimes get to work part-time at Bud Plant. Maybe when you heal and if your chores are done and if you're good you could go back, period.

Are all of your "youngsters" booted from the nest? Are you and your family enjoying the extra space? *(Note: My grandson's had been "living" with us for 2+ years.)*

I hope them damned ole fires are put out soon and y'all can frolic amongst the plants and tree's in the clear mountain air. I don't suppose with your injury yer doing a lot of frolicking. Maybe one legged frolicking.

Spike's swimming in the toilet. It's a pool party. Why not? Its 7,000 degrees down here. Your state's on fire, mine's, (not that I claim Texas,) very hot and humid. There's not much to burn down here.

So, ya used to live in Southern California huh? Me too. Where? Do you hate Cal Worthington? Who don't? I've lived in Redondo Beach, Hermosa, (Beaches), Playa del Ray, and Westwood, (All of that L.A.) I've lived by Salina's, Santa Cruz. I was born in Oakland but raised north of San Francisco in a place called Clear Lake. Unfortunately for me my youth was an array of being tossed around from an early age. My mum was a boozer and what's affectionately termed "a man hater," to some extent. She obviously liked them well enough for some reasons. She did have five kids. She would lash out at any and all men when she drank, and I was the only male. It put me in a position to grow up probably before my time. My father lived in L.A. and I went looking for him after being booted out again. My mother would run me off in a drunken stupor and it was sink or swim. Actually the welfare people told her if I wasn't there she couldn't collect welfare for me. So eventually I ran away, for good and journeyed to find my dad.

I stashed myself in the back of a K-Mart in Lake Port until they closed. When everyone left I loaded up a backpack and escaped out the fire exit. I hitchhiked down the hill all the way to L.A.

I burned up hitchhiking I-5 and highway 99 time and time again in the 70's. I did find my dad. I was 12 years old. He was living a playboy life style and lived in an apartment complex that did not allow kids so he gave me to a house full of bikers in Culver City. It was right across the street from Universal Studios. I used to ride my bike or skate board along the wall that separated the studio lot from the street. They would premier movies at the little theatre outside those walls. I saw "Blazing Saddles" and "Tommy" both rated "R". I was too young to get in but would trade pot for a ticket and go in through the side door. The ticket proved I was legal to be there if asked.

The interesting thing is back then a guy named "Bonner" was cruising up and down the very street and freeways I was hitchhiking on killing young boys. He was known as the I-5 Killer. I coulda been had I tell ya. Some weren't so lucky.

I told you that I had done time in California for stealing. After paroling from Mule Creek State Prison I came to Texas to see my wife and son. I ended up reconciling with my wife who was in Texas. This is how I ended up here.

Our son Daniel is 17 and perhaps coddled more than he should be. A mother's indulgence and a fathers too. I missed a lot of my son's childhood and probably overcompensated. I worked laying concrete and building metal buildings. My wife managed two shoe stores. My son ran wild. One day he said, "Dad I'm running away from home." Well! As you recall I was on my own way earlier than 17 so I said, "Got any money? No? Here." I make sure he's not broke. I already knew he's moving to his friends house in town. "Daniel," I say. "If you need me, call!" And he left.

Well! Mom explodes. "**My Baybeee!!** I dive for cover. You no good, "whadayameanyoulethimgo? "I – I – I – I…" Geese, I was in so much trouble. So I'm on scum status. Daniel ends up coming back of course. He called and I go and get him. But I'm still pond scum.

A few months later, my wife, is at work. I'm home playing pinochle on the internet. Daniel called. "Dad! Guess what? I got a gun; me and Maniac (Daniels friend) are going to Utah." He's running away from home again! Oh my God! "Stay right there," I say. He's at a convenience store in Bonham, we live outside of there. I catch a ride with a friend who drops me off at the store. Sure enough, there's my boy with a packed backpack beside his miniature friend Maniac. (Both Daniel and I are over 6 ft. tall; Maniac is 5' 1".) I took the gun, take the bullets out. It's a .45 Caliber slide action Military sidearm. I put it in my pocket. I tell Daniel he can't run away. And yes I asked him where he got the gun. He was evasive. He also had two more that I didn't know about. He's determined to run away though. So I told him he's "gonna" have to tell him mom, because I ain't getting the "ice Queen" treatment again. So we call a taxi to take us to Paris where his mom works.

We get into the cab. Daniel and Maniac are in the back, I'm in the front. As soon as I climb in the pistol digs into my hip. So I take it out and I actually told the taxi driver, "Look I got this gun, it ain't loaded. I'm laying it here on the floorboard because it's too big for my pocket." "No problem," he says. "Where ya headed?" he asked. I tell him Paris. He says it's a long way and we'll need gas. So we stop and fill up. When he comes back he says, "say, it's gonna cost ya at least $50.00 for the trip. I have a car, all I want is $200.00, ya want it? So I buy this car for $200.00, cash. I pay for the cab ride, $5.00 for as far as we went, went to pick up the car and off we go.

This car has no radiator, no back window, half the lights are out and 15 miles up the road we breakdown. Meanwhile back in town, the cabbie tells a friend of "mine" about the idiot he sold this piece of crap car to. Oh yeah, who? Says my friend. The cabbie tells him and my friend, James, tells him, "Geese stupid, of all the guys to sell that car to. He's gonna kick your ass when he walks back to town." So, this spooks the cabbie and he goes to the police station and tells them I robbed and kidnapped him. That's how I was charged. The sheriff was baffled at how this was even charged and was convinced I would be turned loose.

Well, I had made an enemy in town. He was my ex-boss, ex-city commissioner, ex-Chief of Police. He was a pillar of society. He owned several business, "one" of which he had asked me to burn down for the insurance money. I refused, period! He thought I was having an affair with his girlfriend, not his wife, his girlfriend. Anyway, his surrogate son was the Prosecutor of that county and according to sources whispering in my unlucky ear, I had pissed "someone" off. It was them who broke the rules of Criminal Procedure to get the conviction and for this I've never quit fighting. I will prevail. It just takes time. I look forward to getting out of this whole mess sometime soon. How soon? I don't know. I've proved everything I need to, it's just a matter of time. I know this isn't the first time I've told you my tale of woe, this time I've gone into more detail though. *(Note: I have **all** the names of the people who screwed Walter. I would love to see them in print, now. However they'll all "come out in the wash")*

Well I'm gonna go for now. It's Sunday and I gotta get this in the mail on my way to church. Liz, I don't mind the questions, I'll always answer truthfully. I'll see about the cowboy art for you. I don't make but a few dollars on my art so I have to save up to do boards, but I wanna send you another before I get out of here because I may get too busy at first to do anything like that.

Texas gives us nothing. No personal hygiene products, except a small bar of soap once a day. It's a very bad situation but I eek by and will get ahead and so this thing. I have an idea, as if you didn't know. Let me know if you have the "Giraffalo" picture. Gotta go, I'm running out of paper room.

Yer friend,
Walt.

****

August 8, 2008

Dear Liz;

Hi. How are things? This pen writes very badly. It's a bleeder. Spike says it's not a good sign.

So to answer your questions. Has Ronnald written since he was paroled? Well he sent me a card that I didn't understand but then I never understood him when he was here, so that answers that question. Other questions will be answered as we come to em, but first I have a question. You said you have a friend who lives in Disneyland? *(Note: No, I said I have a friend who "works" in Disneyland.)* How fricken cool is that. How many times have you toured the grounds of Disneyland? The only thing I can remember of my trip there in the late 60's was the repetitive "It's a Small World After All" song. We went with my grandparents when we, my sister and I, were visiting from Northern California. My mom and dad were separated, divorced, sworn enemies, I don't remember, I was little.

You're welcome for your cowboy card. It was from "The Searchers" and came from a movie marquee from an American Illustrator in a book titled "American Illustrators" (from Bud Plant).

Speaking of books, you mentioned Boris Vallejo and Julie Bell's Fabulous Women and asked if I wanted one. **Yes. Yes please,** okay, yup, thanx. As you know I'm a whore for art books. Perhaps a more eloquent way of putting it, "I'm a slut for art books." I read the description in Bud's catalog and it doesn't mention nudity, so we should be okay. Did I say, "Thank you?" It will have to at least appear it's coming from Bud's. Because no one can just send books, know what I mean? When you go there to mail it, tell everyone I say, "Howdy."

I'm sorry to hear about the mean ole momma bear and her baby. *(Note: Momma bear kept breaking into neighbors shed's and chicken coops. She was shot, wounded in her leg. She had been seen again a few months later and seemed to be okay.)* But I'm glad to hear you're up and about tho. Is your pancreas all better? It was your pancreas, right? Or was it something to do with your leg? Your mobility for sure. Do I have a pancreas? Spike told me I sold it to the organ harvesters. Sometimes they ask for donations for a couple of bucks. (Since Texas doesn't pay their inmates to work, they work em anyway.) There are always a couple of hands that go up. "Me, me, me, I'll sell you my kidneys for a couple of bucks." I've volunteered a time or two. I know my goiter, spleen and gizzard have all been removed. The pay's good so why not?

I'm glad you took the dogs when you walked. I'm also glad you trust your dogs. *(Note: I told him one of my three dogs saw a young bear walking up the hill near my home, while I was with them on a walk. I turned around and very "quickly" walked back to the house.)* I'd walk all over the place if I lived there. I love the mountains.

As for my ex-boss, no he is not a part of this legal crap, "on paper". I know he influenced and manipulated the police etc to prosecute me but there's nothing I can do to him, legally. Nor is there anything I want to do to him. He will be him and that's punishment enough. He'd never understand what it was all about anyway. He's kind a like "Boss Hog" of the "Dukes of Hazard." The people he calls friends I wouldn't want to have anything to do with.

If you really wanna call someone try the court clerk in the Eastern District. U.S. District Clerk, Sherman Division (903-892-2921) and ask what's taking so damn long? It's been two years. When are they gonna hear my writ of habeas corpus. Case #406-CV-204. That's all that's holding me up. You don't have to though; I doubt it would do any good anyway. But thanks for offering. *(Note: I did call and was told it was still an open docket and would come due when it happens.)*

I'm getting bored, annoyed, tired or any explicit explicative that conveys my utter frustration of this entire mess.

Oh, I wrote to the National Endowment for the Arts. I'm gonna apply for a grant. Maybe get a studio and produce some stuff. That would be cool. I sent a picture of "Giraffalo" with my letter to them. I asked for info on grant information for starving American artists. Not that I'm starving. I have seven illustration boards stashed here and there (My sister has five) that I can refer to as an example of my ability for whoever decides that. *(Note: He's right, he's really bored.)*

Oh yeah, one other thing. Do you read books? Because I read a book that is certainly up your alley. Tim Dorsey's "Stingray Shuffle". I have not laughed so hard or been so entertained in a long time. I highly recommend it. Very funny! *(Note: He knows I "love" to read.)*

Let's see, where were we? Oh yeah, bear repellant! Don't "they" make a bear repellant?

Do you know what group from Britain was the first to have a number one song on the American charts? Have you ever heard of the Tornadoes? The song was "Telstar". My "roach" just informed me of that piece of trivia. We can all breathe easier knowing that, huh? *(Note: When that came out and I found it was an English group, I played it so much on the jukebox my boss nearly fired me.)*

I did get the pictures of your birth home in Kintbury. (England) Not much of a front yard but the back yard looks really cool. *(Note: The house was right on High Street with just a pavement in front.)*

You asked if I'd heard from Daniel recently. I haven't heard from him for quite a while. He's now 24 with a family in Texas. Hey I'm a grand pappy. I don't like him living in this state.

Okay I'm gonna go for now. I've started work on another board. You never said anything about Western art, so I may start over. Take care friend, write, and send the book. I'm starved for something new. It's hot, so very fricken hot. Hurricane Eduardo did cool us down to 98 fricken degrees. Mother of God it's hot and humid down here! Other than that, everything's the same.

Keep your eye out for that Tim Dorsey book. You'd love it, I did, funny stuff.

Talk to you later, always my best.
Walt.

August 29, 2008

Howdy Liz;

How are things? I haven't heard from you in a lil while. I ain't panicking, I'm just spoiled.

Spike left for the Gulf of Mexico yesterday. Hurricane season is off and runnin down here. We catch a lot of rain, some wind and that's about it. I saw Spike waiting on the roof. His personal seagull came swooping in, picked him up, they barely cleared the razor wire, and they banked into the sun and were gone.

I've got two major projects going. One I finished today. This one pays for the postage for the other one. But not until the second week of Sept. So you should expect it the third week of Sept. Please write when you get it or I will worry. This is something you asked for so...

I have allergies. I have never caught hay fever this time of year before. Someone, (my celli knows everything which is handy.) told me it's from the Mesquite trees. They're bloomin this time of year. Have you ever seen a Mesquite tree? The Wapato Indians use the thorns for sewing needles. When we used to go out and work on the road crew, chain gang, we had to clear out groves of Mesquite trees. You could step on a branch and have a thorn go all the way through yer work boot and into yer foot. It was definitely an "ouch". I had thorn wounds on my arms and hands that took all of 18 months to heal. I ain't kidding. *(Note: 18 months? When I went to see him in October 2016 he had what was left of a Mesquite thorn coming out of his arm. It had buried itself in so deeply and was then just coming out. I kept picking at it trying to bring it out.)*

And then there are fire ants. Any native Texan has scars from his ankles to his knees that took forever to heal. Them there are "nasty" lil bastards. Pure evil! No wonder Sherry lives in here.

Capt. Happy, my celli, talks to Sherry. He's an idiot. He can't help it and I ain't gonna tell him because he knows everything, but ignorance is bliss. Look who's talking huh. Oh yeah, your boards in colour. Three colours. *(Note: I've noticed he's spelling a few words the way I do. I guess that's a compliment.)*

I'll bet it's nice up there in the mountains. It's still 7,000 degrees down here. The heat index makes it seem like 8,000 degrees though.

My nose is runnin. I have body aches and facial cancer. Probably not the cancer one but it feels like it.

I'm kinda just writing to keep in touch. I'll draw ya a lil card and put it in with this. My creative juices are runnin out the middle of my ugly mug right now. I hope everything there is fine and you're okay. Do ya go swimming up there? My God I'd be in the water every waking moment if I could.

Y'all take care and write when you can.

Your friend,
Walt.

****

September 1, 2008 Labor Day

Hi di ho friend to you too!

How's yer Sciatic nerve doin? You say you're on the D.L. (Baseball term for disabled list.) It's not a bad thing you know. I have a similar injury except I think mine is a pinched nerve. When I stand in one spot for too long my right upper leg starts to burn then goes numb. I wonder if it's because my Sciatic nerve is shot out. I don't do doctors though. They have to pretty much trick me into going to see one. Once when Sherry bit me, (it can happen and I "may" have had it coming. I put a plastic bug in her web. She didn't think it was funny. It was Spike's idea.) Anyway she bit me next to my left eye. I swelled up like a balloon. I wouldn't go to the doctor. Why should I, I knew what was wrong. "They" told me I had a visitor and shot me with a tranquilizer gun 13 times. I'm not sure what went on after that. All I know is I got another shot (for the spider bite) and it healed.

Anyway, I'm writing to tell you your plan for sending the book is perfect.

We are hosting another prison population, (extra inmates coming in) because they're sitting in the path of Hurricane Gustav. So we're locked down for most of the day.

Yes you told me you liked westerns. I thought Tom Sellick played a great cowboy also. I've also based on what you said on what I'm drawing on this board or visa versa. I think you'll like it. I'm hoping you'll like it. If not then tell me. *(Note: He's never drawn anything I didn't like.)*

I forgot when you're leaving for your reunion in L.A. Did you say this month? Anyway I hope it's a grand ole time. Thank you for making that call for me and no I didn't think they would tell you anything other than that it is still pending. You calling though may let them know that someone actually cares and could make a difference. And no, I don't have a lawyer. I've done this all on my own. I know, I know, but Spike helped me. It's one of those things where, "if you want something done, do it yourself," and get your favorite bug to help.

I think Sherry's in a bad mood. She has "f – u" written in her web. It makes me wonder if spider's can get PMS.

Since going to Disneyland when I was a wee lad I've always wanted to go back, like you. Until I read about this place called Cedar Point in Sandusky, Ohio. They have a roller coaster that is unbelievable. I wanna ride it and I wanna go now. Besides I can relate to your grandson's opinion of "It's a Small World." The music sucks and it's scary. What if all those little people got lose? I'll bet they're tired of singing that song over and over. No wonder your son cried the entire way through.

I'm gonna cut this short. It's so hot the pen keeps slipping out of my fingers with sweat. I should have enough stamps to mail that board when it's finished.

I know you and Cyndi will have a ball at yer reunion, tell me all about it. Do I seem anxious? That's because I'm eager for some new eye candy. (the book) I'm bored and I'm also an idiot, but that's another story.

Yer friend,
Walt.

****

October 16, 2008

Dear Liz;

Hi, and yes you should have received a letter before this one. I have two stamps to my name and I've been saving them. One for you and the other to the courts. As you know I make my money drawing cards for the masses here. Yet this time of year there are no holidays to really speak of but in another month I'll be back in business. I have been drawing though. I have a friend here who says his ole lady might help me sell a couple of illustration boards. But, if I can do some kind of Southwest art. So I've busted my hump trying to come up with something. I've completed one and am starting another today. But unfortunately my friend has been moved to a different cell block which makes it hard to communicate, let alone do business. So I could be "snake bit."

Spike says it's because I was Hitler in my last life. Sometimes I wonder about that bug.

I got ambushed and scalped the other day coming out of the chow hall. They have grooming standards here at this prison and decided my hair was too long. It sure ain't now though.

Why Liz McGuire! I knew which beautiful lady you were in this picture you sent. You said, "Two beautiful old ladies." on your card. I "assume" Cyndi was the other beautiful lady.

Spike's been a real rag lately. Nag, nag, nag. They took Capt. Happy away the other day and brought someone else. Spike is prejudice. He talks about *me* being Hitler in my last life. He's a big one on that reincarnation stuff. He says if ya were bad in yer last life, ya get treated bad in this life. I pointed out that he's a five legged cockroach that lives in the pipe-chase in a prison. He defended that remark by saying how good he has it as a five legged "water-roach." I gotta agree, as a roach he's doing pretty good. How many roaches have a very large spider for a girlfriend and she protects him.

I've been thinking that Vallejo book was coming right after your last letter and I wanted to have postage to write you when it got here. In your last letter, four weeks ago, you said, "I'll send it next week." I worry when I send out a board and wanted to be able to write back and say, "I got that book." That's the real reason I hadn't written. When I do draw large pictures my card hustle suffers and most of my income has gone to buy these boards. I had four of them. Anyway, I'm not complainin. *(Note: Yes he is, but hey there's nothing much else he can do.)* If you did send the book, I didn't or haven't got it yet. It will get here when it get's here.

My sister wrote and said she'll send me a few bucks so I can get a Halloween costume. (Kidding.) I haven't heard from her for a few months. She's promised to send me money before and hasn't. So we'll see if she comes through this time.

Oh, if I didn't thank you before I'm thanking you now for calling the courts again for me. I believe the squeaky wheel gets the most grease. However, I'm squeaking my butt off and am dry as a bone. I still haven't written the courts with my other stamp. I probably will today.

It's six o'clock Thursday morning. I got your letter and card with Alphonse Mucha last night. I'm a big fan of Alphonse Mucha. You sent me a book on Art Nouveau a while back and I quickly became a fan. I wrote to Alphonse Mucha after I got the book. Spike says it don't matter that he died in 1939, there's that reincarnation thing again. I sent the letter to Leonard Seeblecorn of Nebraska Heights, Nebraska that in his past life he was, in all probability, Alphonse Mucha. I never got a response.

Listen my friend, I wasn't complaining about not getting the book. I was really saving my stoopid stamp for that reason. That's assuming you didn't get to sending it. That's okay, in fact if you haven't sent it, keep in mind it should appear it's coming from Bud Plant, maybe you can throw in some flyers, old catalogs or whatever it takes to mask it's not a real purchase from Bud's. I'll get it when it get's here.

I hope your spinal tap thingy was a success. I'm including an Angel card. I may have sent it before so I'm sending it again.

I hope you're well and everything is okay there. Again, thanks for the picture. I'll write more soon.

Peace, love and Bobby Sherman,
Walt.

****

October 24, 2008

Dear Liz;

Hi friend, it's me again. How are you?

I was up early and have another stamp so I'm using it on you. We're on a mandatory state wide lock down. It's a major shakedown and this came from our esteemed Governor Rick Perry. Rumor has it that some idiot got hold of a cell phone and called someone he thought could complain about prison conditions. It was his state's representative of all people. Anyway the cops are on a serious search for any cell phones. The ironic thing is if there are any cell phones on the premises it's one they brought in. We, "C" wing, got searched yesterday. What a drag that was.

Spike got us kicked out of church again. Just before our lockdown I told you about the last time he got us kicked out right? It was open mike night and Spike talked me into going up and singing a sea shanty, "Moon Walking." I had to have told you. Anyway, a friend, (Spider) told us in the chow hall that "Holy Moses" was coming to the chapel. "Holy Moses" is a big hit with the fellas. He comes in periodically and preaches up a storm. He get's everyone riled up pretty good. He get's more people baptized than chips in bean dip at a Mexican wedding when he's here. So I had told Spider that the Chaplin (Chaplin Athey) makes his followers atheists. Anyway the Chaplin told me and my abomination (Spike) to go and not come back. Spider said they had a flyer up outside the Chapel door that said, "Everyone Welcome." So I checked and sure enough that's what it said, so we went. Spike likes Holy Moses. We got through the door with the rest of the crowd okay. We hadda watch out for a couple of key figures like, "Big Show" or his twin, "Tiny." Both of them are huge, 6'8" and over 300 lbs of religious fanatics who the Chaplin has made ushers. I've been "ushered" out of there by them more than once.

So we got seated and Spike was half in, half out of my pocket. He wanted to wear his Batman cape. I knew better than to let him. His ego is ten points higher when he's Batman. Anyway Holy Moses had no more taken the stage when he spread his arms out, tipped his head back and said to the heavens, "Heavenly Father we all are but dust before thee." At that Spike scampers up to my shoulder and says, "Hey, did he just call us "butt dust?" "I think he did," I say and stand up. "Hey!! Who you calling butt dust?" The whole congregation turned and looked at us, me and Spike. You could a heard a pin drop. Holy Moses is staring. "What?" he says. Chaplin Athey comes out of his office. "*You!*" was all he says. "Duck" Spike said and I do, as one meaty paw swipes at my head. Well the chase scene wasn't pretty. It ended up behind the drum set on the stage with yours truly getting "blessed" with three sets of feet all in the name of...I don't rightly know.

Anyway Spike gave Chaplin Athey a black eye. Spike landed on the Chaplin's glasses, the Chaplin went to give Spike a smack but Spike was too quick. So the Chaplin smacked himself. It was one of those cartoon smacks. Now the sign outside the Chapel reads, "Everyone Welcome, *except.*" Now there's me, Spike and a few other names on it.

My new celli is a "waste of a human life." That's the gang he's in. It's called, "Waste of a human life". It's an offshoot of the losers. Me and Spike don't believe in gangs, well not like them anyway.

And that's the news from Lake Woe-be-gone, sort of. Sherry has gone into hibernation. In the pipe-chase. Every time she comes back she's bigger. She's already bigger than Spike and he's three and a half inches long, so...yikes! She's moody too but at least she keeps out all the other spiders. Which is a good thing because I hate spiders, except Sherry and I hope she knows it?

Take care, keep in touch and know yer friends have survived another outing to church.

Bye for now,

Walt and Spike

****

September 2008

Dear Liz;

Once upon a time (1874) an artist was born. His name was Joe. (Joseph Christian Leyendecker) He was born in Germany but became an American Illustrator. He did the original to this pen and ink attempt of mine. I like this picture and hope you do too. It will be a rare color of mine and I had a fine time with it. Unfortunately there ain't much room for a frame so just nail it to your barn and later when someone claims to have sent you your first Christmas card for 2008 you can point to this and say, "it was Sept. when I got this".

I know it's early but I traded an old book for some stamps and here ya go. I hope you like it. You wanted color and all I had was a red ink pen. My choices were a fire engine, the Oscar Meyer Weiner mobile, or this. How'd I do?

Did you already go to your reunion? How was it? I'm gonna worry about this getting to you until I hear back from you. I might worry about y'all driving 7,000 miles across California until you write back and say you're home. So that should get me two pieces of mail. Tee hee. Well I'm gonna go. I have a National Geographic I ain't read yet, I'm gonna find my local classic rock station (no baseball tonight) and take a break. I'm glad this is done. Let me know when you get it.

Take care
Your friend,
Walt.

****

November 12, 2008

Dear Liz;

Just a few lines to let you know I received the books you sent. They kept the "Vallejo" book. I know, I know, they have a list and there's a book called "The Fabulous Women of…" by David and Anthony Palumbo or something like that. Anyway I've written to the Directors Review Committee about getting my book. I've put in a grievance on it and should get it…eventually. The little synopsis from the catalog did not mention nudity so I "assumed" there was none. These, umm…I wanna choose my words accurately… let's see…"Assholes!" Yeah that's it. These assholes are unbelievable. I pointed out their mistake and they even admitted it but, "So take it up with the Grievance Committee," so I am.

I wrote to the Magistrate Judge, Don Bush, and will write the judge this week, Judge Schneider. The Magistrate investigates and gives his recommendations to the judge. I cited some cases that the judges offered an unsolicited opinion on the length of time the courts take to hear an 11.07 (write of habeas corpus) so we'll see.

My friend D.J. just dropped off a couple of stamps for a future Christmas card so I'm rushing this letter to get it out before morning mail call otherwise we gotta wait. I hate waiting.

Well, I know its short but I'm mailing it. I hope y'all are okay. I'm okay, nothing outside of the norm. I love the fairies book, thanks. They kept the 60's book, I've appealed that also. Heavy sigh. I gotta get out of here, Duh! I'll write more soon.

Your friends,
Walt and Spike

PS: How about that new Pres? I can't believe you didn't like the Tim Dorsey book. I laughed my... ummm...ears off. I thought the Russians were funny, especially the exasperated leader, "what's wrong with you guys?" Just not your cup-o-tea huh? What do you like? Give me an idea; maybe my next suggestion will be better. I read a lot. Bye for now.

****

November 30, 2008

Dear Liz;

Hi my ole friend, it's me your ole friend.

I wrote you a short letter last time saying I got the books. Of course "they" kept the best one. They finally let me see it because the catalog didn't mention nudity and I was very unreasonable about it.

Say, do you realize it's been five years, seven months and eight days since I first wrote to Bud plant? Long time huh?

I'm tired; lately I've been just going through the motions. I've been drafting an essay / article about how shitty the legal system treats someone's rights guaranteed by the United States Constitution. Once you're in the system you cease to be anything more than a nuisance. If you're without a lawyer that is.

I have the equivalent of a D.N.A. test clearing me of any wrong doing and I can't be heard, or I will be heard after four or five years. That's how strong my case is. Yet here I sit. I'll bet you're tired of hearing it too. I'm sorry. Let's talk about Thanksgiving. I can't see the English celebrating Thanksgiving across the pond. Maybe they do?

So wha-da-ya gotta do to become a citizen? Seems like marrying an American citizen and sticking around paying taxes for as long as you have would be enough, right? Frustrating huh? Yeah, I can relate.

So y'all gearing up for Christmas out there in snow country? I was going through my old pictures the other day and came across the ones you sent of your winter-wonderland. I wish I could be somewhere like that right now. I will be. I'm pretty determined.

So how is Liz and Co.? I hope all is well. I've gotta get in here and find something to do or I'm gonna go stark-raving-mad. I wonder if "stark-raving-pissed-off" is the same thing. I'm okay friend, just a bad time of year for me. I want to say something positive before I go.

Did I ever tell you the time God himself came to Adam and Eve in the Garden of Eden? God had a bag in his hand. "I've got something for each of you" he said, reaching into the bag. "There's the ability to be able to pee standing up, who wants that? "Adam almost broke his neck jumping up "ooh me! Me! Me!" he said and God gave it to him saying. "This is for you and all male's after you" God reached in the bag and said, "All I have left is multiple organisms" for you Eve. And that's why women, I've heard...anyway, I'm gonna go. Take care and write when ya can.

Your friend,
Walt

PS: Spike's still in Mexico, he says, "Ola." He's due back this week. I can hardly wait.

****

December 7, 2008

Dear Liz;

Howdy friend! Spike's back.

Ain't this Pearl Harbor Day? Hmmm, Spike says yeah. He's usually right about these things. He says the Japanese beetles get all full of themselves around this time of year. He always wondered why until he asked them. Pearl Harbor Day, go figure. (I don't understand that)

So, is it all festive up there? Seems like every other radio and TV commercial is Christmas and has been for a couple weeks. I'm already choking on "Tis the Season to be jolly", ahh well, but some of the songs are okay, I guess.

Today is football day. I'm in the day-room staking out a seat for the game that starts at noon and it's just after 6am. This joint is over crowded, so on football day if you don't get down here early and stake a claim to a seat, "yew ain't a gonna git one hoss" (that's Texan)

Is it snowing yet? Up there I mean. Down here it's still in the 70's during the day. I've gotta draw three Christmas cards this year. One for you, which I've already started; one for me Pa and one for my stinkin sister. The one who never writes. I do it mainly to guilt her. She used to write and promise's she's gonna do this and do that but never does. That's frustrating from my point of view. I told her she didn't need to promise anything, just write once in a while. I write to her. I think she just doesn't know what to say. What can ya do? Maybe one day I'll just show up and she'll start blubbering. She's one year, one month and one day older than me.

The day-room's filling up. It's after 7am now. Spike's perched on a bench taking bets. Well him and his friend Jughead. Spike advises Jughead in his gambling endeavors. They don't call Jughead "Jughead" for nothing. I have my handy dandy Grass Valley and Nevada City gold mining book to prop my pages up so's I can write letters this morning. It's the one y'all sent me umpteen million years ago. I have six stamps and three letters to write. You're first.

Stamps are the currency here. Everything is stamps. When yer laying up in yer bunk, starving because chow wasn't much or what they did have wasn't edible, someone comes around selling sandwiches for two stamps apiece. Usually they're good sandwiches when you can afford them. The only trouble I have, other than not being able to afford them is they put Jalapeño peppers on *everything*. I don't like the real spicy stuff. I'm in the wrong part of the world for my tastes. They put peppers on peanut butter and jelly sandwiches, oatmeal, eggs, and even Jell-O! If that ain't bad enough, they have these little jewels called "Habanera" peppers that make Jalapeno peppers taste like lollypops. I have three taste buds left and I'm not gonna blow them out proving how tough I am by eating something grown in hell by Satan himself. How about you, do you like the spicy peppers? My sister used to eat them like candy. You know there're hot when smoke comes dribbling our yer belly button.

Spike's inciting a riot over here. He's bad mouthing the Dallas Cowboys. When ever the Cowboys lose, all the state facilities fly the flag at half-mast. I believe Pittsburgh will be beating all the pee-wailing-duky out of the Cowboys today, tee hee.

There's an organization in Philadelphia or somewhere that's doing an art show. I think. Anyway they're inviting prison artists to submit pieces which will be auctioned off after the show and the proceeds given to the artist, I think. The last time I did this I drew a board that sold for $68.00. Good money for me. Only thing is, I didn't get the money; it was donated to the organization responsible for researching the comeback of the four legged chicken. The donation was in my name. So I really need to check this info. Out. Only I don't know anyone, except you, who owns a computer. If I send you the information could you check it out for me? I could really use the money if it's all logic. Spike needs new shoes, seven of them I need a new toothbrush and one of those new fangled writing irons and maybe even a bag of potato chips from the prison store.

Well Liz, I'm gonna go. At least I ain't all depressed like the last letter. My bugs back, so at least we'll be together for Christmas. I hope you and your family get everything you want for Christmas and the whole holiday thing is wonderful, magical, and groovy even. Maybe next year I'll be out. I hope so anyway. There's a new Star Trek movie coming next summer, I wanna see it at an IMAX theater and see it in 3-D.

Merry Christmas friend, take care

Your friends, Walt and Spike

December 17, 2008

Dear Liz;

I got the calendar yesterday. Thank you, thank you, and thank you.

I've been staying busy hassling the courts and judges. I may get leave to attack an issue in the lower courts. That would see me out of here before I turn 47 in March. That would be a blessing. Anyway, like a dog with a bone, I'm on it. So-to-speak.

I need to get this out in today's mail or ya ain't gonna get it till next year. I hope all's well with you and yours. Happy Holidays, Spike sends his best wishes as well. He's in the pipe chase playing poker again. Me? I'm keeping my pecker up, so to speak, and faithfully remain your friend.

Walt

PS: I'll write more soon, it's contagious.

****

mug shot
6-20-2000

IN THE UNITED STATES COURT OF APPEALS
FOR THE FIFTH CIRCUIT

No. 14-40330
USDC No. 4:06-CV-204

WALTER GERALD ANDERSON,

Petitioner-Appellant

v.

WILLIAM STEPHENS, DIRECTOR, TEXAS DEPARTMENT OF CRIMINAL
JUSTICE, CORRECTIONAL INSTITUTIONS DIVISION,

Respondent-Appellee

Appeal from the United States District Court for the
Eastern District of Texas, Sherman

O R D E R:

Walter Gerald Anderson, Texas prisoner # 1092654, seeks a certificate
of appealability (COA) to appeal the district court's denial of his 28 U.S.C.
§ 2254 petition, challenging his 2002 conviction for aggravated kidnaping and
resulting 25-year sentence. After filing his COA motion, Anderson moved to
file a corrected COA brief. The motion to file a corrected COA brief is granted.

To obtain a COA, Anderson must make "a substantial showing of the
denial of a constitutional right." 28 U.S.C. § 2253(c)(2). Such a showing
requires that he "demonstrate that reasonable jurists would find the district
court's assessment of the constitutional claims debatable or wrong," *Slack v.
McDaniel*, 529 U.S. 473, 484 (2000), or that jurists of reason "could conclude
the issues presented are adequate to deserve encouragement to proceed

No. 14-40330

further." *Miller-El v. Cockrell*, 537 U.S. 322, 327 (2003). To the extent that the district court denied relief on procedural grounds, Anderson must show, inter alia, that "jurists of reason would find it debatable whether the district court was correct in its procedural ruling." *Slack*, 529 U.S. at 484.

If his brief is liberally construed, Anderson renews only his claims that the trial court violated his due process rights when it failed to require disclosure of the prosecution's witness list prior to trial and that the prosecution violated *Brady v. Maryland,* 373 U.S. 83 (1963), when it withheld the victim's previous conviction for sexual assault. He briefs no argument renewing the claims that appellate counsel was ineffective in failing to discover and raise the *Brady* claim, that the trial court abused its discretion in failing to give a lesser-included-offense instruction, or that appellate counsel was ineffective in failing to raise several arguments on appeal that had been preserved by objection at trial and in failing to advise him of the appellate court's decision so that he could file a petition for discretionary review. Those claims are therefore abandoned. *See Hughes v. Johnson*, 191 F.3d 607, 613 (5th Cir. 1999); *Yohey v. Collins*, 985 F.2d 222, 224-25 (5th Cir. 1993). Anderson also alleges, for the first time in his COA motion, that the trial court violated his rights under the Equal Protection Clause and that the prosecution knowingly suborned perjury when it allowed Barnett to testify about his criminal past. These newly asserted claims will not be considered. *See Henderson v. Cockrell*, 333 F.3d 592, 605 (5th Cir. 2003).

As to the properly preserved claims, Anderson fails to make the required showing to obtain a COA. *See Miller-El*, 537 U.S. at 327; *Slack*, 529 U.S. at 484. Accordingly, his motion for a COA is denied. His motions for leave to proceed in forma pauperis (IFP) on appeal and for the appointment of counsel are similarly denied.

No. 14-40330

COA DENIED; MOTION TO FILE CORRECTED COA BRIEF GRANTED; MOTIONS FOR LEAVE TO PROCEED IFP AND FOR APPOINTMENT OF COUNSEL DENIED.

/s/ Leslie H. Southwick
LESLIE H. SOUTHWICK
UNITED STATES CIRCUIT JUDGE

A True Copy
Certified order issued Feb 11, 2015

Lyle W. Cayce
Clerk, U.S. Court of Appeals, Fifth Circuit

"Lurleen"

I need someone who is prepared for:

No PROBLEM   -A million questions
Hmmm see Back   -Uncontrollable laughter - caused by you.
No PROBLEM   -My family
ummmm... O-Kay   -My Appetite — not how much but what.
got cha →   -Musical outbursts
I can dig it →   -Random dancing — always
looking Forward to em -My friends
goes without saying → -Sad/Happy Tears
How deep? →   -Deep talks
love it   -My imagination
love em   -My dreams
Yeah Baby Yeah   -Walks in the rain.
You mean like this? -Random ~~Note~~ ♡ notes
about what? →   -Useless Arguments — unless we agree
Done and Done! → -and acceptance of the real me. — oh boy!

110

Dearest Lovey,   2-14-18

Heres hoping this is the last Valentines day we spend apart. I hope you know I love you and look forward to doing things sweethearts do together like walking in the rain and the snow hand in hand with or without the dogs 😊 Sleepin in watching old movies and drinkin hot coa-coa...with booze in it! 😊 Adult sweethearts. Sorinade's on the porch and long wet kisses and warm deep hugs. Heavy sigh!

Love always
Walt
xxxooo

114

For my very Special Valentine,
Elizabeth Anne.

I love You Liz.
Signed.
Walter G. Anderson.
Valentines Day 2016

Absolutely none of the reasons given for denial apply to him. I found out the parole board usually makes their decision before the inmate actually comes up for parole.

PDKAR008AAHNEA   STATE OF TEXAS   02/02/2016
                         BOARD OF PARDONS AND PAROLES   PAGE   1

                    NOTICE OF PAROLE PANEL DECISION

NAME: ANDERSON,WALTER GERALD
SID NUMBER: 06353092   TDCJ-ID NUMBER: 01092654
TDCJ-ID UNIT OF ASSIGNMENT: EASTHAM
HOUSING ASSIGNMENT: DORM 2   BED: 048

SUBJECT: Decision Not to Grant Parole - NEXT REVIEW

     After a review of your case, the Board of Pardons and Paroles
decision is not to grant you parole and has set your next parole review
date as 02/2017. *← wont be Necessary Lovey.*

     You have been denied parole for the reason(s) listed below:
One or more components indicated in each paragraph listed below may
apply, but only one is required.
1D. THE RECORD INDICATES THAT THE OFFENDER HAS REPEATEDLY COMMITTED
     CRIMINAL EPISODES THAT INDICATE A PREDISPOSITION TO COMMIT
     CRIMINAL ACTS UPON RELEASE.
7D. THE RECORD INDICATES THAT LENGTH OF TIME SERVED BY THE OFFENDER
     IS NOT CONGRUENT WITH OFFENSE SEVERITY AND CRIMINAL HISTORY.
2D. THE RECORD INDICATES THE INSTANT OFFENSE HAS ELEMENTS OF
     BRUTALITY, VIOLENCE, ASSAULTIVE BEHAVIOR, OR CONSCIOUS SELECTION
     OF VICTIM'S VULNERABILITY INDICATING A CONSCIOUS DISREGARD FOR THE
     LIVES, SAFETY, OR PROPERTY OF OTHERS, SUCH THAT THE OFFENDER POSES
     A CONTINUING THREAT TO PUBLIC SAFETY.
5D. THE RECORD INDICATES UNSUCCESSFUL PERIODS OF SUPERVISION ON
     PREVIOUS PROBATION, PAROLE, OR MANDATORY SUPERVISION THAT RESULTED
     IN INCARCERATION, INCLUDING PAROLE-IN-ABSENTIA. *?*

     The Institutional Division will monitor your treatment plan progress
and will report your progress to the Board of Pardons and Paroles.

     Should you have any questions regarding this notice you are to
contact your unit Institutional Parole Office.

2-48

TEXAS DEPARTMENT OF CRIMINAL JUSTICE
CORRESPONDENCE / CONTRABAND DENIAL FORM

NAME Anderson, Walter   TDCJ-CID# 1092654

UNIT Eastham   DATE CORRESPONDENCE RECEIVED 4-7-16   DATE OFFENDER NOTIFIED 4-11-16

CORRESPONDENCE: ☐ TO OR ☒ FROM Liz McGuire
13104 Manton Canyon
Grass Valley, CA 95945

The above correspondence has been denied to you in accordance with BP-03.91, Uniform Offender Correspondence Rules

CHECK APPROPRIATE CAUSE OR CAUSES FOR DENIAL AND STATE APPROPRIATE REASON
☐ Content   ☒ Contraband   ☐ Enclosure   ☐ Package / Publication   ☐ Sealed Correspondence

DENIED:
1 - Stamp   I taped a stamp on the back of a photo.
I knew it was not allowed but thought
"maybe" it wouldn't be noticed. Duh!

RECEIVED:
letter + 3 photos

APPEAL:
Should the offender decide to appeal the rejection of said correspondence/contraband, he/she must notify the Unit Mailroom **WITHIN TWO (2) WEEKS** of offender notification requesting that this correspondence/contraband and the rejection form be forwarded to the Director's Review Committee (DRC). Should persons outside the institution desire to appeal, submit by mail to the Director's Review Committee, PO Box 99, Huntsville, TX 77342-0099. The appeal must reach the DRC **WITHIN TWO (2) WEEKS** of the notification date listed above.

Does offender wish to appeal the decision? ☐ Yes ☐ No ☒ Non-Appealable _____ 4-11-16
                                                                    Offender Signature   Date

DISPOSITION: Offender must check the desired disposition at the time the denial is presented.

☒ Destroy

☐ Send to the following person at the offender's expense: _____
                                                          Name and Address

_____ 4-11-16   Womack 4-11-16
Offender Signature & Date   Mailroom Representative Signature & Date

UNIT DISPOSITION: _____
                   Date   Employee's Signature

IF A DISPOSITION CHOICE IS NOT EXPRESSED AND EXECUTED OR LITIGATION HAS NOT BEGUN ON ITEMS BEING HELD FOR LITIGATION WITHIN SIXTY (60) DAYS OF THE INITIAL DENIAL OR FROM THE DRC DECISION DATE (IF APPEALED), THE ITEMS WILL BE DESTROYED.

DISTRIBUTION:
Original- Send to the DRC **IF THE OFFENDER WISHES TO APPEAL.** If not, keep on unit.
Gold   - Unit Copy
Yellow - Offender Copy
Pink   - Mail to sender/addressee of correspondence
I-153 (Rev. 3/12)

119

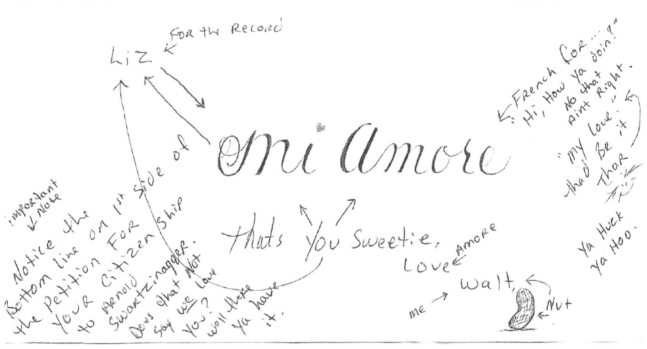

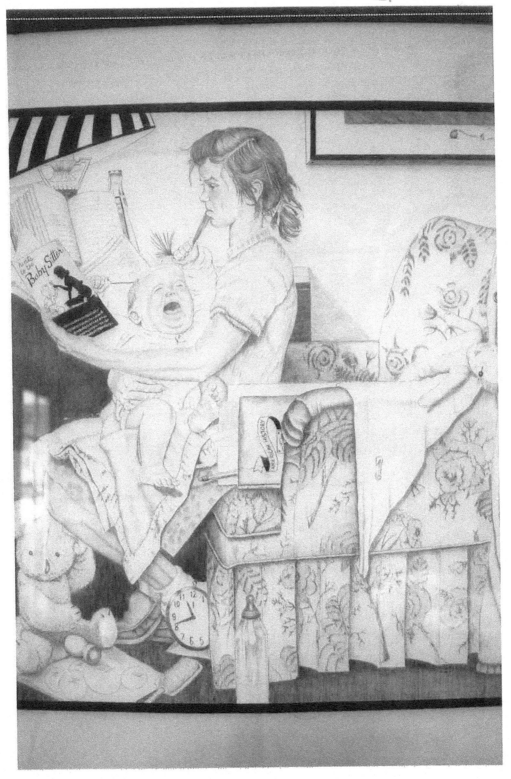

Chapter Seven

January 19, 2009

Dear Liz;

Hi, how are things up in the mountains? How's your New Year coming, so far? Mine's been about the same.

I'm more optimistic about getting out soon but it ain't materialized yet so I've enclosed a… umm..what's the word? Marquee or something like that. Spike's idea. I was just gonna tell you but Spike wanted to make a big production out of it. He's messing with the cling on tape right now. If he's not careful he'll lose another leg.

It's almost 70 degrees down here and its only January. We've got one more football game to go. Do you watch the Super Bowl? Just wondering. I'm hoping the Arizona Cardinals win it but Pittsburgh could do it just as easily. We're about ready to swear in a new President, I hope he's as good as the last one.

They're giving us fried chicken today because of the holiday, Martin Luther King Day, Is that a Federal holiday? The only bearing it would have on my meager existence is whether the mail runs or not. Well that and fried chicken. We rarely get such fare for chow. If one had a couple of stamps one could buy an extra piece of chicken in the chow hall. They ain't big pieces. In fact I'm not seeing the usual flock of pigeons outside, I wonder if there's a connection. Hmmmmm…

Spike's been pretty chipper these days, that's probably because Sherry is in some sort of hibernation thing. Every year she does that and when she comes back it's a shock to us all. She's bigger and hairier.

I gotta make an effort to get into the barber shop for my bi-monthly scalping session. I have them buzz my head every other month, although it seems like longer this time. Probably because my hair seems longer. I gotta do that before the "Nazi Hair Squad" gets a hold of me. They roam around with tazers and zap you into unconsciousness and you wake up strapped to a barber chair and someone practicing being a barber on your head. That isn't always as fun as it sounds.

Well friend I'm gonna go, I just wanted to share some news with you. Hope all is well out there where you are. Take care and I'll be writing again soon.

See ya, lots of love and stuff luv.
Walt and Spike

****

February 22, 2009

Dear Liz

Hi friend, me and Spike have been busy drawing and drawing and drawing again. I've been commissioned to do four boards just so I can stock my food locker, for a change. I'm busier than a one legged man in a butt kicking contest to get these done. I've done two and am on the third.

I got your letter dated the 29th and have been meaning to answer it. I even sat down several times but never finished. I will tonight and it will go out with the mail in the morning.

I got a letter from the county clerk in Fannin County. It seems the judge that presided over my trial, both of them, the first one ended in a mistrial, has retired. The lady that's taken his place is tired of my letters wanting to know when I get a fair trial. She's appointed counsel to represent me in this matter. Cool huh? I'm like jazzed and am convinced I won't have to spend my next birthday here in Texas. Whether that's true or not we'll see. If you're curious you can call him and if you find out something good let me know, if not, then I don't wanna know. I'm happy in my delusion of optimism right now. If I get moved to the county jail I'll write to you from there, okay? Okay!

I'm reading a book from the Association for Research and Enlightenment, A.R.E. This organization is based on the life and readings of Edgar Cayce, a psychic of phenomenal success. The Sleeping Prophet. Anyway this book is on reincarnation. I only read it when I'm winding down to go to sleep. The only thing is the book's so compelling I find myself not going to sleep. Anyway it talks about the Bible a lot and the fact that certain people seem to live a charmed life while others seem to go through more of their fair share of hell. Karma, ye reap what ye sow. Actually it makes sense. I must have been Adolph Hitler in my last life. Have you ever met someone that you feel as if you know them? Or meet someone who for some unknown reason you just don't like them? Well you may have known them in your last life and they were either your best friend or your worst enemy. Day-ja-voo (sound it out) I refuse to write French words, hell I have a hard enough time spelling English. Anyway that's explained as well.

The spelling of your name with a "Q" was not intentional, just a funny "G". Maybe I should take more time in my penmanship huh, or not. Anyway I'll do better, especially on the envelope where it's important.

Thank you for the info on the website. Did you get to see your old friend from England in Roseville? I know where Roseville is, I used to live down that way. Sounds like a regular British invasion. You know of the last two, the first one didn't go over too well but the second one was awesome!!

How far am I from Dallas? If you have a map, find Houston and there you have it. We're a ways away.

Well Liz I'm gonna go for now. I got some news on Ronnald and want to share it with you but am up past my bedtime and it ain't a good bedtime story. But I'll get after it soon. Take care and keep me in your prayers. I "may" finally be getting some action in the courts.

Your very good friend,
Walt and Spike

PS: If that lawyer gives you any flack, tell him you're Hilary Clinton, I'd do it but my voice is too deep. Oh wait, how much of an accent do you have? Never mind, he's a Texas lawyer, he can't be that bright, in which case maybe you had better wish me more luck.

****

March 8, 2009

Dear Liz;

Hi, long time no hear from me. I got your lil card dated Feb. 14 the other day. You wrote my number as 1092659 when its 1092654. I credit that to my sloppy writing and you probably read it off the envelope I addressed the last time. The card went to another unit and travelled to three different country's including the province of China before someone thought to get it to me.

I've written to the shyster lawyer twice and have got no response. I'm worried thinking maybe the judge didn't appoint that attorney for *my* benefit. My last letter to Mr. Bottom Feeder was very blunt and to the point. Spike helped me. I really trying to get out before my birthday, but with one week to go that don't seem very likely. What do you think?

I did get an order from the Federal Courts saying that I should "Shut the hell up, nothing else needs to be filed. We're reviewing your case right now". Wow it's only been four years. I'm not as excited about that as I am about the States action. They seem to be faster. In any event things do seem to be coming together. Hallelujah!

Ronnald's back! Seems he was caught smoking crack with the homeless. He says he was holding it for some guy while he panhandled for wine money. I asked him why he even came back to Texas. He said, "I never left, parole wouldn't let me". Hamburgler sold him the crack and had just left the scene. Spike asked him, "I thought it was someone else…Ronnald made a move to squash Spike, so, I don't know.

We're trying to get Ronnald moved back into this cell and it's looking good because they want him back in the kitchen and that gives a bargaining chip.

My "now" celli is nuts. He takes 10,000 mg. Thorazeen shots. Actually it's an I.V. drip for about three hours every week and sits around slobbering. Sometimes mumbling in a different language about some dude named "Bamboozle the Great". I personally can't see "Bamboozle" but I have no doubt he's there.

I'm sending you a card on Spike's seagull. I'm not sure if I've sent this card to you before, if I have well? Have another one. I'm burned out on drawing things right now but wanted to send you "something" so there ya go.

This place sux. It would be nice if when I get out of here I can maybe, get enough $$ to buy materials to draw originals. Maybe bring "Giraffalo" to life again. That would be cool huh? But getting out will be step one. Do you still want me to call you and say, Hi friend? We will still be friends, right? I consider you a friend. *(Note: If only we both knew then...)*

I've been writing to another person, not quite as long a you. She's a Christian lady (her names Carolyn) that lives in Fortworth. She comes down once in a while; in fact she should be coming this weekend for my birthday. That will be nice. She'll buy things for me from the vending machine. Actually she won't personally feed me, she'll be on one side of a glass screen partition and I'll be on the other. I think she's sweet on me but she yells at me sometimes. One of us is crazy but she's a friend.

Spike says Hi. I'm gonna go for now. I hope everything's good there. It's warming up around here. I hope I don't have to spend another summer down here in Texas. They're gonna spotlight your homeboys, the Beatles, on the oldie music station today. I'll be listening to that.

Take care and all that
Walt.

****

March 25, 2009

Dear Liz;

It's already 80 degrees down here, eeeek! Hi friend, it's me, your friendly neighborhood convict. You could probably figure that one out on yer own, huh?

I've been meaning to sit down and write to you but every time I do I start bitching about my legal situation. I don't wanna do that anymore. I'm consumed by it, heavy sigh.

I wanna write another story or add on to one I've started in the past. I'll bet I could finish "Peter Pan and Spike the Wonder Roach". I think the type of humor (or humour) that I'd need to finish that story would be along the same lines as that Tim Dorsey novel with Sarge in it. Do you remember? You said you weren't impressed with it. (Triggerfish twist). I wanna go to the Serengeti with "Giraffalo," but can't find my way back, yet. I did give him a friend though, I'll tell ya about it, one day. Hint, a snapping turtle and a Badger. It was either that or a defrocked friar and a wino. What do you think?

My shyster lawyer lied to you Liz. No one has written to me but you and my Christian lady friend. Yes she was a little ole lady in a black tee shirt and spandex pants. I can not give her justice with that description. She really looks more like the Southern Belle type except she's about 12 years older than me. I think she believes I'm her husband-to-be. She started to write through a pen pal site, not long after I started writing to you through Bud Plant, about six months after. I've never pretended to be her betrothed. In fact I've been not very nice on more than one occasion just so she won't cotton on to me. But she's fun and funny.

She said she talked to you after you said you'd reached the shyster lawyer. She's very religious and says I can ask her to type any legal document and send it to whom ever. Actually she's been invaluable to my cause. In fact she found the new evidence I'm going back to court on. I owe her more than the description I gave you when I told you about her. I believe she's a Baptist. A Methodist once claimed that the only thing wrong with a Baptist is they don't hold em under long enough when they baptize them. I read that somewhere. You could have sent it in one of the computer printed jokes or from my neighbor who gets them from his ole lady.

So what should I write about, story wise? I have first hand experience with two penal systems of the three in the USA. California, Texas and Florida. I could write about that. But the only problem is in the real prison world Spike doesn't exist and Ronnald never went off the deep end and played Chicken cricket in the hall way. Maybe I could write a book and call it "Ten Men doing Time" and have Spike in between stories. Ten different men authorized by me and edited by you.

Back to my lady friend, Carolyn, she advised me to not write to my lying, sorry, no good, shit eating shyster lawyer again. I wrote to him twice and he never responded. Even after him telling you someone did write. Argh! So frustrating. I wrote to the court clerk and asked that I be informed of any dead lines that are levied on anything pertaining to cause #20118 in Fannin County. My last letter was plain enough without being rude. So I won't blow it.

You mentioned you'd like to hear my voice on the phone one day, me too. I don't wanna wait till the end of summer, my fan won't last another summer and I don't have the money to replace it. Besides it stinks around here in the summer.

Have you ever read the James Herriot books, "All Things Bright and Beautiful"? Great Veterinarian books. Very delightful anecdotes etc. *(Note: I've read all of the books and still have them and saw the BBC TV series.)*

Well I'm gonna go. What do you think of me writing about prison? I hate this place and when I write I do better when I escape into a story. Write when ya can, thank you for the b-card. Your friend,

Walt

****

April 12, 2009

Dear Liz;

Hi again friend. I received your letter dated 3-30-09 last week. Last night I got your postcard about you calling the lawyers office. I'll start with the letter.

127

Country music? Y'all listen to country music? Deliberately? I was raised listening to a Sacramento country radio station "K.R.A.K." When I can and do listen to country its classic country. Seems I'm listening to classic rock too. In fact Saturday night (every other Saturday) the classic country station plays "oldies" which is older than classic, I think. Anyways that's what's on now. Elvis, Chuck Berry, Ball Haley, Buddy Holly etc. Before the British invasion. Anyway Spike likes Petula Clark, as do I. Lulu too. What's not to like. My "modern music tastes are practically non-existent. I am a big Pink Floyd fan. An acquired taste, so they say.

Let's talk about my lady friend, Carolyn. First of all I'd never repeat anything you said. You asked me not to tell her you said I shouldn't tell her that we; her and I, are gonna move in together after my so called, "graduation." *(Note: On the phone Carolyn told me Walter and she were going to live together when he was paroled)* I didn't, haven't won't, ain't gonna and all that. She's nuts Liz. That in itself isn't a bad thing. I can dig crazy women because they're usually not boring. I'm also not cruel in the sense to lead her on and abandon her at the prison gate. I've told her many times I ain't staying in Texas when I get out of here. I haven't got a letter from her in three weeks now. This usually means she's mad with me for some reason I don't know about. I'd have given a small fortune to have been listening on the phone conversation between the two of you. Especially when you told her that "you" were probably too old for me, those were your words. Tee hee. Liz, she's about the same age as you are but you actually look a lot younger in your photos.

She started writing shortly after I got your first "Post-It" note and the books. I had solicited a pen-pal place a year prior to writing Bud Plant. I got no response. It seems the lady that was doing the pen-pal place died and Carolyn was sorting through about 100 letters. She said God directed her to my letter. Actually it was five letters. So she wrote. Not once did I tell her that we, her and I, were gonna move in together and all that. Now, according to her, we're gonna get married, or maybe get married. Carolyn has been a solid friend and has broken up with me on more than one occasion and told me to "get bent" several times. I don't bite into that anymore though. I did once and that was a confusing episode that made me question my own sanity. So I just wait out the strange parts. She knows where I am if she wants to contact me. But, please, for God's sake, "Don't call her!" Not on my behalf. She's a good friend but not near as anchored as you are. Between you and her though and once in a while my dad will write but you and she are my only "pen-pals" so to speak. She's very smart, religious, capable, crazy, helpful and Southern. Did I mention nuts? Enough about her.

I hope your "filthy cold" is better. I've had a cough for about a week now that only seems to bother me when I lay down to sleep. Last night wasn't quite so bad. I've been like a surly old bear lately. My friend's have make comments to that effect. I've been frustrated and short with people. So I've taken a step back to regroup. Good idea. This really ain't the place to lose ones perspective.

I've drawn a horse for some dude, got into a "moon" marathon and genuinely tried to keep busy. I have started a letter to you twice but didn't like what I said. There are aspects to this place that I try and leave out of my letters. In reality it's not a nice place and I try to differ from the norm. I attract people who don't relish in the violence and games that accompany the day-to-day routine of prison life.

I may have mentioned I've done time in California for being a bad thief. In fact I came to Texas to get away from that entire scene. Kind of like breaking a chain. I reconciled with my wife of a long time, here in Texas. Got mixed up in small town politics and here I am. For the record I really <u>did not</u> kidnap any taxi driver. Long story, I think I ran it down to you before. Anyway, perhaps one day we can talk about it in person. The things I wanna do with the rest of my life are better than I've been doing. I'm fighting for the chance to hope to keep you as my friend, you know while I get all this together.

I wanna comment on the "cat thing" you go to three days a week, three hours a day. *(Note: I volunteered at a cat adoption place)* I had a girlfriend who was a vet tech and would visit a feral cat place and administer vet stuff to them. She took me one day. All these little kittens in their cages starved for attention. I was not allowed back. I literally had empathy for them. I also left with two. Only two. Gonzo and Tarzan. Anyway, a man must know his limitations. Mine are cages.

Now about my "solicitor." Thank you so much for taking an interest on my behalf. In the grand scheme of things, odds are, it won't make a bit of difference that you make these enquiries on my behalf, but it does to me. I wanna make it clear that I appreciate it a lot. Your postcard said the secretary will talk to "David," (that's his name) and the possibility of him coming to me or me going for a hearing. I believe it's the latter. If the lazy bastard can't even write a letter he ain't gonna drive seven hours and come to tell me nothing. The next logical step is an evidentially hearing. I should be present for that so they should come and get me and strap me to the hood of a Fannin County police car where they can keep an eye on me. And, drive seven hours where I'll probably get this conviction overturned and begin my third and final trial. I'll win the third one. Knowing what I know now I doubt they'll prosecute my stupid butt. Really! That's not just optimistic speculation, that's an educated guess. Anyway, if it happens, I have your address and will write ASAP and keep you posted.

Well my friend, I'm gonna go. Say, do they have country music in England? If so, is it big like over here. Could a genuine Yank get a gig crooning out old cowboy sings while plucking the strings of his trusty "git fiddle" (guitar?) Just curious. I used to play the guitar and knew about a million songs. Everything from Johnny Horton to the Eagles. You do know who Johnny Horton is, don't cha?

Spike's out and about while Ronnald's concocting a new pancake batter. Sherry's getting bigger and I'm calming down. I believe I've about completed my bout with Texas prisons. Let's hope.

I look forward to seeing the new Star Trek movie that's coming out next month. Wow, wouldn't that be awesome? You're probably not a big Star Trek fan, or are you? *(Note: I told him I've seen all of the old Star Trek movies plus the TV series)* Well I like a good action movie and would love to see that one at the theater.

Take care and "Bee" good! E.T. said that. It wouldn't surprise me to learn that Texas has a few aliens locked up for being stupid enough to land in Texas. If it's true that we're here to help others, what exactly are the others here for? Something to think about.

Well I'm gonna go, again. What do you think of me writing about prison? I hate this place and when I write I do better when I escape into a story. Write when you can, thank you for my birthday card.

Your ever friend,
Walt

****

April 22, 2009

Hey Yourself!

One quick response deserves another. I'm sitting in the day room on a day that's gonna clear 90 fricken degrees. Yuk! Well it's gonna get yuckier. Just one more thing to complain about. I like complaining about my stinking lawyer. I have some groovy explicative adjectives, I think that's the correct phrase to say, "I have some groovy shit to say about my scum-sucking waste-of-a-human-life solicitor," providing he's human. I could go on, but I'll spare you. You probably think, from my speaking of him, that I have a low opinion of that shyster. Not true, in fact I have a low opinion of *all* shysters so it's nothing personal really. I feel the same way about accidently stepping in dog poop bare foot repeatedly! Okay once would probably do it.

The letters I wrote that I did not send were more descriptive of this lifestyle than anything. This place is ugly Liz, and I'm of the opinion that when I write to you I can leave all this crap behind. At least I try to.

I'm getting so frustrated and am probably over anxious about something that is inevitable. I think I have a good idea of how its gonna play out too. I ain't always a good thinker though. I think they'll offer me my freedom if I sign a paper to not sue, or to not bring a suit against them I have the feeling I'm gonna get indignant and refuse on the basis that I didn't do it and refuse a conviction on a crime I didn't do. Besides I've had to endure eight years of some pretty degrading treatment. Enough about that. Spike sends his love. Spike says I'd be a fool to let them off the hook and I believe him. Especially in this economy, what do you think?

I have still not heard from Carolyn. Don't call her, its okay, she'll come around. *(Note: They had a big disagreement.).* When she does come around it will be nine miles of "you rotten bastard!" Trust me I've been here before. I don't make light of her feelings but I think this is a sort of game with her. I used to get upset over it, I don't anymore though. I write to you, my Dad four times a year, my Aunt in Washington and my sister occasionally but she dropped off.

My sister wanted to sell my art for me so I sent her seven boards with various pictures. It took me about four months to do. She still has the boards and hasn't written for a long time, don't know why. My Aunt wrote last month and said she'd take my art to her church and see if any one showed interest. She also offered to sponsor this project. She told me to send her some deposit slips, I did. I also sent her a board I had been working on.

Let me give ya some background on my aunt. She's my Dad's sister. She took me in when I was 11 or 12 years old. I was from a bad home where Mom drank and kicked my stupid butt out at a young age. The next day, mom would call the law swearing I had run away from home again. I ended up in foster care and my Aunt, being the Christian lady that she was volunteered to take me. I mean, I was family. My aunt's husband, Uncle Ted, worked for SeaTac in or near Seattle. Rocket propulsion scientist or some such thing. Anyway this was a solid family unit. My aunt and uncle, their 16 year old daughter, a son who was my age and a younger son, two years old. We went to church every Sunday. I went to school 5 days a week (I know, can you believe it!) Anyway they did regular family things. We lived on the Hood Canal in the Puget Sound. Great place for a kid. But, I was too wild. They took away my buck knife, my cigarettes and my genuine Viet Nam Zippo lighter given to me by a one legged veteran who used to look out for me in the brief time I knew him. I forget his real name; we all just called him Stumpy. True story. Anyway, I had been living on the streets wild and free knowing that when I got caught they would just send me back to my mom. Not this time. I landed in Washington surrounded by Ozzy and Harriet, maybe Ward and June Cleaver would be more accurate. Very Religious. So much so that on the way back to Sea Beck from picking me up at the airport, we stopped to have me baptized in the Lutheran Church. I got beaten up pretty good when I called the preacher a "Fuckin pervert". I know, I know, but I was literally wild. I could tell you story's, true stories but let's stick to the subject at hand.

I ran away for real about seven months later. My aunt and uncle didn't look very hard to find me and I didn't get caught. My aunt feels responsible for me turning out so bad. It's tough raising two boys about the same age but so opposite that even their hair reflected this difference. Their son had black hair and mine was very blonde. He was very naïve and I knew more than I should at that age. My aunt said that I was competing for her love as a mother. Maybe so, I didn't get any from my own mom, but I don't remember that. I do remember pointing out double standards that eventually drove me out. I had fun while I was there but I had fun after I left.

I hitchhiked to Los Angeles to find my dad. I had $32.00 in my pocket and after making it to Bremerton, WA. I stashed myself in a K-Mart until they closed. I got me a back pack full of stuff and off I went, down I-5 after crossing to Seattle. I didn't know it at the time but the I-5 killer was doing his thing. By the grace of God I slipped though. Literally. What the hell brought this on? Oh yeah, I remember, I sent my Aunt a board. Now my aunt and uncle live in Ocean Shores, Washington, they're now retired. She took the board to church. They all ooo-ed and ahh-ed. She said she'd send money to do a series. As of late that hasn't happened. I hate when people do that because unless the person that sends money writes and says, "Hey I sent x-amount to your trust fund account, I won't know unless I actually go to the store. Sounds easy but it's an ordeal and to go and not have money is worst than eating cat food. That's pretty bad, done it. She will send the money, they have money.

I didn't ask and have invested my life savings (seven stamps and an illustrated board) in that board and the other one I'm waiting to send. Two cowboy boards. I wanna make a craft shop order and get some prism color pencils. They sell color pencils in the store for $1.00, but they're pure crap. They don't write what color they are, ya gotta be able to tell what it is by looking at it. I was excited about getting busy and staying busy. Probably what I need, we'll see how that turns out.

I went to the dentist the other day. That's probably why my writings a little off. One eye is swollen shut. They got me tied to the chair by promising me cookies. When they had me tied down and head folded back told me "no cookies" I said, "agheeduroghhh!" Dr. Tooth said, "You should have thought about that before you got in the chair. Now, do you feel this?" I said, "owww!" He told nurse Crotchet, "Novocain" and he gave me a shot in my mouth. He waited 5 minutes and started drilling. "Ooow eey hucken ass hole!" I said squirming. "I can see the patient is experiencing a little discomfort" and he took off his shoe, "Bam, Bam, Bam!" He went up the side of my head. "Very good doctor" said Nurse Crotchet. "How was that?" the doctor said to me. After the doctor came back into focus, "Ahgh goon tah agh ergh eew hock hucken!", "Bam bam bam!" "And now?" he asked, to which I replied "Ing hine, Ing hine!" and he proceeded to put a crown on one of my teeth, after drilling of course. I don't like the dentist. I can't believe he burned me on the cookies though.

As you I feel the same way about music. Did you listen to the Beatles when you were wee lass in England? I did hear Susan Boyle. Yeah she can sing beautifully. It's a good thing my getting out of here doesn't depend on hearing her sing then blindly picking her out of a line up. Which one? I've never seen her, know what I mean. I'd like to sit with her on the porch during a Southern rain storm and play guitar while she sang. That would be cool.

About writing to the Governor, I don't have any problem with it but I think everything that can be done has been done. My Federal writ is due really soon so it's just a matter of time. I used to live in the law library and have greased the wheels that needed greasing. Let's hope I used the right grease. All United States Supreme Court cases cited. So, hopefully before it gets to hot here.

"Go to Church!" good advice. I am, I do, I will, I know.

I got a little long winded in this letter. Thank you for listening. I hope everything there is okay. I really, really, really wanna go and see that Star Trek movie at the movies next month. We'll see. Please keep in touch. Don't worry about Carolyn, I'm not. Spike sends his love and Ronnald says Hi.

Bye for now, your friend,
Walt

PS: Please excuse the profanity. I wouldn't have done it but you said I could. I really did say that to the pastor of the Lutheran Church at the age of eleven or twelve. First impressions. I'll not forget him or him me probably. We ended up being friends.

****

April 26, 2009

Hi Liz;

You mentioned coming to Texas next month *(Note: I went to visit my brother),* and at the time you wrote you spoke of dropping by this prison for a visit. I never really responded except to say it was a long drive from where you were going. At that time I applied for a visit in your name to be added to my visitors list. I put down that you were my 1st cousin / wife from Nebraska, this would explain any accent you might have. This is the South and the wedding of 1st cousins is the norm. I'm kidding about all that except the part about putting you on my visiting list. I got a notice on Friday that you had been approved for visiting. I also read in your previous letter that it is too far to drive, I don't blame you nor do I expect you to alter your plans. But if something happens that changes, you can only visit on weekends between 8am and 5pm

If you think of renting a movie, rent "The Life of David Gale" starring Kevin Spacey and you'll see this prison and its visiting room. They have a hospitality house that rounds off the prison experience, I hear it's nice. *(Note: I went to see Walter the first time in May 2014. I stayed in this truly wonderful hospitality house in Huntsville TX.)*

I'm trying to get this letter to you before y'all take off. I've not heard from no one legal or otherwise. (Cept yew) So be good! I hope your trip is a good one, I hope your brother is well.

If you do decide you can come and these assholes tell you, you can't visit, don't take no for an answer. Demand to see the highest ranking officer on duty. Sometimes these people are a bit unreasonable. Like your drivers license says Liz instead of Elizabeth, petty stuff. Anyway I gotta go and get this in the mail. Again, take care and let me know when you get back. I'll worry, really. *(Note: Now it's my turn to worry.)*

Bye for now,
Walt

****

May 10, 2009

Dear Liz

Hi, how was Texas for you? Don't even ask me cause you don't wanna hear my cuss words.

I got your postcard mailed from Texas dated 5/1/09 and thought about you getting out and about to see the sights of Dallas / Fortworth. Did ja like it? Did ya experience the muggy weather? Well that's nothing, its just getting warmed up. It's been in the early 90's around here and maybe 10% more humid than where you were. You were just in Texas; I'm in "Armpit" Texas.

I hope your trip was a good one. If Mr. Haynes was serious about writing me this time then I should get something this week. You know my federal writ will probably be decided this month too. It would be really, really cool to have a favorable decision by the Feds while Fannin County is dragging their feet in owning up to their "error". Ahhh, heavy sigh...It's a race to the finish. I'm wondering what's gonna happen then.

My fan is all but done. I only use it at night and then I have to douse it with oil and physically spin the fan blades to get it to start. Don't suppose you'd like to make a donation to my fan fund? I'm in dire straights without a fan. This is one item I can't hustle off the streets. Meaning I can't go to someone and trade art work or proceeds from art work and come away with a brand new fan. I have to buy a new one from the inmate commissary and they cost $20.00. Which is actually not bad except the feds take 40% of my income $$ due to federal filing fee's that were waived "in forma paupis", with promises to pay 40% from money received on my trust account. So I gotta come up with about $40.00, and that leaves me $24.00 which I can buy a fan with. Help only if you want. If not then of course don't. I'll write to my dad and maybe he'll send $25.00 I can also write to my sister and if all the planets align she might write to acknowledge my presence. It's a longer shot she'll send money. In all the years I've written and not asked is because I'm pretty self sufficient. I don't get a lot of money because I don't really need much money. I'm a convict that's pretty good at surviving in this environment.

So I don't run out of coffee (must have), toothpaste (that too), and deodorant, etc, things of that nature. Sometimes though I need to go to the store. This is one of those times, unless! They're gonna let my hot sweaty butt out of here!! Then, well never mind.

I have a western scene board completed. I'll trade ya. I'll use the extra $4.00 to buy more boards. They're $3.80 for two boards. Anyhow if you don't wanna, that's cool...no worries.

My Christian lady friend Carolyn wrote. She was pretty insulting at first then she lightened up. But I'm yet to write her back. She's bitter sometimes for no reason. It's not nice. Spike's scared of her and can't be consoled.

Spike's out with Ronnald, visiting. Well I gotta go. I'll get you a deposit form and you can, if you want, donate "or" negotiate an illustration board with a drawing on it (duh!) of your choosing. Example...Norman Rockwell or Frank Frazetta or Paul Rubens or Western Indian. You know I wouldn't ask but I "really" need a fan. This will not affect our friendship, one way or the other. If you do, it has to be a postal money order and it has to go to the Texas Dept. of Criminal Justice, inmate trust fund address is on the form. Make the money order out to my name, my number, in care of inmate trust fund. Please write and let me know because "they" won't tell me. Then I go to the inmate commissary and turn in a request for a fan, wait a week, then pick it up. *(Note: Talk about groveling "nicely".)*

Well Liz, I gotta go and get some machine oil or baby oil. I was hoping, praying, lighting candles, doing yoga chants, Indian dances, anything!! In hopes that another summer would find me somewhere else!! Preferably next to water. Preferably somewhere north of the Red River. Anywhere but here. Heavy sigh.

Take care and let me know you got home okay.

Your friend,
Walt

PS: If you send a money order make sure the deposit slip is fully filled out, thanx again...Me.

****

May 31, 2009

Dear Liz;

Hi, I haven't heard from you since your trip to Texas, I hope everything's okay.

Friday I finally heard from Mr. Haynes of McKinney TX. His opening remark was "I was recently appointed to your case" (five months ago). He's asking *me* for advice on how to obtain the court records. Great, one of us is an idiot...really heavy sigh.

So, how are you? I wish I were up there smelling those Ponderosa pine trees, listening to the wind drift up the side of that mountain you live on, and telling stories of the old miner days. Did you know that Worcestershire sauce was invented up that way? The Chinese used to feed the miner's and do their laundry. (For a price of course) Well, the Chinese men used to put soy sauce on the table. The miners used to pickup the bottle and looking at it they'd ask, "Soy wish-dish-here-sauce"?? After awhile they just called it Worcestershire sauce. Believe me?

About a hundred years later them Hippy's from San Francisco finally named the listening devices on the side of our heads (ears) ears. They used to smoke a lot of pot in them days and in handing a joint to a friend (who was probably inebriated) used to shove it into the side of their heads, saying "ere". Later they just referred to that part of your head as an ear. True story.

I knew this chick that was a hippy in them there days, she told me. Her name was Sunrise, really. I'm only telling you this in case you're ever on Jeopardy or something.

Sayyyy, is your Governor going to legalize pot or what? That would get California out of hock wouldn't it? It should, tax them Hippy's!! Why not? I might come back to California and stay awhile, I think. If I ever get my stupid butt out of here anyway. I'm working on it, it's hard though, and no one seems to want to listen to the truth nowadays.

I should give you the Federal court clerk's phone number. My Federal writ should be open, active and in session. This lawyer Haynes asked permission to speak to you about my case. I had already given it to him (with your prior approval), but I will again. So if you get him on the phone you may ask him anything about me you want.

I have a California prison record for stealing. I've had a self destructive trait ever since I found out I was an asshole. My youth was spent mostly on the streets and I was educated in California Youth Authority. I came to Texas to leave all that behind and reconcile with my wife (her idea) and get away from doing time. I've never had a sex crime nor have I ever hurt a child or anyone for that matter.

I grew up wild. My mom was an alcoholic. This woman would kick me out and tell me I didn't belong. I sometimes stole in order to eat. True stuff. Not very flattering but we all have our crosses to bear. Old news. I'm so tired of doing time and fed up with this kind of life. But, I'm not suicidal;

I'll drag my butt through this summer just like the previous seven summers and keep fighting. But it's taking its toll. I'm venting and I'm gonna quit.

Did I ask too much with the fan thing request? I hope not. I hate asking anyone, especially you, for anything. I hate this heat worse though. That's what it comes down to though, doesn't it? What do you hate more, the humid heat of the Texas summer without a fan or imposing on your very good friend for a handout?

I actually started a picture I've been wanting to do but always thought it was out of my league. It appears that it isn't out of my league. It's almost done and I'll send it to you if you want it, as payment for the fan.

I finally heard from Carolyn, she sent two Christian based stories but really didn't write anything. So, she will, eventually.

Well friend Liz, I'm doing my best to not dwell in my own misery. I know some things gotta give but it ain't gonna be me. I haven't felt anything but frustration lately. This too shall pass though. I always believe I will prevail. In the meantime I'm worried about you, have you made it home from Texas okay?

It seems Spike doesn't come around much anymore. Sherry's webs that used to be so thick and strong are growing dimmer and are unable to hold the weight of my imagination these days. Ronnald gets harder to find and all I know of Giraffalo is he's romping around the bush with another little giraffe named Honey or Sugar.

I gotta go now. I'm off to the showers then to church. I truly hope all is well there with you and yours. Write sometime and tell me about your plants, dogs, family or whatever you want. I'll be here and remain your friend.

Walt.

****

June 25, 2009

Greeting Cowgirl;

Well maybe not "cowgirl" but then Texas girls start yellin "yee haw" you can bet your silver spurs they are cowgirls.

Thanks for the photo. It's a good picture of a good person. Not just because you're helping me get a new fan, which I truly appreciate, but for the past six years you've been a good friend. Again, thanx. I haven't been to the prison commissary yet. We can only go on certain days, but I'll go tomorrow. In which case, I'll turn in a "blue slip" (a request to purchase a fan). They'll then check to make sure I have the funds, then process the blue slip. Next Thursday I'll go and pick it up. My sister sent $10.00, which should be more than enough total.

Okay, your letter, written on pretty blue sky paper with fluffy clouds printed on it. Do you know it dipped down to 83 fricken degrees last night? Add to that I'm on the 3rd tier, top bunk. I'm in hell Liz. Enough about that for now. It's supposed to reach 103 degrees today. 687 with the heat index.

All of your grandkids, kids and kid in-laws and whoever else stay out there with y'all and *you* have to drag the trash down to the road? Maybe you have no house guests at the moment, but next time it's their turn to do that dastardly deed.

You asked how I like my coffee. I drink instant. Taster's choice if I can get it and straight black. I like it as I do my women. Strong and black! Actually that's not true. I'm not one for interracial mating, like Spike and Sherry. It's okay for anyone who's into that but I'm fond of white women, when I can get em. Actually I'm pretty romantically retarded, probably due to all the time I've done. I'm even a bit shy, or so I've been told. Not a big promiscuous, girl chasing whoremonger. Mainly because I'm an idiot when it comes to social courtship rituals.

I was married for a long time. When that wasn't going good I was usually in prison. This is my third trip. I can't blame my wife for going away the second time. This time was different because I didn't do what I was arrested for. I don't think we'll ever reconcile due to unrecognizable differences, blah, and blah, blah. No one's perfect, least of all me, so I'll move on.

Carolyn has been in close contact with Mr. Haynes. She scolds me on my being rude to that "poor Mr. Haynes". He obtained the trial records and asked her if she wanted a copy and convinced her that this case is very difficult. It isn't. This case is cut and dry. I was rude, in a tasteful way. I only pointed out that a passive roll is not what I'm going to be doing. That role got me 25 years last time. He can bullshit her all he wants but I'm not having it. He or his secretary seems to be bullshitting you as well. Your assessment of showing that I was not alone, that somewhere someone else cared about how this court crap turned out is exactly why I asked you to call in the first place.

I thought if he wouldn't write to me or communicate with me perhaps someone who called would get some info. It worked too. Carolyn never called him until she spoke to you. At first she wrote, criticized my friendship with you, (she really is nuts) and she said she had better friends than I did. I answered that she was also my friend.

She didn't write for about a month or so. When she finally did write a couple of weeks ago, she had contacted Mr. Haynes who told her I was very rude. This lawyer waited five months to contact me. He hadn't done anything. He claimed he was unable to get trial transcripts and when he did write the first thing he said is "don't get your hopes up; these things don't always work out". Rude? I was *livid* (let me look that word up); yeah that's what I was. I also, among other things, told him he was no better than my trial / appellate attorney who was also appointed by the court. He took offense because that guy was booted out of the State Bar for a lot of reasons that mainly reflected upon his incompetence. In fact part of the reason he, Mr. Haynes, was appointed by Judge Loraine Blake was because the trial lawyer was such an incompetent boob and there probably was something to what I was saying in my writ. Another fine example of that office feeding you bullshit.

The thing is I didn't fall out of Texarkana. The judge said the attorney was my old lawyer, Mel Bruder, I've never heard of him. Fannin County is my county of commitment. Donnie Jarvis Jr. was my attorney. Carolyn said in a letter from June 11, 2009 that Mr. Haynes has obtained a copy of the record through the court of appeals. This was one of the suggestions I made in my "rude" letter. Anyway I'm going to write the lawyer this weekend.

I'm going to write to Carolyn but I'm letting her cool her heels a little. She's in close contact with Haynes and the only way I'll hear what he has to say is through her, as she's scolding me for being rude. She just don't get it. I'm still here because of a nice talking lawyer who mollified me into trusting him explicitly and it cost me, so far eight years. It ain't going down like that again. Enough of Payton Place for now.

I truly appreciate your help and concern; it is and does make a difference. Carolyn, my alleged beloved, is showing me that she is indifferent to my fight and has taken every thing Mr. Haynes says as a declaration of the absolute truth. His feelings got hurt. He's a lawyer; I'm a convict, oh well. This is starting to sound like a soap opera, "As the Stomach Turns"

Okay, you wanna hear a Soap Opera? I got another one for you. Spike the Wonder Roach, seems to have pushed Sherry beyond her affection for him or at least to the limit anyway. He is at the moment hanging above the sink by a thread. He's in a cocoon with only his mouth uncovered and has been since yesterday. I don't know what happened; Ronnald ain't talking if he knows. All I know is Sherry is hanging our little buddy out to dry for awhile. She sits in her web watching, just watching. It seems Sherry has taken over this cell. I won't buck her. Ronnald's a believer and Spike seems to be learning a lesson. We know he ain't dead because every once in a while a stream of vile cussing of the kind that would, and does make a crack smoking clown and an old gray haired convict blush. I don't think tact is working, but you know Spike won't listen to nobody. (Mostly.)

There isn't much else going on around here. I have someone picking up other things I've needed from the store. I'm drawing a cat on half a board for you. I know you're a dog person but I think you'll like this. It's either that or a fairie. Maybe I'll do that; I have a couple of colored pens. You said you like fairies. I don't know though, the cat is a tiger. *(Note: No, the cat is a Panther and it's on my bedroom wall...)* I get these things started and someone comes along and offers me $$ for them or it. I have most everything I need just now, so yeah I'll do a fairie something cute. It's time I drew something cute. I got a green ball point pen, also red and blue, so...it will be a rare color on half a board. I have everything I need but stamps. They will come though.

I've never done any stone work or pavers. I've laid concrete and imagine the principal is the same. *(Note: I told him I'd had pavers laid on my patio).* Dig the form, sand, manipulate the stones, mortar...what? Nine times out of ten, just doing what needs to be done is the ticket. Anyway I hope that works out. It seems like y'all are going major renovation in your yard. I'd think if the stones aren't too heavy, you'd wanna do it, you being a yard person and all. Or is your yard attraction limited to just plants? If it is you could grow pot for the Governor. Spike's idea.

Well my friend, I'm gonna go and mail this. Ever notice how many times we cross each other in the mail? Meaning as I'm mailing a letter you already have one on the way or visa versa. Great minds think alike. Be good, wish me luck, Ronnald believes it's about to happen, I trust his instincts.

Spike says Hi, Ronnald says Hi and Sherry ain't talking but she waved.

Walt.

****

July 9, 2009

Dear Liz;

Hi friend. I know it's been too long between letters, sorry. I received the money order and managed to get a fan which has me off the floor at night. Thank you very much. Actually of late it's been cooler around here.

My legal battle continues. Carolyn came to visit two weekends ago. She's marrying a guy named Frank or at least this is what she's telling me. I'm okay with it, I hope it works out and she's happy.

I have a half board for you with a little blue fairy. *(Note: A Moon Fairy which I have framed.)* I have to petition the property officer for permission to mail it. You have to be, (and are) an approved visitor in order for me to mail art work to you. This is a new policy. Heavy sigh.

I have legal mail coming on Monday. I really, really, really hope it's from the Feds telling me good news. If it is I'll let ya know. Mr. Haynes has told Carolyn that he still has to obtain the trial records. What did he send you? You said he had sent the initial court record, not the trial transcript then, right? I wrote to the judge and told her I would rather not have a lawyer that ain't gonna do nothing. It's been seven months and he can't even get the trial records. I also told her that I could litigate this on my own and the prosecutor could bare the burden of producing the record to refute my claims. These claims are valid and cannot be disproved by any record. So...we'll see.

I've been meaning to write and have started a letter once or twice only to lose track. It happens. I will probably get that Moon Fairy drawing in the mail by Friday. It's in color so I don't have any faith in it. I'm very color shy. My color self esteem stinks. I hope you like it anyway.

I'm enclosing a vintage letter (from you) that you might recall and a funny thing from someone's computer I'm passing along. If you find it offensive, I apologize. I thought it was funny and wanted to share. *(Note: It was the origin of the word "fuck")* They're talking about the English language so of course I thought of you.

Well take care and I'll fill you in on Spike and the gang as soon as I get my wits about me. Look for that board soon. I'm truly at the property officer's mercy here. I got the stamps, so no problems.

Always respectfully, your friend,
Walt

****

July 25, 2009

Dear Liz,

This pen is gonna be a pain (running out of ink). I have your picture done. Let's try this pen, hmmm, that's an improvement, sorta. I go through a lot of pens, let me tall ya. How ya doing friend? I hope all is well at your place. I'm okay here.

I have legal mail pickup scheduled for Monday. It's a response from the judge. I told her I don't need that lawyer. (This damn pen!! Hold on I'll get another, I know this one will work because it's my drawing pen.) So, where were we? I'm sure the legal mail is in response to that. What I'm thinking is, the judge got all over his butt about un-due delay and what not, sent him a copy of the letter I wrote her and then wrote me and told me she did it. Cool. What I hope is a letter saying, fine, you don't want a lawyer? Good! Your court date is such and such, see ya then. I can handle this.

It's been a couple of days since I wrote that I've had to apply for permission to mail this. I go down today, the 28th, to do just that.

The legal mail was from the federal courts saying I have free reign to pursue what ever I want in the state courts. Yesterday I received notice that my letter to the judge concerning undue delay and the shyster she appointed being unnecessary was forwarded to the District Attorney and my shyster. Cool!!

I have a mail-room pass from someone today. No doubt it's from my whining-ass lawyer crying about his feelings being hurt or me questioning his ability to litigate this "most difficult case". I hope it's from the judge setting a date for me to go back and have a hearing on this issue, my innocence. That's coming. I know it is.

Well, I'm gonna go. Drop me a line and let me know you got this and the drawing. Please save those books you have for me, I'll come and get them, soon I hope.

Peace,
Walt and company

****

September 1, 2009

Dear Liz;

Hi from here. I've been meaning to write but haven't (duh) that's why you haven't heard from me. I'm still here and still trying to get somewhere else.

I told you I was in a computer school that's still going on. I missed today due to the guards screwing up the count last night and me not being able to shower last night. So I showered this morning missing a day of class. For that, 52 lashes and I don't get to celebrate Christmas

with the other good little convicts this year. I'm hoping I won't be here, again, still.

I wrote to that worthless lawyer of mine asking for some kind of progress report. It's only been eight months so far and I've seen nothing. I mean I only have a viable claim. Why they're dragging their feet is beyond me, except they're assholes. Hmmmm...there might be something to that.

So that's how I'm doing. How are you and the family? I'm in the day room watching the girls play the U.S. open. Katrina Buttstankovich and some other Slovakia type girl with a very short skirt and very long legs. Anyway I think they're playing tennis. Who care's. Serena Williams looks like they shaved a man and taught her how to play tennis. Sorry, that's not very nice is it? I've become very cynical since being here and in my old age. I'd rather watch Stewie in Family Guy. But...what the hey? Can't have everything.

I'm hoping Hilary Clinton will show up and rescue me like Bill did those two girls in North Korea. Spike had me write to Hilary and ask for rescue. She should reply any day now...maybe... maybe not. At the same time I wrote to Chelsea (Clinton) asking the same thing. Maybe I shouldn't have put both letters in the same envelope. Oh well, I haven't been accused of being the sharpest tool in the shed.

Have you been digging in the yard lately? It's Southern California that's on fire this year, right? Six quadrillion acres on fire, right? Well that won't help the budget.

Well Liz, I know it's short; I'll do better next time. Maybe my mind will be in a better place next time. I must get off my lazy butt and draw some cards. I need postage stamps. So long friend, till next time. Take care,

Your friend,
Walt

****

Labor Day September 2009

Dear Liz;

You are more than a little bit welcome to vent in your letters to me. Lord knows I do my fair share with you. What with the courts being assholes and all. Not to mention my no good shyster lawyer. So "friend" (that's you) if you wanna talk about it, I'm here. I just can't respond with any kind of useful advice. Well, I could but I don't know what to say, for example, your friend, the thief. You knew the law would catch up with her and that's good. I'm very anti-law, except when deserved. The fact she got let out on her own recognizance proves that the law ain't always just. I do like it when you talk about your plants though. You seem to enjoy that more than your friend. *(Note: My "friend" stole from us. Unfortunately she was on drugs and felt she needed money for more. My "friend" is now clean and has been for several years. She and I are back to being friends, she is back with her family and all has been forgiven.")*

Where's Spike? He's around here somewhere, I'm sure he'd have something cleaver to add to that. He was mad at me last week and stayed at Festers cell. He went to school with me and wanted to be involved in my computer class project and I said, "No!"He left, sulking all the way.

Hey, I want to ask you if you'd call that stupid lawyer again for me. I'm writing to him more time than I'm writing the courts. (The Texas Court of Criminal Appeals) I'm going to file my own paper work and Mr. Haynes can kiss my cockroach. I've asked for a progress report, he may or may not respond due to my knack of pissing him off with my casual enquiries.

You probably think I've been rude or flat out disrespectful, but I honestly haven't. It's in my best interest to get this dude on my side, but after eight and a half months of dragging his feet it's obvious he's not interested.

Well Liz, I hope you're well and everybody there is okay and happy. If you see anyone from Bud's tell em Howdy from Texas. Write when you can and say what you want. I don't judge anyone except, lawyers. Them I call like I see it. I sure wish I'd see something good out of this lawyer. If you get him on the line, which I doubt, he's elusive when being questioned on his performance, tell him how vulnerable and little I am. And how much I need his stupid ass to actually do something productive! Or, maybe you could just wing it.

Take care Liz and know me and Spike and Ronnald are thinking of ya.

Sincerely,
Your friend,
Walt

****

September 17, 2009

Dear Liz;

Hello my friend. Wait, someone's yelling at me. No, that's the voices in my head again. My bad. It happens, but not often.

I'm trying out a new pen that's why I'm writing cursive. Looks good huh? It's Saturday night and I'm tired of reading. We're on a lockdown. I'm still waiting on the prison to shake down "C" wing. What a hassle! Rumor is we will get it Monday. Saturday and Sunday the prison has a skeleton crew and isn't geared up for the bigger cell blocks. "C" block has a bad reputation for...I don't know, they just treat "C" wing bad sometimes. Screw us around on our commissary day, (not that I go very often) we're last to chow most of the time, then the foods cold. We get the grade A asshole guards, (mostly ghetto mamma's with attitudes that hate white folk.) Not good for me.

I had to put this down for awhile and am now back. Did ja miss me? Spike is looking at the bird feeder photo you sent, the one that has the Praying Mantis on it. I told him Praying Mantis are nothing to fool around with, especially the females. He thinks I'm making it up. Maybe he'll learn the hard way. I gotta write to my dad this weekend. I still haven't done that.

This letter was put down for a while due to our extended lock down and my lack of funds to mail anything. This lockdown has dragged on and taken its toll. It started from someone trying to escape out of administration segregation. (Ad Seg or more commonly known as "the hole") He had acquired hack saw blades from somewhere and had cut his way out of his cell and was working on the window so we all got slammed. It's been a long tiring lockdown. I haven't had anything to do to keep my mind or myself occupied. My card stocks (materials) were taken, and I had no boards to draw on, it figures, huh. Also, no stamps or coffee either. O.M.G. It's a miracle I'm even alive. I'm tough.

I wrote a smashing motion for Summery Judgment to the courts and sent it a couple of weeks ago. My lawyer still has done nothing, so if ya want something done, etc, etc.

Spike's getting ready for his annual trip to Mexico. It's about to be the holiday season. So Sherry has webbed her cocoon for hibernation. Ronnald is on nine kinds of psych medication from the psych. He's out of it. Slobbers all the time, but hey, he's happy. How are you?

I've gotta go to church tonight and do some networking. I gotta get my hustle on so I need material. I know people at the chapel that like me, so maybe I can get some blank folders, hook up with a glue connection, envelopes, and maybe some pre-orders, and collect some stamps and we don't need to worry about the lawyer anymore. (I think) unless the judge refuses my motion. In other words the motion is a "shit or get off the pot" motion. And it's out of David Haynes hands, unless the judge refuses it due to me having representation and that representation has not been heard from. This is where I find out where the judge stands or sits. Anyway, I'm hopeful. Something's gotta give. Heavy sigh.

Well Liz I'm gonna go for now. Sorry I couldn't write before this. I'll bet ya I've got a letter on the way from you as this gets mailed. We've been doing that a lot lately. As I've said before, great minds think alike. Okay, you take care and be good. Spike says, "Hola" and Ronnald says, "Argh".

Peace,
Your friend,
Walt

Sept. 25, 2009

Dear Liz;

Hi you! I wanted to write sooner but I didn't have stamps. I picked up three today but it was rough. We're still locked down and have been for awhile. We'll probably stay on lockdown until they decide to shake down the unit again. Something or someone caused this one but I don't know what or who. In the meantime it makes it real hard to hustle up the things I need. I did manage to sell a birthday card for three stamps. One stamp for yew (that's Texan for you), and one stamp to piss off my lawyer some more. Actually I don't write to piss him off, I just get the feeling he gets pissed off when he see's a letter from yours truly. I don't tell him how to do his job or pretend to know more about the law than him. I do sometimes make fun of him for not being able to get a simple court transcript after almost a year. This is my intention today anyway. I'm probably not really going to tease him too much, because I need him. But really!!?? Still no court transcript?

I got the photos of your lil statues, they're cool. *(Note: When I worked at Bud Plants we would, sometimes, get little statues back damaged. It was my job to take them back and re-send or credit the customer. I was allowed, if I wanted, to take them home and glue them back together. I have quite a collection of Frank Cho, Frank Frazetta and others. I told Walter they are his if he wants them.)* It was in a letter you said you were going to weed out your book collection and set aside the ones you were going to give to a starving artist and did I know any? Well not exactly in those words, you ended your hint with an, eh hem, remember that? Actually I came across the letter yesterday while going through my stuff, starting the down sizing process for the trek to the tables. I've told you the process for shaking us down before, right? I think so. (I don't remember)

I like the photo of the Praying Mantis. Is it just one? The same one or do you think maybe more than one. He or she ain't camera shy is it? Actually it's a good bet it's a "she" since they're mating ritual includes her biting off "his" head in the act of procreating. Perhaps only when he / she ain't up to the task...Hmmmm. What a way to go though. Have you named her? *(Note: Her name was Lucy.)* Spike don't like the looks of her, gee I wonder why. Sherry does though, I'm not sure why.

It goes from sweltering hot and humid to cold in the span of two days. That's Texas. I can deal with the cold a lot better though.

So, what have you been up to? So far my computer class is a success. After four tests I'm one of the three that have not missed a single question on the tests. They test us after each chapter and that's okay. What system are y'all operating off of, Windows XP? Seems to be the most popular. Windows Millennium, the new one is Vista and the instructor says ain't worth the hassle. He's an ex Nasa engineer. Computer engineer geek. He's old now but has been involved with computers since the 60's back when they were as big as your refrigerator. He's pretty smart. Of course Spike doesn't like him, says he's too rigid.

He makes us do the "Pledge of Allegiance to the flag..." Did you, as a girl in England, have to do a patriotic pledge each morning at school? *(Yes, God Save the Queen.)* I remember as a wee-lad in grade-school having to stand there with the rest of the brats, hand over heart and saying in a monotone voice the "I Pledge Allegiance to The Flag of The United States of America..."

I gotta write my dad. He's old and this month is his birthday. He lives somewhere in Phoenix Arizona. He don't write much, but what's there to say? He's an asshole, but I forgive him. He feels guilty about how rotten a father he was to me when I was but a lad. I once told him not to worry about it. He'll probably be a fabric softener strip in a Chinese laundry service in his next life. I'd like to be a reusable rubber glove for a Jewish Gynecologist for the rich and famous. You know that glove won't be thrown away. That's probably disgusting to you, but you're not deprived like I have been and am now. Again with the heavy sigh.

Well my friend, I'm gonna go for now. Thanks for the photos. Glad you liked the Arabian proverbs I sent. I thought it fit. Take care and I'll write again soon. Soon as I get more stamps. I hope this lockdown doesn't persist too long. It makes it hard to stay ahead of the creditors. Spike sends his love. Ronald's in the kitchen making peanut butter sandwiches and boiling eggs, which is our lockdown diet, standard issue. One heavier sigh before I finish. Heavy Sigh. Pathetic huh?

Sincerely,
Your friend,
Walt

****

October 21, 2009

Dear Liz;

Howdy yourself! I filed a motion for summery Judgment with Fannin County Court. I wouldn't do that kind of stuff but aside from not being able to find the court record, Mr. Haynes or his secretary don't share strategy with me so I'm in the dark. Yeah I write to them and they have an idea of what's going on but I don't, so the judge can accept it or refuse it as "Hybrid Representation".

I got a letter from that judge saying my attorney or the D.A. can request a hearing on this matter. Nine months is a long time to sit idle while someone decides to. This is the same thing my trial lawyer did with the appeal. Thank you for your prayers and help. If you talk to Mr. Haynes secretary Donna again, tell her thanks for giving you heads up. Maybe whatever is gonna happen is gonna happen right directly. I hope so.

Now to your letter. I told you every time I write or you write we cross each other in the mail. We did it again! We're psychotic Liz! We have E.S.P.N. or something like that. What am I thinking right now? I'll project something. You're thinking if those damned kids don't stop throwing pine cones yer gonna beat the living shit out of them. That's if you can catch them. Either that or a purple goat dressed up in a French maid uniform? That one might be Spike's brain waves. No, wait, that's the voices in my head giving me the score on the Philly's-Dodger game.

So, where does the Praying Mantis go in the winter? I've heard they're smart bugs, so maybe they head indoors, but where? Maybe with the Keebler elves, you never know. *(Note: I told him they die after laying their eggs.)*

I used to live in Washington. The Western side of the state is beautiful while the Eastern part ain't as nice. Maybe the Cascade Mountains keep the weather separated, who knows. I don't know the area you're going to, Brewster is it? Is that by the Puget Sound or over in the grass lands by Walla Walla?

You have a great Granddaughter? Cool! You also said you got the front of your house finished. Does that mean your patio pavers are done? No, we're not on lockdown anymore, but we were for quite a while. No, you can't send loose stamps, thanks for asking anyway. The only things you can send are books from a bookstore or money orders to the trust office. But you have to have one of those little forms to do it. So don't even think to send money they'll just send it back to you, and I'm not sending you any little forms so don't even think about it. I'm funny about that. The fan thing was an extraordinary situation and I was panicking. I don't need yer money as much as I need your friendship. I've got that and that's more-n-enough for lil ole me. Besides if I let you or anyone send money I'd just get lazy and fat or fat and lazy. Maybe for Christmas or a birthday but I'm really hoping to be gone by the next come around. I really should be gone now.

You might shoot me your phone number again in case I get to Fannin County Jail on my way to court. The charges will have to be reversed though. So if you ain't into that don't send the number. Also give me an idea when you normally retire for bed so I don't call at 2am. When the phone rings that late it's either someone's in jail (which would be me) or someone's hurt or dead. There's a 2 hour difference between here and California. Is Texas forward or backward?

Yes the books you're holding for me are tantalizing. Hey I bet when I get to Fannin County Jail you can send a book or two directly to me. I'll bet they would let me have them, would that be okay? Not all of them but a few to help me wile away the hours waiting for my next court date. I think I can recite your address by memory. They may not let me have my property and I many not remember your phone number but I'd be able to write.

What's an orthopedic? Do I got one? What's wrong with yours? You were a Girl Scout? You raised two fingers and did the "Girl Guide" thing? I was a Boy Scout in Bremerton Washington. We (some of we) raised three fingers, (I raised one, guess which one), always the rebel. A rebel without a clue, and recited pretty much the same schpeel, except for the King and or Queen thing. When you were in the Girl Guides they had a King in England?

Liz McGuire, I gave you leave a long time ago to be as nosey as you wanted. As far as my dad is concerned, he lives in Phoenix Arizona or a suburb of Phoenix, Fort Hayes. Yeah he would welcome me when I get out. In fact he's on the route I'm gonna take when I get out of here. I will see him again. He's old. He was not a good father when I was a lad but I'm not gonna get into that unless you ask. I'm all the time telling you what a shitty childhood I had. It probably gets as tiring hearing it as it does writing about it.

My dad sends me $25.00 on Christmas and my birthday. I get "maybe" a paragraph of casual "how ya doins" two or three times a year and that's okay. I write to him and tell him I love him and that his baseball team, the Dodgers, suck...but mine, the Astros, suck worse. When I get out I'll go to see him. I let him know I forgave him for being an asshole. I'm gonna need forgiveness one day, maybe not from him but...

Well Liz, thanx for a nice letter, I'm glad you're okay. I hope your whole family is groovy. You're making a Mexican casserole. So how many Mexicans do you put in your Mexican casserole? I don't like spicy foods, too hot. Take care friend, write when ya can. I haven't heard from Carolyn in months. Yer the only friend left and I'm glad I have you. Cool.

Bye for now,
Walt

****

November 24, 2009

Hey yourself friend;

I started writing several times but went off on a negative trip and never sent what I started. I'm not feeling negative toward you, I've just been...surly? I'm not sure, but disheartened maybe? I'm closing in on nine years of this place and I'm not a happy camper about it. It would be different if I were guilty of my crime or if everything was done right to get me here. I guess those two things go together because if everything was done right I probably wouldn't be here.

I filed a summery judgment into Fannin County. No response and Mr. Haynes don't respond to my letters to tell me anything. It's sooo frustrating. I've let my entire drawing hustle go to pot. My motivation is nil and I'm not having a very productive Holiday season. This is my best producing season usually. I'm still alive though, that's a plus. I still have you as a friend and I really need a friend right now. Your letter was the best thing in my week.

I made a Thanksgiving card in computer class. I'll send it to you. *(Note: I still have it)*. This class is "computer maintenance". Nowhere in this system (prison system) are inmates allowed to have access to the internet, so I can't go online or I'd email you. Oh that reminds me, there's a place you can go called "Jpay.com". You can buy stamps and send me an email, if you're so inclined. If you have something important to tell me I would get it within 24-48 hours from you sending it. I think there's a phone call procedure too, I'm checking on it. That's only if you wanted to actually talk to my stupid ass. Well not my stupid ass literally. I think you have to register or something. You're an approved visitor so there shouldn't be a prob. So check it out on that site. I can't find your phone number anymore and don't have any money to call if I had it, so I'd have to reverse the charges or there's another option, I ain't sure what it is. Someone said go to Jpay.com and they should tell ya. Again, only if you want. You mentioned a year ago that you'd like to "say" Hi, so just sayin, I don't want to sound pushy. Sup to you.

Thanx for the picture of Mt. Shasta. They don't have mountains down here. There are a few termite hills or mesas (that's where they cut the top of the mountain off and leave the bottom). I'm not sure what they do with the top part.

You said something about a back fusion surgery. I don't know anything about them except you can get some good pain drugs, but also you actually need those drugs too. So it probably ain't a whole lot of fun when you need to take pain killers.

You said you'd named the Praying Mantis, Lucy. I thought about writing a story on her and her lost lovers, get it? They lost their heads over her. It don't take much to make an old convict smile. I'm tired of being a convict; I wanna be something or someone else. I'd like to be Batman. Let's face it, Bruce Wayne's richer than rich. That's how he can afford all those neat toys. Bat Mobile, Bat plane, Bat boat, Bat bazooka. Ya think he's got Bat booze? Why not? I used to wanna be a pro bowler but Spike asked how I'd feel if my fat thumb got stuck in the finger hole of my bowling ball and came off while bowling or better yet didn't come off and I went sliding down the alley face first. So, no more pro bowling dreams. I'd also like to learn golf. I like walking and walking around a gold course smacking a little ball with a club that sounds cool.

Yes, I wrote to my dad and will do so again. He doesn't write much, you're the only one who writes. Carolyn hasn't written in three months. She came down to see me and never wrote afterwards. She's older than me, I hope she didn't die. I wrote to David Haynes and asked him to call her. Whether he did or not I don't know. He's not written back to say anything. My last letter from Mr. Shyster was in May.

Thanks Liz for caring enough to call Mr. Shyster. One day I hope to thank you personally. You sound like someone worth knowing and will be one of the very few things about this whole rotten experience that I can honestly say was a positive thing. Thanx for being my friend.

I hope your daughter-in-law thing works out. I can't say I've ever been down far enough to steal from my family. I'm not from a family tightly bound enough to actually be from a part of anything substantial, whatever that means. Anyway, I hope she's never down that far again, and maybe she can, one day, ask you to forgive her and mean it. I'll put her in my prayers. I still pray. My prayers lately ain't very nice but I'm always apologizing for my attitude toward God and His will. What can you do?

I read a lot of Edgar Casey and think there's something to that reincarnation stuff. I may have been an asshole in my last life. If that's true and I truly have this "doing time" thing coming, then I must have been Hitler or Mussolini. (Speaking of which I did not know Mussolini was a spy for M-I5, interesting).

Well friend, Thanksgivings gone by the time you get this. I hope you were blessed and remain blessed. I'm frustrated but still standing. I'll put some thought in on a Lucy story. Thanx for writing, I needed that.

Take care and Happy Christmas,

Your friend,
Walt

****

December 2009

Hi Liz;

Just a short note from me and Spike wishing you a very Merry Christmas. I hope it's a good one. I ain't been doing any drawings, well I did for me to get these stamps, other than that...?

I have three cards; I like this one I sent best so...yew can have it. Spike stayed here for the holidays. Usually go goes to Mexico. He's getting old ya know. He can't outrun stomping feet like he used to. Sherry's hibernating and Ronald's cookin in the kitchen. Tis the season. Me? I'm moving forward. I hate that another calendar is about to expire and I'm still here. Could be worse, though I can't think of anything just now.

I'm okay, I hope you are too. I don't have many friends but I'm awfully glad yer counted among the one's I do have.

Merry Christmas friend
Peace,
Walt

****

Chapter Eight

January 3, 2010

Dear Liz;

Howdy friend! Well here we are again, another year. I'm doing all I can to git out a here and hey, maybe 2010 is my year.

I think January 2010 is when Fannin County is going to do something. I wrote to the court and as you said January 8th the judge comes back. Maybe she will say, "Enough!" If she denies my writ, it's already waiting on a Federal bench. I sincerely doubt Fannin County will let this get out of their county because if they do, they will have no say over how this turns out. In other words if they deny me, the Feds won't. If I get what I want, an acquittal, then Fannin County is liable for almost nine years of wrongful incarceration. That's big money for yours truly. At least $56.00. I'm not sure, maybe a little more. Spike's crunching numbers right now. I'll get back to you on that.

Donna (David Haynes secretary) never wrote. I didn't really expect her to, you know? I can't say she never wrote, she just never wrote to me. On third thought, I can't say she never wrote to me, she just didn't mail me what she wrote. She's never said she was mailing anyone anything. Right?

Okay, now on the phone information. You must be an approved visitor in order to receive phone calls from me...you are...so ya gotta go on line to www.texasoffenderfriendsandfamily.com, there you can register. When you do write, and tell me or go to Jaypay.com and email me. (I'll get it within 24 hrs) or write. Either way I'll call you. I'll have to reverse the charges but I hear it's reasonable. I haven't had a stamp to write or I would have. *(Note: Because I was "told" by a family member to not write to Walter he and I didn't speak on the phone until November 2014. Even though I continued writing to him and he me. We were friends, nothing else. He needed a friend and in a lot of ways I did also.)*

I started a story about your Praying Mantis named Lucy who was listening to the oldies from your window sill. I'm in the day room on a Sunday morning; rumor has it we'll be going on lock down in the morning. You can never trust them rumors. But you never know they could be right. I've been so wound up over this calendar turn over I've been neglecting my normal routine. This isn't all that normal anyway.

Okay now about Lucy the Praying Mantis. The story with Lucy started in the spring. There was a one-eyed bird sitting in a tree watching Lucy intently as she gathered up the right twigs. Two male Praying Mantises watched from under the leaf of a plant and talked about how sexy Lucy was and that they'd like to mate with her. At one time there were three male's but one of them decided to mate with Lucy and was never heard from again.

Lucy found a twig; actually it was an oversized pine needle. She held on to it and flew up to the window sill of the house where she could faintly hear the music coming from inside. She watches as the lady of the house does her home cleaning ritual. Dion is the "Wanderer" on the radio. Lucy starts to sway to the music. Just then another bird lands on the branch beside the one eyed bird. "Hey" he says in bird language. "Hey" the other bird answers. "What's happenin?" says the new-comer. "Watchin that bug on the window sill", says one-eye. The new bird looks down and as he see's what the other bird is looking at he jumps off the branch without a second thought. "Lunch!!" he squawks and spreads his wings in a power dive for the dancing Praying Mantis on the window sill. The two male praying mantises under the leaf of the plant hear the squawk and look up to see the hungry bird. They look at Lucy who continues to dance to Dion. The bird, in its excitement squawks a final squawk of triumph as it closes within striking distance, knowing it's too close for the Mantis to get away. It opens its beak as it braces for landing. As it stretches its neck for lunch, Lucy spins lightening fast and jabs her pine needle into the eye of the bird.

The lady in the house hears a screech and looks to see the bird flapping its wings frantically trying to back peddle off the window sill. "Blimey!" she says, and the bird is gone. The lady looks out the window as the bird fly's up to a nearby tree branch and lands next to the one eyed bird. The lady goes back to her cleaning as she hears the bird still screeching. Meanwhile on the other branch, ole one-eye said, "Ya got a stick in yer eye, didn't ya?" "Really?" says the new one eyed bird in a sarcastic squawk. "Yeah, want me to pull it out?" he asks. The new one-eyed bird says, "No, leave it in, I kinda like it" then he says, "of course I want you to pull it out asshole. Why didn't you tell me she was gonna do that?" "Well" he says, as he gets close, "you didn't ask". The old one-eyed bird plucks out the pine needle and lets it drop. I think that's how Lucy survives the spring, what do you think?

Do you ever say "Blimey" any more? Have you ever said "Blimey?" I should start saying it. I can do an English accent. I can do a Scottish one too. Also Texican, Midwestern, and am working on my Eastern Block/Russian accent. They might not fool an authentic English Bird but these yah hoes around here don't know the difference. I've done my English accent to guards asking stupid questions like, "Hey, wha dar yew doin in my hallway?" I use my English accent, "why guvner, I'm walking in your hallway, is it really yours?" They look stupefied. "Wha dar yew a Mexican of sompin?" Why bother? Why not!

I'm gonna go. I hope everyone there is healthy, happy and all that. A popular Norwegian (which is what I am, or sort of) "may you live as long as you want and never want as long as you live" and be happy. Happy New Year friend. I'm so glad you started writing. If God's willing and the creeks don't rise, maybe this year I'll get to meet you. It could happen.

Bye for now,
Walt and Spike.

****

January 31, 2010

Dear Liz;

Hi. I'm sorry for not writing sooner or much in this letter. I ain't seen it in its entirety but I know it ain't much.

I got a card I'm sending with this, I thought of you when I saw it. No envelope for it so I've gotta bend it to fit.

I have eight letters going out in the morning. None to that no-good-worthless-rotten-assed-bottom-feeding-lawyer of mine. I ain't wasting any more stamps on him. If we were all parts to a great big celestial car, he would be the hood ornament. He doesn't do anything He's just there for show. You could be the blinker. I'd probably be the exhaust pipe. But we'd be something useful, right?

I'm writing everyone from the Governor, Rick Perry, to all the bleeding-heart civil liberty union organizations and innocence projects I can. I want them all to call that judge. Maybe someone will. It's been over a year since she's had the case and ain't done nothing.

You asked if I could really sue for money if I beat them. Yes, and I intend to. I really didn't kidnap anyone and, in a fair trial, they can't prove I did.

I should have taken more time with the Lucy story, it's not very good. *(Note: Actually I quite liked it.)* I've just been so wrapped up in trying to get my case moving again. It's bogged down and I'm getting frustrated, again.

I feel blessed to have met you Liz, and I ain't even met you yet. Thanx for your friendship. You know Edgar Casey says we have Celestial friends. Maybe we knew each other in another life. God I hope it wasn't a Nazi-Jewish thing, because I'm pretty convinced I was a Nazi in my last life. You know that Karma thing. My last life was spent being an asshole, and this life spent atoning for my evil ways because I sure ain't been bad enough to have deserved doing this much time. (Life time total is closing in on 30 fricken years!) Too much, oh well what can ya do? I'm still fighting and am burnt on writing.

I'll write more over the week. Keep me in your prayers. I hope you and your family are safe and happy. Probably cold, it's cold here. In fact it's below freezing here in armpit Texas. It's not snowing though. Take care friend,

Sincerely,
Walt

****

February 18, 2010

Hi Liz;

I got your letter last night. Nobody writes anymore but you. Carolyn got married; at least she said she was last time we spoke. She hasn't written since last June or July. It's been a while since my sister wrote. Donna, Mr. Haynes' secretary, said she wrote, but other than that letter from her I haven't heard from Mr. Haynes office since last May. My aunt writes once in awhile. She purchased two boards from me at Christmas and gave them for presents. That was nice for me and she claims whoever got them really liked them. I've been commissioned to draw two more of the same. Not for a great deal of money but enough to keep me for awhile.

I've been busy with a Mandamus writ. I get tired of this place and you're right, I probably was a little depressed the last time I wrote. Then I got mad and wrote to the Texas Court of Criminal Appeals about the delay after delay. I've compelled the higher court to order the lower court to rule on my case. I should hear back from them around the middle of March, which is my 48th birthday. No judge likes to be told what to do or when to do it, but I've had enough. With what I've got going in my legal corner I don't care if they like it or not, "just do it!" So ya don't gotta call Donna no more. I mean you can if you want to but it ain't necessary.

I feel so drained lately. Usually I can sit down and busy myself in school, art, run off down the Serengeti with "Giraffalo" or Spike can show up and I can get out of here (mentally). Imagination is a gift when properly stimulated.

I think my visit to the Swami roach (in the prison water pipes) was some fine imagination. Have you copied that story yet? *(Note: Yes, it's in a future letter.)*Liz, if you wanna submit any, all or part of that stuff I send you, you're more than welcome. Except for a corny joke here and there, it's all original stuff and all of it really happened right between my ears at one time or another. Sometimes that stuff spilled out over the top and flowed out of my pen easy as you please, others it was a job just to keep it alive. To have an audience as willing to read it as I was to write it is what truly keeps that going. I feel blessed to have acquired a friend in the way I have, writing to you I mean.

Alright, my next page will be written on the back of my last progress report from my Vocational Computer Maintenance Program. This way you can see my current grades and it might convince you that I could actually know what I'm talking about when you say your computer is slow. What is your operating system? We can't get on the internet but we work on Dell computers with a duel operating system (windows 2000/xp) if you're having trouble with speed, is it only when down loading? Have you ever opened up your computer and installed memory modules? More memory could help. It's easy to do and probably has already been done. If you opened up your computer you'd see these "slots" all over the computer board. (The mother board) You can expand all kinds of crap inside your computer; you just have to be careful with static electricity off of your body. Simple static electricity can fry a microchip so ya gotta ground yourself. Except for inside the power supply, nothing on that computer is over 12 volts. Most of it is actually under 12 volts. There's an internet program called "Glary Utilities", they offer a maintenance program off of the internet free to home addition computers. Once you download the program you'll have tools to manage your computer. Most of these programs and tools are built into your computers operating system. Tell me which operating system you're running and I'll tell you what you can do. Most of this stuff you may already know, maybe not though. I'll include a short cut key chart to Windows and you can see if any of that is useful. *(Note: I still have it).* If I don't know about your operating system, I'm smart enough and have the resources to find out. Don't believe Spike when he's evaluating my stupidity or intelligence, I'm actually sporting an I.Q. well into the double digits. I hope some of this info is helpful. Have you ever added or expanded your computers memory?

No I don't guess giving your credit card number out over the internet is a good idea. I see TV and all the identity theft going on. A good way to prevent that is to keep it out of reach from assholes that do that kind of thing.

I'm gonna go for now. Survivor comes on TV tonight. "Heroes and Villains" Groovy! Actually I only watch that for the intellectual stimulation. I don't ever notice the bikini clad girls on it. Are there bikini clad girls on Survivor? I don't get to watch Family Guy anymore, my favorite. Other than Survivor and maybe a movie now and again, (commercial TV movies) I don't watch much TV.

Did you see Avatar? If so, was it as good as they say? I want to see it in 3-D. I'll bet that's cool as hell. Well again, I'm gonna go. Take care and thanx again for being such a good friend. Sometimes it ain't what you give; it's the manner in which it's given. Thanx for giving me some of your time and friendship, it means something.

Most respectfully,
Your friend,
Walt.

****

March 16, 2010

Dear Liz;

Hi friend. Thanx for the "warmest fuzzy that ever wuzzy", *(Note: His birthday card was a fuzzy bear and to date he still has it.)* as well as the coldest trees this side of…picture you sent…somewhere colder to be sure.

Soooo we're still locked down as the cops finish trashing the rest of the joint. We got ours yesterday. I packed up and lugged all my crap down stairs to place before some asshole who, if you're lucky, will go through it detached, bored, disinterested and give it back, unharmed, to be drug back upstairs and reassembled until next time. If you ain't so lucky you'll get some pencil necked geek that wants to go through each scrap of paper hoping to find something, anything, that he or she could write a case on and make an already miserable experience more so.

I was fortunate. I had been commissioned to draw a couple of cowboy boards and spotted an officer that's expressed an interest in seeing something that I've actually drawn. He heard I could draw, I knew this officer was fair and not of the latter category, so I caught his attention and had a relatively painless intrusion into my stuff. Anyway, I thought I'd write and tell you a little bit about myself. You get bits and pieces, so here's one.

Because I was worried about not getting any birthday cards this year, I shoulda known. I did but...okay, my mom. I may have told you of my childhood so I'll be brief about most it. My aim was to get to boy scouts. But to get there you have to have some background. I was born third in line to a women who probably didn't have a lock on what "it's" all about. That in itself isn't as naive as the combination of that and believing that most everyone else had in fact come with some predefined notion. My mother drank, heavily. She also had a knack for running off the men in her life. I don't remember much about my father. He left when I was little so I grew up in a house full of women, well girls anyway. My mom kept ending up at her mom's place and by the time I was aware of being aware of anything, she'd had two more girls. Both had different fathers. So I had my grandmother, (who refused to raise my mom's kids) my mom, two older sisters and two younger sisters.

I was situated in a small town called Kelseyville, way up in the mountains of Northern California. (Lake port, Clearlake area) right at the foot of Mt. Kenocti. I was all over that mountain, sometimes until after dark. My grandmother always held something from the dinners I missed. She often held it hostage until I bathed but after raising three sons of her own she knew boys.

My mom was indifferent. I did good in school without trying and used my devious little boy ingenuity to ambush "Aunt Flo." My stinkin sisters got visits from "Aunt Flo" and I never even got to see this person. I never caught her! One night, late, my mom woke me up to watch a scary movie. She's done this before. We watched "The Night of the Living Dead" Zombies! Yikes! Anyway the following night, after drinking heavily, she convinced me that I didn't belong there and kicked me out.

I walked into town in the middle of the night crying my eyes out. I was eleven. This is mountain country, grape vines for miles on one side of the road, a pear orchard on the other, and moonless. Just me and those gawd damned Zombies. The cops found me and I wouldn't tell them who I was or where I belonged. They found out but this started a trend. Mom would get soused and boot me out. Later she would realize that she couldn't collect welfare for me if I was "kicked out" so she always claimed I ran away.

I got a probation officer and a reputation for running off. One day, after being kicked out, in the day light hours I walked all the way to Lakeport and got there before Kmart closed. I stashed myself in the store, waited until the stores cleaning crew left then I went shopping. I left through the fire door and walked under the weight of the back pack, with travelling gear, to the highway. I caught a ride and two months later found my dad in Los Angeles, I was twelve. Anyway, that didn't work out and I ended back with mom. Not for long though. I'd been in foster home's, detention center's, lived on the streets in San Francisco and L.A., all before the ripe age of 13. (I know this because I know where I was at age 13) I remember being picked up in Boise Idaho and spending time in the Juvenile section as they tried to figure out who I was. I used that time to rest up. I'd got better at "shopping" and was self-sufficient. I had money from selling cigarettes. I had cigarettes, food, clothes and knives. I had eleven knives and an assortment of Zippo lighters. The knives were for the fags and the Zippo's were cause I smoked.

My favorite knife was a Buck 119. My father's sister, who I'd never met, volunteered to take me in as a foster child. She and her husband lived in Seabeck, Washington, by the Hood Canal, right on the Puget Sound. Heavy forests and the ocean. They had a teenage daughter, Gigi and a boy my age, Shawn. Their youngest Ryan was three, I think. Shawn was my complete opposite. I was blonde and Shawn had black hair. My Uncle Ted worked as a Rocket Scientist for SeaTac and/or Boeing. This family was as straight laced as the Cleavers and had no idea how wild I was.

When I was about nine years old, my mom married a Staff Sergeant in the U.S. Army and we all moved to Germany to live for awhile. We flew on a big Jumbo jet. When I was transported from Boise, Idaho to Bremerton, Washington I got to ride in a small Cessna type plane. I decided I didn't like flying. I knew who Buddy Holly was and what happened to him, plus a pilot with a sense of humor didn't help. I was free to smoke and did. When we touched ground and stopped I had already planned my escape. I didn't know my aunt and uncle but by now my life had got easier to map out. I'd wait till I got wherever "they" were placing me. I'd be polite or rude until they turned their backs or went to sleep, then "Adios Mustachios". I was probably resigned to the fact that they were gonna run me off anyway, so...the people in Idaho gave me back my backpack with all my knives, lighters and cigarettes.

It should also be noted that "the Cleavers" were devout Lutherans. The church was a very important part of their lives. I'd become quite the callous little shit in my wonderings. When faced with questions like, "what would Jesus say if He knew you were smoking cigarettes?" which is what happened. I lit up on the way back from the airport.

Picture this; my uncle, receding hair, glasses and passive. My aunt: A large women, (not fat) tall, very religious and the obvious matriarch of the family. Gigi was there. She sat bored as teen-agers get when things that are beneath them are forced upon them. Like picking up her wayward cousin from the airport, "He's gonna live with us, won't that be a blessing?" Shawn in the back seat between me and Gigi, asking all kinds of boy questions and me sitting behind the driver's seat on the drive back to Sea Beck. Nighttime, Kingswood station wagon, I light a smoke. "We don't smoke" my aunt says. Gigi looks over with new interest. "So", says I. I'm in Levis, a tee-shirt and yup, a genuine imitation black leather jacket. "You need to put that out" my aunt says. So I roll down the window and fling it out into the night. My aunt gasps, "That's littering" she says. "You want me to go back and pick it up?" I said. My uncle gives me "that look" in the rearview mirror. "What would Jesus say if he knew you were smoking? You're too young to smoke". My cousin Shawn said, "Jesus doesn't like smoking" and here is a defining moment. I turn to Shawn and say, "Yea? Fuck Jesus, how 'bout that? "Oh-my-God!" My Aunt was over the front seat pounding on me like I was on fire. The car stopped and my Uncle had to literally pull her off me. It didn't take long to find that button. Everybody in the car was traumatized except me of course. I'd been jumped on before but these good folks had never encountered a seasoned little bastard before. I shrugged off the encounter as all in a days work. Some serious thinking was going on in the administrator's office though. My aunt and uncle took me to meet the pastor of their church, whom I had no sympathy for. I had seen things no twelve year old should have seen. Done things just to survive that no twelve year old should have done. Where was Jesus when all this was going on? It took me awhile to convince me that Jesus was there but I wasn't trying to hear Him then. The more my aunt forced religion on me the harder I refused. My poor aunt, she truly tried.

I was introduced into a five room school house. Grades one and two were in the same room. I came in at the end of fifth grade and got to meet everyone. I made friends with two girls, Paige Jones and Sharelle Linux. One blonde and the other dark haired, both tomboys who liked me. They both thought my cousin Shawn was a dork. I'm skipping over a lot but me and him didn't get along very good. I ended up sleeping in the basement; me and them gawd damned zombies! I was too macho to admit of being afraid of the dark basement. Paige was my friend and an only child. She lived by the school. Her parents loved and trusted her. They gave her anything she wanted, horses, motorcycles (later on), whatever she wanted. Paige was a good girl. She was the only girl that could give me a run for my money at tetherball. Sharelle was shy but I was attracted to her laughter. I was the class clown and she was a good fan base. I knew neither girl as well as I would before it was over.

Shawn was in Little League Baseball, so I had to be too. Not because I wanted to, but fair is fair. I had never played baseball and barely knew where to run after I first hit the ball. I also had to be in Boy Scouts. Our scout master was a very wise old sailor who I think hated everything and everyone. I remember our first Boy Scout get together. It was arranged to bring three packs together and we'd camp out for a week. The entire group would start a three mile hike to a camp ground that they visited every year. We would set up camp and do Boy Scout crap till it was time to leave. Shawn was sick and didn't have to go. Gigi later told me it was planned that way. It didn't matter; I'd been there long enough by then to have my own life. In fact I had turned thirteen and started sixth grade.

Both Paige and Sharelle had started to fill out and I was aware of this. I was late to the rendezvous. (I was scoring a lid of pot by then). Old Sea Beck Highway started by Paige's house and wound through the woods for miles. It wasn't used anymore except for the Boy Scouts and swallowed up by the woods. I stashed my back pack and banged on Paige's door. We listened to records in her room for awhile and then she gave me a ride on her motor bike for about 2 ¾ miles up the road where I walked the rest of the way into camp. Our scoutmaster made me haul water for not hiking with pack number or troop number 5150. (That ain't the real number but close enough). I remember smoking pot in the darkness with some of my friends and moving the outhouse back so the next idiot would walk up and fall in the hole. It happened to be a visiting Scout Master who was, obviously, not pleased. In fact he had skinned up his leg and forehead falling into the pit and we had to all go home so he could get medical attention. You can't have an open wound when falling into a half full outhouse pit. Eeeeww!

I had some good times there. I ended up leaving late that summer. Again I found my dad in L.A. He gave me to a house full of bikers. I did okay there. I learned a lot. We lived by the movie studio in Culver City. The only rule was, "don't bring the cops to the house". I learned work ethics and was treated like an equal as long as I acted so. I was caught again and ended back with my mom. By then it was too late, I was seasoned and refused to stay in any one place. I was deemed incorrigible by the courts and sent off to a juvenile detention place until another foster home would take me. Then I ran away again and found my way back to my dad. He turned me in, and he refused to keep me. I was sent to the California Youth Authority until I turned 17. Pretty rotten huh. Oh well, life is anything if not always fair. I did an awful lot of hitch hiking between Northern Calif. and L.A.

I was very lucky because the I-5 killer (who was on the rampage then) didn't get me. I was trolling the very area he had been moving through. Looking for lads exactly like me, and finding them too. Maybe Jesus was watching me, who decides who gets nabbed?

Anyway, that's a brief synopsis of my childhood. I had some good times and some bad, just like any other brat, just more drastic I suppose.

This letter started last week. We're off of lock down and I've just now scored a stamp or two, sometimes it's like that. So I'll mail this in the morning. I don't know why I wrote all this, my motives were good when I started.

I got a card from my Dad. I think he feels guilty in his old age. He sent $25.00 and a card. He's done that for the last four years. I never even had to tell him my birthday. Anyway I have made my peace with my mom before she passed and my dad.

Life is life my friend and I think we're given just what we need to get through it. Sometimes it ain't enough so we gotta make do with what we have. Some people don't know how and fall prey to things like booze and drugs. (I ain't got nothing against either if done properly, but if abused... well, you know) Some lessons are learned the hard way. I hope ole Edgar Casey was right and this is all prelude to something better, we'll see that's for sure.

I'm gonna go for now. Take care and thanks again for the card.

Affectionately and respectfully,
Walt.

****

April 22, 2010

Hi Liz;

Well I started several letters over this week but went nowhere with them. I've been in a kind of funk and haven't wanted to relay it to you.

I've written the court coordinator asking what the hearing was about on the 1st; so far I've heard nothing. My "hood ornament" hasn't blessed me with any news. I don't expect him to but it would be nice. I suppose I'll spend the next week in the law library searching for some avenue I've overlooked. Nine years is too damn long to get the run around. I ain't wasting a stamp on David

Haynes (my hood ornament) anymore. All I know is he turned out to be everything he denied being. Another summer. Heavy sigh.

My computer class graduates in four weeks. The final exam is in three or four weeks. I'll probably go back out to the bus barn and into the welding shop to work. This prison has been slated to go "single cell" in June. A lot of folks will be shipped to various prisons around Texas. I really don't want to be one of those poor bastards. I don't like moving. I might as well find something to do that I don't mind doing and do it well.

Baseball season is here; in fact I have the Houston Astros on the radio right now. They lost the first eight games. Not a good start for the home team.

It's been in the 80's around here. Not much humidity yet. But that will change. Is it still cold up there?

I re-read "Shogun." Good book. All good English ladies should read it. A lot of English history in it. Not like the last book I suggested by Tim Dorsey (which I thoroughly enjoyed but you didn't) I still smile thinking about the ex-KGB guys in that book. I also read "The Shack" It's a big "you gotta read" on the Christian circuit. I didn't like it because of the subject matter. A novel. I can understand why it got good reviews though, sort of.

How are you and your family? I hope y'all are doing great. I'm gonna mail this letter in the morning so it will go out before the weekend. Not much going on here. I'm studying for the final computer maintenance exam, it has 40,000 questions! And if you believe that, then...never mind. It has 100 questions, all of them based on 22 chapters of a text book approved for something called "A+ Certification (A plus) we won't get certified but we could if we took the proper test, but that cost's too much. Passing is enough for me.

Well my friend, I'm gonna close and go to bed. The Astros are losing, again. I have a chapter test tomorrow (usually on Fridays) I'm ready for it, but I need my ugly sleep. Take care and write when you can.

I've just had an idea. I'm gonna draw an original picture with a detailed picture of the moon. I've got an Astrology book for this purpose. S'wat I'm reading these days.

So again, I'm gonna go, see ya. Great picture of you holding Emily Ann.

Always,
Your friend,
Walt

****

May 9, 2010

Hi Liz;

I got your letter last week and am writing back now, (in church) to let you know I'm writing... in church.

I have hay fever and a 600 question final exam test first thing in the morning. I've already done part of the 600 question test. I haven't heard from Donna or her "hood ornament" boss. Maybe this week. (Hmmm, seems I've said that many times before). So I have no idea what went on Friday. I hope it was good news for me. I'm due for some good news. If they didn't find the records, I don't know that they will do anything. My case is such that the record will reflect the errors that render the last trial unconstitutional. So the record will benefit my cause! I doubt I'll get millions but I'll get something, I may have to wait. (I'm good at waiting) we'll see.

TRILLIONS! That's what I'll ask for. One trillion is okay, I guess. Actually I try not to dwell in that aspect. One thing at a time. First I gotta get outa here.

I've got hay fever, did I mention that I'm allergic to idiots. The idiots are pollinating. I didn't get hay fever in California. Not there aren't idiots in California, I don't think those (in Calif.) are "bloomin idiots" Think there's a connection?

It's a Mothers day sermon. My mom's done passed so, does that make it okay to write a letter while the preacher is up there yelling and hollering and stomping his feet about momma? Who knows? I felt I needed to write this and mail it on the way to chow, so it will go out in the morning.

My computer class ends this week following the "big test". I guess I'll go back to the welding shop (bus barn) and work on Texas school bus's until...until I get my trillion gawd damn dollars. As I've said so many times before, I need to get outa here, I'm working on it. Thanx for calling people for me Liz, if nothing else it helps me.

You mentioned getting or not getting Mothers Day cards. Oh my God! My wife expected something for bearing our son (Daniel) rightly so too.

We stopped having kids after Daniel was born. The next Mothers Day she got flowers, candy, cash, yard work, sex, a puppy, a kitten and a nice card to boot. I still have feelings for her even though I don't hear from her anymore, but wha-da-ya-gonna do? Heavy sigh.

I hope Mothers Day was a good day for you. As much as you do for your kids and their kids you should have a 1957 orange and white Chevy with a big bow on it in your driveway. Maybe when I get my trillion dollars...you thought I'd forget? Naw I've got a mind like a steel trap. The hinges are a little rusty but all in all it's steel...and definitely a trap.

Well friend, service is almost over. I'm gonna go now. I have a card started that I wanted to send with this but it will come later. This has to go out indigent. They won't mail home made cards through the indigent mail program. I don't know why, that's the way it goes. You'll like the card, it's...funny.

So I'm gonna go. Take care and write when you can.

Always your friend,
Walt

****

May 31, 2010

Well howdy Podner;

How y'all doin? I received your letter dated 5-17-10 last week. It's taken me a couple of days to answer. I'm back to work in the bus barn. I got my final grade from the "Computer Maintenance 101". I'll send it. I missed one stinkin question. One stinkin question throughout the whole course. I'm a failure! Spike is so ashamed he won't talk to me. Ronnald spit in my dinner. Sherry webbed my eyes shut again while I was sleeping and was working on closing up my nostrils when I worked my way back to consciousness. Yike's! I'm a failure!! What an idiot huh? *(Note: Even missing one questions he still got A+)*

As for David Haynes he ain't sent nuthin. Surprised? Oh wait, he didn't say when he would write, just that he would. My bad. Okay, I'm all better.

Don't for a moment think I'm mad at you. My wrath is solely for "the system". This includes David "hood ornament" Haynes. His lackadaisical attitude only confirms my suspicion of his roll in this epic story. He's there to stonewall, delay or otherwise confuse the issue, which is not representing me as a habeas corpus petitioner in the State Court, but following a script by the state who is at fault for violating rights that are or should be guaranteed by the Constitution our lives are governed by. He ain't there to help me, so I'm not wasting my time writing to him anymore or the State Courts. I've petitioned the Federal Courts to consider the state portion of my writ exhausted. I'm hoping someone call's the State Court judge and gets off their butt's. The problem with the Federal Courts is they take so long to do the simplest things. If David Haynes wanted to "He" could have called a hearing a year ago. But he didn't. He won't write to me and if it wasn't for you I'd have no idea what they were doing at all. So, thank you. I'm always hopeful when I hear from you that David or Donna has told you the record has been obtained and that I'm going back for a hearing. I feel once I go back I won't be back here. I have your addressed memorized, 1313 Mockingbird Lane...no wait, that's the Munster's. Do you remember them? Anyway I'll be writing to you first if there's word. Carolyn doesn't write any more. She married Frank; I hope that worked out for her.

I'm happy to have found a friend as grounded as you are. I'm just a regular guy, translated to "nut job", with an over active imagination that's got caught up in a bad situation. I believe in reincarnation and also believe what the Bible said, "you reap what you sow". To me that's real. I must have been really bad in my past life because I've been dealt a bad hand of cards. I also believe that God gives you enough to handle what you gotta do. There are rougher lives to lead but there are better too. I take the best of any situation and leave the rest. It's getting harder to do that these days. I will meet you one day and thank you in person for befriending me when I really needed someone. Until then, thanx for writing and calling David Haynes, sending me books, helping me pay for this fan (which is still going strong, thank God)

The next chapter of my legal battle will be interesting. I'll tell you what they're gonna do. First Fannin County can't afford to let the feds take this. (My opinion, I could be wrong) Because if the Feds do bypass Fannin County then Fannin County won't factor into any more legal process's that involve me. The Feds could acquit me of all charges since there's no evidence, except Darin Barnett's accusation. Not enough. If that happens, Fannin County's liable for $80,000.00 per year of wrongful incarceration by Texas law. That's over $700,000.00 so...why would they let this go without having control over this process? If they reverse the conviction themselves, they can wheel and deal. That is preferable by me because I'll leave here sooner. The Feds will have a hearing and I'll have to sit here another six months waiting for them to decide.

I went digging for that final grade-score page and found a picture they took for graduation. I'll send that too. *(Note: I still have that photo and love it.)* Okay, let's dig up your letter and see what I missed. Oh that reminds me. I gotta draw that card for you too. I can't do it this letter because I'm sending this through the indigent program. I've got to draw a Fathers Day card this week and I'll do it then. I'll get stamps from Fathers Day cards I draw for other people.

Your letter mentioned was I interested in the statues you have and yes, save them for me. The photos you sent of them are great. Put them with the books you're saving for me. I'll get out sooner or later. I'll tell you what, you save those things for me and when I swing by my sisters to pickup some boards she's holding for me, I can swing by there and pick-up those things. We can do a swap if you like the pictures I've drawn, Okay? One is a Norman Rockwell (old man fishing with his dog) the other is a Native American drawing. It's something to think about while I sweat the courts.

Well if you talk to David Haynes you can tell him I've filed a "motion for relief" in the Federal Courts, Eastern District and Sherman Division. Part of the prayer I requested was for the Federal Courts to share the record, the ever elusive record, with David Haynes and the 336th judicial court of Fannin County. He can contact Federal Magistrate Judge Amos L. Mazzant, civil case #4:06-cv-204 see what he says. Hell maybe this time he'll have the record. If he does ask him what he thinks. That would be interesting. *(Note: For the record, I did call and left a msg. I've never heard back from David Haynes).*

In case you're wondering about the white canvas clothes in my picture, that's what everyone here wears. Thanx for the computer humor. It reminds me of a story of a little boy sitting on the sidewalk shaking up a jar or turpentine. A Catholic priest came by and sat down next to the little boy. "What cha got son?" The little boy watching the bubbles in the jar, answered, "I got the most power fullest water in the world here." The Priest looked at the jar and asked, "Is that Holy Water?" The little boy looked at the Priest and said, "No, why?" "Well" said the Priest, "you rub a couple of drops of Holy water on a pregnant ladies belly and she'll pass a boy." The little boy stared at the Priest. "Oh, that ain't nuthin" he said, "you rub a couple of drops of this one a cat's ass and he'll pass a motorcycle." Did I ever tell you that one before? Cute huh.

Well friend I'm gonna go now. Y'all take care, ya heah? Spike, Ronald and Sherry say Hi. We're all fine and impatient. Thanx for contacting my "hood ornament" I hope he has good news. I'm doing nothing but getting older in here, as you can see from that picture, it ain't doing me any good. You, however, are aging a lot better than I am, you don't look your age. It must be the tea. Do you still break for tea? Have I ever asked you what a crumpet is? Is it like a cookie? I like cookies.

Take care,
Walt.

****

June 20, 2010,

Dear Liz;

Good morning to ye lass. It's 80 degrees at 5:30am, probably the coolest it's been all night. I live on the third tier of this cell block so it may be a little warmer. Nothing unusual for this part of Texas.

Well that hearing was last Friday. I received a copy of a letter from Mr. "hood ornament" Haynes trying to retrieve the missing trial record. The latter was dated June 14th requesting missing portions of the trial record for a June 18th hearing...Hmmm, doesn't leave much time to actually deliver. I've written to several organizations, including the Federal Courts to try and put pressure on the State Courts. My guess is it had some effect and Mr. Haynes was scrambling at the last minute to make a show of it. What do you think? This has turned into a regular soap opera hasn't it? Anyway, I'm still optimistic, we'll see.

How are you? I hope all's well with you and your family. I'd love to go swimming today, perhaps get stoned and lounge around beside a body of water, picking a guitar and crooning out some old folk/country songs or make songs up as I go along. That sounds like so much fun. One day I'll do it, you'll see. *(Note: It was too cold when he did come home but the first "warmish" day we went to Rollins Lake and did just what he wanted to do.)*

I'd like to ask a favor of you. No I don't need money or anything that cost's money. I'd like you to post something on a couple of bulletin boards on the internet for a friend of mine. His name's Ray Hill. Ray has helped me with my case. He actually went to school in Grass Valley by the way. Anyhow, I told him I'd ask you. I don't know much about Face Book or any of the other social web sites but I know there are sites that have public bulletin boards. So will you or can you post the information I enclose with this letter? Ray doesn't charge me for helping me and he could, so I told him I'd try. If nothing develops well, we tried.

I drew the card I've been trying to get to you. I like it. It's from one of the books you sent a while ago. I hope you like it too. I'll bet I have a letter on the way from you. It usually happens that we pass each other. You may be waiting to write until after the 18th (the hearing) to send me some fantastic news, or just some news. I gotta tell ya Liz, without you I'd not know what's going on with Mr. Haynes. I do feel we're getting closer to some action though.

Well it's about time for the doors to roll up so I'd better get this in the mail. If you're wondering where to post the info on the internet, anywhere there might be a free public viewing place. As

I said I don't know about Face Book so shoot your best shot but if you don't wanna, then don't. I just told him I'd ask you.

I'm gonna go. I hope all is well and y'all are happy. I feel like I'm finally getting close to some relief. God I hope so. It's so hot!! I'm closing for now, take care and write when you can.

Your friend,
Walt.

****

June 27, 2010

Dear Liz;

Howdy. Just a few lines to let you know that Donna came through. She must have mailed me right away. I received another letter or copy of a letter going to Billy Gant, the prosecuting attorney for the state, from David Haynes. I'm glad to see he's doing "something." I just wrote a "thank you" to Donna and told her I have a legal assistant named Spike. I also wrote to the court coordinator. I'll probably write several more letters over this week. Maybe, MAYBE, we'll get some action this month. God I so hope so, then? Well then they will start a new trial and the process starts all over.

They can only try a person three times for the same offense. I've had two trials already. They will offer me a deal to avoid trial. "Time Served." Y'all can go home right now, sign here." They'll make it sound like they're doing me a huge favor. I will decline. They will then start the scare tactics, "You will / could get a life-sentence, you'd better think about that." I have thought about it. I've been in here nine years for a crime I didn't do, so, "bite me!" See ya in civil court. Actually I've got really good grounds for them not prosecuting a third time. I've been busy these nine years.

Soooo, how are ya? I've been working at the bus barn. I think I told you that. I started back in the welding shop but there wasn't enough work for all of us so I talked my way into a clerk job. (Air conditioning)

I've dug up some case law on missing records and sent if off to the court coordinator and David Haynes. He probably doesn't need my help. I wonder if that judge is putting pressure on everybody to just "Get the Record!" I hope the Federal Judge has put pressure on her. Anyway we'll see how it turns out. You're right though, I also feel like something's about to break loose. I wanna go swimming, I wanna retire.

This ain't a long letter, but there you have it anyway. I heard "The Battle of New Orleans" by Johnny Horton the other day and thought of you and how much you "love" that song. NOT! Yeah, I'm an asshole but you still like me don't cha? It happens after a prolonged period of being kicked around. Spike's the one who mentioned you while we were listening to Johnny H. So...yeah, I blamed it on Spike.

Here's hoping you and yours are Healthy, Happy and Blessed. I'm off to church this morning. Take care my friend and thanks for your concern and friendship. It makes a lot of difference.

Very truly,
Walt and Spike

****

October 10, 2010

Hi Liz;

How are ya? Me and Spike are packin up and getting ready to travel. If you've been in contact with Donna you already know. Usually they won't bench warrant anyone back unless they have action. I HAVE ACTION. Let's hope I have favor as well. I know they're gonna offer me "Time Served" and I'm determined to NOT take it. Even if it means coming back and resuming my fight. I hope I can stay strong. Please keep me in your prayers.

I have wanted to write but I know you said you couldn't anymore. *(Note: Even though I did continue writing, he couldn't write back to my home address, so I told him to write c/o me to Bud's, where I used to work.)* Spike's been pestering me to write Bud's to see how you are. I've waited so as to not ruin a good thing.

I may have to sit in that stupid county jail for a few months waiting on the court of criminal appeals to affirm the judge's recommendation. We'll see. If so I may ask for a couple of those books you've put away for me. Spike hasn't decided whether he's going with me or not.

The paper I sent you, I don't need it back. My clerk job gives me access to a copy machine so...I told you I was hired as a data entry clerk in the bus repair shop, it pays the same as the welders position, nothing. But at least I don't come back with my nostrils full of soot and sore shoulders.

I've got several letters from you and each time I got the itch to write back. You could get a P.O. Box; I don't think it's that expensive. I would love to continue our friendship but completely understand why thing's are as they are. I don't like it but respect it and would expect nothing less from a person of your caliber. I keep you and your family in my prayers. They let me into the Catholic Chapel once in a while (did you know that "Catholic" means Universal?) and I sit through their service, I don't take communion but I do get a Catholic blessing now and again.

I'm listening to a radio station that plays "Cruising Saturday Night" every second Saturday of the month, "Oldies!" but being a country station they don't always get it right. Right at this moment I have Connie Francis singing, "Who's Sorry Now". The next song is Peter, Paul and Mary singing, "Puff the Magic Dragon". I try not to miss this program, I really like Oldies. "A Prairie Home Companion" comes on right before this, which I also listen to. Also a "Thistle and Shamrock" (Celtic music) on public radio on Sunday night. They're good drawing music or for letter writing. I only write to you, my Dad (three times a year) and or the "hood ornament." I wrote to my Dad about the final hearing, his letter will go out with yours. His will stop in Arizona.

Fannin county, (the county I'm going back to) was on the Texas State Network news for killing someone out there after serving him a warrant. I hope they don't do that to me and Spike; yeah he's going with me. I'm downsizing my stuff in case I don't come back. If I do, I can't bring anything except legal work back into the system. So I'll have to replace everything, fan, radio and hot pot.

I got a couple of illustration boards and am planning to draw a couple and hopefully sell them to the yah-hoo's there in case I gotta come back and replace everything. A cowboy sleepin in a wheelbarrow is one that I've started, that should be a good one. A vintage "Steam Boat Willie" is another. Anyway hopefully they'll keep me waiting. Waiting word from the court. I'm nervous about their intention. I can not, must not make a mistake at this stage. So please keep me in your prayers, oh yeah I already said that huh, well then maybe it's important.

I miss you my friend. I went through all the pictures you've sent and I've collected over the years. I've missed much. I get mad about it when I dwell on it.

There's a lot of wrongful convictions and prosecutorial misconduct in Texas. I'm collecting information to take on all of that. I'm nothing if not determined. Go Me!

Well my friend I'm gonna go. We've been shook down, the weather is perfect and I'm ready to go and do battle. You may have time to write but keep in mind; if they come and get me they may return your letters. If they do that, have a different return address on the envelope so you don't gotta explain nothing. I'd hate to be the cause of any friction between you and your family.

I hope you're well and everything is groovy. Hey, are ya ready for Jerry Brown, again? Who saw that coming? Okay, gotta go. Spike and Ronald send their best.

Peace, love and Bobby Sherman,
Walt.

****

November 7, 2010

Dear Liz;

Hi ya toots! That's an old American greeting that's jovial yet still respectful. At least that's how I'm intending it.

I've been here since the 26th of October. No sign of my "hood ornament" I've been kept in a single cell in "segregation" due to my transient status. The solitude is a welcome to the chaos of an open-cell block at the other prison. I'm ready to proceed, today, Now! So let's proceed already.

How are you? I hope you're okay, well and happy. All of that and more. I got your Halloween card (it was re-routed to me) on Friday night, Thanx, it was a nice thought.

Liz, I got an unpleasant request to discuss with you. Let's get it out of the way and then talk about other stuff. When they took me out of the prison, they refused to store my property. All the stuff I've accumulated over the past nine-eight years. I can't bring it back in either. I'll be going through intake again and can only bring in legal work and five stamped envelopes will be allowed. (Five letters also) I've written to my dad and called him collect. The call cost $10. He asked me not to do that again unless I'm dying. He said he could send $25. I need another $25. to replace my hot pot and fan. These are necessities. You know I don't ask for $$ unless I absolutely need it. I need it. I know this sounds stupid but, can you loan me $25. to recoup my appliances at least? I can draw and hustle coffee, stamps etc, etc. Consider it either a loan or an early Christmas present from you. I have nothing to offer in return, due to the present situation. I can draw that last reclining cowboy in the wheelbarrow, on a full board and get it to you in time for Christmas. It would make a fine Christmas present for someone.

In all the years we've been writing, I've only asked for financial help once. My fan died. I hate doing it but it's done now. If you decide to do it, you can't send it till I send one of those forms for the trust office. I can't do that till I get back. I'll wait till you respond. I'm sorry if I'm imposing, I really don't mean to. This whole mess is messing with my normal roll with the flow, taking it in stride, I can handle it attitude. I've written to a Baptist Church in the area to ask if the pastor will take my letter and all my pictures until I get back. I explained everything to him and think he will. Believe it or not he was my neighbor when I lived here before. I got a lot of stuff, pictures, etc. that have become important to me. Pictures of my dad and pictures of people who have passed since I've been locked up. Anyway, if you can swing it let me know. Write to me at Ellis Unit. Odd's are I'll go right back there, even if I don't they'll re-route my mail to wherever I am. Thanx Liz one way or the other.

My dad made it sound like he was eating dog food and couldn't really afford it but did it anyway. I told him it's been a coon's age since we've spoken to each other and all he's doing is complaining. I really didn't say that but it struck me, as old as he is, 80 something, he might wanna tell me he loved me in case one of us doesn't survive to see the other, God forbid. It was good to hear his crotchety old voice. He used to call me "God dammit" True, he'd say, "God dammit, will you get out of that tree, or God dammit will you stop doing that" Ahh the good ole days.

Okay, enough with the beggin. As much as I don't want to be here I'll be glad to get back there. I missed the World Series. I bet about a million pushups on the Giants. You probably weren't interested in the World Series were you?

I have one book in here. Stephen Kings the uncut version of "The Stand." I read the edited version years ago and enjoyed it. This version has 500 more pages, oh boy! I've read myself into a void where I wake up or come too sitting with my back to the wall banging my head against the wall and drooling down my front. Not a good sign. I have learned to appreciate Stephen King's editor. Holy moley I gotta trade this book for something else. Sometimes the night jailer will let us swap books with each other.

My cell door opened last when they put me in here. There's a tray slot that opens and closes when its chow time, other than that, nothing. There's a small area with a shower head sticking out of the wall. Actually that's kinda cool and handy. All in all, your entire bathroom's probably bigger than my entire cell. The best part though is no cellie and solitude. I also asked the Baptist pastor for a King James Bible, so maybe I'll get something else to read.

I've been over my legal work 50 times and I'm ready! The law is on my side also. I'm not sure about my "hood ornament" though. I have a Texas Constitution article memorized in case they try to stonewall me. It says I have a right to be heard. I wish Spike was here. I almost got beat up, literally, by the Lieutenant in charge at the prison when they came to get me. It was early 4 am and he informed me that, when you get bench warranted back to the County jail, the prison is not responsible for your property. You take it with you. Nine times out of ten the inmate doesn't return. I happen to be that 10th one though. Heavy sigh. It would be great if I didn't go back but all this judge can do is offer up a recommendation for a reversal.

The Texas Court of Criminal Appeals affirms or denies the recommendation. (Nine times out of 10 they go with the recommendation but that takes awhile, upwards of six months) Fannin County will not house me for that long when I'm technically a State prisoner and can be housed in a State prison. So I'm going back. If I'd known I could have left most of my stuff with a friend there, but I didn't know. What an idiot! I sure hope the pastor shows up. Another heavy sigh. The good news is I just saved a bunch of money on my car insurance by switching to Geico. (Couldn't resist that)

Has it snowed there yet? This county jail is ultra modern. It's designed to hold 500 prisoners. Three hundred of them are Federal prisoners and it's privately owned by some wise guys in New Jersey I think, no kidding. I've been in some old county jails before, mostly when I was a juvenile and always on the run. I really hope to be out before my birthday in March, but odd's are...nothing is ever fast around here. Speaking of which, where's chow? The food is much nicer here but the portions are small. It certainly won't kill me to lose a few pounds. I exercise and shower on a regular basis. They don't have soap, only shampoo packets.

Well ole friend, I'm gonna close this and mail it. I hope I didn't catch you at a bad time by my request, piss you off or overstep my worth. I hope you know I wouldn't ask if I felt I didn't have to.

I'll pray you and your family are doing well, please keep me in your prayers. You'll probably get this before Friday and I should leave the following Monday or Tuesday so I'll be right back at Ellis Unit by the time you answer.

Till then, take care and thanx Liz, whatever you do. You know I really have good morals...you're laughing aren't you? Bye for now

Always your friend,
Walt

PS: If you want that board with the reclining cowboy, you can always say you got it from Bud Plant's. Slap a frame around it with a glass face and it would be a nice Christmas present. Sup to you. *(Note: I have it. It's a cowboy reclining in a wheelbarrow.)* Oh yeah, I heard Calif. was talking about putting pot on a bill this November for recreational use. What happened, did it pass? Keep me posted! Not that I, uhh, used to smoke weed...umm

I'm just curious.

****

November 13, 2010

Hi Liz;

It's me again. I just want you to know that the hearing didn't go too good. I don't know if you already know this from Donna but I said I'd write and let you know.

We, the shyster and I, proved our case but got turned down anyway. It ain't fair I tell ya. The judge didn't deny my claim on its merits; she denied it as "being out of time." It's because of Fannin County that things have taken so long!! I asked if I could respond to that but she said, "**No!**" I feel as if I've been punched in the stomach by Hell Boy or some such character. I figure by the time you get this I'll be back at Ellis Unit. What a waste. Well I guess I have to present this mess to the Texas Court of Appeals. They won't hear it. Then it's back to the Feds who "will" hear it. (But for how long?) The only good news is I've got all the evidence on record that I need and eventually I will win, but not today. It's getting harder and harder to remain standing but I will.

Thanx for being my friend in all this. I hope Thanksgiving is wonderful and y'all gain 10 lbs in all the right places. That ain't meant as a curse. I don't mean to be a bummer but wish with all my heart we could be celebrating, but evidently not yet, not yet.

In closing let me wish you and your family well and write to me at the address I put on the back. I ain't got no more books. I can only bring back law books into the facility. So if you sent some and they were returned that's why. If so could you re-send them to me? I'd be ever so grateful.

Take care, your friend,
Walt

November 23, 2010

Hi Liz;

It seems that I'll be here over the holidays, including Christmas.

I'm in a 24 man tank now. Well over half are teenagers. Teenagers! Ugh! I'm still waiting on an order from the stupid judge.

I'm writing for two reasons. One just to touch base with you my friend. I feel I need a friend right now. And the other is hoping to expound on my "loan" letter. There's a phone in my tank and they sell phone cards from the commissary. It's $11.00 for a $10.00 phone card. I don't know how long a Texas call would be but if you sent the $11.00 I could call you at a pre-designated time. Hearing a friendly (yours) voice would be groovy right now. I always wondered if you still had an accent. I could use this money in one of two ways. The phone or paper and stamps. That decision is up to you. A collect call is $10.00, they'd charge you and believe me they stick it to ya pretty good. If money went into my account it's a little less, in fact we could get two calls out of it. There's a two hour difference.

So if you want you gotta send a money order with your letter to this address. It must have my name and number on the money order or it's sent back. If not please write anyway, I'm dying in here. It's like a Romper Room with these kids. I drew a picture on an envelope for a guy for this stamp. It's better than giving up food to someone for a stamp. They don't feed enough for that.

I don't think I can have books or nothing so a cheery, "Hey, Hi, How are ya?" I'm already working on my response to the Texas Court of Appeals, which is my next stop. **I will win, I have to**. I have proven my claim irrefutable but no one will listen, that's crazy huh?

You can send a card with a nice picture on it or a nice letter with pictures or whatever.

I'm gonna make this short. I would love, after all these years, to hear your voice. I'll be here through Christmas. I hope you and your family are well. Take care and thanx for lookin out for me. *(Note: I do remember this request. I so wanted to send the money so he could call but he would have to call my home number and that wouldn't have been good, at that time.)*

Your friend,
Walt

Address: Walter "Super stupid" Anderson, Fannin Co. Detention Ctr. Bonham, Tx 75218

If you do decide to send $$ for a phone call, let me know the best time to call. I will call unless you don't want me to.

****

December 10, 2010

Hi You;

I got your letter dated 11/23 yesterday. I'm still in the county jail waiting to go back to the joint.

Last Friday I talked my way into being trustee. I was excited. Trustee's get to order pizza on Friday night. I don't have the money to do this but I did a drawing for a guy and today we were supposed to split a large pizza. It's been "years" since I had a pizza. (From Pizza Hut even) I'm so lucky. No really! Let me explain. Saturday I got to work in the kitchen scrubbing pots. I'm okay with that. The food here is better than Ellis Unit, Huntsville but the portions are small. Anyway, Saturday I gorged on fresh salad, of all things (no fresh veggies in prison) that and ham and cheese grilled sandwiches, Yum, Yum!! Sunday we had chicken, Oh my God! I waddled out of the kitchen. Monday we had a riot and I ended up with six stitches in the back of my head and two broke ribs. Today I'm laid up in the hospital wing.

I was scrubbing pots in an enclosed area when white guy, backed in, fighting off four black inmates. In Texas the jails and prisons are mostly black. Apparently, from what I've learned, the blacks had a tobacco stash and it got busted. They blamed some whites and wanted to fight. I had no clue as to what was going on. Being new in the kitchen, I was blissfully in my area scrubbing a kettle sized pot thinking about the chocolate cake baking when all hell broke loose. I fell over that kettle sized pot caching the rim in the ribs with some black dude on my back. I'd like to say I gave as good as I got but I ain't sure. They gassed us and separated us. I ended up in a hospital wing with a young man (Doogie Houser) telling me I can't have no pain medication for my ribs because of my head injury. Forty eight hours later I got some pain meds. Then I got some more. It was good and helped. Anyway, yesterday they dropped your letter through the bean shoot (slot in the door) It lay on the floor for an hour while I maneuvered out of bed and retrieved it. Ouch! I had to laugh involuntarily real hard while my ribs watered my eyes. It hurts to breath. I saved up my morning medication and took it with my evening medication. Pretty smart huh?

I'm up at the little desk like thing sticking out of the wall, writing you. I'm still not sure how much longer I'll be here. I believe until after the New Year. So, when you write back, if you write back, put Bud's return address on it. I'm sure my mail will be forwarded but, what if it's not. I'd feel like 10 tons of shit if you got into trouble writing me. I think I'm starting to feel my evening medication. It's nice being in a cell by my self.

You asked if I was going to file with the Federal courts (in the wake of this denial) it was the Federal courts that gave me permission to go back to the State courts. I've been in the Federal courts since 2006. This latest denial is a mere formality. I'm supposed to proceed to the Texas Court of Appeals. And then, when they deny it, and they will, my state remedies will be exhausted. You see, my State writ progressed into a Federal writ and during my litigating the Federal writ I found new evidence to support my claim. In order to present this new evidence to the Federal courts I had to exhaust it in the State courts. This process is rare and only a case that has merit would be allowed to do this.

It is the hope of the Federal court that the State court will clean up their own mess. They didn't. But this hearing proved every single allegation I made and there ain't a doubt in my mind that the Feds will grant me relief. (Hopefully an acquittal) They just take so long though. So, in answer to your question, yeah I'm still fighting. In fact I've already mailed my plea off to the Appellate court and at no added cost, I petitioned the State judge to rescind her ruling. I was rather rude pointing out that her incompetency has hindered her judgment citing Presidential law that refutes her interpretation of the law. I don't foresee her granting me any motions or sending me a Christmas card. Oh no, I'm far from done. My meds are kicking in.

Spike, by the way, didn't make the trip. I'm glad too; he would have been in the thick of things in the kitchen. I've already received word from the "black population" that I was not the intended target and no hard feelings. I feel so much better now. Politics!

Okay I'm gonna go now. I got no Christmas card to send, Merry Christmas anyway. Thanx for the computer funnies, I laughed until I literally cried, but it felt good.

Bye for now,
Walt.

PS: I've been thinking about "Giraffalo." I should write that damn story, what do you think? Do you still have the opening story I wrote a while back *(Note: Yes!)* I remember what I wrote just not how I wrote it. Send me your thoughts.

****

December 23, 2010

Dear Liz;

Hi. I don't have much time and only one piece of paper so I hope you get this at Bud's. I traded something off my dinner tray for this stamp and really want to mail it before the weekend. Tomorrow being Friday and I'm unsure if mail runs Christmas Eve. or not but I don't wanna take the chance.

Last Thursday the Jail Administrator came to me at 4:30am and asked if I was well enough to go back to the joint. I said yeah, wanting to get out a there that morning, so I left. I came to Palestine Tx, via various stops along the way to pick up, drop off, visit kin folk, slop the hogs, attend a shot gun wedding and once to speculate on this years cotton crop. We were dropped off at an intake unit. This one, where we were scalped, stripped and robbed of everything we owned except legal papers. Even letters I'd received while at the jail. They took all cosmetics, shampoo, toothpaste, soap etc. Anyway that's why I'm in a hurry to get this money slip to you.

I'm in a 54 man dorm on a top bunk with 600 mg. Ibuprofen twice daily to stave off the pain in my ribs. I thought I was going back to Ellis Unit but so far I haven't. I spent 5 days in the medical unit where a doctor yanked out the stitches in my head with his teeth, I think. Un-taped my ribs and took my Lortab prescription pain meds. Bastards! Anyway I'm hoping you did not send money to the county jail. If so I'll get it eventually. If not, here's the slip for the Trust Office.

This is definitely the worst Christmas I've ever had. But I'll survive. The good news is that the Court of Appeals has already come back refusing to hear the matter and I'm already back in the Federal courts. This may be the "Darkest before the Dawn" thing. I hope so, I could use a break.

Anyway, I'm sending two slips in case one gets broke. Kidding! Send it to the address on the slip just like last time. Write me when you do so I'll know when to go to the store.

I'm in pretty bad shape but still refuse to toss in the towel. I hope everything there is okay. Y'all be good. I'll write a more in-depth entertaining letter when I can. In the meantime...I remain your friend,

Walt.

****

PS:Anyway, I'm sending this to the address you wrote on your letter. And since you didn't give your last name I'm tempted to write Willoughby. I hope this finds you and yours well and good. I hope your pinched nerve, is that right? I hope its better. I'll drop you a line next week at Buds in case this doesn't make it.

Thanx for the letter and card. Keep your fingers crossed on my legal thing that looks like it just might happen.

Take care, your friend,
Walt.

****

Chapter Nine

January 17, 2011

Howdy Liz;

It's "James Earl Ray Day" here in Palestine. Not Middle East Palestine but close enough.

I got your re-routed Christmas card with your home address on it. Should I write that address down or stick with what werks? (Sometimes I deliberately misspell words to hide the fact that I'm an idiot, good plan huh?) I was trying to figure out how to spell "odysee or oddisy."

I'm already back in the Federal courts. The Feds gave me permission to go back to Fannin County to exhaust State remedies (give em a chance to clean their own mess up) I ain't heard from them yet. But I every reason to believe that I'll get my case overturned through this next step. I was hopeful with Fannin County but they chose to not deal with the problem. Even though I proved my case, which I did. I'm being punished for even pursuing my post conviction rights by being housed here in this "arm pit" of a place. But again, I will prevail.

I'm feeling better these days. My side still hurts when I laugh (which I don't do often) or turn the wrong way. My head has healed and hopefully I'll make store this week to get essentials, toothpaste, deodorant and art supplies to make cards to keep ahead of poverty. Valentine's Day is coming and I can hustle up the things I need through my home made greeting card business. First I gotta get to that store. Thanx to you that will probably take place this week. If not then eventually. I don't know how long I'll be here but send the calendar anyway. Even if they move me I'll be in the Dept. of Corrections and will receive what you send as long as my number is on the address and as long as there ain't no explicit nudity. The last one you sent (Frank Frazetta) was perfect. Is it another Frazetta? You and I share an appreciation for ole Frank. I really like Alphonse Mucha. He drew the card you sent me. I'd like a new catalog from Bud. I have to start a new collection, realistically though I believe I'll be out this year, preferably before my 10 year anniversary in June. You understand I must keep telling myself that every year.

I'm trying to entice David Haynes to take this case "pro bono" for the final stage and then take the civil suit after receiving an acquittal or dismissal. In fact I'm writing him today and sending it out through the indigent mail program. If I have money on my account it will come back tomorrow night. Then I'll be able to go to the prison commissary Wednesday. If not then I'll have to wait two more weeks. But this and David's letter will go out; we'll see how that plays out. Legally I'm in the right...so what, but again I'm on the mend and optimistic about the New Year, again. Eventually I will wake up one morning knowing I'm leaving this place for good.

I've been thinking about canvassing publishers and concentrate on laying down some genuine chapters in one of two my stories. I'd like to write a publisher and get some kind of idea what's expected and or relay the fact that I don't own a typewriter. Can you work with my chicken scratch? Here's my idea, are you interested in typing any?

I just finished reading a book called "The Girl with the Dragon Tattoo." It was number one popular book of 2010 by Stieg Larsson. Very good book, I think the publishing company is Random House but it doesn't give an address. Any ideas about publishers? You could go online and type in "Children's Books" I'm stagnant and need to move forward. I'm all caught up on my legal crap.

How's everything with you, are you snowed in? It snowed here a few days ago.

Well Liz I'm gonna go for now. Thanx for looking out for me. Every time I start thinking God's treating me too bad I think, well...that ain't a good way to start a positive thought. Let's try again. I've read "The Grapes of Wrath" by John Steinbeck and I gotta tell ya, it could be worse. I'm glad to have a friend.

If you get bored and wanna look up publishers for Children's stories send me some ideas and I'll pester some of them until they agree to read something like, "Giraffalo, Wyet Woodchuck or Peter Pan and Spike the Wonder Roach" I liked "Peter Pan and Spike the Wonder Roach" I was a little crude and it's probably not fit for children, but...Well I'm gonna go now, y'all take care and keep yer powder dry!

Bye for now,
Walt.

****

February 15, 2011

Dear Liz;

I got your letter dated 2-2-11 on Friday.

I went to the store (prison commissary) yesterday. Between you and my niece, I was able to purchase everything I needed and quite a few things I wanted. I wanted to write this yesterday but after spending the entire day trying to get into the store, (starting at 6am) I slept. Thank you so much for the $$ and the calendar. I haven't actually received the calendar yet but I'm sure I'll love it and appreciate it.

Bud's catalog could be a good thing. There are more than just a couple of guys that would order books given the chance. I think Bud Plant or Bud's Books refuses to send Texas prisoners' orders due to the returns. I wonder if Bud could screen the orders and check for nudity in the books, if so, I'll do some prevention campaigning on what they order. I'll remind them that they can't order anything with nudity and if they do and it doesn't come they'll have to settle for a "like" book or reorder. This could generate some business for our friends at Bud's, wha-da-ya-think?

I have to think up some good characters to put in Giraffalo, like Mir cats, or is it Miercat? And a Badger, if they have those in Africa. It's on my mind.

As for me staying in Palestine, it seems so for now. However, if they move me, my mail will catch up as long as my number is on the envelope. This is a transfer-facility mostly full of new prisoners. It's designed to house us until we are classified and shipped to one of any number of prisons strung throughout Texas. (Well over 100) However, some people get stuck here for upwards of two years. It seem's I might be one of those. I'd leave long before that amount of time. Federal court is slow, but not that slow. So for now this is where I'm at.

Upon reentry I have lost all my property except my legal work. As for my pictures, I had a preacher I used to live next to in Bonham, pick up and keep them until I got settled while I was in the County jail. So, I will have those, they should be arriving here soon. This reminds me I have an 8"x10" piece of a board. I was thinking of drawing that picture of you and your friend at your H.S. reunion and sending it to you. Could you have it? I don't like doing portraits but…I'd give it a shot if you wanted it. If you couldn't keep it you could send it to your friend. Talk to me about it.

I have enough $$ left on my books for a radio when I do finally go somewhere else. Let's hope I leave via the courts, soon. There are no electrical outlets for radio's, fan's etc in this dorm so ya can't buy them here.

I really, really believe the Feds will grant me action this year. I pray it's before the summer months. *(Note: Didn't happen and still hasn't.)* In the meantime I'm working in the "garden squad". It's like a chain gang without the chain. We work outside the prison, shoulder to shoulder swinging what's called an agie, pronounced ag-ee. It's a big hoe. We've got some idiot with a gun on horseback riding up and down the line talking shit and some other idiot calling out cadence. "And we're rockin on it, one and a two and a three-four step-one and a two and a…" out in the fields. We only work half a day, weather permitting. 'Cause we're old "Cool hand Luke".

You said you went to the Monterey Aquarium, I've been there, very cool. John Steinbeck country. Salinas, Monterey and Santa Cruz. Did you go to the board walk? Probably not up and runnin this time of year.

When I was in that computer class we talked about marketing strategies and selling you a computer not compatible with your printer is one neat scam. Did you get that taken care of?

My sister asked me what I wanted for my birthday. I'm going to shoot for a "Paul Bonner" book. That guy seems to be the next…umm…Paul Bonner? Anyway she may send it or not. I'll get a board drawn and maybe trade it for something from Bud Plant's catalog when one of these assholes makes an order. I'm pretty resilient.

I ain't holding my breath on your friend who "said" she'd like to write me. She's probably got better things to do than write letter's to some nut in a Texas penitentiary. You probably do too but you I've been working on for a lot longer. I am an acquired taste; *(Note: Is he ever!)* just ask Spike, he'll tell ya. I sent him a message with someone "catching the chain" to Ellis unit. (My old unit)

They don't ever come here from Ellis, only too Ellis and not me. I could, theoretically, go anywhere. I don't care anymore; my focus is on that Federal Magistrate. I'll keep you posted though.

I'm going to do my best to complete Giraffalo. Maybe I can generate an interest before I get out of here. No doubt they will release me with nothing but what I'm wearin and carryin. So I should put forth an effort to exploit any asset I have. I have my imagination, which just might come in handy if I can reach the right people. It's time, don't cha think?

Well my friend, thanx again for lookin out for me. I'm set now. Any feedback from you is always welcome. I hope asking you to dig out those stories ain't asking too much. I'll bet they're packed away in a box somewhere. Take care.

Sincerely, your friend,
Walt.

****

March 14, 2011

Dear Liz;

Hey you! I've been meaning to write, and answering your letter has been on my mind but I've taken on an additional project. My "war" wounds have healed and my ribs don't hurt anymore, unless I turn quickly the wrong way. This dorm isn't violent. It's loud and in my opinion, disrespectful. But no one is fighting the old dudes.

I'm trying to get out of here. (My new project.) This facility is a warehouse for new boots (new inmates) and it seems guys back from bench warrant. Normally if you're gone over 90 days you have to be reclassified and put through the "intake" diagnostic program. If you hadn't been gone that long you normally went back to your original unit. This didn't happen with me, maybe because of my injuries. In any event, I don't like it here more than I didn't like Ellis unit. So, I'm on a mission. I miss Spike and Ronald too. I may not go back to Ellis unit but I will go somewhere, hopefully soon.

My legal status does not involve David "hood ornament" Haynes anymore. He no longer represents me. I am back in the Federal courts where I've always believed I'd get relief from this bogus conviction. I'd hoped I'd get it from the State courts but that wasn't the case. All they did was drag their feet for two years and then sidestepped the issues. The Federal court seems to take an average of four months to do anything. I was granted leave to attack what's called a "Brady Violation" in the State court. ("Brady Violation, if proven, is the equivalent of a constitutional violation and the only remedy is a reversal. I have and will again prove this in my case) At that time the Federal magistrate closed my Federal petition for habeas corpus and pretty much said to the State courts, "You take care of this or I will." That's a good thing BUT I've had to petition the court to reopen my case. I've been pestering them for three months to hear the case. The clerk in the court wrote and explained my suit "ain't even open yet." (It is now, but then it wasn't) I received word the other day in a formal "order" that my case is now on the active docket, so four more months puts me in the middle of July. *Shit!*, but thanx to you and my dad I have enough money saved for a brand new fan and radio when I leave here.

Baseball season starts in two weeks; I hope I'm back in Ellis by then. I can get back out to the bus barn and get back to my usual program. In the meantime, I'm going to put forth an effort to get some solid writing done.

I've also been trying to draw your smiling face. I hate doing portraits and hope these two attempts are better than the last time when your son drew you. I feel like you look better than I could ever draw and that may be because I'm bias and think highly of you. Here ya go anyway. What do ya think? *(Note: they were or are good but I don't like pictures of me anyway.)*

I have a question concerning your warthog character in Giraffalo, what name would you have him? Would he be gruff, lovable or surly? Not a villain. Could he be an adoptive uncle to Giraffalo? Let me know.

Gotta go. Write when you can, Take care.

Your friend,
Walt.

****

March 25, 2011

Dear Liz;

Friday I got the Bud's catalog and the calendar, thanks. Some people want to order. I've been telling them to have their folk's do it via the internet. They scratch their heads and say, "wuss that?" So I run down how to tell their folks about them "new fangled talking TV's" Some already know about computers. This one feller had got his computer to upgrade his business when he was out. He raised chickens. This also got him thrown in prison.

I should explain. His name is Chuk (spelled just like that) His business was "Chuks Chikins." Chuk's okay. He's your typical Texican. He out thought himself was all. Common mistake when you're not used to thinking. Anyway, Chuk's neighbor, who was also a customer, asked him if he could figure out a way to raise a three legged chicken. (This neighbor's name was Roy) Now Roy had a wife who liked the drumstick. Roy liked the drumstick and Roy's boy, Roy Jr. also liked the drumstick. Trouble is, chickens only got two legs and three don't go into two to good. So Roy asked Chuk to see what he could do. Chuk did it too! I don't know how but Chuk started raising three legged chickens. You'd think that was a good thing, but Roy and Chuk couldn't catch them chickens. They were real fast! The picture I saw was a blur but you could make out nine legs on three chickens. They were too fast to trap. You could'nt coax them with food, and they would tease the dogs.

Well, Roy and Chuk decided to shoot the little peckers. Only thing was when they took aim at the chickens, there was a funeral procession for the Sheriffs "Aunt Iola" behind the chickens and they ended up shooting at the funeral procession. So Chuk's here and so is Roy. To date no one's caught one of them three legged chickens.

Well I hadda put this down for a day. It's now the weekend, no biggy. Someone stole my boot last night. We're issued State boots so it ain't like I'm "out" anything. I wonder what kind of an idiot needs three boots...maybe someone stole someone else's boot and this is how they replace the missing boot? I got mine back or one like it. I'm a little different in my methods though. Since everyone likes to sleep-in (I'm an early riser) I got up at 6:30 am and stood upon my bunk and gave the loudest Johnny Weissmuller Tarzan yell I could muster, dragging it out as long as I could while people (guys) started yelling things like, "Shut the fuck up", "Hey are you crazy?" or "Shed-up!" etc, etc. all the while throwing whatever is handy...boots! I had a pile of boots to choose from. It's thinking like that that will win my case. Speaking of which, I wish they'd hurry up. I'm just waiting on the Federal Magistrate. He usually takes about four months to do anything. It's been one month since he officially opened the case.

I'm glad to hear Miss Em's doing so well. Are you going to get her a lot of noise making toys? Kind of "punish your kids." It's your right you know Grandma. Drums and police cars with loud sirens. Yeah she's a little "loidy" but what can ya get a little loidy that makes a lot of noise at 5:30 am? Do they make Barbie's mother? It comes in a plain box and all it's got on the outside of it is "Bitch". Maybe Barbie's mother-in-law. Was Barbie ever married to Ken or anyone else? I know they had a "Ken" doll. My sister's had all that stuff. I had "witch hunts" and such as a boy. I burned a few Barbie's at the stake when I was a wee lad.

It's heating up around here, almost 90 degrees yesterday. You guys should be getting some flowers in your garden pretty soon. Have you seen Lucy (your Praying Mantis) lately?

Anyway I'm gonna go. I got the stories you sent and am hard at work on Giraffalo. I'm pestering my niece Desiree for publishers' addresses. She's going to college to be an "editor" so she should have this info. At any rate, we'll see if we can't breathe some life into Giraffalo. The lead bull is "Bruno" now, not Spike. "Spike's" gonna have to be something else. Something a little less serious. I miss Spike. Gotta go now. Y'all take care.

Sincerely,
Walt.

PS: Thank you so much for the calendar and catalog. I really, really like the old west theme. I wish there were more Indian stuff, but all-in-all I like the old west stuff.

Thankee kindly.

****

April 24, 2011 Easter Sunday

Hi Liz!

It's me! I know you knew but I wanted some kind of entro. "It's me!" is the best I was gonna come up with on a Sunday morning. I've been meaning to write back but got busy.

I've been at the Federal courts again. They don't answer very often so I have to practice "due diligence" claim. Remember? Well to better understand what a Brady claim is you can go to yer talking TV and Google "Brady v. Maryland." It will show you a legal case that was from 1963 (at least). Back then they arrested some guy named Brady and stomped all over his constitutional rights. He litigated his crap all the way to the U.S. Supreme Court who granted his claims. Any such claims that are similar are called "Brady Claims" and might as well be law's because they pertain to our Constitution.

Many of these Constitutional rights fell over from England. None more important than the habeas corpus which is what I am under. Now, Brady had a trial in which evidence favorable to Brady was withheld during his trial. Evidence that could have changed the jury's whole outlook on the situation that Brady was convicted on. The very same thing happened in my trial. I've proven it but the State courts are ignoring the fact that they screwed the pooch on this one and refuse to even look at my proof. That's crazy but it's true. It also renders my trial unconstitutional and under Federal Law the only way to fix it is to reverse the conviction and send me back for more of the same. I've got a good eight years of law library studying under my belt now and when I do go back I won't be so naive. I've had two trials and doubt a third one will even happen, so...

Say, while you're Googling stuff try "Turtle Books." I sent them a letter about Giraffalo and other such stories. I ain't heard back, yet, but it's early so keep your eyes, oops I meant fingers crossed.

How was your Easter? Did ya get to spend time with that baby? Ain't it time to get her some drums, whistles or noise makers? Tee hee. Imagine mom and dad's expression when a big ole box from grandma arrives with whistles, horns, drums, sling shots, B-B guns and fire arms etc arrive. Of course she'll be pampered real quick while one of them hustle off the box of goodies...Maybe its better I'm not out there. My sister's kids need an uncle with a sense of humor. Imagine coming home with tattoos (removable of course, but the initial shock...)

Thanks for the internet pictures. I laughed hardest at that fat Giraffe that was funny.

I guess I've been cleared medically, for light duty. Ribs take a while to heal. I've been put in the laundry and moved to another dorm. The new bunk is right by the TV (noise ass stinkin TV) but also by the fan. So I can't have my fan or even buy one, the community fan hanging from the ceiling is the next best thing. My last bunk in "C" dorm, I could see the fan, I could hear the fan, but I couldn't feel its wind. Over here I have a good bunk for the fan. Thank God. I only hope the Feds hurry up though.

Well I gotta go. I think I got you a few customers coming from the internet, should be soon. Y'all take care.

Your friend,
Walt.

****

May 2011

Dear Liz;

I missed yer freakin birthday!?! Son of a *!*&! now, see if Spike were here...no, Ronnald was better at remembering things like that. I'm so sorry. Heavy sigh.

I'm so sorry to hear about your dog. We should all be so fortunate to have lived the life Daisy did. She looks beautiful and happy in the picture. I can't tell you how I'd like to be sitting where she's standing in the picture, beside that lil creek. I'll bet cha I'd still be there when it got dark. Then I'd probably freeze my ass off trying to find my way out of the woods, maybe even fall in the creek. If I remember correctly it gets cold at night and very dark there. I'd have to bring a flash light and a guitar and a joint and a box of Cheese crackers. I guess you could drink the creek water, Pepsi would be nice though. I'm not much of an alcoholic drinker, I'd get lost too easy. Anyway, thanx for the pictures.

I'm reading Edgar Cayce who makes a good argument for reincarnation. But also why things happen as they do. It's very interesting. His biography "There is a River" or "The Sleeping Prophet" is also very interesting. If you're interested, it will give you an idea of how much man has re-arranged history to suit his own needs. It's all part of living.

Sorry I missed your birthday Elizabeth Willoughby. Are you impressed I remembered your "royal" name? I can't believe they ain't offered you to become an American Citizen. When they do, my opinion of this country will improve, until then…?

I'm rebelling!! I can't really make a stand in here due to the fact that no one will care and if they get tired of my crap, throw me in the hole. There's spiders in the hole, big hairy hellish lookin things. They carry knives too. So for lack of a better way to put it, fuck that!!

A cold front from Canada you say. It's already 90 freakin degrees down here in hell – I mean Texas. Open a bag of potato chips and they wilt before you get them to your mouth. (Humidity)… Oh "Crisps, that right? Potato chips are Crisps, blimey!

I was happy to get your letter, thanx. I've put in a legal argument to the Dept. of Corrections committee stating that this legal library isn't equipped to handle my legal needs; therefore I demand to be moved to another unit with a better law library. I'm tired of this place. My new bunk now gets no air. They have maneuvered the fans around for better circulation which disrupts the air flow I was getting. Yeah, I know, bitch, bitch, bitch. Actually all they did was add another fan which redirects the air, so…see ya! It should get me moved. Maybe back to Ellis Unit, we'll see.

DAMN! I can't believe I missed your birthday! Well had I drawn you something you couldn't really keep it. I should draw you another card anyway. I can't do it now because it's Thursday and

I want this in the mail and leave here Friday. Maybe over the weekend. I don't know what a late birthday card looks like; when I find out I'll send it to you.

I liked reading about Miss Em calling you. That was pretty cool. I'll bet it brightened your day. It did mine, thanx for sharing. Speaking of, I don't hear from Spike or Ronald but I'm hoping my legal razzle dazzle will put me back over there with them.

The Houston Astros are in last place! And I miss messing around on the computer at the bus barn where I worked. I don't get to hear no music here. I still have not spent the money for the fan. I'll have to hustle up a radio but I can do that. If I can get back into the office I'll have access to a whole slew of music on secret hard drives stashed in cleaver places. (Hogan's Hero's thing) In the meantime, I don't watch much TV. I can hear it because it's three feet from my bunk and from 9:30 am till 10:30 pm it's at top volume. I've learned to tune it out. Otherwise my days are spent putting up clothes in the laundry (ribs are better, no pain) and reading. Oh I've been doing okay with drawing cards and providing my necessities, coffee, cookies, hygiene, stamps etc. They have stopped feeding us three meals a day over the weekend. And during the week we get a sack lunch for several meals. Budget cuts. I ain't starving.

I'm still waiting on the Federal courts; soon...next month puts us at half of 2011! It also commemorates my 10th year spent in captivity for something I didn't do. Maybe the courts will take that into consideration and get off their butts! Let's hope.

Well I'm gonna go for now. Take care and thanx again for the pictures and letter. I hope all is well there with you and the family. Be good and all that. Have fun in Bakersfield. I'd say "Hi" to Buck Owens while you're there, but he's dead, so...do you even remember him or have you listened to Buck Owens? Hee Haw? That may not have been your genre of entertainment. *(Note: Actually I watched it every week)* I, however, was very diverse in my music appreciation as a young man. Still am. Not so much the new stuff though.

Take care, your friend,
Walt.

****

June 9, 2011

Dear Liz;

Hi you. Today marks exactly 10 years I've been locked up on this crap charge. My address has changed again to Eastham Unit, 2665 Prison Rd #1, Lovelady Tx 75851. This prison is a notorious Texas prison. Google it. I'm sure you'll find some American history that will raise some eye brows.

I've been meaning to write, but have been preoccupied. I recently found out that medical, at the Gurney unit has taken $6.00 out of my account for a co-payment program. That cuts into my "fan fund" I had saved. This unit is not a transfer facility so fans and radios are allowed and available through the prison commissary. When I went to order my new fan they told me I was short. I put in to find out why and was told that medical has booked my account for co-payment. I've put in a grievance but...anyway, yesterday the heat index was 102 degrees. I'm not on the 3rd tier any more. I was when I got here. In an orientation wing, 3rd tier, no fan, miserable! I survived. I'm on the 2nd tier in a wing that's 80% black and chaos reigns.

"They" say it's always darkest before the dawn. It seems to be the norm in my life. I'm trolling along and just before things get better they get worse. I don't know how they can get any worse than they are now...That's not exactly true. I have a white cell mate. That's probably God looking out for me. My new celli is a religious fanatic but manageable. I'm doing the best I can and am hangin in there best I can. Lovelady Texas is about 30 miles from Huntsville so maybe I can get Spike over here. Why he'd wanna come to this dungeon I don't know. Maybe for a visit, he wouldn't have to stay.

I hope you are doing well and all that. Life goes on. Perhaps that Federal Magistrate will take note and hear my case. Really, that's all I'm waiting on. I believe that "oral arguments" will be the next step. Either that or he could just recommend a reversal, that's all he'll do. When he makes his recommendations, a bonifide Federal Judge will co-sign and that's that. "Unless" he recommends to dismiss which I can't fathom. The law says...Brady Violation = Reversal. And I have proved my case. Heavy sigh.

I'm learning where to go and where not to go in this prison. I'm hoping to not be here long. But history will attest to not knowing what's really going on. Remember a few years ago, me believing this is my year. How many years have I been saying that? Jeese! Enough about that.

How's spring and summer in the mountains? Wish I were there. I will be one day. I'll come there for a visit and hopefully stay. But I don't know where I'll end up living. Hopefully with a settlement from Texas I can buy my own little place. That would be a blessing.

So, I'm gonna go. I got this little card for you, I understand why you really can't keep these things, but I hope you get it. You'll figure it out. Take care and I'll look for ya in the mail.

Respectfully, your friend,
Walt.
Hope ya like the card anyway.

****

July 3, 2011

Dearest Liz;

Me thinks you underestimate your worth to me as a friend. You claim you wish there was something you could do to help me in my quest for freedom. (Not in them words but close) Your letters and pictures sent just because you consider me a friend is and has been enough when all other winds in my sails have died down to keep me going. I am blessed to have a friend such as you and truly appreciate you, so, accept it and shut the fuck up about it.

If you get curious about where my case is in the courts, I'm pretty sure you can boot up yer talking computer TV thingy and search for, US Eastern District Court…wait let me get you the address with the official wording. You want the Docket schedule. Look for Anderson (that's me) v. Director of Corrections Civil Action, No. 4:06 CV 204.

When my case works its way to the top of this Docket then and only then will these slow ass bastards (legal term) hear my claim. I should, in all likelihood, actually receive what's called "Relief" from this conviction and either be remanded back to Fannin County for further prosecution, (which I highly doubt, they have one more chance at another trial and legally they are at a disadvantage) besides if they chose to try me again and loooose? It would be the same as giving me the keys to the town of Bonham) Anyway, I'm thinking I'm close to the top of that list, if you look that up let me know how far away I am from the top. The only other option they have is to just let me go. I'd have to stay in Texas until I work out some sort of compensation for over 10 freaking years of wrongful conviction. Then I'm travelin. I will be in contact with yew and truly am lookin forward to meeting you. Even if it's only briefly at Bud Plant. But I'd get to email you under the guise of an email Non de Plume.

Oh to change the subject, I got a fan! I wrote my dad and asked him to send me $10.00. I still owe Federal filing fees and they still take 20% of all incoming money and I had saved enough to buy a fan but the damn Medical Dept. had taken a co-payment fee for something they shouldn't have. Anyway, when I explained the problem to him he sent the money and a week after I wrote him I got a fan. You'll be happy to know that now I ain't gonna die of heat exhaustion.

This prison seems to be punishment for some reason. It's a notorious shit hole that's been around a long time and has housed Clyde Barrow of Bonnie and Clyde fame. I think I told you all that. Anyway, it's been my experience through life that things get worse just before they get better, so I'm due.

Oh that court is "United States District Court Eastern District of Texas." Search that and if they want more info, put in "Sherman Division" that and my civil action number, already given, 4:06 CV 204.

Anyways, how are things in your garden? Is Nathan keeping the bug population down? Do you still have Lucy Praying Mantis hangin around? Spike's in the Rocky Mountains. He's due to arrive back here in August when it cools down. Ronnald sent word on Spike's whereabouts through some derelict that wandered into my cell block the other day.

I live in a cell next to a tattoo artist who, for the use of a radio, has me drawing tattoo patterns for him. It's a livin. I lost all my little card pictures and art crap when I went out on a bench warrant. But I did save all my photos through a Baptist minister friend. I know, that's old news. I did have to choose which pictures to lose or keep. I chose my photos. Duh, huh? So if you spy any really cool pictures of things like dragons and things of that nature, cowboy art and / or gladiator stuff, keep me in mind. One of the things I also saved was a couple of birthday cards. One that you sent with the "Warmest Fuzzy that ever Wuzzy" Some stupid little kitten that's so cute.

Anyway, I'm makin it here. I've been outside several times and have been sun burnt to the point of…well never mind. Sometimes words escape me. Man, there's a first!

Well friend, I'm gonna close for now. Take care and thanx for the picture of the frog. I have a frog tattoo on my right arm. I got it when I was 19. I don't have 1000 tattoos but I have a few. I've never thought to truly conform and get "sleeved." I dare to be different, know what I mean jellybean?

Okay, see ya. Yer biggest friend,
Walt

****

August 10, 2011

Dear Liz;

Hi you! How are things? I hope everything's roses. Thanx so much for the photo of you and Miss Em. She's getting bigger and you're getting smaller. Perhaps it only seems that way because she's getting bigger.

Still no word from Spike. I don't think he wants to come home. I don't blame him. This is an ugly place. Too ugly for any friend of mine. It's a good thing I'm big and seasoned. I know when to shut the hell up and move on when necessary. I really thought August would be the month they finally decide my case. Maybe they will. I wrote to the court and asked for a copy of the docket to see where I am on the list.

My old dad seems to be fading. I get a post-it size note from time to time and I can't make out most of it, but at least he scribbles. My niece quit writing. Probably because she's busy with her career and family. Other than yeew and my dad I don't hear from no one. I ain't whining, just sayin. Seems I could have answered your letter a little sooner then huh? Well, I really have this feeling that something monumental is about to happen and wanted to write with some good news. It ain't gone down yet so...when it does you'll be top of the list to let know.

It's still hot, but at the end of this month it starts cooling off. This was a bad summer. I'd love to be by one of those crystal clear California rivers, soakin up some...river.

I went to the library and found another Tim Dorsey book. I remember you didn't much care for "Stingray Shuffle," but I laughed and was entertained. I read "Shutter Island" and was impressed with the story and the way the author brought it all together. Have you seen the movie with Leonardo de Caprio? If not, it's a really good book. Anyway, I enjoyed this other Tim Dorsey book. Not much different than the one you read and didn't like, so I'm not recommending it to you.

I've been drawing tattoo patterns for the Mexicans. It keeps me in coffee and stamps etc.

Say, what's going on in England? I heard on my radio they're rioting and raising hell. It's not over soccer is it? The radio stations in this area aren't big on news but they did say that some chickens were spotted doing well over the posted speed limit in several West Texas towns. Causing accidents and problems for the local dog population. The dogs can't catch em. It appears the chickens have three legs! Remember "Chuks Chikins"? It was all fun and games till some farmers dog runs himself to death trying to catch a three legged chicken.

Once in a while I can tune in the BBC at 7am and listen to that news. It's not all the way from England, its broadcast over a public radio station that only comes in early in the morning. Anyway I was just wondering what all the rioting in London is all about. It sounds serious. I don't like riots. I don't condone that sort of behavior at all. Let's talk baseball...*(Note: he drew a funny face and a bat and ball)*

Now you've heard me talk about the Houston Astros. It's the only games I could get on the radio so sometime after I started writing to you (four score and 80 some years ago) I started listening to Astros's Baseball games on the radio. I'm still listening and they stink!! They have the worst record in baseball. (Period) Anyway, they're on as I write this letter. They're in Arizona playing the Diamondbacks. They've scored 9 stinkin runs and still lost. 9 runs is amazing but they still lost. Arizona has a chance to take the lead from the World Champion San Francisco Giants (in the National League West) Okay enough about that.

How's your flower garden? Are you growing this year? Nothing grows out here. We're in a desolate part of Texas. Grass for cows, cow shit for mushrooms and flies. Lots of flies. I've had, as well as most of the inmates, a heat rash since June. Sometimes it feels like I'm wearing a fiberglass shirt. Icky! In a couple more weeks it should taper off. All the little birds are either gone or have burnt to death from the heat. Maybe that's why the flies are all around. The flies have a reflective type of skin and don't seem to be affected by the heat. I might be in hell and don't know it.

Well I really feel like August is my month. I did my figuring and figure August 19th is like a deadline. Don't know why. Perhaps I'm an idiot savant, who knows. *(Note: He's my idiot savant, now.)*

I have an opportunity to make $50.00 if I can draw 50's type vintage pin-up girls. Do you have anything like that in that stash of yours? I only know of "Gil Elvgren" or "Bunny Yeager" or "Betty Page" or George Petty" or "Alberto Vargas" and I know there are more names even earlier. None, (that I know of) were nude. If there's anything on your computer on those guys and want to send me pictures, they can even be in black and white, I'd appreciate it. If I can get some material on this stuff I can probably do one illustration board and get more customers based on what I produce in the first one. The guy who said he'd give me $50.00 for a drawing like that, (for his Dad's birthday) spends a lot of $$ on prison art and I believe I can sell him on it because I have a unique style as well as a different taste. Most of these prison artists are just that, prison artists who glorify prison and that life style. Not me. I'm different, as you well know. Listen friend, if I ever ask something of you that's impossible, out of the question or ya just don't wanna do it, that's okay too. I've been making my money lately. A couple of stamps here, a couple of stamps there and would like to get ahead a little and believe that "jon-ra" (30's, 40's, 50's pin-up girls) will be a hit, unique! I got no material. Do you have anything? *(Note: I sent him some pin-ups and told him I'd spoken to Betty Page on the phone a few years ago when she called Bud Plants.)*

Well friend, I'm gonna go. First news I hear I'll write. Keep me in your prayers.

Walt.

****

August 25, 2011

Dear Liz;

This is a trail of my Federal Writ. I've made some comments and aside from all that you can see how far I've come. *(Note: He sent the legal paperwork of the Fed. Writ.)* Bottom line is I'm still waiting. I don't know where I am on the docket. I thought it was a four month wait; I've been waiting six months since they re-opened the case. Anyday, I hope. In the meantime I must keep busy. I wanna get some of those pin-up girl boards done. I lost so much crap on this last bench warrant hearing.

I drew ya a card. It's sweet and I'm sure I've never sent it before. I liked the picture. Please believe me, I ain't makin a move on a married women. I ain't sayin you ain't worth a shot. I'm sayin I respect you and our situation. I treasure our friendship and look forward to meeting you one day and telling you in person. I may be a few french fries short of a happy meal but I am grounded pretty good. It's just a card, I hope you like it.

It's Thursday and I'm trying to get this out before the weekend. I asked for any material on the vintage pinup-girls of the 20's, 30's, 40's or 50's. I drew some vintage bathing beauties and a couple of these "high rollers" (inmates) went gaga over the style of art. I'm thinking any help in this area would do two things to make my time easier here. #1: It would fill my locker with food I don't normally get for chow and things I need, hygiene etc, Instead of drawing cards like the one I sent you, for a few stamps, I can make a lump of commissary for a board. And #2: It would keep me busy. Every night I look for a mail room pass (for legal mail) and am disappointed. I think about it all the time because according to the law I'M RIGHT! And I honestly believe that this next decision from the courts will be for me. In the meantime, I'm stuck in a very bad prison and I'm doing all I can to stay out of the way. I ain't nowhere close to giving up. I'm looking forward to the day when I can give this stupid assed conviction back. I've worked hard for it. As you can see from the reverse side of this letter. Those pages are not important to me by the way; don't worry about keeping them on my account. I don't need them.

I've thought about how I might meet you later on in the future. I would probably contact Bud Plant (and I pray everyday for their prosperity) and have them call you. We would meet, shake hands or salute, which ever. We could sit and talk in an English accent. "Ere now!" You could introduce me to your family as your idiot cousin. My English accent would be convincing. I can see it now. Someone see's me walking up and says, "Who's this coming?", "Oh that's my idiot cousin Nigel from England, and I hired him to pickup dog shit in the yard". All of a sudden someone would yell out the window, "Hey, what the hell are you doing?" My response would be, in a Cockney accent of course, "oim pickin up the poo then" Then I'd look down at an enormous pile in front of me (I know you have big dogs), "This eres a real corker it is?" Then you'd say, "That is not a corker, you bloody fool, that's a Rattle Snake and you'd better move your Limey Arse away from it before it bites you" "Blimey!" I'd say, "Ee all most bit me wonker, wot?" First of all I probably ain't never gonna meet your family, this I understand and am only yucking it up.

I just read Ken Follett's first book in a three book series called, "The Fall of Giants" It's about England just before and during the First World War. A lot of history, which I'm partial to. If I were English, I'd hope not to be name Nigel or Tristan or anything like that. King George the 5th was runnin around at that time. I've never known England under a king. Was George V the last king of England? I did learn that "Big Ben" was actually the bell not the clock.

Say, if you have a good clear picture of Miss Em's little face and a good clear picture of your face, close up and "not" smiling, I could draw the two of you together. I would give you my best work. This is called a "bribe" for some of that vintage art crap. I'd do it anyway but I'm sorta desperate. I'd return the photos; I'm going nuts here for something to do. It's about to start cooling down so I can go outside and work out soon. It's supposed to be 108 degrees tomorrow but only 78 at night instead of 86. You take your blessings when and where ya can.

How are you Liz? I haven't heard from my niece Desiree since the first part of June, she must be really busy with her life.

Oh, I just thought of something...no that was someone yelling. Let's see, what's new around here? Nothin, what's new around there?

Okay, I'm through beggin. I hope I didn't over do it. Please think about the drawing and shoot me a couple of photos of you and Miss Em to draw. Why a picture of you without a smile, you ask? Because you're always smiling, which is great, but I can't see your eyes properly. My favorite picture of you is you at work, feet up on your desk with your hands clasped behind your head and smiling, real big. Anyway I gotta go. If this task with the vintage pinup girls is too much, don't worry about it; just send the other photos of you and Miss Em anyway. I hope you like the card. I copied Norman Rockwell to do it. Pretty cool huh? (Note: *That card and subsequent bigger drawing are on my wall*) Bye for now.

Respectfully,
Walt

PS: I believe the "gavel thingy" (action #31) represents what's to be ruled upon next. Everything else is litigated. That particular bit of litigation is "the final question" Everything is in there can only be one decision that would not be a judgment. That's a call for oral arguments. Which means the court would appoint another "hood ornament" and after he familiarizes himself with the "facts" I'd be bench warranted back to a Federal court for another hearing. I'd probably refuse the hood ornament and ague it myself. Stupid? Maybe but I'm tired of my fate being in other peoples hands. Know what I mean? (Note: *I cannot find that legal info. He sent, but I do remember it.*)

****

September 10, 2011

Hello Liz;

I got your letter yesterday evening. I was gonna write tomorrow (Sunday) during a radio show that comes on an alternative rock station called "Lost and Found" by some D.J. named Dr. Luke. He's one of your home boys. Tonight the local Country station (if they're not airing Pee Wee football) will play "Cruzen Saturday Night" The 2nd Saturday of the month they play three hours of old rock and roll. (50's, 60's) I look forward to this program as well. Last month, for whatever reason, they didn't air and gave no explanation. I would have written to em but don't have the stamps to waste.

Did you get the letter written on the back of those court papers? With the Norman Rockwell card? I ask because in this just received letter you didn't mention anything. You did ask if I'd heard from the courts when I do hear from the courts it will be a "recommendation" by the magistrate and I'll have about 30 days to wait on the judge to rule by agreeing with the magistrate or doing something else. It gives me a chance, as well as the Attorney General for the State, to object to the recommendations if we don't like em. One of us ain't gonna like what the magistrate has to recommend. Let's hope it's the Attorney Generals office.

The TV room here in Eastham is half the size as Ellis Unit for the same amount of people. So they're often crowded, noisy and uncomfortable due to the people who have staked a claim on certain benches. It's a trap. I've been down there and "studded up" to let em know I ain't scared. But to be honest I'd rather go outside. The recreation yard is bigger than Ellis and that's where I usually end up.

You mentioned a Betty Page calendar; you also said that none of the pictures are nude. Actually I didn't want nude. If I drew nude they wouldn't let me mail em out. Betty Page, as well as Bunny Yeager, were two legendary pinups. Betty Page is a real person, beautiful too. Duh, huh? See, you can learn a lot from a dummy. If you truly don't mind tearing up that calendar I could use the pictures to make illustration boards and maybe sell em in here. That one guy has kinda lost interest but once I get a board done…

If I was to draw you one of the boards the rules here have changed. I couldn't mail it to Bud Plant because they're not on my "approved mailing" list. It would have to go to your street address, which is on my list. I could write ahead of time and tell ya I'm mailing it on "X" day and you could be ready five days later to pick it up at your mailbox.

So that's a big *"Yes"* on the Betty Page calendar. Send her sexiest and provocative pictures first. Is that the right word? In exchange for a bag of coffee, I have to draw Freddy Kruger for somebody's tattoo pattern. That's my other task for this evening.

I wanted to write you first. Priorities. Actually I've been feeling like shit lately and took stock of all the people I thought I could write to and feel like I had a friend. After careful consideration, your "it". Have you ever been "It?" Everybody's been "it" at sometime. When I was a lil boy I was "it" so often we all stopped asking, "Okay, who's it?"

Anyway I need to stay busy. I've researched and filed everything legal that needs researching and filing. I only work three days a week, from 5am to 11am (6 hours) the rest of that is spent knowing Any Day...Heavy sigh.

Oooh "Sea Cruise" Old Man Rhythm is in my shoes...good song. I don't know who sings it. There's a lot of "one hit wonders" back then. I don't think that guy was a one hit wonder. I just can't remember his name.I'm gonna go for real now. Oh yeah, Dennis LeHane "Shutter Island," I hope you get to read it.

Then tell me whether or not I've restored your faith in me to pick a good book. "Shutter Island" ain't nothing like "Stingray Shuffle", the one you didn't care for.

On that note, the Beach boys are playing so I'll leave you. Take care.

Your friend,
Walt.

****

September 25, 2011

Howdy Liz;

Look who dropped in to see me, Spike and Sherry. He's right here and sends his warmest regards. Not his exact words but I ain't repeatin what he said. Should I break one of his legs? I'd have to do it when Sherry ain't lookin. Anyway, he is a Roach.

I got your letter dated 9-16 last Friday. I started the enclosed picture on Friday, I hope you like it. *(Note: It's a beautiful drawing of Emily which hangs on my wall)*

You mentioned in your letter that you didn't know how you'd introduce me to your family. I was always under the impression this was something that would never happen. I always thought I'd go to Bud's and give you a call from there and you'd come there, give each other a hug, exchange email addresses and I'd ride off into the sunset. I'm as anxious to keep you from having any problems over me as you are. You've been a wonderful friend and as your friend I'd feel like shit if you and your family had a falling out over my stupid butt

I hope you really like the picture of Miss Em. You know I'm an art whore and you've given me so much stuff to draw over the years. And that ain't the only reason I write you. I'm just sayin, in my mind, this is a good thing for both of us. The last Spectrum book you sent (years ago) was originally denied. But, when I appealed to the Directors Review Committee, it was given to me. I lost Spectrum three, eight and 11. Those were my favorites along with Mucha (someone liked it better than me), Franklin Booth and the Black and White Frazetta. Testament (by Frazetta) was okay but I bet his best was in Icon. I never seen that one but had Testament for while. I truly hope this drawing makes you happy. I tried my best and have an idea for a caption. "All the boys think she's a spy...she's got Betty Davis eyes" Sherry said she's never laid eyes on a more "beautiful child" That's good because Sherry has eight eyes.

You asked me about what new calendar I'd like for next year, God I hope I'm not here for another calendar year.

The weather has changed here too. Its 98 degrees today. Hey that's fall weather for Texas. Southwest Texas. My fans on but not blowing hot air.

It's killing me to have to bend this picture. Ya know my pen started puking ink, note the upper right hand corner of the picture, while scribbling in her hair. Bad thing. The pen I'm writing with don't look too bad. There's a point where I feel like I'm gonna shade it too much. Anyway, had you got your camera to work your wonderful happy mug would have been in it too.

I wasn't making fun of the British names in a spiteful manner. Nigel is a "fine" name, so is Trevor (Howard, good actor) and about the movie "Elizabeth" with Helen Mirren, I will, at some time, watch it. My grandmother on me Da's side was named Helen. There was a movie called "Elizabeth" with Kate Blanchard, maybe six or seven years ago. Don't know if it's the same Elizabeth, but I'll put your version on my "to see" list.

I'm glad your new dog "Echo" is working out. I've always wanted a Rot and a Jack Russell Terrier. I'm not a big fan of small dogs but I'd like a Jack Russell.

Well my friend, I've got just enough time to get this in the mail. I don't even have time to proof read it. I hope you can figure everything out. I hope everything with you and your family is great. Take care and write back when you can.

Bye for now,
Walt and Spike

****

October 24, 2011

Dear Liz;

I got Casey Kasem's Top 40 on. It's vintage, Oct 1970 and I thought what a better time to "finally" write to my friend. Spike's here, he says, "Hi" Sherry's in the locker lookin smug these days. She saved Spike's little butt the other day from a gang of lizards, but we'll get to that. First... (#37 Yellow River)...(#36 was "Looking out my Back Door", Creedence Clearwater), did you know they never had a #1 hit? "Wow". Anyway I'll be cutting in the notable tune info. I got time, paper and your not going anywhere. Well maybe you are but for the time being yer stuck with me and Spike...and Casey Kasem.

October 31, 1970, where were you on that date?

Okay, the package you sent got denied on Oct. 14, 2011. The reason is it happened to be opened by some stupid freakin asshole with nothing better to do. I've appealed it and hopefully will get the calendars this week. If not I'll send em to my dad and have him turn em around. "They weren't purchased from a business address on the return address" Since they were used you could have sent them direct. Of course we know that wouldn't have been a good idea in case they got returned. But, for some reason, since they weren't new or whatever, they were denied. I'll get them one way or another. I have the name of one of the committee members and wrote yesterday explaining that, #1: Nothing in that package could be considered contraband or inappropriate. #2: The calendars were probably originally purchased from a business and finally, I hope Santa Clause takes presents away from who ever denied these calendars. Maybe washing their own socks will give them something better to do than mess with people who actually try to do things, in such a manner, that would comply with rules that are stupid at best. Happy Halloween! Spike suggested I call her a name I won't give here but it's an "acronym" for can't understand normal thinking.

I thought about doing it but Sherry said I shouldn't. She didn't say why but I'll go with Sherry on this one. Women's intuition, know what I mean? So I'm waiting. I also intend to write this person, Jen Smith, and specifically ask about the books you mentioned. Maybe I can get prior approval. Being Art Books sometimes they allow "some" nude pictures. I'm not sure how it works but...having "prior approval" for the Western Book and maybe Frank Cho (I like his monkey boy); anyway, it seems like a good idea. (Another brain maneuver from our eight legged arachnid premadonna) Spike on the other hand is an asshole, this is a fact. He almost got killed and ate.

Do you remember Ellis Unit had the Huntsville Derby? Like the Kentucky Derby but they ran it across the ceiling of cell block 7. Well, Bonham has "The Fall Lizard Roundup." Lizards are a big thing here. A lot of guys have lizards as pets. They catch flies in the chow hall (or what ever they can catch) to feed these miniature Dinosaurs. These guys buy, sell, trade em and even mate em. These lizards are much pampered.

Well just before the lizards do their hibernate thing the officers allow these lizard collectors to congregate and show off their pets in the south gym. There's four long tables pushed together with white sheets stretched tight over the tops. You'd think it was a runway for super models. Spike wanted to go so we put his Batman cape on and went. Spike rode in my t-shirt pocket, when we got there he jumped out and parked center stage. (Hang on, #32, Hang on Sloopy.) Anyway, there were some pretty respectable little monsters there and at first they didn't know what to think of a three and a half inch Roach wearing a Batman cape. Then it hit em, this isn't a lizard, this is a Double Whopper with cheese!! They all surrounded Spike and just as I started to reach for him Sherry showed up. She dropped down from the rafters. She landed right over Spike. For just a moment there was a circle of lizards surrounding our duo with Sherry standing over Spike. The owners of the lizards still standing around the table, still not comprehending what they were seeing. For a moment it seemed like a Mexican standoff.

The biggest lizard, I think his name was Brutus was owned by the guy standing next to me. Brutus opened his mouth and hissed, spreading his body out and doing his little lizard challenge dance. Sherry lifted her butt and shot a web down his throat, fast as the Sundance Kid. She flicked her rump a couple of times and slammed Brutus once on the left and then on the right. Then she twirled him over her head and flung him 30 feet over the heads of the people standing around.

All this and she's pregnant. This happened in the span of five seconds. The owner of Brutus broke the spell by screaming.

The other lizards turned and broke for the floor. Sherry webbed two and dragged em back across the table. Somebody fainted and some soiled themselves. The 60 others abandoned their critters and broke for the door. I grabbed Spike and headed for the door too. The last I saw of Sherry, she looked like Charlton Heston in Ben Hur as she rode two lizards across the table. We didn't see Sherry for a while. When she came back to the cell she went into the locker and fell asleep. Some guys wanted to do me harm because Sherry either ate or traumatized their lizard pets. I told em I'd send Sherry over while they slept to take their complaints. That shut em up some. Spike however is makin the lizard owners pay a lizard fee if they want to keep lizards on HIS prison line.

I've been busy writing to Senators, newspapers, innocence projects, universities and ANYONE and EVERYONE I can think of to try and get some publicity. I seem to be stuck back at the end of the line in the Federal courts. My case was reopened in February 2011 (it was on that court paper I sent you a while back) so I gotta wait how ever long it takes to get to my petition. In the meantime I'm gonna start writing to people. Texas State Senator John??...let me ask Spike. He says it's John Whitmire. Anyway, I wrote him but ain't heard back. I wrote a couple of newspapers and (don't know why but...) I wrote to that stupid judge that screwed me on the evidentiary hearing I took part in about this time last year. What I should do is write everything down Texas has done to me with no accountability and send it to our good ole President Obama and ask him. "How can you invade other countries because you don't like the way they treat their citizens when here at home...?? That's what I awt to do.

I wanted to cook up a big ole turkey myself this year, but that doesn't look like it'll happen. Pretty soon them judges will be taking the holidays off and that's IT till next year. Heavy sigh.

Meanwhile...me and Spike and Sherry will enjoy the holidays best we can and I'll find some Christmas thing to draw for (#23, Bobby Sherman "Julie, Julie, Julie do ya love me?") you. I'm so glad you liked Emily's picture. I probably could have done better on a board but can't mail a board through to Bud Plant any more.

If you want to send more books let me know the exact name of the book(s) and I'll get prior approval. I'll try to get a repout going with this committee member and maybe I can get some special consideration. Anyway, I'll tell ya this, "it ain't hot here no more!" It ain't Arctic weather like what's going on there, but by God is ain't melting my teeth and torching the sparrows either. Yay! (Happy face).

Ya know? It's funny you mentioned white hair on Spike. Spike's hair ain't white but mine is. Sherry's a red head. Spike ain't got any hair that I can see but mine is just about as white as it can be. Cool huh?

About Sherry's pregnancy, I'm not sure that ball of...whatever she keeps watch over is babies. I think she has..."things" in there where she is. Maybe trophies or prisoners. She won't talk about it and I really ain't gonna pry to much. She's got my fat disgusting waste of a human life celli in line and I'm okay with whatever floats her little boat. She bullies Spike sometimes but NO ONE ELSE DOES. I feel no symphony for him. Tee hee.

Well y'all I'm gonna go. I'll keep ya posted on things. Be it the Directors Review Committee and the calendar saga or the courts. I'm getting the feeling I'll be put on the back burner til 2012. In the meantime I'm gonna keep pestering people until someone takes notice and asks "Why?"

Saturdays I listen to the vintage top 40. Sundays I listen to one of your homeboys from England, the name of the program is "Lost and Found" good music. You can look up his show on lostand-found.com. Anyway I work in the garment factory during the week, that's about it. I go outside sometimes. Sometimes I go to that crowded day-room to watch baseball. But not anymore because baseballs' over. I'm staying out of the way and sometimes, SOMETIMES I sit down and write you, and that's not bad.

Thanks for the nice letter and thanx for the calendars. I'm ever so grateful to Bud Plant for allowing this friendship. (#17, the Partridge Family "I Think I Love You") Was there really a Partridge Family? (#1, Led Zeplin "Immigrant Song") Fucken cool!! Sorry, couldn't resist that. (Smiley face)

Well I'm gonna close. Y'all take care and I'll do the same.

Bye for now,
Walt, Spike, Sherry

****

November 27, 2011

Dear Liz;

Well it's about freakin time huh!?

Hi my friend. Okay let's see what's been going on here. First, Spike and Sherry are at odds. I hate that too because they put me between them. I can't go against Spike because he's my lil Roachster. On the other hand Sherry is big and can web my eyes closed, hide and jump out scaring the ever livin shit out of me, literally. Anyway, it all started over a damn Cheerio. Spike and Sherry are both too good to eat a Cheerio. A plain old Cheerio? Sheeeit, but a doughnut seed? Sheeeeit (Texas slang) I gave Spike a Cheerio and told him it was a doughnut seed and Sherry "yoinked" it. So they are mad at each other. I could give him another but I told him it was the only one. Anyways it's in her stash egg thing. I ain't messing with it.

The yellow piece of paper I sent is a standard denial form. It's the very one used to deny me the calendars. As you can see they gave me NOTHING. Not the computer images you sent from the Chinese Wal-Mart or the lady police officers from around the world. Anyway I wrote that J. Smith at the suggestion of the mailroom lady who yoinked the calendars in the first place. I wrote her three letters before having the denial overturned and finally getting the calendars last week, along with the computer images.

I also asked about the Robert McGinnis book and Frank Cho. She said that is wasn't their policy to deny obvious art because of brief nudity. Sexually explicit art is another matter. She checked the computer for denials on Robert McGinnis and Frank Cho and came up with one on Frank Cho for a book exclusively on nude women. She said she herself probably wouldn't deny a "How to Draw Nude Women," which is what she said this book was and that's on the list, unless it was tasteless. Anyhow, I think I'm developing a rapport with her. She did say had you sent those calendars directly from a residence they probably wouldn't have been held up. But now the books have to be sent from a vendor. So thank you for the calendars. Betty Page is so freakin pretty. She has a smile that when genuine, and I think I can tell which one's are for the camera and which one's the camera caught, is truly a blessing to behold. Every picture I have of you has you smiling with a smile that is contagious. Different than Betty's but definitely unique and hard as hell to draw. I've tried. She, Betty, was photographed before the air brush technique.

Anyway, you asked for a Christmas scene and I'm sending it with this letter. I drew two original pictures this year; one was a Rose in front of a Celtic cross and this picture of Santa. Would you like a nice rendition of the Rose and Cross? I'll do the Rose in red ink if you want. Let me know, it's not too big, but it is an original. *(Note: It is beautiful.)*

I'm sending another Santa to Senator John Whitmire with an ultimatum that if he doesn't help me get some action...I'm gonna tell him Santa owes me and I'm gonna call in that favor. I've asked him to call the Federal Magistrate and light a fire under his butt to hear my petition for writ of habeas corpus. Now!! Can you imagine the little Whitmire's when they get all excited hearing Santa on the roof and then...EEEEW, what's that in the fire place? Yuck. I'll do too! Spike's idea. He pointed out that my ideas ain't been working so...he's got a point.

So how are you? I hope all is well. Casey Kasim did 1978 last week. I listened til I couldn't listen anymore. Today was Nov. 27, 1971. I liked most of the pre-disco-prefunkadelic. Even though the #1 song was the theme from "Shaft." It was a good song. It was funky but tastefully done. Anyway Cher was #2 down from #1, "Gypsy's, Tramps and Thieves" #3 was Bread "Baby I'm a Want You". Sonny and Cher had another hit in there and of course the usual from that time, Michael Jackson, Neil Diamond, The Osmond's etc, etc. WARNING! WARNING! beware profanity ahead but necessary, you'll see...That stupid-fuckin song that got stuck in everybody's head is now implanted back in my frontal lobe and because I'm your very good friend I'm gonna share. You should skip this next part. (Note: with musical notes written on the page) "I'd like to teach the World to sing in perfect harmony, I'd like to buy the World a home and keep it company..."Tee hee. Casey said it was a Coke commercial jingle first. I'd bet it was the other way around. I remember the Coke commercials but always thought it was a pop song first. I'm so stooped. How can you stand to be seen with me? Oh yeah, you're not.

Well, with the holidays upon us, I'm resolved to the fact I ain't goin no where this year. Heavy sigh. And I landed in one messed up prison too. I must have been one bad assed dude in my last life. I've really gotta be workin off some bad Karma. I know I ain't been this bad in this life. I wasn't any nastier than any other nasty little boy. Another heavy sigh.

I've been going outside, when not working, and walking the track and wracking my pea sized brain trying to figure a way past this delay-delay-delay shit. I try staying busy. I don't have no more boards. (I'll get some). This Santa card pattern will probably get me three stamps per card

I draw so...Every stamp has a street value of .35. I go on a card drawing trip and build up a stash, I'll be okay. I'll be a human Xerox machine. Thank God I have the snap to do that. It's a hustle that will keep me busy. I ain't complainin. In fact I'm really not depressed or anything, I'm "just" here.

I hope Thanksgiving was not too stressful for you, I know all that you do every year. And I bet everything I own that this letter passes (in the mail) from one from you. I waited on this last week, in case you wrote but can't wait no more.

I'll get a board and draw one of these pictures with a real cool border and it will probably be sold before it's done. That old dude commissioned some bean eatin Mexican to draw him a picture that will pale compared to one I'll be drawing. Spike's here and Sherry is too, I'm gonna finish weathering out this storm. Speaking of which, I'm glad it's not hot anymore. Last week it was 80 degrees with humidity just above being under water, can you believe it? Geeze! Today it's in the 50's and these assholes are crying about no heater! "Would someone pleeeze help me" but I'll survive.

Oh! I finally got the transcripts to the hearing I went to in Fannin County a year ago. I sweet talked the court reporter. She probably sent me the transcripts (free of charge) just to shut me up. Anyway I have all the proof I need to win!! If and when I get up on the court docket, whenever that is.

So take care, enjoy the holidays and know I've got nothing but good thoughts for you. Bye for now.

Your friend,
Walt

****

Chapter Ten

January 11, 2012

Dear Liz;

Hi, I'm writing while waiting for chow. It's 2:50am and I'm up for breakfast. (A rarity) I now live in a dorm. So instead of one cellmate I now have 79. Spike took Sherry back to Ellis Unit, to live with Ronnald and Davy Jones. I may have mentioned old man Davy Jones. He lived next door to me in cell block seven. Anyway, his exact words were, "he don't wanna live with people who don't get along." imagine that. I can't blame him really. Some of these guys, and not just certain individuals, are beyond reason.

I've been busying myself pestering a magistrate judge. I'm due for another "Shut the fuck up" letter. I get one once in a while. I'm working my way up a docket. And, I suppose, after going to the back of the line again since January 2011, it don't matter that injury is compounded with every year I spend in prison. I still gotta wait my turn again. I'm waiting but I'm also practicing my diligence.

I'm sorry to hear a member of your family is having a hard time. Surgery is never very nice especially in a sensitive part of the body. He's in my prayers and yeew too. I'm sure what affects him, effects you as well.

I got your two letters backwards. The one where your going to Bakersfield followed the one "we went to Bakersfield", one day apart. I drooled over the turtle-burgers. I haven't seen bacon in almost 11 years. I'd make one or two of those turtle-burgers and serve them with tater tots.

Okay I'm still waiting on chow here. It's supposed to be scrambled eggs. The last time I went to breakfast was probably two months ago. It's served, literally, in the middle of the night.

I'm back, see that didn't take long. Not scrambled eggs but fried eggs. I think they fried them a couple of hours ago so they were a wee bit rubbery. I like fried eggs over easy. Not here, they're all fried hard. Still I like eggs, so...

I really like the picture of you and your brother. I can also see why you're so proud of your age. You don't look as old as I do and I turn 50 in March. I really wanted to be out here by then but... perhaps I will. I'm ever the optimist.

I sent the judge a get out of jail free card from a Monopoly board game. I haven't heard back from him but I'm thinking it probably wasn't my best move, legally. It was mainly a gesture towards "HOW LONG JUDGE?!" I accompanied a motion to rule/judge/litigate or do something! I cited some law and quoted the U.S. Constitution and the "speedy" part of the rules governing habeas corpus dated back to the Magna Carta adopted from the Mother Country England in 1697. Anyway I laid it on thick and put the get out of jail free card in there with a personal note saying, "Whatever it takes" Spike said I should have done it a long time ago. Yeah, we'll see. *(Note: It seems when you tell the legal entity what they should be doing, legally, that's when they don't do it.)*

I hope this letter finds you well. I'm glad the surgery didn't turn out as bad as you said it could have. My only health problem so far is arthritis. I ain't complaining, I'm making plans. I'm gonna get me a prescription for pot when I get out. I can't imagine going into a pot store and getting to pick out what I want. I'll bet the hemp shops down in L.A. have every kind of fast food and junk food restaurants surrounding that area. I know that's where I'd put my doughnut shop or hamburger joint. Anyway I ain't done nothing but pester the courts and go to work.

I still go outside in the mornings when I don't work the garment factory. When they let us go outside that is. Last weekend it rained and we might get wet if we go outside. It was 68 degrees here yesterday. Can you imagine? They keep the heat jacked up so much in this dorm? They say it gets worse before it gets better. If that's true then this is a good thing.

You mentioned liking Tom Selleck. He was in one of my very best favorite cowboy movies, "Quigley Down Under" I used to like "Magnum P.I" also, but Quigley was a real good movie. Have you seen it?

I just finished a book about England in the Bronze Age. It's supposed to be based on fact. "Wolves of the Dawn" by William Sarabande. It's an Irish and England thing. Anyway I was impressed with the story and even more so when the author claimed, at the end of the book, that these were real people in real places.

Well, I guess I should get ready for work. I gotta sew towels all day. Could be worse. I used to work in the fields. In fact when I first started writing to you in 2003 it was in medium custody Ellis Unit old death row and I was in the legendary Texas fields. People, including Clyde Barrow, used to cut off toes to keep from having to go to work in the fields. That movie, "Cool Hand Luke" with Paul Newman, showed them boys in a chain gang. It's basically the same thing but your out in the field hoeing cotton, corn or whatever and picking up that crap. Once in while we'd do road work. All the time with an armed field boss on a horse over ya. They'll shoot ya too. Anyway I'm getting too old for that now, even though it kept me in good shape.

On the tattoo subject, I agree with you about covering your body with ink. I don't have many tattoos. I was gonna get em but stopped when I realized that wasn't me. I do have a few though. The Celtic Cross on my back is the biggest.

I'm gonna go to work. It was great to hear from you. Take care.

Sincerely your friend
Walt

****

January 26, 2012

Dear Liz;

Hi ya, yer self. I just went through all the pictures you've sent lookin for "Green Monkey", now there's a picture I'd like to have. Or, the whole plant! See, if you'd said "look stupid, I got this plant that I'm giving away, can't keep it..." What did whoever you gave it to do with it? Now that's a stupid question huh? I would have worshipped it then smoked it. Maybe its better this way. It would probably be as big as one of those pine trees in your yard by the time I got out. *(Note: He doesn't know this but I kept some. Who knows if it's okay when he gets here)*

Speaking of which, I got yelled at! But the Assistant Attorney General got kicked off the case. She, the lawyer representing the Director (that's who I'm against, the Director of Corrections) responded to one of my letters to the court and seemed to get mad. The judge (Magistrate) admonished me for filing frivolous motions and the current Assistant Attorney General responded.

Whenever I file anything into court, the clerk makes a copy and sends it to the Atty. Generals office in case a response is necessary. In this case, it wasn't. But she responded anyway. More than likely thinking it was an opportunity to point out what an idiot I am and that relief in this case must not be granted. Sooooo, I responded claiming that the Assistant Attorney General is worried that the grounds of my petition are such that addressing a frivolous motion based upon a petitioners frustration over being strung along for six years and still seeking justice as set forth by the United States Supreme Court is more appealing. I also pointed out how off the mark the Attorney General's office was on those very grounds. Basically questioning the intelligence quota of the job requirements over there. That got the response that got her booted off the case. To be fair, an attorney named Michael Bozarth was the assigned shyster and totally sidestepped the issues. This was before I actually found the evidence the prosecution withheld at my trial. What I did do was get the transcripts to that evidentiary hearing I went to last year, entered into the record...and told to shut the fuck up and sit down somewhere. My admonishment ended with, "The court will hear this as soon as possible." so...I probably shot myself in the foot in that the new scum-suckin lawyer assigned to defend the director will ask for six months to familiarize himself with the case. Heavy sigh. Will someone please kill me!

Oh, I obtained another get out of jail free card from another Monopoly game and sent it to the court. That probably wasn't my smartest move also. But, that could have been the frivolous part, I ain't sure. Anyway at least I got someone's attention. I do not have an attorney anymore. I gotta do this on my own, unless the court thinks I need one.

I've been pretty wrung out lately. I need to start drawing Valentine's Day cards. It's my big money making season, as well as Chistmas. All my best patterns for the good cards are gone though. I can free hand roses I guess. I'm about out of everything except time and don't like anyone enough to wanna draw anything for em...well, except you of course. But I'm talking about around here.

I hate this dorm and everyone in it. Can't go outside because it's either raining, wet or muddy. I got no good books to read. Oh, that reminds me, I seen an add in a magazine on a TV series on HBO called "A Game of Thrones" by George R.R. Martin. That book series was very good. If you want a real good medieval type fantasy story, they don't get any better. I put that up there with "Sho-Gun" by James Clavell. Anyway, that might be easier to find if your lookin for some exceptional literature.

I'm glad Bud Plant called you in to help pull orders, I'm glad they're doing okay. This shitty economy is the pits.

You asked if we got bacon, No! and I don't know why they don't give us bacon. Both Ellis Unit and Eastham Unit have hog barns. I think these prison farms raise hogs and instead of keeping the meat for us they sell it on the private market because they make more money. We get pork roll or sometimes a very small pork chop, but never any bacon. We get, when it's served, egg's, biscuit and grits. The biscuits are like baking powder biscuits. Not much flavor and very dry, but hey, a biscuits a biscuit, right? I've been eating this mass produced chow so long I'd probably die of a system overload if I got some good food with taste. Maybe my taste buds have died...Hmmmm.

I'm gonna turn 50 in less than two months. Is it gonna hurt? I'll tell you what hurts, it's since I was less than three months into being 39 I've been doing this shit and I'm a little cranky. I'm sorry Liz, I don't usually write letters like this and I may not send it. I'll end it on a positive note. I may be "bonkers" too!

I hear there's a movie out with a Jack Russell Terrier in it. A silent movie even. I heard em talking about it on the public radio station. I wanna Jack Russell Terrier. I seen the one on the Jim Carey movie, "The Mask" and wanted one ever since. Ther're supposed to be smart. Bonkers would be a good name for him or Foamy the Wonder Dog unless it's a she. Hmmm, now we have a dilemma. I've seen puppies being sold in the news paper for ungodly amounts of money. Do they really cost that much for a puppy? How's Echo and Dobby doin?

Well friend I hope I ain't depressed ya and everything is okay where you are. I'll try and do better next time. Because there will be a next time. I'm just cranky. A cranky old dude who can't go outside and play. Maybe I'll instigate a riot between the Mexicans and Blacks! No that's not a good idea. In fact that's not really even funny. I aught to be ashamed of myself. I ain't, but I aught to be.

Let's see...oh yeah, I should be drawing cards. Well take care and write when you can. You're the only one who writes. Carolyn's been married and gone for a couple of years now. I could write just to see how she is...no, better not. I'm thankful for my one friend. I'll be okay. Bye for now.

Sincerely,
Walt.

****

February 21, 2012

Hey Yourself!

I got your letter dated Valentines Day. You are the onliest one who wished me a Happy Valentines day, thank you. Actually when you think about it, where I am and who I'm around... that's okay, what an idiot I am.

Yes you thanked me for Miss Em's picture. Okay I'm convinced you really did or do like it, thank you. I'm glad I could do it for ya. It's a hit or miss thing, drawing that is. I did make a good commission on the cards this year. After whining in my last letter, I spent as much time drawing sweetheart crap and living in an 80 man dorm, the cards were sold before they were finished. Before you think my fallen talent carried the day, there wasn't much competition. There were or are other artists but their cards were standard "prison" art and who wants a guard tower with some girl's face surrounded by graffiti type tag art? Anyway, I was the only one drawing true Valentines. I had a Celtic Cross with a rose drawn and it had more time in it than I wanted to sell to one of these ya-hoo's. But I got offered a bag o cookies for it and in a moment of weakness...cookies are $1.20 and that's not bad for these cheap-assed-cow-shit-eatin rednecked bastards that I live with.

I'm so descriptive sometimes, ever notice that? I had thought to send the card to you on example of what a hand drawn Valentine's Day card might look like. But I did not want to give you the impression that I was trying to be anything more than your friend. I'm careful because I like being your friend and even though my opinion of you is higher than I let on, you might start demanding money to remain my friend and I'd have to pay it. What a load of horse shit, huh. Actually, you would have done that a long time ago if you were gonna do it.

Hey, I just did the math. BBQ on August 18th? Can I come too? I looked all over this letter and didn't see my invite to bring my fat ass to this shindig. I could bring chips or something. Also you said you could ask your friend for another Monkey Tree plant. I'll make you a deal, you do that for me and get it going and when I come up to your BBQ I'll bring you an illustration board and we'll trade. It's an art raffle! You can either sell tickets or everyone there can have one entry just by showing up. Some of those might like to have an illustrated piece of art by that guy who started writing silly stories back in '03. Some might anyways. Wha do ya think? This would give me incentive to get the hell outa here. Just think, a BBQ with friends I never met, plus a Green Monkey plant or some such thing. Okay, I'll redraw the Celtic Cross rose card if you want it. It'd be my pleasure. If ya want.

Do you remember a few months ago I wrote a letter on the back of a legal thingy with all those court entries? Starting in May 2006. Did you get that? Well, when I got to Ellis Unit, I practically lived in that law library and have litigated this federal case all by myself, so yeah I can speak legal jargon. I'm embarrassed to say that my grammar and spelling does lack and I don't always get to clean up writs or responses. But being the genius that I obviously am, I found a ruling from the United States Supreme Court that says any writ or court action drafted by a pro se ("pro se" means without legal representation) litigant must be taken in a more liberal light and can not be dismissed due to being an idiot or some such wording. But, it's a good case to cite and I think I have a certain magistrate starting to see things my way. I have everything in I can think of. Now I wait. I think I'm close. Which means I think I can really make your BBQ party, so if you don't think it would be a good idea you should say so, otherwise let me know what I can bring and your opinion of the art raffle type swap? I can research the law to make sure I can have one plant, I think I can, who knows? Maybe by then it'll be legalized across the board.

I didn't get the funny email on the Walmart people, just the questions (Bible) from the kids and where's the cat? I laughed at the kids answers and found the cat, I don't like to brag but within two days. I know, it's hard to believe but I wouldn't lie about that.

That Rose drawing you speak of from the Rachel story, is it yellow? *(Note: Yes it is!)* Speaking of which I started another story the other day and it got too big so I stopped. I'll bet when I get out of here and get in front of a computer with word perfect I could lay down some pages of several ideas I have. Including <u>Giraffalo – Wyet Woodchuck</u> and this new story that's kind of a medievil tale or fantasy. I can put those together and send em to an agent or publisher? I read in the Writers Almanac where some publishers don't require agents, just advance permission to send what ya got. I'd like to illustrate "Giraffalo" though. That would take time, but I'd really like to.

Going back to your BBQ, are you going to have pizza there? On second thought, never mind, I don't wanna know.

Well I'm gonna go. Your letter made my day. I was glad to get it, thanx friend. Take care and remember...Oh yeah I almost forgot, I think I asked you this before, is it going to hurt to turn 50? Should I brace for impact? My hair's almost all white. Anything else? Is my goiter gonna explode or anything? Spike said it would, the little pricks lucky he ain't here or I'd feed him to the Cambodian down the way. (Chop Socky Willie) Let me know if I gotta prep for this.

Thanx,
Walt.

****

March 19, 2012

Dear Liz;

Hi. Thanx so much for the B-card. You wrote "belated" on it but I got it actually on Friday 3/16 which is my birthday. Your timing was impeccable. Thanx again. I got a card from my dad earlier in the month. I'm not sure if he was being funny or his old eyes...knowing I got my sense of humor from him probably the former, anyway it was a sympathy card. Like you'd send to someone who's loved one had passed. It simply said "Happy B-day, love dad" with all the Hallmark sappy words, "sorry for your loss" type stuff. Anyway, yours made it on the very day and again, thanx for that. (Nice card by the way, true too)

Well, you've probably been busy and haven't had a chance to respond to my last letter. I was curious as to your reaction to me begging an invite to your August 18th BBQ. You probably needn't worry, at the rate the courts are going, I'll have finished my 25 year sentence before they do anything. I was serious about the plant though. If your of a mind to grow another one that is.

I'm actually waiting to go to work and writing this on the way out the door, so-to-speak. Well friend I'm hoping you and yours are well and happy. Take care and write when you can. Always my best.

Yer old friend,
Walt.

****

March 20, 2012

Hi Liz, it's me again;

I got your letter tonight and wanted to write you something about the BBQ. Don't give it another thought about me not being able to come. I completely understand and wouldn't have it any other way. But about that plant you mentioned, you called it God Bud. OMG! Are you serious? If I can get out and do so legally, can I get one? Just askin. This could be a big incentive for me. I'll even type up all those letters for you and dedicate my first book to "my good friend Liz whose green thumb paved the way" or to "Liz and WordPerfect" Long live Giraffalo!

About the redneck thing. There is a distinct difference in a country bumpkin and a redneck trust me on this. You are not a redneck, country bumpkin, maybe. There's nothing charming about a redneck women. Besides, redneck's in general can't write like you. Nor do they have all their teeth on the top or bottom. Check Jeff Foxworthy out on your computer. He'll give you an abridged version of a true redneck. I happen to live in redneck central and you are not one. "Country Bumpkin" by Cal Smith, it's a song, ever hear it? It's one of my fave's. *(Jeff Foxworthy is my favourite comedien and has been for many years.)*

My legal status, after I win my case, and I WILL win but I won't have parole. I know I've been saying this for years. If anyone knows this it's usn's. I want the kidnapping charge wiped from my record. *(Note: Why not give the kidnapping charge to Darin Rae Barnett, the taxi driver who accused Walter of kidnapping him. Walter was "kidnapped" by the legal system.)* I may have to wait for compensation but I'm determined to come away with enough to get me a place of my own and settle down to write and talk to my God plant. If the plant is worthy of its name, perhaps I'll even get an answer. Really, if you have other plans please let me know because I'll be getting my hopes up and pestering someone to get me the hell out of here and situated to have a thing like that. Are you gonna put it in a big transportable pot so I can slip a dolly under it and wheel it away or put it in a U-Haul or something?

Have you ever read "Of Mice and Men" by John Steinbeck? I'll be like Lenny and the rabbits. So please tell me yay or nay, we'll figure out the details later. If there's a will there's a way. I'd like it to be a girl plant too, so we can give it a girl name like Roxanne or something. ALRIGHT enough about that. Sometimes I get so worked up with a fantasy. *(Note: Between the two of us, that's a fact.)*

Yes they have a legal library here; in fact it's why they sent me here. The transfer facility I was in, Tennessee Colony, didn't have an adequate law library and I complained, so they sent me here, as punishment I'm sure, but the law library's good.

Back to the BBQ. August is a long time away. Those people who have declined may change their minds. Don't take it personal. We can send Spike and 10,000 of his relatives to talk some sense into em if you want. Spike would do that for you, for free.

Yes I remember Peggy Sue; I saw her picture in one of the Christmas cards from Bud Plant. I have several pictures of your ex-co-workers from those cards. It's nice to see someone's face when you refer to them.

Don't you worry about getting old, it happens to the best of us and I can assure you that few look as good as you doing it.

Have you read the book "Sho-Gun?" is an epic adventure with forbidden romance that will rock your world little country girl! It's truly a fine read. Anyway, I'm not sure why I felt compelled to reiterate the literature but there you have it. *(Note: I got it after he mentioned it and yes it kept me reading when I should have been working.)*

I scribbled this out in record time, I'm in a hurry. Thanx for the computer funnies, they are always welcome, even the not-so-funny but interesting are also welcome. But none so welcome as a well written letter from my friend. Thanx. I'm gonna go now.

Take care, always,
Walt

****

March 24, 2012

Dear Liz;

Howdy, it's me again. On Friday I was called down to the mailroom to have the Gil Elvgren calendar held back claiming sexually explicit images on certain pages. I'll get it back because I have never seen Gil Elvgren do nudes. Risqué yes, but as long as there are no nude images I'll get it. Unfortunately a rookie was at the helm in the mailroom that day. I'll have to wait how ever long it takes the Directors Review committee in Huntsville to review it. There are no nude images, right? The reason I ask is there are grievance procedures I can take to ensure this won't happen again. but in case I just don't know about Gil's "Nude" pinup paintings, I thought I'd better ask. Please let me know as soon as possible, I assume you sent the calendar from Bud Plant because no one else likes me enough to send one.

Now on to the calendar. I haven't seen it but of the entire pinup artist's, he is at the absolute top of the list. Vargas is up there also. But I've always believed Gil's depiction of the images he puts out are the most entertaining to look at and if I were gonna plagiarize anyone...So! If you only jot down a note claiming No!, No nudity in that calendar, risqué yes. And when I say nudity, all they're concerned about is "naked-nipple" or a direct "naked vagina" shot covered is okay. Naked butt shot is okay. I can't believe I said vagina. I'm blushing profusely! *(Note: Yeah and with your white hair...)*

Alright, on to another topic of importance. I wrote a publisher and explained how we started writing and that you've save all of these letters. You saved all of them? OMG that's gotta be upwards of ...let's see, 2013 is when I first sent the first letter begging books from the service dept. right? You kept...13 thousand letters? Did I mention I was an idiot? Alright, so I wrote to this publisher who specializes in prison type literature. I told him about our pen pal type relationship, how it developed and that you saved all the letters I've written. I also told him I could not save all of yours due to space, and whatever crap I've had to go through moving around from prison to prison. So we'll see what develops. The reason I'm bringing it up is if they are interested in em, would you want to deal with em or wait? Or do you have some other publisher in mind? Would you want to turn over the whole lot if there's genuine interest? So that's two important questions I need answers to. Actually you ain't answered the God Plant questions either so make that three questions. I may have another question at some point, would that be okay? That question don't count though. *(Note: Well obviously I'm doing something with those letters now. Plus I'd prefer to market the book outside from prison walls.)*

Okay you, I'm gonna make this short. Keep it business like. I do need to know about the calendar and nudity. My guess is no. But before I put in a grievance form I wanna know for sure. I intend to ream someone out on unnecessary censorship, bastards.

How's things with you Liz? Ya wanna talk about it? Your birthday's coming up isn't it? More questions. Thank you for the calendar. I'll probably get it back, I hope. Take care..

Always your friend,
Walt.

PS: I had a good PS too but friggin forgot it already. This old age crap is getting old real quick. Did I mention I was an idiot?

Bye...

****

April 15, 2012

Dear Liz (that's yeew);

Tis I (that's me) again. I received your 4/7/12 letter the other day and am just now getting a chance to answer it. Let me again compliment you on answering every question put down in my previous letters. Thanx. Your birthday falls on Mother's Day this year. I'm sure you know that by now. How bloody wonderful for you. It should be wonderful, by God! If your regular appearance is as youthful looking as your photos, you are absolutely blessed. No I ain't stroking you because I want something I'm stating an obvious fact. Say before I forget, one of the coolest looking photos you ever sent me was...BESIDES the one where you're kicked back at your work station. Your feet are up on your desk. Your fingers are behind your head. There's a big smile and the happiest look on yer face, yeah besides that one, I have one with a little bitty girl in a red outfit walking, (Izabeau) next to your Rottweiler Missy Ann, in your woods, right? The dog appears to be big enough for that little girl to ride. What became of that Rott? You now have Echo and Dobby, right? I was just wondering. *(Note: I told him "Missy" had a stroke and we had to put her to sleep.)*

Oh, the courts are making a move. On 3/22 the magistrate issued an order to the Attorney General to show cause why my petition for write of habeas corpus should not be granted. They gave them 40 days to do so. So that's a good sign.

Also while it's on my mind, you asked what you had said regarding the God plant. You were wondering if I was under the impression that you agreed to give it to me if I were free. In answer, you did not and I am not. Speaking of free, it looks like I very well could be out pretty soon. I know, here we go again! But you never promised me anything. I asked but you never committed. I can imagine why and will probably die a lesser man because of fate, but that's the way the... (My E.S.P.N. has kicked in and I've been told to "oh shut the bloody hell up!")

Your home girl, Adelle, is really putting a large foot print into musical history. She's very good. Only 21 years old and she literally smoked the Grammy's and hooked about a trillion fans with her unique singing voice. Have you heard her? Of course you have! She sounds Black sort of but she ain't.

On 4/12 the Directors Review Committee upheld the decision to deny the Gil Elvgren calendar. I don't know why and have written again, the head person at the Directors Review Committee in Huntsville. If there's no nudity, and I believe you, then some asshole has probably denied it to claim it when I can't have it. I hope that's not the case but this system is so corrupt. If you want to, but you don't have to because I think I can get the thing reviewed by someone in authority, you can call and ask, "What the fuck?" Call as a Service Dept. representative from the company it was sent from and explain there's no nudity, so what gives? You'll need my number and it was denied on 3/22/2012 and upheld on 4/12/12. Sometimes they get backed up over at the committee and end up rubber stamping a whole bunch of shit without really looking into what they're doing. Really and truly! There's no excuse for it being denied. Can you tell I'm really put-out about it? I know what these assholes are capable of and sometimes all it takes is a phone call from the outside. I don't have the phone number but you can call the main phone number for Huntsville and ask.

Whatever you decide is okay with me but I know it has to be sometimes. ` I'm just ever so grateful you thought of my stupid ass on my birthday. I know, I'm getting mushy.

Speaking of birthdays, what can I do for yours? Would you like a nice serious hand drawn card or a funny hand drawn card? Would you like me to pen you a story? Bring Spike, Ronald, Sherry and maybe the Swami Roach around to your house for a party? I got a story rattling around in the old bean about an old man and his granddaughter I was thinking about it the other day. I was also thinking about starting a story about a knight from a wagon wheel kingdom called, "The Right Hand of the King" That one I should write. I've always wanted to write a good fantasy story. Damsels in distress sort of thing. Do you remember the movie with Oliver Reed and Michael York, "The 3 Musketeers?" Swash buckling with humorous overtones. That's the type of fantasy I'd like to write.

The publisher I wrote to answered my letter. They informed me of a nationwide contest that promises the top three entries would get published. A drag! That's what it was. However I wrote Breakaway Books and explained that if Hemingway, Steinbeck and Benny Hill all fathered a child with writing ability, I'd be it! I wrote and told em our idea for a book, and explained how original an idea that would be. (Note: This book was and is the original idea.) I have another idea that's so original and controversial, (good combo) that someone will do it one day. If someone hasn't already. It's called, "If I Were God" All of the book would contain a bunch of, "If I Were God, love birds would have heart shaped wings" There's also some serious "If I Were God" things too. But it could stay cute and not so serious. Like "If I Were God" Jesus would be a baseball player. (or soccer) Bet something like that would appeal to someone. Of cause you'd get some people, with too much time on their hands, opposing this idea saying, "Sacrilege"! But history has shown us that the controversial things like that get a lot of free publicity and sell a lot of copies. What da ya think? Simple enough. Got any "If I Were God" ideas? No kidding, I'd like to hear them. No politics though! People should have bloody knees from praying and thanking God that I really ain't God. I'd draw a little love bird with heart shaped wings (Note: He did on the last page of the letter)

Well my friend I'm gonna go, I'm about out of gas here. The stinkin Astros are back playing baseball so that will keep me busy for awhile. The Attorney Generals 40 days to respond to the magistrates order are up on May 1st. When he does respond I get to answer. Then the magistrate makes a recommendation to the District judge, which is usually followed within 30 days, of that he will hand down a decision. A favorable one I'm hoping. It should be. The law is on my side. Keep me in your prayers, you're in mine. Take care

Peace, love and Bobby Sherman, bye for now,
Walt

****

April 28, 2012

Dear Liz (that's you);

Howdy y'all! Well the final decision to not give me the calendar is in, see the enclosed crap, (he sent the pink denial slip) That J. Smith is the one who overruled their last decision for me to keep the last pinup calendars. Remember that? So I wrote her and appealed, stating that these people are assholes and can't be trusted. I'm starting to think there might be some exposed "breasticals" somewhere on this calendar, but that would be saying you overlooked them. I want to take your side over these moronic pieces of...umm...they're probably reading this...moronic pieces of "sunshine?? Okay, let's leave it at that. I have the six stamps to mail this back to Bud's. I still want it, can you hold on to it for me? Even if it's for 11 more years? Geeze, let's hope the hell not!

I've run every possible scenario the Attorney General could do in response to the magistrates order to show cause...except one. It dawned on me yesterday it's possible the Attorney General might not respond at all. His deadline is up on Tuesday 5/1 and I haven't received anything, I'm sure I would have by now. By law anything he sends in regard to this petition to the judge, I must also get a copy. If he responds and the magistrate rules in my favor, he can appeal. That might drag on another six months to a year. If he doesn't respond I can motion the court to rule in my favor by default and he can't appeal. It takes five to six days for legal mail to reach me from the courts, so...let's see…his time's up on Tuesday the 1st, if he mailed it on Tuesday I've got till...6,7,8… Wednesday...carry the one, subtract...February!! No that ain't right. I figure I'll wait till the following Monday, then if I don't hear from him by the seventh of May I'm in the clear and Tuesday the eighth my motion to grant me relief from a bogus Felony conviction goes in. That will be a great scenario for me. Keep yer fingers crossed.

I ain't heard from you since...what time is it? Where's my teeth and I can't see a thing! I'm 50 now, I have these rememberin problems. It's a good thing I ain't a true Texas or I would be sporting portable teeth. I still have all my original choppers and most of my hair on my head.

Did I tell ya my sister finally wrote? My Dad had a heart attack and a stroke so she thought that would be an apt occasion to drop me a line. I don't know anything except he's laid up and can't talk. He can point and grunt though. Sounds like nothings changed. Believe me I'm not making light of my Dad's condition, I wish I could do something but can't and I've accepted the distinct probability he won't last till I get out of here, also, I've made my peace with him. I'd really like to see him again and catch a ball game, play chess, watch the new three Stooges movie with him but if I can't I'll do what I can and that's write to him weekly and tell him dirty jokes that I know he'd appreciate and will annoy his wife because she'll have to read them to him. She might not like them but my dad's sense of humor and mine are pretty close to the same. Of the two of us I have the biggest imagination. I don't ever remember not being able to make him laugh, so I've been doing that by writing and telling him I love him. I wonder what Kandas, his wife, thinks of my vows to give him a Viking funeral. I wrote and went into great detail of how it should be done. Spike and Ronald were there when I wrote the detailed six page letter. Anyway Kanda said she may move before I get out. In my last letter to her I explained how I'm not really crazy, no that's not right, I am crazy just not really crazy. She married my dad so she may not be as much of a prude as I'm thinking.

Okay you, I'm really disappointed in not getting the calendar. I'm a big fan of Gil Elvgren and even if there is some nudity, and until you tell me differently I won't believe otherwise. I'd wanted you to send it anyway, if given a choice. Will you keep it for me? Maybe it's an omen. Maybe I won't need a full calendar and that's gonna be the calendar that'll be there when I get out. I'm startin to get excited about this crap again and I'm not in the mood for another let down. After thinking about my claim there may not be anything for the Attorney General to dispute. The transcript of the evidentiary hearing covered every element of the claim I'm making and the U.S. Supreme Court has ruled repeatedly ya can't do what they have done to any conviction. Heavy sigh.Okay this week I'll be sending the calendar back. I don't need another; I want just that one, kay? Let me know when you get it, please? I don't need all that paperwork I sent you, back, unless you never receive the calendar, and then I will need it.

Take care, bye for now,
Walt (that's me)

****

May 5, 2012 Cinco de Mayo, Ola Signora

Hi Liz;

Okay as you might have guessed from the bloody size of this letter and card its yer Birthday-Mothers Day gift. I'm at the very moment waiting on chow down at the local choke and puke.

I'm really surprised the whole joint ain't on lock down due to a ruckus on the recreation yard yesterday. Rumor is someone died. But I've seen people who these assholes swore were either kilt or had died by some such disease, the infirmary failed to diagnose, walking around fine and dandy a week or two later. "hey look it's a freaking miracle," I'd say pointing to the so called dead person, "someone said they'd seen your toe tag" So goes the saying "don't believe nothing you hear and only half of what you see".

So, how the hell are you? Did you get the calendar back? It was sent May 1st. I got Casey Kasem on "Vintage Count Down" show. Last week was 1979 (yuck-vomit-ick-geeze what a waste of... unless of course you liked disco/funkadelic/Kool and the Gang fan? *(Note: yes I told him Disco was one of my favourite dance music eras)* I believe I started listening to Classic Country at that time. I do really like the 50's, 60's and early 70's music, be it pop or rock or country. What they called "Hard Rock" back then was okay, mostly. I liked the British bands, Zeplin, Stones, and Beatles etc. not exclusively though, I just like music, any or most music if it's good. There's some good music coming out now but most of its crap. That English fella, Luke Camden, not sure of the spelling of his last name, "Dr. Luke" runs a radio show called "Lost and Found" I think you can check him out on face book at "Lostandfound.com" I like his taste in music, new, old or whatever. 'Ee speaks wi an accent. Not that bad, I'm practicing for a story I'm writing for you there are Cockney English speaking Angels. No I ain't writ it yet but I've got a pretty good idea what I'm gonna write. It should be fun.

I got a copy of a request from the Texas Attorney General to move the court to extend the 40 days given to show cause to May 31. It's a 30 day extension. I'll probably hear the courts decision to do just that come Monday. I have a lay-in (pass) for legal mail on Monday so, the court will probably grant it...heavy sigh!

Sunday May 6, next day.

Okay I just finished your card, I hope you like it. I chose not to write in it, (for obvious reasons) I want you to be able to keep it or give it to someone you like. If I were to write in it I'd say "Happy Birthday my friend and Happy Mothers Day too. We should all be blessed with a mother like you.

I hope your birthday is groovy and Mothers Day is a blessing beyond comprehension. I guess I got another month or two to wrestle with the Attorney General. It's already in the 90's here and humid. My fan, the one you helped me get, is chuggin along just fine. (Thank God) Let me know you got the calendar back and what all the fuss was about. They weren't budging at all on that calendar. I'm curious as to why. *(Note: There was a small picture, which I missed, with bare breasts)*

Well take care. Again Happy Birthday, hope you like the card. *(Note: Yes I did and still do. However his Cockney accent really sucks.)*

All my best,
Walt.

****

May 10, 2012

Hi Liz;

Just a quick note to request a favor from you. Remember how you separated the pages of those other calendars and mailed em to me? You have or had that denial slip, yellow form with the page #'s on it. You probably have a good idea which pages are unacceptable. Could you separate em and write on the month side so it looks used and send the ones left? You'd have to put Liz McGillacuty PO Box 1689 etc...as the return address. I have a client who's also a Gil Elvgren fan and can make a few bux drawing a couple of his girls.

The Atty Gen. asked for and got 30 more days. I'm going fucking crazy here. I must find something to occupy my time while I wait. I know I just wrote but I was talking to some idiot who wants to pay me to do a couple of Elvgren boards. Do I have any material, not yet? He looked at these other ones but wants the Elvgren. Maybe a Betty Page. He ain't worthy of a Betty Page unless he pays. I could use the $$ so...wha da ya say? Have you already disposed of the calendar? *(Note: I did what he asked but it was rejected anyway.)*

Am I an idiot? Two questions, take yer pick. Okay so there ya have it. Hope all is well. Just make the return address look personal, I guess. Get back to me soon as you can.

Thnx,
Walt.

****

June 21, 2012

Dear Liz;

Hi. Sorry I haven't written of late. It's our mid-year shake down, or was. We've just come off a three week lockdown-shakedown. I'm just now acquiring a stamp to write. Actually I got commissioned to draw a birthday card for three stamps. Now I can write you, my son and my ailing dad. He's unable to write back but until I hear he's "gone" I'll continue to write. My son's another matter. He rarely writes, but once in a while he does.

I have access to a writers market book and am amazed at all the addresses of magazines, book publishers and or periodicals that solicit short stories, poems, exposes' and any other form of writing one could want. The same guy that has this writer's market book said I could use his typewriter but I'd have to supply my own ink cartridges. They are $2.50 out of the inmate commissary. Boy when it rains it pours too. It is the time of year when there is no market for cards so stamps are hard to come by let along cartridges.

They took my radio in the shake down. I could not provide property papers on it but my fan is legal though. Thank God!

I'd like to write a few of these legal publications and run down my legal situation and the state of our post conviction Appellate process but I'm beat up from the feet up. I did finally get a response from the States Attorney General and replied in kind though. So that's all done. He was pretty hard on a fella I have to say.

Jason, my new neighbor in this dorm is the guy with all the good stuff. He's actually a published author and pretty damn smart (academically) to boot. Anyway I showed him the Attorney General's response and he told me, in no uncertain terms that I was screwed. He has litigated two civil suits through the Federal courts and is familiar with law. He offered to help me, the best he could. He said, "Replying to this brief could quite possibly be my final down fall." Not very encouraging. I told him I'd accept his offer of help, in the way of typing, correcting any grammar, spelling and or punctuation mistakes I made. He said he would, for a card or two. He'd also help me articulate or present my reply in a better light. I spent two days on it, referring only to my own research materials that I've collected over the last eleven years. This stuff they could not take from me when I came back into the system in 2010 from that hearing.

I delivered it to ole Jason who went over it and proclaimed me way smarter than he originally gave me credit for. He said outside of my spelling errors and a few grammar changes this 15 page brief I wrote was a masterpiece. It went into the mail a week ago. It was typed and lethal, I hope. It was all backed by the U.S. Supreme Court Law and basically accused the Attorney General of siding with a criminal element over FACTS presented to prove constitutional violations against a U.S. Citizen for no reason. According to the law. Anyway, if this were baseball I swung for the bleachers and nailed it. Spike would be so proud. Then he'd take all the credit.

How's things up in the mountains? How was your trip? I hope all went well. Still no word on my dad. It's hot and getting hotter. I miss listening to baseball. I'm glad you liked the Adam and Eve story. *(Note: Not one of his intellectual best, more on the corny side, but yes I like it.)*

I wonder, there's a Christian publication poetry contest that I could enter if someone would go online and get me an entry form. I have a good idea for a poem for Em. Their web site is utmost-christianwriters.com; you can down load the entry from, free of charge. The prizes are $1000. For 1st, $600. For 2nd and 10–$100. Prizes for 3rd. I'm sure I can maybe nail one of them $100. Prizes. I can't imagine spending $100. at this store, I'd probably ration it. It's easy to do when you don't get $$ often. I really don't NEED $$ except when I don't have nothing. It would be nice though. The deadline is August 31st, I think. There are other contests but if I can only enter one, it would be nice to replace my radio and maybe a hot pot. Hot water is not supplied, there are several places I could enter or submit that Rachel story. Everybody wants type written manuscripts or emailed manuscripts. There's some law magazines that I'd like to write to. Heavy sigh.

Last time this stupid ass court had all the responses and replies in they took over 20 months to do anything. I hope that ain't the case this time. However long it is, I need to get busy and *DO* something.

Well I look forward to getting the calendar. If they allow it. I hope your garden's doing good and all is well there. I'll write more when I know more.

Would you please check on that entry form for me? Ya never know. With my ole dad laid up I can't ask him for $$. Not that I do, but, if I really needed to, I could, like the fan a year ago. Between you and him I got that fan. That was an emergency though. He's older than dirt, on a fixed income and now paralyzed from a stroke. I wrote his wife several times asking for a status report but nothing. I wrote my sister and his (my dad's) sister too, but nothing. Hmmm, me think I may be on scum status. Another heavy sigh. Well friend, I'm gonna go. Take care and write when you can. I enjoyed the computer printouts.

Walt

PS: I'd be happy to draw that lil Angel card again. If you already have it you can give it to Jen at Bud's for being our co-conspirator. Let me know, I'm ever so grateful for her help.

Bye for now.

****

July 30, 2012

Dear Liz;

Howdy lil cowgirl! Okay ye ain't no cowgirl. Me neither. I ain't even no cowboy. I can speak cowboy though. "I recon y'all orta... (snort while dragging wrist across nose, spit, adjust hat)... git yer rig and head on out to pasture" Translated that means...who knows? I didn't say I understand it, just I can speak it.

Alright, I got your letter with the heavy burdens that have been placed at your feet in these trying days. I'm sorry you lost your uncle. Eighty nine years, wow! I should be so lucky. I hope he was as well adjusted to life as you seem to be. In all the years we've been writing I've never heard you complain unnecessarily or talk bad about anyone. You may not always like the way things are or the way some people are but there's a difference between being observant to the stupid sons-of-bitches that make up our daily lives, and complaining needlessly about frivolous things. *(Note: He complains, a lot, about his legal issues but to me they're not frivolous.)* Hey speaking about stupid sons-of-bitches, how about that one shooting up the movie theater? There's one that qualifies, hands down.

I have been busy and if there ain't a drawing in here for Jen there will be next time. The poem entry form's deadline was July 15th so it was late. Don't *EVEN* trip on that. Unbeknown to me it also required an entry fee of $20. so I couldn't enter any way. Even if I *HAD* the money to enter I would not have done it. But here's what I have done. On June 11th I mailed "Rachel" (the story about the nursing home) to Pen American Center and entered into the Fiction Category of their Annual Prison writing contest. The deadline is August 31st. On June 25th I mailed filler (joke type story, 1000 words) to Arthritis Today magazine. They claim, if accepted, they pay $85. to $150. for a good filler. I enclosed an S.A.S.E. in case they didn't want it. I haven't heard nothing yet. I used my Aunt's address as a return address if they send a check. I know no editor would want to fill out one of those Trust Account slips to buy a filler. I have no one else and hate using my aunt. (holy roller, extremely religious and in her 80's) I'm not sure she likes me a whole lot. She doesn't need any money, but they send the magazines to me. If they send something to her she'll eventually get back to me. If I could I'd rather send that crap anywhere else, well almost anywhere else. Okay that was my first submission to the magazines.

The guy with the typewriter said I could use it but I have to buy my own cartridge, that's fair. I tried selling my kidneys again but I sold all three of em already so I had to get creative. I traded Betty Page (whaaaa!) for an ink cartridge and six stamps. I wrote another story called "Second Chances" (5700 words) and typed it up and sent it to a magazine called "Subtropics" in Florida. It was 16 typed pages.

Do you remember the "Swami Roach" story where the boilers under the kitchen in Ellis blew up killing Ronnald while me and Spike made it out only to get kilt in a shootout with the dirty screws? Well, "Second Chances" had nothing to do with that. Blimey, me think someone has just called me an "arse hole." Actually the thing the Swami Roach did, I used in a story where a feller got a second chance through a phone booth. Long story, happy ending. I sent it July 9th. The 2012 Writers Market Book says they want fresh stories by new authors. If accepted its $1000. I also included return postage. I can't afford the ink cartridge to retype it. I still ain't heard back from them.

Pen American Prison Writing Contest has four categories, Fiction, Drama, Non-fiction and Poems. I took my new story and entered it in the drama category as a screenplay. I called it "The Phone Booth" that finished up my ink cartridge. Not bad for a 16 page story, plus an 18 page screenplay. The screenplay was formatted differently and took less to fill a page. The Pen American Center had sent a writers handbook to show me how to write a screenplay. They used parts of Sylvester Stalone's "Rocky" and some other guys screen play "The Taxi Driver" an early Robert De Niro movie as examples. Sheeeeit! If Rocky can write one, how hard can it be? They don't pick their winners until the spring.

Okay I can't do no typing anymore but I'm gearing up for when I can. I drew and sent two Christmas cards to two magazines that ask for seasonal material six months in advance. One magazine is "Hustler" (a raunchy girly magazine) I sent the card of Santa crapping down the chimney, did I ever send that one to you? *(Note: Yes, he did and unfortunately I still have it)* Anyway, "Hustler" might buy it. I had Santa sitting on the chimney, pants down around his ankles and reading a "Hustler" magazine. The other magazine that got a "crappin Santa" was one called "Flick". With my luck being what it is, "Hustler" will buy the rights to the drawing and mail the check with the original drawing to my Aunt, who upon opening the envelope and seeing Santa doing his business down someone's chimney has an instant heart attack or I'll get an ear full. I doubt they'll return the card though. I told em it wasn't necessary.

Anyways, if any of that pans out, I have two more stories written. One of "Giraffalo" The magazine that wants things like that is " High Life" I had to condense it to 800 words max. I have a major imagination when firing on all cylinders. I also have a story about a little boy who invented time travel. That one's pretty cool. That one's ready to be typed along with Giraffalo. I drew another picture of Giraffalo with his mum Hazel. And since Hazel has been such a good mum cow I gave her a calf. A little girl calf. And me being a sentimental stupid son of a cow myself, I named the calf, (Giraffalo's only friend at first) "Liz." Don't worry she's a real cool little water buffalo who sticks up for her adopted brother. I've done some research on a futuristic story and am working on that next. A blood sport story with a tragic ending. A friend of mine challenged me to do it.

I also have a lay in pass to pickup legal mail on Monday. Hopefully it's not something they're denying me. Hopefully it's from the courts telling me that the're ruling on my case. It's been almost two months since everything's been completed. I waited till Monday to finish this in case I got good news.

It wasn't. It wasn't bad new though. It was confirmation that they had received my reply last month. Yay! I really want out of here. It's hot and obnoxiously rotten. It sucks the life out of a person. If I were guilty then I would deal with it, but as long as I stay busy, I'm okay. I'm getting to the end of my tether. Anything and everything is starting to lose its appeal. I'm tired. I didn't commit the crime to start with and, after almost 12 years, I've yet to have a judge even comment on the merits of my case. They broke the law to get this conviction. I've proven it in open court and all they can say is, "yeah, but..." Yeah but my ass. What you did is illegal and it's costing me my life. Blah, blah, blah.

My faith in the law and everyone representing the law, is so fragile that I think I would probably do better to write fiction. If I can sell just one story, I can finance my attack at the media and legal magazines on the mishandling of the so-called great writ "habeas corpus" Something like that I'd not ask for payment, which might compel an editor to consider what I was saying and maybe even printing it. If God wants me to do that he'll tell them assholes at any magazine to purchase my shit. Well maybe not in those many words.

Okay, I don't know what prompted me to go on a rampage like that, I'm really sorry. I initially started this letter to cheer *YOU* up or at least try to. I always look forward to hearing from you even when your feeling low. It's okay. All of that and this is a part of life. Yeah I know I've said this before. It would be different if I did the crime "they" say I did. Oh and I hate Texas, I don't know if you knew that.

I have a nine page story here, front and back, that I typed, I sent it to that magazine I was talking about earlier. You're welcome to it if you want. It's a good story with a real cool twist at the end. When I type up "Giraffalo" its gotta be under 800 words. So far this letter is over 1200. I can send you a copy of that instead. I gotta do some drawing, not just for Jen, even though she's on the list, and get some stamps and ink cartridges, and get some more crap in the mail.

I hope you're okay and...Gasp! what about your BBQ? Shit Batgirl that's already upon us! What about your God plant? Did you grow those seedlings? Take pictures for now. *(Note: The seeds did not grow)*

I'm writing that stinking judge again and demanding I be let go *RIGHT NOW!* There, that should work. Sorry about all the profanity in this addition of "Oh shit he wrote another long one. I've told you what the problem is, no one else writes me so you get the full Monty, as it were.

Okay, you take care now and I'll keep you in my prayers. If you write back soon you might be able to ask Jen what exactly she would like in a drawing. A fairie, a dragon, a warrior type gladiator man type thing, an angel, or something cute or cool? Otherwise ya get what I feel like doing at the time. It might be drawn well but if I'm in the mood to draw the north end of a south bound mule, you'll look at it and, "eeeeew!" is that what I think it is? "Yeah, but look how well it's drawn"

Okay, gotta go. Be good.

Me

August 12, 2012

Hi Liz;

Okay I'm mainly waiting for six reasons. One: To say Hi and send Jen her drawing. Two: To say Hi and tell you the calendar arrived and they kept it. I'm appealing it and should get it. I'm raising hell, again, it's getting old. Thank you for sending it. And three: To make sure your okay. Coming from one who knows "when it rains it pours" and I hope it ain't still raining on you. How many reasons did I give? Jeesus let me see...three more huh? Okay, four, was for something else and so were five and six. That about wraps it up then.

"Giraffalo" has left the building! I sent him to the children's magazine called Highlights. They gave an 800 word parameter and I sent em 940. I'm ever the recalcitrant rebel etc. Anyway I sent an illustration with it. This seems familiar to me did I already tell you this? My memory is going, I think. Anyways he's out and about, wish me luck. I've got one more complete story ready for typing if I can get the ink cartridges to do so. I seem to be making out though.

"Billy Schultz and the Fantastic Time Machine" (about 7000 words) will go the "Asimov's". It's a science-fiction magazine named after the famous science fiction writer of the 50's, Isaac Asimov or something like that. They don't pay a lot but the prestige would look good on a resume'. I have several more story ideas rattling around in my brain pan but ain't writ nothing down. What do ya think of "Psycho Squirrel?" I like the sound of that for a story.

Well, I know its short but I got this card done and wanted to get it to our friend Jen like we promised. I hope, she likes it. Let me know. I ain't melted down to nothing yet but with this heat I am definitely in danger of it. Take care. Let me know how the BBQ turns out. Till I hear from ya,

Walt.

****

October 10, 2012

Dear Liz

Hi, I received your letter and pictures last night. I was happy to get em.

We've been on lockdown status due to a staff shortage so I've been pretty stagnant lately.I entered "Bill Schultz and the Fantastic Time Machine" in L. Ron Hubbard's Writers of the Future Contest. (forth quarter.) It was hand-written and all corrected. I don't have another copy except for the mess that was the first draft.

I've enclosed two stories that I wanted to send to a women's magazine that wanted romance stories under 800 words. But I can't afford to type them or the postage to send them. I'm lucky to get this stamp to send this letter actually. I had one emergency stamp in case the stinkin stooped assed courts ever decide to get back to me. But, I am writing YOU instead, probably a safer more satisfying event anyways.

The listing for the woman's magazine is romance only! So I thought, hey why not. I plan on winning that L. Ron Hubbard contest and I'll be freaking rich!! Well maybe not rich but well off in here. You can check em out on yer "talking TV" (computer) Go to www.writersofthefuture. com I'm in the 4th quarter of the contest. I have no idea what the web site consists, of but on the form letter they sent back, they said I can go there and do something. Anyway maybe they post the winners or contestants.

I'm really sorry Echo (my dog) didn't work out. You apologized about crying on my shoulder. Don't be silly. #1: I have big shoulders. #2: I've cried on yours on more than one occasion. Friends do that so shut the fuck up about it. Okay that was designed to make you smile. It's called shock value, and to make you call me an arse hole. Did it work? *(Note: Yes! He did in April 2003 and is still doing it today 2016. Bloody man.)*

Okay I used the stamp I originally had to mail the two enclosed stories to a friend's mom who will mail the two enclosed stories to that women's magazine in her name. If accepted, I gotta split the $$. I'm okay with that. You of all people know I can puke a story out when I want. These two stories came in, in mere moments; it took longer to write em than to conjure them up.

I got a story back from Fantasy & Science Fiction magazine with a rejection notice that pretty much said publishers, as a rule don't accept material from convicts. It's typed, double spaced and 45 pages long. I like it and hocked my radio to afford the ink cartridges to type it and, the six stamps it took to mail it with return postage. We should come off this lockdown pretty soon and I may be able to hustle up some more stamps. Would you like me to send you the story? "The Queen's Dancer" I would like to and I value your opinion. It's all typed up and, oh yeah, I said that, didn't I? *(Note: "The Queen's Dancer" is one of his best fiction story's. The story line is excellent and the characters believable.)*

"Billy Schultz etc" is being judged by a Scientology group, (L. Ron Hubbard) I should hear back by Christmas. I figure since it takes the stinkin courts an average nine months to do anything, I should have my answer by March. I've come to terms with it. In the meantime, I'm gonna try and write. I wish I had someone to mediate so I can do it without revealing my prison status. My inmate friends mom, who's mailing these stories, seems like a stand-up person. If that pans out I can hire a secretary-type lady who advertizes in the prison legal newspaper to do all that. I'd be a fool not to, we'll see. *(Note: So three guesses who eventually get's the secretary job?)*

I'm okay, I ain't dwelling on my crappy position in life these days. I'm actually doing something constructive and after nearly 12 years I feel confident I'm nearing the end, so don't worry.

So what else in your letter? Yes I received the newspaper clippings and am enlightened and impressed in Bud's origins. *(Note: My old boss, Bud Plant, got a great write-up in the newspaper on his 40 year being in business and his success.)*

You also asked if you mentioned that Jen liked her drawing. No, I read your last letter wondering if she liked the genuine Ball and Chain Enterprises card drawing and figured that because you're the classy brawd, you are you and just didn't mention it because she didn't like it and you didn't want to hurt my little feelings. I literally blew snot all over the place, blubbering about the drawing. Do you know how long it took to draw the "hair" alone? (Am I putting too much on this? I am, really sorry) I'm very glad Jen liked the drawing. If I ever do any more drawing, I'll keep her in mind because I don't have anyone else to draw for. Your situation, being what it is, probably prevents you from keeping things like that. I honestly understand that. *(Note: In case I hadn't mentioned, I had been told I could not write to and couldn't accept letters from Walter)*

So, onto another subject. Fergy, the Duchess of York, she's the redhead right? I'm partial to red-headed women, not exclusively you understand. Usually they are mean and unpredictable. None I've ever met can cook but they make up for it by...umm...never mind. So Fergy wrote a children's book huh? Great, great and she's Royalty and all. So how are you Liz? (speaking of Royalty)

The 'Psycho Squirrel" story didn't go no where, but I slipped one in the Billy story. I'll rewrite that in long hand and send it next time, maybe you can type it up. Unless L. Ron Hubbard has it on display on the website.

Okay it's late and I gotta get up in the morning to catch the mail carrier. Being locked down they come to the dorm and pick up the mail. We're getting one hot meal a day now so otherwise its peanut butter sandwiches, prunes and hard boiled eggs. Vomit! Take care and let me know if you like these two stories. Take care and all that.

Peace,
Walt

PS: Thanx for the pictures of the lake at sunset with the two grownups holding the hand of a child. Is that you, Shelby and Emily? Good picture. Is that Folsom Lake? If so it's pretty low ain't it? *(Note: It was Lake Shasta in Northern California.)*

****

October 29, 2012

Dear Liz;

Hi, I'm hocking my teeth and done sold another kidney to get the postage to mail this but I gotta.

I've written two story's and sent them to two different magazines only to have them rejected for I believe they just don't publish from prisoners. I'm writing a proposal to you to try and convince you to sponsor me in the next stage of my writing.

You mentioned buying a calendar for me. I doubt I'll need one really and truly because by March I should be leaving or have left. I have to believe this, so I need to put a serious effort into putting together a bank so I'm not getting our destitute like. If I've learned nothing at all from being in Texas I've learned that there is NOTHING but $100. gate-money and a "good luck son" waiting for me when I'm released. Even, if they acquit me, I'd still have to get a "hood ornament" and litigate this through court or start it and settle. Until that happens I need to get a place to stay, feed myself, clothes and keep all that till I can convince someone to hire me to shovel shit. Which is not a very high career goal but I figure, shovel shit now and rule the world later. Know what I mean jellybean? I'd do what ever it took to pay the rent legally and move up the ladder gradually until I can land a lucrative writing job.

All that said, my proposal is for $40.00. That's what I think I can make the following happen. Out of $40.00, 20% still goes to the Feds for the old filing fees but I think that's down to about the last $10.00. Anyway, I thought it was done but the last trust statement I got showed $10.59. I lose $8.00 right away. Four ink cartridges at $2.50 apiece is $10.00. After paper, correction ribbon and stamps. That should leave enough left over for a couple of 4oz bags of coffee to keep me going. I've had to take up drinking tea. Coffee is too expensive. It's $2.50 for a box of 100 tea bags that will last forever. But I'm a coffee man. Have you ever, or do you still drink tea? Stupid question!

My friend Jason has offered me free use of his typewriter as long as I can provide the ink cartridges. His mom has offered to be a go between in mailing my stories so no prison return address. And yes, Jason is the Jason from Friday the 13th. I know, I know, I'll explain later. At least it ain't Norman Bates huh? Anyway I trust her and Jason. She sent "Billy Schultz and the Fantastic Time Machine" and two romance stories to different magazines. "Asimov's and Women's World" I have three other stories waiting to be typed. I think I told you about "Jragin?" Big mean monstrous dragon getting his balls charmed off by a lost little four year old girl? Did I mention that? Cute story. Anyway, part of this proposal includes two examples of my polished writing skill. I don't have a good copy of Billy Schultz, but since these have been rejected, (rejection slips enclosed) I have good copies to present to the Liz McGuire Board of Directors. Are you ready?

Example #1: (with illustration) "Giraffalo" It was condensed to meet the "no more than 800 word count" in the guidelines. Very condensed. Example #2: "The Queens Dancer" this story was sent Sept. 4th and rejected Sept. 7th. They didn't even read it! It should have been titled "Cat Dancer" It's an example of what I can do when I try. It's also a fine example of what I have to offer as an author. Should I continue? Or, judging from this story, should I face reality and "not quit my day job?" Part of the proposal is answering that question because, realistically if I'm living a delusion what's the point, right? So, please read "Cat Dancer" and give me your honest opinion. I trust your opinion and value any comment I believe it is some of my finest writing. "Jragin" is cute and should be written. *(Note: Both stories are wonderful. They're both very different from each other.)* A friend of mine once said that I'd be a fool to not pursue my writing talent. "Cat Dancer" is enclosed. My only other copy is hand written, with scribbled notes and in short, a mess. I wish I had more copies to mail around. I almost have enough short stories to mail to a book publisher. That's where the real $$ is. Anyway, I've enclosed one of those money slips in case you wanna sponsor me in this pursuit. If I succeed I'll be able to put aside money for my release. I would pay you back with interest. But only if you're interested.

You once told me of an English saying, "Keep your Pecker Up" I try to do that on a daily basis even though it's hard sometimes. I think God give's us *JUST ENOUGH* to do just that sometimes. I write these stories to leave this place. If I can make a living doing that then I wanna know I can take my readers with me. There's a prison saying that goes like this, "It could be raining pussies and I'd get hit in the head with a dick" Sometimes I'm unlucky like that. So, there's my proposal. I hope my timing isn't as bad as that saying would indicate.

It's before Christmas and if I had anyone at all to ask other than you I would. Not because I don't think you'll do it but because I feel awkward asking. I feel like I'm an asshole having to put this on paper. If you can help, this is what your helping. (See enclosed) *(Note: He enclosed "Giraffalo" and "Cat Dancer")* I wanna un-condense "Giraffalo" and send "Cat Dancer" to another destination, maybe to that L. Ron Hubbard contest. (Go to www.writersofthefuture.com) It's their first quarter deadline December 31st. If you sent back a typed copy, I could enter or send it from there. If it's sent from there you'd have to get the ad from the computer site. Anyway they didn't have a problem with my prison address. I honestly hope I'm not causing too much problems with my problems. I hope you get to read this story leisurely and enjoy it. Let me know all of the above.

Alright I'm gonna get this off. It's late and I've been working at getting postage for this since yesterday. Thanx, as always, for listening and taking the time to write me back. Lying that the story is good just to save my feelings onother run through the mud. *(Note: I've never lied about telling him his stories are good. There has been one or two I haven't liked the story line, and told him that. Otherwise he writes a great story)* Yer a good friend Liz and I hope to be as good a friend to you one day.

Bye for now
Walt

PS: You don't have to do anything with these copies of the two stories. If you want, after viewing "Cat Dancer," you can go to that website for the L. Ron Hubbard contest and get their address and send them this copy or make another copy for yourself. Send them the story, putting my prison address as the return address for the 2013 1st quarter entry. If you want or you can stash it with the rest of the other letters and such and write me back saying, "I read your story and it sucked!" See what I mean about being an arsehole? Sometimes it comes so easy. Is it because I'm a man? Are there any arsehole anonymous meetings I can attend when I get out? There awt to be one on every street corner in Texas. Okay, gotta go, Bye

Me.

****

November 25, 2012

Dear Liz;

Hi friend. I sketched this piece of stationary listening to football last week. I got your letter with the blonde men jokes. I never heard no blonde MEN jokes, but I enjoyed them. I'll send em to my son for Christmas. He's very blonde, like his momma. The little bastard ain't so little anymore and from what I heard he's getting so many tattoo's he's looking like a circus freak.

You wrote this letter on 11-12 and commented on the two short stories but did you get the big story? I know, I know, I put the squeeze on you for $$, something I hated to do but I'm sorry. I know and I hear the economy sucks, money's tight and you got a lot of other things that probably demand attention more important than my problem. Did you like the story though? Don't tell me "yeah" just to spare my feelings. I'd like an honest opinion. It's long and...what? Go ahead, wha'd ya think? *(Note: "Cat Dancer" is quite long and well written. It has a good story line. I didn't enjoy it as much as others he's written though but I'm not an expert)*

Yes I still have the pictures of you and Cyndi. I have every picture you ever sent. I could not keep your letters because we are limited to our space. I'm sorry to hear Cyndi has bone cancer. I don't know about bone cancer. I thought it was leukemia or some such thing like that. That's why I don't go to the doctor. The last time I went he wanted to examine my prostate. "How the hell are you going to do that amazing feat of magic?" (I know where the prostate is) "Well, first we tie you to the table face down and spread yer butt cheeks..." "Woowah, hey asshole, you can forget that shit!" and that's the last time I saw a doctor. But it only proves my point.

You mentioned Veterans Day. In Midland Texas, they had a parade for the Veterans. They had two trailers with Vets and their wives, moving down the road and waving to the crowd to show their appreciation. The traffic got backed up and the second trailer ended up parked across a railroad track, yeah you can guess the rest. Google Midland Texas and you can probably get a better account of what I know. Had the news reported that incident there in Calif.?

I'm glad to hear Echo is doing okay now. I hope Thanksgiving was good for you and the minions didn't work you too hard. If you're thinking seriously about having a hip replacement it's probably not good to be running around waiting on folks. But I'd bet money these people are aware of this and are considerate enough to get up and help. My Thanksgiving was less than last year. Because of budget cuts to Texas's State budget, it affects us here in the klink.

I've been pestering a law professor at Texas University School of Law. He hasn't responded yet but heads up an innocence project and I've been pestering him to contact the court clerk and ask "what the fuck!" I'm sure he can word it better than that but...well, you know.

I know this is short but I wanted to write and say "Hi" Okay I'm gonna go for now. Take care and try not to kill anybody. That's good advice; I don't know why the hell I said it but just thought I'd share it with you.

Bye for now. Yer friend
Walt.

PS: We're closing in on 10 years, can you believe it?

****

December 10, 2012

Dear Liz;

Hi, I ain't got nothing to draw on so all I have to give ya for Christmas is a story. I thought about what you might like and came up with this. Let me know.

"The Queen's Dancer" or "Cat Dancer" I sent a while back, well I may need a copy of it. There is an e-book place out of Las Vegas that, (if they respond in kind) I may submit that story and a few others. I went through my records (story archives) and found that my hand written notes to the "Queens Dancer" are incomplete. I rewrote some stuff into the typewritten copy you have. Like the part where they all bonded after the spankin. It needed to be in there, don't you think? *(Note: Yes I did. If more youngsters were "spanked" today there would be less disrespect.)* Anyway, I hope that won't be an inconvenience. The story enclosed, "Departure 153" was easy to write, like Rachel was. I hope you like it. *(Note: Yes I did and do. It's very sweet and poignant)*

Well that's it. I hope Christmas is great for you and your family. I'll draw something new after I get a new drawing pad. Maybe Satan...or Santa. Did you know both names are spelled the same? Santa owes me, I saved his life one time, but that's another story. Speaking of which; could you, if you remember or get the chance, punch in on your computer www.writersofthefuture.com and see if they have a list of winners for their 4th quarter contest? I entered "Billy Schultz and the Fantastic Time Machine". I feel I'm due a break and maybe that will be it huh? *(Note: I did and he didn't win or get a mention.)*

Okay I gotta go. Let me know if you like this story or not. Take care and don't work too hard this season.

Merry Christmas my friend,
Walt

****

December 30, 2012

Dear Liz;

Hi. First of all, thanks for the lovely Christmas card. It was very uplifting. Also the $$ was a great surprise, thanx much. There will come a time when I will repay you twofold.

I plan on compiling all the stories I have written and sending them to a book publisher that specifically asks for short stories. If I get someone interested, I may need you to send them "The Queens Dancer" That story I don't have a copy of, at least not the type written and polished one, (such as it is) I'm investing $30.00 in having all (seven I think, not counting the Dancer story) copied, retyped, edited for spelling and mailed from the outside world by Jason's mom. Jason will also contribute $30.00 and between us we'll pitch our crap to a book publisher. We ain't getting no where with these magazines. Maybe it's the end of the year and...who knows? I'm also pestering "Mother Jones Magazine" over publishing an article on the treatment of U.S. Citizens in the Judicial Dept. I MUST STAY BUSY.

There are a couple of irons I have in the fire. I'm not in the dorm anymore; I got in a bit of trouble and lost my job. No biggie there. Now I don't work for free. Whaaa! But they moved me back to the south end of the prison and back into a cell. That's really not so bad but I was comfortable where I was. Anyway, both locations, cell and dorm, have their plus'.

In our computer funnies there was a term or word I didn't get. They are obviously English. The guy talks about going to jail for stealing swimming pool inflatable's and then says, "I gotta lilo" What's a lilo? Usually I can piece a meaning together by the subject but I'm stumped here. *(Note: I gotta "lie low")*

So yer getting new parts next month huh? (New hip) Are you gonna be the bionic babe? Or bionic bird as they might say across the pond.

Weather permitting, I usually get up and go outside to walk laps as the sun comes up. I like the early mornings (out there in Calif.) Waking up still in prison is always a bummer but that will change one day. After two and a half hours of continuous walking, my left hip starts to pain me too. But I think it's because I sleep on a futon on a metal slab and my hip presses into the hard surface when I sleep on my side. Perhaps I'm in denial and one day I'll also need a new hip. Hey, does that make us Hippies? Well for you. I'm not quite there, yet. I hope that all works out Liz and I'll keep you in my prayers, especially on the 22nd.

You stated you didn't understand why my son Daniel didn't speak up for me at my trial. He and his friend, Maniac, (cool name huh?) the one he was running from home with, were scheduled to testify and Maniac did. He said he was there and never saw me point a gun at anyone and order em to do anything. The prosecution would have claimed that seeing as Daniel was my son, would have led him to claim that due to the family ties, that Daniel would have lied. It wasn't really necessary since Maniac gave witness. So it really compounds the State's error in allowing witnesses to take the stand without background checks, which by law I'm entitled to. My criminal history in California kept me off the stand because the prosecutor painted all the witnesses as saints. When the truth was 90% of the witnesses weren't even eligible to testify. They couldn't give testimony as to the guilt or innocence of the charge. The one who could and did testify, the lying son of a bitch taxi driver, had a worse record than mine. The prosecution withheld all this. All this has been proven three times over and sits on the desk of a Federal Magistrate. Einstein defines insanity as doing the same thing over and over again and expecting different results. I ain't sending nothing else to that court. I'm gonna pester the media until someone publishes my claims. Put a little heat under the pot so-to-speak. I hope anyway. I'm gonna do what I can. In the meantime, thanks for the lovely card. Its second favorite behind the birthday Warmest Fuzzy that ever Wuzzy card.

I'm gonna go. Besides I've run out of paper. Take care and write when you can.

Walt

****

Chapter Eleven

January 8, 2013

Dear Liz;

Well it's about time! (ME writing YEEEW.)

I've been bouncing around through the medical system over an irregular heart beat that causes dizziness and shortness of breath that hits maybe twice a week. The medical staff is sure I need "this" type of medication until it starts again. Then it's another type of medication. I'm hoping they'll get it right soon. It doesn't appear to be killing me, its just inconvenient. It stops me from doing whatever it is I'm doing, like pushups or walking briskly around the prison yard for exercise. Outside of that I seem to be fine.

I sent a motion to the courts explaining my cardiac problem. The magistrate asked for proof so he could bump me up the court docket. The medical people here said they don't have to provide documentation of anything unless I pay some stupid fee. After fighting back and forth with them I just turned all that over to the court with a chronological history of everytime I'd been whisked out of here in an ambulance or hustled off to a cardiologist at Galveston University. We'll see. It's unbelievable but true to still be waiting on a ruling by an appeals court, but I am, I think, worst case scenario...ahh well. Let's not do that anymore. *(Note: He's been having "episodes" with his heart for quite some time and this is the first I've heard him mention it. Bloody man!)*

We've been writing for 10 years now and I remember thinking and conveying that I'd be done with this legal crap based upon my innocence and the fairness of the courts. What was I thinking? I can tell you that whatever that was I ain't thinking like that now.

I had a dream back in February that I'd get my action in August. I didn't see which August though. Actually I'm half assed convinced that it's about to happen.

SOMETHING is about to happen. It's no wonder my hair has turned white huh?

I read a book called "Lamb" or "The Gospel of Jesus by His Best friend Biff" I was as entertained as any book I've ever read. The author is Christopher Moore and the guys a hoot. Its a novel about the years the Bible doesn't talk about and very tastefully done. I'm right now half ways through Jeffrey Deaver's rendition of James Bond. Ian Fleming's family chose him to write a new James Bond book. The reason I'm telling you this is because a lot of the story (first half) is placed around

London. While its not a bad read, the author is very (my pen just died, a moment of silence please... okay) So, where were we? Oh yeah, Jeffrey Deaver, an American bloke (I'm trying out British terminology) He used "crikey" which I thought was Australian, even though like America, it's a British Colony. I've only heard "Crikey" from the Ausies. What say you? So far it's a decent read. Since yer an English women perhaps you'd like the location descriptions. Some things will never be cleared up like the "Chicken / Egg" thing. And what the hell's a Piccadilly? Wait, is it a flower?

How's yer hip? I hope yer up and about without complications. I don't get no news anymore. Since the bastards took my radio I don't know what the weathers like out there. No doubt its better than here. Besides the Astros are scheduled to loose or is it lose? (Seems like the double "o" in "loose" should be "lose". I get those two words confused all the time) They're scheduled to lose more games than any other baseball team...ever!

Hey, guess who wrote? Crazy Carolyn! No kidding. She wrote and explained how her marriage to Frank went to shit. How she missed me and that being married to a black man wasn't all that great. Okay I tossed the "black" in on my own. Actually I believe ole Frank is a Mexican or Spanish at least. His last name is Herrera. Anyways Carolyn wrote and said she wants to resume our friendship. Yada, yada, yada. The last time she did this I wrote and told her sure, whatever, I ain't mad. Hell I didn't wanna marry you in the first place. I believe she married ole Frank to spite me. She wanted me to propose to her back in...you and me had to have talked about this, so you should remember. Anyways, she was pissed that I wouldn't lie to her about us. I ain't staying in Texas when I get out. I ain't marrying nobody that I don't intend to stay with and Carolyn ain't the type of women a man like me is gonna stay with. I also stopped lying a long time ago. Telling a story is different, a harmless story. Oh that reminds me, I should hear back from E-books by Crooks this month. Keep yer fingers crossed. You've only read two of the four stories I submitted. I guess that will change when I get them back.

Okay I'm gonna close this off for now. You take care and even though I ain't writ in a while don't make me less of your friend. I ain't dead and if anything breaks in the court or with a publisher I'll let you know first thing.

See ya,
Walt.

****

February 2, 2013

Dear Liz;

Hi, how's the hip? I hope everything went well. *(Note: because I was told I couldn't write to Walter but was, I still couldn't write for five to six wks after my hip surgery)* Did you get the...umm... gothic card? Did everyone at Bud's sign it? Did anyone sign it? I couldn't because I wanted you to be able to keep it. You did keep it didn't you? *(Note: Yes of course.)*

Speaking of keeping things, I need at least a copy of "The Queen's Dancer". The rest of my stories are being professionally put together due to a joint venture with Jason, 50/50 split and credit. He's really my editor. He had nothing to do except spelling and punctuation with the "Queen's Dancer". Well, it was his typewriter I typed it on.

Anyways there's an outfit called ebooks-by-Crooks.com that Jason contacted. Everyone else avoids us like the plague. Probably due to Jason is bald and I'm gray / white haired. Or maybe our "con" status. Anyways, the story you have is not among the stories we sent to the typewriter, email brawd (Jane) in Ct. and since it's my favorite and the longest story we have, I want it included. You can go to this website and see if it's a bullshit place or not. Jason has already instructed Jane (the typewriter lady in Ct. we paid $65.00 between the two of us for professionally formatted story layouts ,and she downloaded the stories on a disk. She will email em to whoever we tell her to) It's worth it because we can wheel and deal without putting a prison return address on it. Anyways Jason has already contacted this ebooks-by-Crooks.com place and got a letter back saying, "ahh, yeah, send what cha got" This is a start.

I'm not living on the same dorm with Jason anymore due to them moving me over a job change. But we are still partners and I trust him. I am the imagination behind this partnership. He's a published author of non-fiction but I got the stories. Besides he's a rare person and likable. I say rare in the sense that, in this environment he's trustworthy. I know he's bald but what the hell? Okay, so when you get a chance would you pleeeeze shoot that story back? I think I have notes and a rough outline at what I wrote but thats a finished product. I don't have access to the typewriter anymore. I wish I had two copies. One to keep and one to send off to this E-books place but it ain't necessary.

So, what have you been doing? I bet reading, watching TV and hobbling around. I'll bet Dobby misses your walks. I bet you miss your walks with Dobby. I got a friends radio and am listening to Casey Kasem. He's doing February, 1978. I like the shows in the early 1970's before 1975, pre-disco era. The big football game's on tomorrow. I'm going for the California team. I'll listen on the radio. It will be crowded, loud and obnoxious in the day room where the TV is. I'll miss the commercials but I'll also miss all the madness. I seem to be getting too old for all the rambunctious bullshit. I wanna see the game but the trade off is acceptable.

Well I'm gonna cut this short. I'm struggling for something to say. I'd like to know how your doing and hope all is well. I'll wait to hear from you when you can write. I hope my request for that story back ain't too much work for you just after they opened ya up. Don't throw nothing out of joint worrying about it. I have time and I can wait.

Geese, I'm closing in on March for another birthday. I have a sneaking suspicion I'll hear from the Feds all around the same time. Maybe by your birthday I'll be able to call you and wish you a Happy Birthday. That would be nice, let's hope! Okay I gotta go, take care and know your in my prayers,

Walt.

******

February 5, 2013

Liz;

Hey, I had an idea! A good one! One you'll either say, "Yer a freaking genius" or "You're a freakin idiot". I know I wrote yesterday asking you to send that story back. Don't! (pretty good so far right?) You say you have all these old letters from when I first started writing, right? Are they in date-order? You said you wouldn't part with them unless you could guarantee publication. I think this place (see enclosed book mark) may be perfect. *(Note: It's a self-printing publish co.)*

Jason got a letter back saying handwritten material is okay. The guy splits 50/50 profit and swears everything is above-board. You could contact him if you wanted or wait till he answers my letter. I told him about the "Queen's Dancer" and those letters. He could air them and get a following. We'd be freakin rich! and published! So just sit tight. Don't do nothing. Well you could write. I'd really like to know your okay. Do you still have all them letters? *(Note: What do you think I'm doing right now with them my idiot savant?)* Talk to me! Please write.

Walt

PS: Don't lose this book mark, I ain't got another.
(Note: I still have it and use it frequently as a book mark.)

******

March 7, 2013

Dear Liz;

Hi, I hope you are doing well.

I have gained access to another writin machine, temporarily. Each machine seems to be different, temperamentally speaking. I'll get the hang of this one here momentarily.

I still ain't heard from you in a while so of course I'm a bit worried. How are ya? Have you kicked anyone off in the ass yet? That seems to be the real test to me and your hip. Pick your specimens carefully though. If you boot someone you have to deal with on a regular basis and your new hip is working real good well, you do the math. They might be burping up stuff they should be shitting out and... Alright, I'll stop now.

Okay, let's talk business first. Enclosed is the letter I received back from ebooks-by-Crooks. It seems to be a form letter. I'm not surprised. What I'd like to do, but only if your up to it and only if your up to it, is send them "The Queen's Dancer" with the enclosed cover letter and this return address. You know, so when they respond it will come back to me. Wha-da-ya-think? Read the cover letter and if it sounds too stooped then, I don't know. I'm just trying to get something started here.

The "Spike" letters will have to be rewritten, that's obvious. That's a major undertaking perhaps I'll undertake once I get out of here. But I can get my foot in the door with some of this other stuff. Maybe catch the eye of a regular publisher in the mean time. Wha-da-ya-think? If this is too much for ya let me know. Like a dumb ass I never made a copy of the final draft. I have my notes but the story, as you read it, is the finished product. Did you like it by the way or were you just humoring me because I'm fragile? The only thing I'd really like to change is the title to "Cat Dancer"

Alright, let's breach a subject we've been avoiding. No, don't stop me; it's something that has to be done. I'm about to turn 49 again, and I still haven't got my fat butt out of prison. Not for lack of trying, but still. I just found and wrote a Christian prison ministries that seems to specialize in wrongful convictions and asked for a little help. The site is "Centurion Ministries." *(Note: I also contacted them at a later date. I've never heard back from them and neither has Walter. Not even a "thank you but can't help you" letter. I mentioned before that Walter's case is not high profile enough for any of these so called "Innocence" programs.)* I think if you put an ".org" after that you can check them out on the web. Anyway I'm basically waiting on the stinking courts to do something (still) anything. Nothings changed in that regard. I think when things really do start to pop for me they'll roll pretty fast. Again, we'll seeeee. Some day.

Usually when I write, after a while between letters, I'll get one right after I mail yours. If I get one tonight I'll be happy to add on to this one. I still have to type that cover letter. I hope your up and around a bit and can do this without too much hassle. If not, don't worry about it. Alright, you've probably heard this before but I read it the other day and thought it was funny. You may be in the mood for something funny, who knows?

An old man walks into a crowded doctor's office and, as the bored waiting patients listened he told the receptionist, "I need to see a doctor." The receptionist asked him "Why?" to which he replied, "There's something wrong with my dick." The receptionist adjusted herself in the seat and told him, "Sir, you realize there are better ways to express yourself that doesn't offend the people around that might be, well, you know, listening." She indicated the other people looking on. The old man looked at them, hiked up his pants and asked her, "Well, what do you suggest?" the receptionist kept her voice down but the waiting room was real quiet as they listened. "You could say that maybe there was something wrong with something not so…risqué." The old man smoothed his thinning hair back as he thought about this, and he left the doctors office. A few minutes late he came back in and informed the receptionist that, again he needed to see the doctor. She looked up at him and asked what his problem was. "There's something wrong with my ear." He said. The receptionist smile a satisfying smile and asked him, "What is wrong with your ear?" To which he replied, "It's broke, I can't piss out of it" The entire waiting room busted up.

Well, I really hope your okay. Did you get your get well card? I'll bet your getting spoiled and haven't a care in the world. I hope that's the case anyways. That about does it for me. Take care my friend and get better. Till I hear from ya, I'll remain myself.

Your friend.
Walt.

* * * * * *

March 17, 2013

Dear Liz;

Hi ya toots! Feelin better? I got your letter dated March 2nd that said you ain't having so much pain in yer hip. That's good, I'm very glad for you. I'm hoping not to put too much strain on you by asking about that stoopid story again,

I just sent e-booksbycrooks "Jragin" (the story of a little four year old girl who charms the balls off a gigantic green dragon) I'm sure I've mentioned it. Anyways, I requested they send a copy back. When it gets here I'll send it to you. Now the other story, I'm hoping you already sent it to them with my return address and that cover letter I sent. If not could, you, please? I told them about the story and that a friend of mine, who just had both her legs replaced…(what, me exaggerate? Surly you jest!) Would send it when she was able. Are you able?

You mention that you had "stuff" at Bud Plant's from me. That probly means you never got the card until…how you gonna heal properly without that Wizard card commanding you to? Did you like the little fellows in his sleeves? Yeah that's Bud himself and Alberta. Not really. Near as I can remember, you never mentioned Alberta smoking a pipe. *(Note: I LOVE that card, it's drawn beautifully)*

Alright, nothing new around here. I'll bet you've already sent that story to Las Vegas and have written me back to tell me to shut the hell up about it. Things usually happen that way. If not, remember I ain't yellin at ya. I'm just reminding ya, friendly like. I built it up to them people and they might think I'm lyin. At any rate they now have one of my stories. let's see what happens.

Okay, I'm gonna go for now. Take care and write when you get the chance. I really miss hearin from ya.

Bye for now,
Walt.
PS: Happy Easter!

* * * * * * * *

April 11, 2013

Dear Liz;

Hi it's me again.

I got this postcard (enclosed,) from e-books in Las Vegas and I'll bet it's a mistake. See, I sent them a story called "Jragin" but enclosed a cover letter for "Cat Dancer", well not a cover letter but a synopsis of "Cat Dancer" as well as "Jragin" (it's required by them.) What I think happened is they got the manuscript and pulled out the one for "Cat Dancer" thinking the following story was "Cat Dancer." The reason I say that is because I ain't got one of these cards for "Jragin" I sent another story called "Second Chances" and if you sent "Cat Dancer," then they have three stories right now. Over the weekend I'm sending them "Departure 153" with instructions.

You asked in a not so recent letter (I ain't complainin. I know yer recovering from Bionic surgery) if I wanted you to send any of your drawings back, in one word NO. Those are exempt from the story thing. I don't need "The Spike Chronicles" right now. I can't type them up at the moment But if you haven't had a chance to send "Cat Dancer" to the Vegas address, with my return address, would you? All the rest of that can wait. My instructions with "Departure 153" will be to offer it as a free download to promote the other three stories. What do you think?

You only got to read "Departure 153" and "Cat Dancer", formally known as the "Queen's Dancer". If you ain't sent it could you cross out the "Queen" and pen in "Cat." So it becomes "Cat Dancer?" Anyway, I'm hoping to be able to afford my own typewriter from this deal. If I can get a steady income from this then I can put some money away for my release. Pizza (my fav food) ain't cheap. It might, if I play my cards right, put me on the map as an author. Who knows? Hey, I could even win the Pulitzer Prize. I can just imagine my acceptance speech. "Eh hem, first I'd like to thank my mom and dad and Jim Beam for my conception. If it weren't for hard liquor and the over sized back seats of the 1957 Chevy...alright, maybe I could work on a better speech.

How are you these days? I'll bet we cross path's letter wise that always seems to happen with us. There's not much new to write about around here. I'll bet those Praying Mantis' miss you in your garden, I really hope your alright and getting better and better. Sorry these letters are so short, take care and write when you can.

Bye for now,
Walt

(Note: I found out much later, when we finally spoke on the phone, that during my hip surgery recovery time that I didn't or couldn't write, he was very worried that something "had" happened to me and there was no one else he could really contact to find out.)

****

May 16, 2013

Dear Liz;

Hi, I'm late on your birthday card. I know.

I've been busy runnin out to the local hospital. Three times over the last month I've been pulled out, strapped down and sent to Huntsville Memorial Hospital due to heart complications. Apparently I wasn't dying or nothing but whatever was going on made it necessary to back an ambulance up to the prison and send me to the free-world hospital. *(Note: I don't care what he said, he could have died if the situation wasn't taken care of.)*

I leave tomorrow for Galveston, for a Cardiologist appointment, and will be gone another week to ten days. My ability to hustle artwork or trade various blackmarket commodities has suffered more than anything. I had to stay under observation, for a time, each time I left out of here. They don't know why my heart is doing what it's doing. Rapid-irregular rhythm-skipping beats and generally screamin to get out of my chest. I've asked for medical marijuana but so far…not! So I borrowed a stamp and a cup of coffee, plagiarized another card I thought was appropriate and included it in this envelope.

I haven't heard back from e-books (Louis Napoleon Publisher) but I just received your card the other day. My mail is in limbo. I've sent them four stories, (well you sent one) I sent them a letter asking to please confirm they were all received.

Outside of that, all is well. Spike came to visit due to my illness and made his mark on your card (special edition).

Well, I have to drag all my property down to the property room in a minute. I'll mail this on the way. I'll drop you a line after I get back and let you know all is well.

Spike sends his best, bye for now,

Your friend,
Walt

****

June 5, 2013

Dear Liz;

Howdy. I got your letter dated May 27th the other day. I've been meaning to answer it and let you know I ain't dead or nothing. In fact the cardiologist ran some tests and said, "We'll call ya back down if these tests show ya need some fixin or something" I go back next week. So what happened was my heart started an irregular rhythm that progressed from a subtle sort a thing to a "Hey I need some attention down here!" Actually the first time I went to the infirmary they accused me of faking to get out of work. They hooked me up to an EKG machine and next thing I knew I was in an ambulance to Huntsville Memorial Hospital. That happened three times before they set me up with a cardiologist at the Houston University Medical Branch.

This is a six hour bus ride starting at four am with 49 other idiots all chained to each other in a bus designed to hold 50 but should only carry 40. The ironic thing is when I was at Ellis Welding I used to put these bus' together. Now I ride one. Anyways the ride, though packed down there went right through downtown Houston and out to Galveston Island. After being stuck in a stinkin prison, for years on end, my neck was sore lookin at all the sights. Especially when we got to the ocean and I saw all the ships. After we got there Doogie Howser took an EKG and ordered a stress test while I wore a heart monitor. "What's that?" I asked. "It's a machine that monitors your heart" "No, not that! What is a "stress test?" I asked, he told me not to worry that I'd be staying over at the hospital and would be treated well. Spike said, "Fuck that! we ain't interested!" Vulgar little bastard, but that's Spike.

"Who's this?" Doctor Junior Mint asked and I introduce him to Spike. The young doctor, I swear he looked 14 years old, yells to an Indian guy with a diaper wrapped around his head. That guy sees Spike from across the room and brandishes a fork. "Uh oh" Spike said and the chase was on. I lost sight of Spike for the rest of the day.

I was taken out of the holding tank and put in a room with a TV that had 5,376 channels of crap on it. It took me an hour and a half to finally land on comedy central and Family Guy, South Park etc, etc. I saw "Kelly Hero's" one of my all time favourite movies. I got settled and a nurse came in with a tray of real food with juice and pudding, O.M.G.! I ate it, puked it up and ate it again, it was that good. My heart monitor was hangin around my neck with all these little leads stuck to my chest, ribs and sides. I fell asleep watching the Stooges.

"Mr. Anderson, Mr. Anderson..." A nurse woke me up. "What the fuck do you want?!" (I can't blame that on Spike) But I woke right out of a dead sleep believing I was still in prison. "Well, okay Mr. Potty mouth, open up and take your medicine" she said. She looked like Mrs. Cunningham from Happy Days and I was immediately ashamed of my language. I mumbled I was sorry and took the pill she offered. "What was that?" I asked her. "Oh, it's to relax you in preparation for surgery" I said, "Oh" and lay back down to get back to sleep. "Wait!!" I said sitting bolt up-right. She stopped, almost out the door. "Surgery?!" I said a little worried. "Yeah, silly" she said "your scheduled for surgery at 9am" and started to leave again. "Wait" I yelled again. Again, she stopped and looked back. "What kind of surgery?" I asked. She laughed and tisked me as she left. I ain't here for surgery I thought. About 15 minutes later two orderly's came in with another nurse. The orderly's were Cuban and big. They spoke Cubanese and proceeded to strap me down. The nurse was a small blonde with freckles. "How are we this morning?" she asked. I was trying to communicate with the Castro brothers when I noticed this woman, pint sized, was shaking up a can of shaving cream. "Hey! Wha da ya gonna do with that?" I asked as Castro #1 cinched down a strap across my chest, being careful not to get the monitor in the strap. "I'm going to shave your head silly." She giggled. "We can't have all that hair in the way when the doctor does his surgery" "What!?" I said, starting to fight the restraints. I ain't no brainiack but they shave the area there gonna cut. "You mean I'm having brain surgery?" I asked, panic in my voice. "Of course" she said lathering my head up. "How else will we remove the tumor?" she said starting to drag a razor across my head. That's when the tranquilizer started hitting me and my words slurred together. She shaved me bald and drew a dotted line on my head and left me strapped to the bed.

An hour later they came in and wheeled me out and into an operating theater. I could have sworn I saw Spike looking down from the audience window. Last thing I saw before they put me out was Dr. Doogie Howser in a surgical mask coming in with a scalpel. I woke up in a puddle of drool in the holding tank gripping a green bologna sandwich. Other convicts looking at my shaved head with the dotted line drawn on it. I was still groggy as we all got chained up and boarded the bus for Eastham or what ever prison these other guys were from. After an all day bus ride I got to Eastham and saw the regular physician's assistant, who explained that the pretend brain surgery was the "stress" test. We'll get the results on how your heart did in the next few days. My answer to that is another trip to Galveston next week. Yay! I can't wait. Spike ended up in someone else's pocket but make it back to Ellis Unit. He said it was close though.

My arthritis is causing my writing to be sloppy. I'm gonna go for now. I'll write you when I get back. I really and truly don't know what to expect. The cardiologist said if I needed another appointment, one would be scheduled. If something bad does happen, I'll get word to you. I'll write to my son and give him instructions on how to contact you through Bud's. But let's hope that ain't necessary. I hope to be able to report court news in August. For now take care and keep me in your prayers.

Yer friend,
Walt

PS: I just finished reading "Killing Lincoln," what a trip! Great minds think alike. *(Note: I read it first and told him I knew he'd like it)* I also read a Christopher Moore book about Jesus. I enjoyed it immensely. (It was tastefully done but with a comedic twist) He's my new favorite author.

****

July 22, 2013 Read this first

Dear Liz;

Hi, how's things in the mountains? I hope all is well and yer hip is behaving itself.

Things are pretty much the same down here. I have neither heard from the courts or Las Vegas (e-books). I wrote them and pretty much said "Shit or get off the pot" Earlier in their first letter they said, "If we don't use yer stuff we'll send it back to ye, arg!" Perhaps not in those exact words. Did ya like the pirate twist? I'm very creative sometimes. Anyways, I revisited the "Rachel" story and sent it with my ultimatum. That makes five stories they have, approx. 100 pages. If they can't see what a great story teller I am by that, then their loss. When they send it back I'll find a publisher out of this Writers Market book and shoot my best shot there. Speaking of which, I think I have a guy that wants me to draw a board for him so I'll have a little money to play with. It is my intent to invest in the Spike stories so if your ready to send the first installment go ahead. I'll buy some ink cartridges if this guy is for real.

You don't know how many so called "people" tell me, "Oh yeah I want you to do this" or that "Only to have them fade into the woodwork when it comes time to get started. " Lately I tell em, "yeah, yeah, yeah, you buy the boards and bring them to me and we'll set something up". Nine times out of 10 they don't. I have to rent a typewriter and furnish my own ink cartridges to type. It's not a bad deal. I was hoping to be able to generate some income through this e-books play by now. I'll keep plugging along. Honestly though I'm startin to think my clean stores are not their regular genre' and they don't know what to do with them. They may jump all over the "Spike stories" who knows.

I write to leave this place mentally and all its bullshit. I have traded for that Christopher Moore book "Lamb" or "The Gospel of Jesus Christ according to his best friend Biff" and intend to send it to you when I get ahead of my stamp collection. You're probably thinking, "Oh Blimey that's what I need right now, a religious book trying to convince me I'm a sinner." Not that kind of book luv. I was doin my English accent, how'd I do? It's a most entertaining story written very tastefully about the years Jesus and Biff travelled about the Middle East before he was the Messiah. Well it covers that too, I know you'll enjoy it and I'm gonna find a way to send it to ya. It'll have to be later though. I have it and am...gonna...yeah well, you'll see. *(Note: I do have "Lamb" and he was right, I really enjoyed it as I also enjoyed "Fool" and "Coyote Blue" by the same author)*

Okay, so send me the first installment of Spike. You should have no problems. If for some reason they stop them, I'll have the postage to send them back so...don 't worry! and I'll get busy. Unless I get a letter from you today, I'll mail this short and sweet, take care and all that.

All my best, respectfully yer friend,

Walt.

PS: Aren't you getting ready for your High School reunion thingy?

****

July 26, 2013 Read this one second (he put both letters in one envelope)

Dear Liz, again

This is not the first time I've written you while you were writing to me. I have your postmarked letter dated the 22nd (actually written the 18th) along with the computer jokes, which are always a hit. Yes I remember drawing both of those flowers you have stuck to your work clipboard, along with other drawings I see. You have other fans I see, I'm not surprised. And none I'm sure bigger than I.

The problem with my heart is thus. No, that's what they call it "Thus"...I'm kidding. Actually I took four trips to Galveston Hospital. The last one they finally diagnosed me and started me on some pills that seem to actually have an effect on my heart. For the better too! No one is more surprised than I. When the cardiologist told me what it was the intern vomited on the spot. "What!" I said, "That's right you have cooties" I rolled out of the way of the intern just in time, "You mean like when we were all little kids and got kissed by a little girl, cooties like that?" He nodded and I vomited. Oh come on, you knew I was an idiot 10 years ago. You can't possibly be surprised when I come up with crap like that, right? The real explanation is thus. My upper heart wasn't firing with my lower heart. It was pooling in the upper chamber of my heart causing all kinds of problems. I seem to be fine now. It was periodical at worst but the periods were getting longer and more severe. *(Note: Yes but it doesn't end there.)*

I just sent the Rachel story to e-books. That makes five stories they have. I told them about the "Spike" stories and they should be reading that today. I revamped "Rachel" and told them the story of Redneck my friend back in 2003 when that story unfolded. The facts turn out to be more intriguing than the fiction.

So, send me the first batch of "Spike" stories / papers / letter, whatever they're called, and I promise to take care of them and return them in person one day. If you want them back it would be a privilege. Maybe I'll get motivated and finish the "Peter Pan and Spike the Wonder Roach" story...can't wait.

Okay I'm gonna go, take care and I hope yer hip is good and perfect. Hi to Alberta and Diane. If Alberta needs cheering up I know someone who's up for the job. Yep the ever faithful Spike. I can write a story where her ex gets abducted by Aliens and they give him the anal probe. Tell everyone there I say, "Hey!" Bye for now,

Yer first biggest fan
Walt.

****

September 23. 2013

Dear Liz;

First of all I got the Spike letters, thanx. I have sat down to write you a hundred and, lets see… I'm thinking, a hundred and twenty, at least multiple times! But something always got in the middle of it. I would have sent you the letters I had started but they wouldn't have made sense...not that they do anyways. Well, some do, sometimes.

How was your H.S. reunion? I hope you and Cyndi had the time of your lives down there in sunny Southern California. Did you surf? I know, I'm an idiot. I hope all went well.

Nothing new to report around here. I'm waiting on a letter from my "mentor" I told you about me getting a mentor, right? *(Note: No he didn't but I'm glad because she really helped him.)* The Pen American Center contest I entered last year thought I showed promise and even though I didn't win anything they paired me up with (so they say) either a graduate student from some hoity toity university or an accomplished author. All I know about this person is her name is Megan. I'm supposed to wait to hear from her before I write.

She has the "Rachel" story and an attempt at a screen play I had written in attempt to enter two different categories in that contest. So when "Megan" writes I may hit her with the life and times of Walt, Spike and Ronnald. I don't know, I may not like her and have Spike do a psychological evaluation to see what makes her tick. Spike says he can do an evaluation just by studying her hand writing. "What if she types her letters" I asked him, he said, "she'll sign her name at the bottom and that's all he needs" The little shit claims to have been an analyst for the C.I.A. This would explain his familiarity to Richard Millhouse Nixon. Anyway I'm waiting for Megan to write whatever she plans on writing and I will respond accordingly.

Fall is upon us! It's cooling down around here again. Jeese going back over those old letters and realizing how naive I was to the court system is disheartening in a way. Fantastic as it sounds I am still waiting on a Federal judge to hear this petition for writ of Habeas Corpus. At the Federal level.

Liz, in your last letter you mentioned that if you could you'd send me some lolly. Every time I've asked you, I always think twice, you have sent me something. And that was always after I exhausted every other avenue at my disposal. Mostly I don't need money, I did need a friend. Looking back over these letters it gladdens my heart more than any amount of money could do...Ah gosh, I'm all choked up here...sniff, sniff. But you get the idea. Liz, you are the lolly. Thanx and all you had to do was be "you" (or yeew, that's Texan) Okay I'm done sucking up to you for now. I meant what I said though. No I ain't getting ready to ask for anything. Even though do you realize reading these first letters, I sound like an art book whore! Here's the interesting part, it worked! I look forward to returning these letters, in a binder, to you in person one day or offering them to you anyways, if you want them back. *(Note: He had asked me to return some of the letters he'd written to me, specifically certain dates for legal questions.)* In the meantime would you like me to draw you another big board? Or would that be too hard to explain? It would be a Christmas present. I don't know what it would be so maybe something Frazetta like since we both have exquisite taste in art. I think I can find something to do. I could write you a story instead, you could even tell me what kind, who's in it and how you want it to end and I'd tailor make you a story.

By that time, I'll have heard from these asshole Federal courts by then, and all of this will be easier. Heavy sigh. That's me keeping my pecker (chin) up as y'all say across the pond. Yes I still have all my teeth. I ain't from around here even though I may sound like it sometimes.

Okay Liz, I'm gonna go for now. Take care and tell everyone Hi for me.

Your friend,
Walt.

****

October 21, 2013

Dear Liz,

Thank you for the Halloween card. Your letter and card was the highlight of my month, so far.

I finally heard from the Federal courts. The Magistrate recommended my petition be dismissed and a Certificate of Appeal ability to the 5th Circuit court be denied. His recommendation referred to my claim in such a way that it was as if I had not litigated anything. When one attacks a conviction through Habeas Corpus, the appellate judge decides whether there is merit and if there is merit, issues an "Order to Show Cause" why this petition should not be granted. The State Attorney Generals office is charged with answering this order. All this has been done, years ago.

The Attorney General argued points against my claim that I proved were not true by using their own records. None of that was visible in the Magistrate's recommendations and findings. I was allowed 14 days to object to the Magistrates recommendations which send both briefs to a "De Novo Review" by the district judge. This judge makes the final decision. If there are questions of law or a discrepancy, I will be issued Certificate of Appeal ability and allowed into the 5th Circuit Court. One step below the U.S. Supreme Court for Texas.

I've been surly, angry and an asshole lately. It felt as if someone had slugged me in the stomach when I read the Magistrates recommendations. Of course I responded, but I'm at a loss for words. And for me that's awful hard, on how latterly one sided and unfair our courts are. There is no accountability for the lower courts who, as in my case, literally broke the law to obtain a conviction. I'm not having a good October.

I had some pretty fair expectations. Well it ain't over! I've done all I can do for the moment, so keep me in your prayers. You know it's strange; I had answered this crap from the Magistrate and then find a case in the books that wasn't available the other day when I was cramming for my response. Anyways, I'm getting past that right now. The District Judge over see's all cases before that court. We'll see.

This picture of your reunion with Cyndi is better than the other one I have of you and Cyndi at a previous reunion. I tried to unpeel the other one from my photo album, to check the date, and it's stuck, so I've stuck it beside the picture I have of you and your brother. Now this new picture will go, "Liz, how do you two look younger in this recent picture than in the other one that's two years ago?" I forget when was your last reunion, last year? No that can't be right, maybe it's... come to think of it every picture I have of you you're smiling, they all look (the smiles) genuine too. Perhaps that's the answer.

I will win in the courts, I have to. I'm right and innocent of my charge. Kidnapping a taxi driver. None of that was addressed in this last batch of shit from the courts. It was all "Procedural" errors made in filing the papers. I found a case, U.S. Supreme Court case, so it's law, that states on a claim like mine you can't dismiss on procedural error, even fabricated ones. What kills me is hearing on the news how homosexual's are getting their rights to bugger each other, when I can't even get my right to a fair trial according to the Constitution!! Alright I'll quit.

Hey, I heard or read a good golf story the other day. Well it's a good one if your not Arnold Palmer. Arnold Palmer (major gold celebrity) died and went to Heaven. St. Peter met him at the gate, "Arnold, welcome to Heaven" he said. "Let's see." St. Peter said, examining his book. "You've led a pretty good life son" Arnold smiled at St. Peter. "I see you only used the Lord's name in vain once in your entire life. That's impressive but, what happened that you slipped up that once?" Arnold shifted his feet around and sheepishly told St. Peter, "Well, it was during "the Riders Cup" (A big gold competition between the U.S. and Britain) "all I hadda do was make par on a par four and the cup was ours" Arnold told him. "Well I shot true from the tee and watched as the ball went down the middle of the fairway and kept going into the tall rough grass beyond the fairway" St. Peter listened and said, and that's what caused you to take the name of our Lord in vain?" "No of course not" Arnold replied. "I used a five iron and came right out. Only I ended up in a sand trap beside the green" St. Peter again assumed that was the reason to cause Arnold to use the Lords name in vain. "No, I was pretty sue I could chip the ball within easy putt distance of the cup. My American team mates were excited as we hadn't beat the Brits in 10 years! All of America watched on every T.V. Network as I chipped towards the flag. I knew I had made a good shot when the crowed erupted in cheers and when I climbed out of the sand trap and seen my ball six inches from the cup; I knew we were going to win" St. Peter, exasperated, said, "don't tell me you missed the GOD DAMN PUTT!! I ain't read a better gold story in a while, like it?

So, you like Vodka with apple juice? Hmmm. I've never been much of a drinker. I would rather smoke a joint and drink Pepsi. I have a low tolerance for alcohol-booze. I'm a good designated driver. I might stop at a fast food place for French fries though…I wonder. Do they call em French fries in France?

You know the last time you sent "lolly" I went on a story binge. I typed up five or six stories and sent them off to magazines, etc. remember? Now I know I won't get anywhere that way but I could try and get an agent. No I ain't heard back from Megan yet. I sent her "Rachel" and "Cat Dancer" They have to go through the Pen American Center place that set up the mentor program. Maybe I should write a true account of my lousy treatment from the courts, see if I can't generate some attention that way.

Anyway, I'm going to send the trust fund slip to you. I went a long way on $40.00 you sent last year. Even though anything is a blessing and $25.00 is like a Christmas morning at the Rockefellers. Actually since I had to concentrate on the legal brief I let my card business slip and am about out of essentials. Liz, I appreciate any thing you do for me, be it a letter, card, jokes, books or calendars. I never needed money to make me happy to hear from you. Shoot whatever you want or can and know it's enough and always appreciated. Thanx. (*Note: I told him a long time ago, if he felt he needed some cash to ask and I'd send some, if I could, whatever I could. He's **never** taken advantage of me*)

Speaking of calendars, as you know I'm a Frazetta fan. I remember you once said you also like his art and his son-in-law, Ken Kelly? Or someone like that did the cover of the Bud Plant catalog and I had commented that his art resembled Frazetta's, you said he's related or pointed out a connection to Frank, remember that? (*Note: No I don't but not to say I didn't mention that*)

You know, speaking of making "Giraffalo" into a movie, I could write the screenplay and enter it into a screenplay contest that's held every year to get new fresh ideas noticed. The first screenplay I wrote got rave reviews from Megan. I agree I too can see Hazel and Giraffalo as a movie. The next Lion King? Sheeeeeit! I'd be a Trillionaire! Disney / Pixar!

Hmmm, there's no telling how long this asshole judge is going to take getting back to me. I would use your donation to type it up and maybe get Megan, when she writes, on board. She wrote and seemed pretty excited (or gullible) about seeing more of my crap. That's why I sent her two stories. I liked "Cat Dancer" and sent it claiming it was my best to date (my opinion) "The Phone Booth" was the story I turned into a screenplay. I have that back, wanna read it? I'll send it anyway, it reads very quick and you will see signs of the Swami Roach. Maybe I should write some of the "Spike" stories and work up to the Swami Roach story. Ahh well, we'll see.

Well I've got side tracked for a while, thanx to you, it's a good thing. I'm gonna go and get this mailed. I'm glad your reunion was a blast. What was the one song that stuck in your head the most from your reunion? Was it while you were dancing or because you were dancing? *(Note: It was "I could have gone on dancing".)* You know that song "Sugar Sugar" by the Archie's? I've always wanted to write up a scene where "Giraffalo" meet's a little girl Giraffe and they do the puppy love thing to the music of "Sugar Sugar". Like the "Lion King" the music or soundtrack would be a selling point. In a screenplay one can pick the music to accompany the visuals. I need something to think about to take my mind off the lousy court crap and maybe this is it.

Okay, Hi to Alberta, tell her I'm glad she's happy. All I gotta do is look at your smiling face to see that's the secret to longevity and staying young, happiness that is. Hi to Diane and anybody else that's interested. Thanx again for the Jack-O-Lantern card. It ain't as wonderful as the "Warmest Fuzzy that ever Wuzzy" card, but its close. Want me to draw you something for Christmas? What? Let me know.

Bye for now, your friend,
Walt

PS: Maybe enlarge to 8x10 one of the photos of you and Cyndi and I'll draw it, you can give it to her, just a thought.

W

****

December 10, 2013

Dear Liz;

Hi my friend. How is life treatin ya? I hope all is well and all things considered you and yours are well and happy. However, all things considered, you may still have a house full of people.

I LIVE with a house full of people, for the most part. However, due to another trip to Galveston I am in a lockup wing waiting for a bunk to open up. I'm in a cell by myself though, which is not that bad. Technically I'm "in transit." I'm not mad about this. However, when they finally do find me another house it could be with a cell mate that I may not like. This is ever the concern. But for now, and until at least the first week of January I am a bachelor. (However you spell it.) It's always noisy in lockup. Well from about 3pm until about 5am it's "free yell time!" Three tiers of cells stacked one upon the other, with inmates who have nothing better to do than, yell down the run to another inmate about whatever. Most of the guys on this wing are at Eastham for the first time and want to know what kind of joint it is.

I have a couple of good books I saved for this occasion. I have my radio and am looking forward to a couple of weeks of no people, only the ones I can hear. They have to compete with the voices in my head though.

I had some Christmas cards and was busy drawing stuff for customers prior to my trip to Galveston. I sold them all for some things I needed and wanted. I needed coffee. I have all my hygiene stuff and knew I'd be back here at least a month so I put some stuff together so I will be as comfortable as I can be. They let us out one at a time three times a week for a shower, that's it. Oh and any important "interviews" like parole. Yeah I saw parole but the chances of me making my first parole… They vote on you. A panel of assholes vote "yay or nay" on an individual basis. Jesus wouldn't make his first parole hearing. It's a joke, really, are very slim. I am not even entertaining the idea. I did not shoot myself in the foot at the interview though. Even though I think it was designed to see if they could make a guy mad, you know to determine whether or not he was suitable for social contact with normal people. So I went through that.

I spent the rest of the money I'd hustled up on re-typing "Cat Dancer" and sending it to the L. Ron Hubbard Writers of the Future contest. That's done! Yay, yay!

I think it was ordained by "the forces that be" here's why. I had sent it to Megan, my mentor, who I have not heard from since I propositioned her…,..No, nothing like that! I've received three mentor letters from her on three different stories. Anyway she gave some constructive criticism on "Cat Dancer." Since I thought it was my best piece I re-wrote it, changing what I thought needed changing, rented a typewriter, typed it up and sent it to L.Ron Hubbard. You may be able to follow its progress but maybe not, I'm not sure how that works. But it's in the 4th quarter and the website is simply www.writersofthefuture.com. It went from a 45 page story to a 50 page, 16,500 words. My limit was 17,000 words. So it seemed all the planets lined up and I no sooner had it typed and in the mail when they called me out for the chain bus to Galveston. That process is a five day ordeal.

Thursday night I took all my property down to the property room. They inventory it and send me back to sleep. Early Friday morning it's off to the chain room to wait for Officer Dingbat to complete the paperwork for any inmate leaving the unit. Then it's out to the back gate to wait on the bus. Bus comes, we're all chained together, (hence "chain bus") and its off to various other prisons picking up and dropping off inmates until we reach the Byrd Unit where we lay over for the weekend. Then Monday morning about three a.m. we're fed, chained up and it's a six hour drive to Galveston. (John Sealy Hospital) where we're mass produced into groups from one million other prisons across Texas. All of us having appointments for anything and everything. We're stuck in a waiting room full of sick whiny dorks all wanting their mama, not me. I got a seat by the window as I was one of the first in there, and watched the ships come and go in Galveston Harbor, that was cool. At six p.m. we're done. Some stay over night so they are culled from the herd. We have had two sandwiches and a juice all day.

Now from six p.m. to midnight it's back on the bus. We pull into Byrd Unit at 1:30am. By the time we get to a cell it's three am. They feed breakfast at six am Tuesday morning. It's back on the bus and a ride all over the southern part of Texas to various other prisons, dropping off inmates and picking them up until we reach Eastham about noon. We had a peanut butter sandwich and a couple of prunes for lunch. We sit in the chain room til about 3p.m. and then we get housed in lockup until a bunk becomes available.

Here is where I'll spend Christmas and New Year, But! I'm by myself, yay! And I'm entered into the 4th Quarter Writers of the Future contest with what I consider my best work. If I can get some recognition and I will if I win, I'll be able to get the attention of publishers and or agents. I'd like to write a couple of full length novels. One in the same setting as "Cat Dancer" and of course "Giraffalo" I believe "Giraffalo," if properly handled, would be a mega hit. It has that "feel" about it. Don't you think?

I ran across this lil cartoon in the Lubbock News Paper and how could I not think of you and Dobby? *(Note: Dobby, my dog, was not allowed on the furniture, so I thought this was cute, plus I drank wine.)* Lubbock is Buddy Holly country, along with Mac Davis and Waylon Jennings too.

Okay I'm gonna close and get this out in today's mail. If I wait any longer it won't go out til tomorrow. Here's hoping they don't work you too much this holiday season.

Merry Christmas to you and our friends at Bud Plant. Take care and all that.

Always my best, your friend,
Walt.

****

Chapter Twelve

January 1, 2014 HAPPY FREAKIN NEW YEAR!

Dear Liz;

Hey you! Thank you for Christmas 2013. *(Note: I sent $$)* The day before yesterday they brought us our commissary that we ordered last week. I got your card about 10 days ago and since I'm stuck in lockup, still waiting for a bunk in General population, I have to wait for the commissary to run ad-seg (lockup.) They get our order the day before and bring what we ordered the following day due to holidays etc. It took a few days. I got the calendar on the same day so my Christmas was the other day.

I'm stuck in the flu zone right now. It started with a sore itchy throat and gradually progressed into the flu or a real bad cold. I'm in a good place for it though. I dread them bringing me a "move slip" with this cold kickin by butt.

I got my "Cat Dancer" story back the other day, It seems that the L. Ron Hubbard Writers of the Future Contest has either moved with "no forwarding address" or folded up their tent. I'm checking on it.

Oh guess what? On December 22nd Carolyn came to see me. She was on her way to Houston to see her son for Christmas and talked her way in to see lil ole me. She got rid of Frank and thought she'd check to see...who knows but they let her in even though she's not on my visiting list. I have no visiting list anymore but she refused to take "no" for an answer and voila! That was nice, I guess. At first I thought it was a mistake. Anyways she swears she's going to write, we'll see.

Okay, I'm dying here, I have cough drops thanx to you and if that doesn't do anything, a bag of Jalapeño potato chips might. I promise you this I won't die with them on the shelf! As soon as I see the Angel of Death approaching...I'll be fine. (Funny smiley face)

Y'all take care. I'm gonna go. I'll write more next time. You know why sharks don't bite black people? They think they are whale turds. Sorry, heard that yesterday and just had to pass it on. It was in Spike's Christmas card. Yeah, I know, he's a real good person (bug)

Bye 4 now,
Walt.

****

March 11, 2014

Dearest Liz;

I haven't the words to comfort you in your hour of need. There isn't a doubt in my mind that your family and friends will flock to your side when you need them. I wish I could be one of those. Don't worry about me, write when your ready. I'm gonna go forward and if for some reason something changes here, I'll write you. *(Note: My husband became very ill)*

I'm pestering a production company about a script where I've combined three of my stories to make a pilot. The three stories are, "Angels Inc", "Second Chances" and "Rachel." I've been working on that screenplay and pestering a production company. We'll see how that turns out. Something has to give. So far 2014 ain't been worth a sour squirt of bird shit!

Our dorm is on quarantine status due to a stomach virus. I had it a week ago but am now over it, but the rest of the prison is wrestling with it now.

If you get the urge to vent, or anything like that, I'll be happy to shut the hell up and just be here for you. I've been listening to an A.M. radio station lately and three times this week Roger Whitaker's "Final Farewell" has played, each time I've thought of you. I don't know if he's singing about a person or South Africa itself, but I hope, for you, that in your lifetime someone thought of you like that. The Liz I know is beautiful and if I never hear from you again, I have been blessed to have known you just the amount I have. But I'll see you one day and that day you'll know how it feels to be hugged by your friend. I'll stop writing when you ask me to, but you take all the time you need. My prayers are with you and your family. Peace!

Always your friend,
Walt

****

April 13, 2014

Dear Liz;

I've started this letter several times and each time I got side tracked or something else pulls me away. Like yesterday, they (the cops) came in to our dorm and made us all go to the TV room in our boxer shorts while they tore up the place. That's always fun. The time before that I had just started writing when they called me down to the Chapel for a special choir practice. It seems I've been chosen to be in "The Warden's Choir" what an honor! I don't see how I can't accept. "Let's hear ya sing!" Okay...eh hem...Laaaa-La-La-La-La, the singing would abruptly end as a Bible, a hymnal and / or a boot were thrown. "Shut the hell up!" "Hey, you watch yer fuckin language, this is a fuckin church!" Yeah, that went well, they figured out why I got chose when they went lookin for a guitar player. They have a guitar player but not one who can flat pick blue grass styles like lil ole me. So that's my contribution to the choir, don't sing just play. I can dig it. It gets me time on the guitar. I really like playing music. Some of those guys are pretty good at it too. Better than I am so it's always an enjoyable experience...except when they throw things at me. They don't do that when I'm holding the only acoustic guitar. They have a 12 string but I play the six strings when I can.

How are you Liz? Liz this Easter card is the second nicest card I ever got. From anyone. The top spot is also from you. I have it still, maybe one day if you're lucky I'll show it to you.

I got a little money for my birthday and have written a screenplay. I told you about it in the last letter. I'm going to send it to the Screenplay Festival next month. I'm writing them with an S.A.S.E. (return envelope) to find out if they still exist. The information I got on them comes from a 2012 Writers Market magazine that so far has proven to be useless. So if they are still up and runnin I'm gonna send them the screenplay and see what they think.

Okay, I'm gonna make this short. I'm often caught thinking about your little ole self doing what must be done and wish there was someway to make all that better for you, but there isn't, and you can take it from me the only way to go is forward. Because you can't reach the end of your journey without going forward. I read an interesting book by Edgar Casey last week and he puts a lot of this "life's trials" in perspective. It's just something we gotta do.

I'm going to the 5th Circuit Court of Appeals, finally, probably next month. This is where all the old writ writers of the Texas Criminal Justice system say, I'll finally get some attention. What I do with it is up to me. Boy I'll tell ya what I'd like to do with it!

Thank you for my Easter card last week. It, as usual, brought some joy and happiness into a miserable situation. More than that it brought some love with it and for that it's easy to say that I love you too and wish for you the best of everything. Thanks for just being you Liz; it's easy to love you when you do that. *(Note: I have to mention, I told Walter I loved him because of his caring attitude towards me and my situation at the time)*

Always,
Walt.

****

May 10, 2014 Note: one of my favourite letters

Dearest Liz;

Hi you. I've been gone from this place for a week. I left the day you wrote the card and got back Thursday. I got your card yesterday. This is the third letter I've started and have come to the conclusion that I don't have the words to pass on to you that would properly convey the feeling I have for you in your time of need. I can do this though, I am here for what it's worth. If you wanna write and vent about how unfair things are or how stupid your in-laws are I'm here. (not that they are, I'm just sayin, who would I tell?) I've been lost too. Not lost like you mean but lost just the same. I do not know what you're going through but I can imagine and with that said, as a person who genuinely cares for you, my heart goes out to you. You wanna talk about it? I'm here. If not, I'm still here. I'm always here for you. *(Note: I sent a card telling him of my husbands passing in April.)* None the less let's distract each other, me first.

The following truly happened. On April 29 they woke me up about 11p.m. and told me, "Yer on the chain, pack yer shit and take it to the South shower" I asked where I was going, "Medical" was their response. Great! I'm going to John Seely Hospital in Galveston. In case I haven't mentioned, for the past two years I've been having trouble with my heart off and on. It goes into "a-fib" and goes wop for a while. An irregular heartbeat that renders me immobile for the duration. Anyways, it got me hauled out of here in an ambulance several times which put me on a cardiologist list in Galveston. I've been five or six times prior to this, each time it seems for nothing. My last time was in October of last year. I refused it in January and got read the riot act by the resident quack here at the prison. Anyways, I was told I could not and better not refuse the next chain to Galveston. So I didn't refuse again and here we are.

So I packed up all my stuff and hauled it down to the south shower where they inventoried it and took it to the property room for storage. Early the next morning I went down to the "chain room" and waited for the bus with six other idiots. A couple was going to the Walls Unit in Huntsville for parole, lucky bastards, and the rest were going to the Byrd Unit for a layover overnight to catch the Galveston bus the following morning at, "oh God thirty". That trip is a three hour ride chained to another fool. Fifty inmates in a bus seat designed for two kids.

When we got to Galveston they unchained us and packed us into a waiting room with a toilet, a TV and a row of wooden benches to wait for whatever department has you scheduled. I was third into the room. The two in front of me made their way to the TV. I went straight for the window. There are two windows that look out, from the 4th floor, on the Port of Galveston, which to me is more entertaining than anything on TV. I got to see a huge cruise ship docking, several super tankers and cargo ships, the Gulf of Mexico and seagulls. We were thinned out as the morning progressed and, by, 11a.m. me and four other inmates were called out for the cardiac department.

They took us to another smaller waiting room but there were only five of us. This room also had a TV and another window with a different view of the same bay. I love the ocean, I am a water person. So one at a time we were called out to get our vitals taken, blood pressure, EKG…etc. Since I'd been up and going since 1am I was feeling fateeged. Yeah I know "fatigued", you knew what I was saying though, right? It's when I'm over worked or tired that triggers my "a-fibulation" bouts. I feel its coming too. I mention this to the nurse who was taking my EKG. "Yeah well, right now yer fine so go back and wait for the doctor." So I do just that. About 12 noon they come in and give us a newspaper thin turkey sandwich, you could read a newspaper through it it's so thin, and a carton of milk. I choke down the sandwich and drained the milk. We don't get milk at the prison, we get powdered milk. This was cold and so good; it also triggered my "a-fib" thingy. Very irregular rhythm, very uncomfortable and, it was getting stronger the longer I waited. "Good" thought I, maybe we can get something done this time.

I was called last, about 2p.m. I go to an examining room and was told to remove my shirt, which I do, and then wait. It's another hour before a med student comes in with a stethoscope. By this time my heart feels like it's about to jump from my chest. He greets me and takes a listen. "Oh my goodness Mr. Anderson," was what he said and then he left the room. Two minutes later a tall man came in eating out of a bag of pork skins, "How do you do? Lets hear this thang yer talking about?" He wipes his hand on the front of his white coat and hands the bag of pork skins to the med student. He takes out his stethoscope and takes a listen. "Hot damn boy, yer hearts in a-fib. Lay back." He goes to a wall phone and starts barking orders. The med-student is holding the pork skins bag away from him like it was a dirty diaper. Oh I forgot to mention, the med-student was from India. The officer that was stationed outside the door comes in "What's going on?" he asks. The doctor on the phone is issuing instructions to someone and he stops and tells the cop "We're admitting him," and goes back to his phone call.

So, I got admitted to the hospital. They put a blue wrist band on my left wrist and a white one on my right. They made me strip down to my boxer shorts and put a hospital gown on with some nifty red hospital sox. I was put on a gurney and wheeled to an elevator. Always in the company of a T.D.C (Texas Dept of Corrections) officer. We went to the 7th floor and into a room with two hospital beds. One was occupied by an ancient old man who neither spoke nor moved, other than being helped to the bathroom. Between us there was a TV and I had the remote. The nurse's station was right outside the window to our room. The T.D.C. officer was only seen at count times. They still must make sure I don't escape. They ran numerous EKG's and did many tests. They finally got the a-fib to stop only to start up again after I showered. It went on till about 11p.m. It quit when the nurse put some super-duper medicine in me that made the whole world a different color (yeah, yeah, "colour") Sorry, couldn't resist.

Anyway, they tested and observed till Tuesday morning, the 6th. It was like I was on vacation. My heart never did go back into a-fib. I had 27 channels of crap on TV, the food was fantastic, I don't ever remember sleeping in a more comfortable bed and the window in my room had a great view from seven stories up. On Tuesday morning there was an extra pill in my medication. It had a "60" on it. "Huh, what's this?" I asked the nurse. "That my dear is a morphine pill" she told me. "Your kidding me!" I said. "Nope, you're going to electrocardiology for an electrographical-hee-mo-goober procedure. (That was the best of my recollection) "Well, alrighty then!" I say and down the hatch it went. For those who don't know, morphine is an opiate with certain side effects, one is constipation and other…well…I'll get to that. And, it makes you loopy.

Okay, so about 20 minutes later, I was talking to the cartoon birds who were flying around the room. Everyone was happy on my planet and off to Electrocardiology we went. First though I had to remove my boxers and put on a gown untied in the back and a paper hat. O-kee do-kee. I got on the gurney and we went for a ride. The T.D.C. guard was a women who looked like Jack Elum (the actor) her eyes went two different directions and she looked mean. She never spoke, only grunted. I was handcuffed to the gurney, one wrist to each side with leg irons on. I was really menacing. We went to the free world side. I watched the over headlights go by as I lay there feeling the effects of my morphine pill. Another side effect is I'm starting to feel queasy.

We travel for, it seems, six miles through a maze of hallways, locked gates and various check points. I have a toe tag for the check points. Anyway, we finally arrive at this pre-post operating area. I'm wheeled into a stall with curtains on two sides and a wall of various medical devices on the third. I can not see behind me. A female doctor is clicking on a computer screen and asks me who I was, did I know what was going to happen, who's my next of kin, just in case...things like that. She said they were going to cut me between my legs and my groin and feed a wire up my artery into my heart where they were going to induce my a-fibulation and then burn the inside walls of my heart to tighten things up in there.

First they were going to freeze the area to stop any bleeding as the wire was fed into my innards, great! "I'm going to start you on a mixture of oxygen" she says putting a plastic oxygen mask over my nose and mouth. "You'll be under anesthesiology for this procedure", great! "First though we have to shave your groin area" "Okay, I guess." The doctor leaves and I'm alone. I can hear the guard breathing, somewhere behind me. I'm still high on morphine. The ceiling looks groovy. Just then in walks two nurses. One walks down one side of me and the other walks down the other side. They are in their early 20's and very attractive. They are carrying on a steady stream of gossip. "He said – she said" one checks my toe tag. "Hi Mr. Anderson, oh look Cherry, he's a prisoner" she giggles and then, "Are you a bad man Mr. Anderson?" A muffled response from me. "We have to shave your groin area so be still. We wouldn't want to...oh look Penny!" Says one lifting my gown to expose my stuff. "Yeah, well that's so cute, it's like a penis only smaller." Here we go. I feel them shaving me with an electric razor while moving Bobby around as they do their thing. (Bobby, as in Bobby the one eyed meat puppet.) Forgive me for being crude, but these things really did happen. "Oh look it's getting bigger, don't point that thing at me!" more giggles. I, on the other hand, am mortified and my muffled complaints go un-noticed. "Uh, oh, you've done it now" My ogre guard get's up to take a look. God, I'm so embarrassed.

It seems opiates have this effect on some men with the smallest amount of attention needed to obtain...umm...full erection. That and the fact I've been in prison for the last 13 years. It had a will of it's own. If they told me "Okay Walt, you can go home with 20 million dollars right now if you stop that, make it go down, right now," I wouldn't have been able to do it. My blood pressure was being monitored and it got the attention of the other female doctor that had left earlier. We heard her coming. The guard quickly went back to her seat. The two rotten nurses tucked my "joy stick" between my thighs and pulled down my gown, just as the doctor came around the corner. "Why is his blood pressure up?" she asked. "We don't know" they said, "but he's ready for..." and they left.

The doctor asked me if I was alright, why was my face so red etc. I had no answer. I was concentrating on trying to deflate my pecker before..."and here we go!" came a voice as an orderly showed up. "We're gonna have to unhook these cuffs" which the guard did. They started to wheel me away. The O.R. wasn't far and we wheeled up against the operating table with the over head lights hanging down. A large screen monitor was beside the table with all sorts of sections. Two orderlies lifted me from the gurney to the table. I kept my knees together and made it okay. But still for some reason my "problem" would not go down. I later found out it was the morphine and the mischievous little vixens that shaved me.

I made it through being hooked up to nine million wires and monitors. I could feel myself trapped between my thighs and with only the hem of the gown covering my mid-section. I thought I'd be okay. Then another female doctor walked in. She had on a mask and her hands were gloved and raised. The anesthesiologist was also female and there were two female nurses with one male orderly. *Boing*! Bobby sprang forth. "Oh look who's glad to see me" said the doctor. She was attractive and witty. "Someone put the tent maker at ease," she said as she came in and started giving orders. I felt the drugs start through my I.V. I wanted to be asleep, but all I got was woozy. There were a couple more jokes about my "tent" and the doctor said, "Why isn't he asleep?" The anesthesiologist behind me said, "I don't know" "Oh hon. your standing on the hose." "Oh," then...mercifully I was out. I have never been so embarrassed before in the whole history of my life. Later that same doctor explained that opiates do that to some men. Well, once instigated the opiate will take over and...well, you know. "Omar the tent maker," that's what she called me. Really heavy sigh.

Anyways now I'm stuck in lockup for 30 days. Whenever someone leaves the unit, when they come back they go into transit for 30 days. That's where I am now.

I'm also going into the 5th Circuit Court of Appeals. That court is in New Orleans and one has to be invited. I was invited, after being denied in the Eastern District Court. They claimed a whole bunch of crap that didn't even apply to my case, but it's like them old timers told me, when I started off, *No* Texas court will overturn another Texas court. You have to wait till the 5th Circuit. Well I'm there now. I *can* win here. I *will* win. In fact, I'll probably draft the writ this week. I have five stamps and because of the lockup status there's no way to get any more. Three are going to be for the writ and the other two I'll gladly use on you. I'll write again when I finish the writ.

I still have to draw your birthday card. It will be in with this, but you already know that huh? I'm thinkin flowers. I know you like flowers because you grow them. Are you growing any this year?

I'm on the bottom row back here and only pick up three radio stations. One Mexican station, one classic country and one classic rock. The classic country is okay, the classic rock would be okay but it seems like all they have is 30 songs. It is a good morning show with "Deeeen and Rodge" out of Houston. Informative and dorkey.

I'm gonna go. My hand is aching. I hope you like the card. You are in my thoughts and my prayers. Write me when you can, I'd love to hear from you.

Take care my friend
Love always,
Walt

PS: Did you walk to the mail box to get this? Was it beautiful? Tell me about it. *(Note: No I don't walk to the mailbox; it's three and half miles away, but if I did walk it, it is beautiful.)*

****

May 22, 2014

Dear Liz;

Hi you. I know I said I'd write sooner but I only got one stamp, outside of my court stamps, and I wanted to wait and see if I'd hear back from you that way if you said "well wot are ye doin luv?" I could say "Absolutely nutin" Mail ain't run today, yet, so there's an off chance...yer probably busier than a one-legged man (only yer a girl) in an ass kicking contest.

I'm still stuck in lockup waiting on a house, as we put it here. I could go to a cell, an 80 man dorm or two man cell. There's more room to move around in the dorm of course and one doesn't have to worry about getting an asshole for a celli. We're about to go on our major shakedown so a dorm is preferable all around.

The story enclosed "Departure 153" is one I think I sent you awhile back. Megan, my writing mentor from Pen American, did all the writing on it. This will give you an idea of how critical she is. But I think its helping. I was going to rewrite the story but wrote a screenplay instead. The screenplay got rave reviews from Megan. It takes approximately one month to send her material and receive it back. I told her she could write direct, and that I won't abuse her address but so far she's ignored all attempts at anything unprofessional, no wait, she did ask if I would draw her a cat. I did. Megan is a college professor who teaches creative writing. The letters from me I send along with my stories, she ..."Mauls!" I've asked her, "since yer gonna annihilate (obvious use of the dictionary) what I write, would you please make a freaking copy as it's hard to get time on a typewriter, so she does now. The screenplay, "Angels Inc" she received handwritten and although I have a typed copy, I wasn't going to send it because I was waiting on a response from a screenplay festival that never wrote back, *Bastards!!* I even sent a self addressed stamped envelope.

So I have typed, double spaced and polished, the pilot screenplay "Angles Inc", short stories "Jragin", "Cat Dancer" and "Second Chances" but no one writes back. No publishers anyway. I'll bet they all respond at once.

I'm still waiting on the 5th Circuit Court to send me an order to send my brief. The last order they sent said, "Don't do nothing till we tell you to" So...here I wait. I figure all that will come at once. If I got a letter saying, "Yeah, we'd like to read yer crap, send what ya got," I couldn't and I wouldn't. I *will* win my suit in the 5th Circuit Court. I *know* this! Without a doubt! So I have to be ready. They will put a time limit on it anyways, so I gotta be ready.

Alright, if I don't hear from you tonight I'll add to this. If I don't, then I won't. Read around Megan's comments and tell me what you think of her assessment of my writing. I'm sure I sent you this story before, if not, I should have.

A very good friend of mine once said to me, "Keep yer pecker up". She told me it was a common phrase from where she came from. I hesitate to tell you that because...well...as Forest Gump might say, "you ain't got no pecker Lutenant Don!" So *you* keep your chin up and know that like it or not you have a bunch of people surrounding you, who love and care for you more than words can tell...Count me among them. Take care my friend.

Always. All my best,
Walt.

****

June 3, 2014

Dear Liz;

Okay, I ain't gonna rag on ya about not writing. You have been a busy girl and I got a long letter from you today. I was very worried. I think you no sooner mailed that letter than you got my other letter with the "Departure 153" story. The one that, *"evil, know it all college professor mauled!"* (Just kidding) I need to write her back but I only have one stamp and I hadda trap a rat and trade it to my neighbor for it. True story, if you believe it.

Oh the Omar story? True 100%. I embellished some of what I said but it actually happened. I've never been so embarrassed. I should be going back to Galveston for a checkup this week or next. Then my transit status starts all over again for another 30 to 40 days in lockup. While the solitary term sounds like quiet, it's anything but. I'm sure I've told you before that we have three tiers of cells, 18 per tier, all open faced bars and the only way to communicate is to yell down the run.

Now an old convict like me doesn't have a lot to say but Texas prisons house mostly black inmates and they, if you haven't ever noticed (your sheltered or just blessed if you haven't) are *loud, all the time!* This prison serves breakfast at 2:30 a.m. and these idiot's stay up yelling until breakfast, about...basketball players mostly, but also past crimes, sexual conquests, possible football picks and any other thing. It is not quiet. The only so called quiet-time is between breakfast and lunch. You can sometimes feel the noise. But I have no celli and being in a five foot wide, nine foot long cell is okay. I don't see any of these idiot's and I'm used to the noise.

Let's talk about the enclosed items. (*Note: He'd returned the note or letter I had written to him in 2003*) I think this is the second...umm...note or letter you wrote to me. I had it in my photo album, next to the photo of you kicked back in your cubicle with your hands behind your head. And big smile. The only time you smiled bigger is the picture of you and Cyndi and you and your brother Jon. I believe I sent you a photo from my computer maintenance graduation class. My hair has gone completely white. I don't wear a mustache any more as in the others I sent. It's too hard to eat sandwiches with big mustaches. I have forgone all vices except pot, but that's gone too, until I get out. I quit cigarettes, booze, illegal drugs, yoyos, boomerangs and shooting arrows straight up in the air and dodging them coming down. Coffee is not a vice it's a necessity, cookies and pizza do not qualify either. I actually gain I.Q. points when stoned and am happier stoned with a guitar in my hand than any other mind altering substances.

I've lost several people in my family. I lost my sister Kim, my brother Patrick was killed in a car accident, my mom died of a stroke, my sister Katy drank herself to death, and my dad has gone. I know about missing someone, certainly nowhere near your situation but I still talk to em even though they ain't here and it helps. I read a book by Edgar Cayce called "There is a River", that also helped. You know you can write me and lean on my shoulder any time. Oh, I still have big shoulders.

I haven't heard from the 5th Circuit Court yet. I still have my three court stamps. I'm afraid I'll be stuck back here with no way to hustle any stamps so if you don't hear from me for awhile it's not because I don't wanna write, on the contrary, I can't write. I should start drawing again. I can draw for you, wha-da-ya want? I can draw some of these flowers you sent photo's of and you can colour them. (How thoughtful of me to spell it your way don't cha think?) I might have a piece of art paper somewhere; just give me your request. I remember searching for that piece for your B-day card. I still have all those old pin-up girl calendar pages you sent a while back and I keep some of the stupidest things tucked away.

I have been up for parole and will be again in Jan. 2015. I truly believe I'll still beat these assholes in court. I shouldn't call them that, it really degrades assholes everywhere and if I were one I'd be offended. My 13th anniversary for being locked up is June 9, 2014.

Hey! I got that screenplay I wanna share with you. When I get a grip of stamps I wanna send it to you. It's what the "Rachel" story evolved too. It's typed and formatted properly and Megan had nothing to add. In fact she said, "You have peaked, were I to grade this it would be A+." I got all choked up and blew snot all over the place. Actually I evolved to this piece. I started writing silly stories to you and your co-workers back in 2003. That was my start. I also have "Jragin" another short story typed double spaced and absolutely adorable. It's inspired by the picture you sent of Izabeau and your Rottweiler Missy Anne walking down your road. I'll enclose it in case you don't have a copy. Also, would you send these photo's back. I have no other pictures of me and my mum. I love this Izabeau picture. The story, "Jragin" is of a four year old little girl lost in the woods and runs into a huge green dragon. (Draconious P. Cinderbreath) I should have named the little girl Izabeau, I went with Maddy instead. Anyway she charms this dragon and, well you can read it.

Okay you, I'm gonna close. Thanks for the pictures. I'm pretty imaginative and I may find a way to get ahold of some stamps. So let me know about reading those things I mentioned, "Angel's Inc" and "Jragin" "Jragin" is suitable for reading to Miss Emily. Take care my good friend and I look forward to hearing from you. As soon as it looks like I'm gonna win my case and get out I'll get your phone number and call you, with an English accent. I can do it too.

All my best,
Walter

****

June 4, 2014

Dear Liz!

I'm a freaken genius! Or I'm an idiot. Either way I know I can't write with this pen. I told you I'd find a way. Okay, I only got the three stamps so I don't think "Jragin" will fit in the envelope. This piece is called a pilot screen play *(Note: Angel's Inc)* and it's the only typed copy in egzistance (Amarilan way to spell that word) Hey, you knew what I was talking about right? Okay then stop yellin at me...wait, nevermind, those were the voices in my head, sorry luv. You know I'm not really crazy right? At least not like that. Well, for the record...wait, I got something comin in...uh, huh...uh, huh...okay! The voices in my head say it ain't necessary to explain this to you. Someone else? Maybe.

Please don't get mad at me. I sold the pin-up calendar you sent for Christmas. I didn't get near what you paid but I'm drinking cheap coffee and mailing you this piece. I'm anxious to hear your opinion on it. I wrote a bunch of places that advertized in the "Writers Market Magazine" for screenplays but only received the entry form to the Screenplay Festival, I'll enclose it, its a crock. Read the disclaimer. Even if I had the entry fee, I'd not send it to them. They are pretty much saying "No matter what, if we lose it, steal it or plagiarize it you can't do nothing about it" At least that's what I got out of it. So...try to visualize it while you're reading and think of the songs I picked out for the scenes. (Especially Rachel) If you don't know them, especially the last one, check them on Google. That Billy Vaughn song is perfect.

Okay, keep this entry form somewhere safe, maybe one day, after I get out, I'll push to get someone in the business to see it. I'm actually proud of it. So proud in fact I hocked my most precious calendar to send it to my most precious friend. Hey, you're actually to blame for me evolving into the writer that I am or strive to be. So...push that chest out and take some pride in it too!... umm, that doesn't really sound as good going to a women, the pushing the chest out part. A guy now...anyways. Enjoy.

Please don't drag your feet writing back to let me know you got this. I'll worry until you do. I hope you like it too.

Bye for now,
Me

****

June 16, 2014

Dear Liz;

Hi yourself. Yeah, I'm sending a money slip and a phone number. I'm still locked up waiting out my 2nd transit status and there might be a third. You wrote in your previous letter that I could call and reverse the charges. I would but there's a couple of problems. First: I ain't got your phone number. Second: Texas has set up a phone system where both you and I have to register our voices on their phone system. I don't know what that entails but someone gave me a toll free number that you can call and they'll splain it to you. Third: I think I can call collect, but I know I can purchase minutes in the prison commissary...**if** I had money. I'm using indigent postage on this letter and will have to pay that back.

I also believe the 5th Circuit Court of Appeals has my account strained up for 20% of all incoming money. So, if you sent $25.00 the courts would take $5.00 and the indigent postage would be...hmmm? I used it twice...that's .49 times two...let's see...there ain't no six's but I gotta carry the one...$86.00. No wait. You love this part of my letters huh? So I'll have $19.00 out of $25.00, I would spend $10.00 on minutes? Liz, I've been locked up since June of 2001 and have not used the phone once. I got two calls from the Chaplin telling me my family members have died but the phone in the dayroom (TV room) has gone unused by me. Who am I gonna call? If I spend $10.00 on phone minutes what am I gonna spend the other $9.00 on? Probably stamps and coffee. What an idiot huh? So since you're getting extra pocket money working at Bud's and you don't know what to do with that new found wealth...Jeese, what am I saying? You're a women, I've never known a women who didn't know what to do with extra money.

I would love to hear your voice on the phone. Did I mention I have a lisp? Well that's because I don't. I wonder if, and, how much of your English accent is left. I can do an English accent. It probably sounds more Australian. I do better accent's when I have a drink or two. I like the Scot accent best. I'd love to be able to master it, I think a couple more sittings through "Rob Roy" and I'd have it. (*Note: Because he's my friend, I'll say, "Yes, he does a good accent"*)

Thanx for sending back your Post It note letter with the pictures. I've had it for so long, my photo album's plastic sleeve cover still had ink from the writing stuck to it. It's back now.

Have you read Dennis LeHave, "Shutter Island?" very good book. I'm not big on the "Odd Thomas" books for the reason you mentioned. I might feel different if I read the first one. I started and never finished "Odd Hour" "Phantoms" was the 1st and best Dean Koontz I have read to date. I'm not big on reoccurring characters like Stuart Woods, "Stone Barrington" or Lee Childs, "Jack Reacher". Jeeze don't get me started on Jack Reacher. But I suppose the exception to that rule is Robert Crais (I think that's spelled right) "Elvis Cole" I like, and Joe Pike, have you ever read him? Private Eye in L.A. modern times.

You know I've been thinking about the reincarnation question. I told you I read Edgar Cayce and his "Sleeping Prophet" readings he did on people and how he mentioned their past lives. I dug through all my crap and found the A.R.E. information (Association for Research and Enlightenment) (www.edgarceyce.org) Okay, Hugh Lynn Cayce, Edgar's son, wrote the book on reincarnation based upon the life reading that his dad, Edgar, did when he was doing life readings. Some strong points to his arguments are things like deja voo (how ever you spell it) or have you ever met anyone who, for no apparent reason, you just don't like? Or that you _do_ like? You may have known these people in your past lives. Interesting. Edgar Cayce was a pretty religious man and said that reincarnation was in the Bible, at one time, until spiritual leaders took it out at the command of certain leaders. Why? The reason provided was that slaves, if they know that all they had to do was cash out and poof no more slave. He gave other reasons, but that's the one I remember. Prisoners too, if they knew they were coming back. Besides he goes on to point out Scriptures that point in the direction of reincarnation. Like "No one comes to the Father lest he be born again." Baptists would argue that Jesus is talking about Baptism but the Bible doesn't say that. Also, what you reap so...wait. "what so you sew so shall you reap" What you do in this life dictates what you get in your next. He says there are eight dimensions and we are in the third and basically infants in our growth. I remember all this. It seems that we tend to find each other in our lives. Like you and your husband seem to have been married to other people in your early years but you managed to find each other. _We_ could have known each other in our past life and, against all odds, look what happened. By God we've made each others acquaintances yet again. All this sounds better stoned. (Pay no attention to that) There are some compelling arguments for reincarnation.

There's a movie called "What Dreams May Come" Robin Williams (not a comedy) about reincarnation. That's a real moving movie. Poignant and I recommend it. Try and have someone there with you when you watch it. If you do, or have seen it, tell me your take on it. Hell 10 million trillion Hindu's can't be all wrong, right? Don't take this the wrong way but I think in _our_ last lives I was Batman and you were Catwoman. And Spike was Robin. Yeah, I know, I set down some real interesting points to a good topic and tag it with Batman / Catwomen crap. Really! Would you have it any other way? _(Note: No!)_ I like Batman and what's not to like about Julie Newmar's Catwoman. "Holy rubber suit Robin! Wait in the Batmobile while I interrogate this wom...um, suspect"

Okay Liz, tomorrow is commissary for lockup. Every other Tuesday. I am allowed five indigent stamps and this will have made indigent letters numbers one and two. I have to write the Eastern District Court for a copy of the court docket for my Habeas trail. I obviously won't get to make store tomorrow but if you take pity on a fool and send some lolly I'll make it in two weeks. The call will have to wait for the moment until I get off transit status as I'm locked up 24/7. You could call this number and ask em what you have to do to register for this phone thing and I'll do the same from my end. I can't get out to run around and am at the mercy of the idiot in the next cell. I asked over the run what do I gotta do and after listening to everyone argue about it at 36 billion decibels I got this toll free number. If they don't know they can steer you in the right direction.

1-877-452-9060 or go to tx.govtechsupport. If this ain't right let me know. I'll do some double checking while I wait. If I can get an officer to actually stop and do anything.

Okay, "What Dreams May Come", don't watch it alone. Do you want me to send Spike? I'd watch it with you if I could, this way I could explain what the baseball terminology means. I'm full of shit; (really!) there ain't no baseball in it.

Well I'm gonna go for now. Take care and I look forward to hearing (literally) from you. When I get more stamps I need to write Megan and check on some endowments for arts grants. I don't know why I haven't done this before. Tell all our friends...I mean your friends Hi! *(Note: All who know me know Walter, so yes they are or will be his friends)* Tell Bud thanx for the catalogs, I really enjoy them, or should I thank you, I mean you're the one sending them to me.

Thanx Liz, keep the faith.

Always,
Walt

PS: I put two slips in the env. In case you wanna rewrite my mistake I made.

****

July 24, 2014

Dear You;

Hi it's me, finally! First I went back to Galveston again and got back the other day, the 22nd and ended up on "N" line, a cell block. Their commissary day is every other Thursday and today, the 24th just happens to be store day, so, now, thanx to you, I have stamps to write with and coffee.

I am writing while listening to my favorite radio station. No cell, except the last cell, get's A.M. on the radio. There's a radio station that plays a variety of oldies and the Astros Baseball games. I landed in cell I-18, first tier cell 18, so...yay. Oldies like John Denver, Peggy Lee, Brenda Lee, Tony Bennett and Dean Martin. ("When the moon hits yer eyes like a big pizza pie, that's amore") *(Note: All written with musical notes spread around.)* Some of these aren't anything I'd pursue, I'm not a big Michael Booblay or Frank Sinatra fan or Tony Bennett but I'd rather hear them than what's on other stations.

I'll be here for at least two more weeks. I have one more trip to Galveston left. They're gonna do an ablation procedure on my heart. They did one back in May but this time they're doing the left side of my heart. It's more risky, since thats the side that sends blood directly to my brain. I told em not to worry too much, I got two brains, one the size of a b-b and the little one in case the other one goes out so I won't need much blood. They have me on coumadin and fleckaynide (not sure of the spelling but that's what they sound like) Very nasty side effects that fleckaynide shit. The coumadin is a major blood thinner. This is supposed to stop my heart from going into a-fib. We'll seeee.

I wanted to write you several times but had no stamps. I bought 20 of em with your $25.00. I keep thinking your going to be eating dog food now because of me. If I weren't stuck back in this lockup transit status shit, I'd be able to draw cards to make ends meet. I did buy a drawing pad and plan to draw some cards for when I get out but this medicine makes me so shaky. Maybe after the operation do you want me to draw you something? I think the last thing I drew for you was the get well wizard card when you got your robo-hip put in. "When the World seems to shine like you've had too much wine, that's amore. When you walk in a dream but you know your not dreaming Senora, that's amore" *(Note: Written with musical notes around it)* that's such a cool song. I'm such a sap and you know it and still you like me! Hey, you know what was the very first song they played when I tuned in on Tuesday? Of course you don't know how could you? I'm so stupid sometimes. It was that Roger Whitaker song about England. I still think he's singing about leaving South Africa. What a beautiful song though huh? And you told me it was played to your mum by your dad in the mornings. What a nice way to wake up.

I always like the computer downloads you send, but the letters are always better of course. I'm glad you had a good time at the family get together BBQ, I'm also glad to hear that Nathan is moving in with you. What about Carl? Is he staying in Bakersfield? The temp here is 98 today with a heat index of 19000. It's a bit hot being in the cell which puts the sun on my wall and warms up and stays warm. Still I'd rather have the heat and the radio station. I don't get to hear the Astros or this kind of music somewhere else. In a dorm I have to have a window bunk and that's a 50-50 chance, so right now I'm okay. It's not that hot yet, with my fan.

Alright I'm gonna close and get this out before the weekend. I'll write more later and maybe draw something. Thanx again for the $$, it was above and beyond. I think I'm gonna take a chance and mail "Cat Dancer" to a publisher. It's been "Megan-ized" and corrected accordingly since you read it I like it more. Take care and I'll keep you posted and you do the same.

Always,

Walt

Liz's Second Letter

Hi, I just got another letter obviously written before the one I got the other day (dated July 24th) It says, "sorry can't send $....." but the other one did. I probably won't never need $$ again as I'm going to hospital in two weeks and then will get out of here (lockup transit status) shortly after.

I wrote to the mailroom asking for all info on the phone setup. We'll get that together you and me. I have no phone access in lockup though. Yeah I know I've said that before, so disregard that last sentence.

Back to reincarnation. According to Edgar Cayce, it doesn't exclude us from interacting or even being with our loved ones from previous lives. He stated that time, as we know it, is infinite and our minds, as they are in our present state, can't grasp the enormous amount of experiences that lay before us. Our entire existence takes us through eight dimensions and we in our present state are only in the third. We will see each other again and in the end become what God intended, together, forever. Yeah I read a lot of Edgar Cayce. He made sense so I went with it. I also liked re-runs of Gumby and Pokey. Oh come on, you knew something like that was to follow, don't tell me you didn't.

I look forward to talking to you. Few friendships in my life have developed so naturally. I look forward to meeting you and giving you a hug and telling you how much better my life has been in here because you were crazy enough to respond to my silly letters in 2003. Thanx Liz, your friend always,

Walt.

****

August 14, 2014

Dear Liz;

I'm not sure what the enclosed "mop 2 payments" paper is for but in case you thought you were losing your mind misplacing this...been there done that. *(Note: I accidently included a receipt for the purchase of a mop in with the letter.)*

Yesterday I came back from Galveston and because of the annual lockdown / shakedown and maybe they have extra bunks, I was housed back in two-dorm, so I'm presently not locked in a cell 24/7. I have one more trip to Galveston for a "cardiac ablation." That's the name of the procedure. I thought this last trip was for the surgery but they wanted a cat scan prior to the procedure, so that's what happened. These trips take a lot out of me, but when I get back there's always a letter waiting for me. Tonight I got your letter, you know the one where you misspelled "you're" and thought it might register in my consciousness. Actually Megan, in one of her first lessons, yelled at me about repeating that very error. I owe her a letter too. She told me she eloped with her boyfriend. She says her two cats approve. Cool! She doesn't usually get personal except within the boundaries of her mentorship.

These telephone registration forms from the internet *(Note: Which I sent him)* are a lot more helpful than yelling over the run hoping the asshole that yells back knows what he's talking about. I'm gonna send one of these to my sister and maybe she'll put some minutes on my phone account and I can talk to both of you. She doesn't like to write and would probably jump at the chance to talk with her little brother without having to write.

I'm so glad you're okay and moving in a positive direction. Can I ask you a question? Not another questions, God what an idiot! Not you, me! What is exercise? I've asked a couple of geniuses around here and we think it has to do with Birthday cake. Actually all kidding aside I've been exercising pretty regular too. I weighed 268 in May when I had the first ablation. I'm at 254 right now. I want to get to 240 and maintain there. I'm 6' 3". I also carry a lot of weight in my upper body, shoulders, chest etc. My chest started sinking into my midsection. I lived in denial till I weighed myself in Galveston and "eeeeked", "Hey" I yelled, this N.A.S.S.A calibrated digital weight machine piece of shit is broke!" "No sir" said a nurse, "yer just fat" Which cleared up any misconception I once harbored. I started working out in my cell. I threw my back out doing sit-ups though. I was fine the day I did them, the next day though...It's a good thing I was locked down with nowhere to go. This time I started getting ready to go anyway.

My second parole hearing comes in January (2015) and I'm still waiting for the 5th Circuit Court to invite me to proceed. I thought I was "in" but not yet.

So far this summer has been mild. It's 95 degrees right now with humidity though, so it feels hotter. And unlike California Texas doesn't cool off at night. The low tonight will be 80 degrees, but I have a good fan. It won't be long, October is just around the corner.

I also like Tom Selleck in "Magnum P.I". but I really liked him in "Quigley Down Under" I always thought they should have made another Quigley movie.

The computer pictures of the clouds were pretty cleaver. I wonder if those were photo shopped. I liked the "Fear" ones you sent in your prior letter.

I'm thinking about writing another screenplay about two 30 something year olds who are crude in their behavior, rude in their dating approach, slobs in their general approach to life and very lucky. I'm gonna name it "Pigs", of course it will be a comedy. I've thought about writing stories about the stupid things that really happen to these geniuses in prison, mostly due to their own stupidity. It's also a comedy.

The guy who gave me this "lined" paper wants me to draw a picture for his sister, so we'll do some horse trading.

Well Liz, I'm gonna close for now. Go ahead and register whatever you need to register to get the phone thing working so I can call. I know it won't be until I get back from my last transit status. From the last (I hope) procedure. You never know what these people will do. I do look forward to talking to you. I'll take care of it on this end. Take care and know I appreciate ya. Chow!

Always,
Me

****

September 7, 2014

Dear Liz;

Atrocious? My spelling is atrocious? Well I'm cut to the quick! Scarred even, for life. I may never be able to recover from this…this…_insult!_ But then again I may, in fact get over it, like I already am. It's a good thing you can spell "atrocious" or we'd both be confused.

I got your letter Friday. I'm answering it tonight, Sunday, as I fear tomorrow morning or Tuesday morning I'll be on the road again to Galveston for that second cardiac ablation. It won't interfere with our current timing on the letters, that is as long as I send one back to you before I go. I loved the photos. I especially liked the one where Emily is pulling her wagon with Petra looking after her, just like Missy Anne and Izabeau. I loved the background and would love to walk down a road like that one day. _(Note: He will; the road is on my property.)_

The Praying Mantis photo is a big hit down here, they have them here but they are never or rarely seen. When the May flies come you might see one once in awhile. But the wasps, hornets and yellow jackets are plentiful. There are ground hornets that are as big as Humming birds, I kid you not. Over on the Ellis Unit we had em all the time. They would get trapped in the cell block and the guys would go ballistic which never helped. There was always some idiot who would do battle with them, trying to trap them in a shirt. Once I saw an idiot get stung. He had to go to hospital it was so bad. Of course when we saw him in the chow hall a week later I took advantage of the situation, "Look it's a miracle! Praise Jesus, he's alive!" Being in the Bible belt and Baptist central one doesn't praise Jesus in jest. Unless you're a tree huggin hippy from California, Yankee bastard whut don't know no better. You and I simply call em "smart asses."

These yahoos in Texas are quick to fabricate what they see. I think it comes from the days before TV and radio. Often I've asked people down here, "Who ya going to believe, *him* or your own eyes?" I had a friend in Ellis Unit, D.J., who was real bad about that. Several times I'd tell him, "Jeeze D.J., I was there for Christ's sake and I don't remember it happening that way". He still wouldn't believe me, but what can ya do? His name is Don Bullock but still to this day he has no idea why they call him D.J. when his initials are D.B. Maybe they're worse spellers than me!

I'm glad Nathan is there with you. It's cooling off down here, it's lower to mid 90's but lower 70's at night, that's a big difference, but still very humid. But at night one can sleep without sweating out all your inner liquids. You need that to keep yer innards lubed (he spelled it loobed) up.

Hey, football season is here! The Texans won and the Cowboys lost to them faggoty 49ers. (not my words) During the Texan's game there was yellin and cheering like we all just made parole. During the Dallas Cowboy's game it was quieter than I've ever heard it. Several times I was asked, "Say...ain't choo from California? Sheeeeeit." Then I'd say, "I'm proud of where I come from, I'm from Nebraska" "Is that in California?" would be the next question. "Nope, we don't even got no football team, grounds too muddy, alligators won't allow it," I'd say as Tony Romo (quarterback for Dallas) would throw another interception (not good.) I really miss intelligent people and good conversation.

So you don't got no belfry but you've got bats for it huh? Ain't that a unique situation? Or is it? It sounds like it to me but then again I don't live in the usual. I need to round up some decent books to take back to the dungeon. I might have an illustration board lined up to take back there too. It will give me something constructive to do while I'm doing nothing. Maybe I'll do some writing. I'd be better motivated if that publisher I wrote to wrote back interested in what I'd done.

Well Liz, I'm gonna go for now. As always it was nice to hear from you. I always enjoy seeing your letters arrive and you always chase off the distractions before opening the envelope. It's my time with a friend from home, yes Nebraska. So homegirl be well and write when ya can. I'll drop a line following my ablation. Til then I remain lil ole me.

Back to ya,
Me

****

September 13, 2014

Dear Liz;

Hi, it's me again.

Yeah, I know I ain't heard from you yet! But I'm writing anyway. My last letter to you was written in haste. I was under the impression I was on my way to Galveston hospital again. I'm due, in fact, I'm overdue.

So, I dumped all that in your lap. I'm so...well...I'm...actually, it's *you* who's so...maybe I should explain what the hell I'm doing and you can assess how much of a role you're willing to take in this. On one hand you're helping a poor idiot savant *(Note: He's **my** idiot savant.)* to become a published writer of yarns. I wanna hook one of these publishers and become their best kept secret. I'd really like my own typewriter and...actually none of that is relevant since I believe I'm either going to make parole in 2015 (hopefully January) or the 5th Circuit Court of Appeals will agree to hear my case and appoint counsel. This will be the best scenario of the options available to me. In any event, after my release I will start writing full length novels with a spellcheck option on the computer complete with flashing lights and one of those little horns you squeeze the bulb and it honks. Yeah! I have stories that reside in my head that need to be told. I would love to contact Scott Gustofson and see if he'd like to illustrate "Jragin". That would be a huge blessing. I first saw him in the Spectrum books you sent me. I really like his art.

I came out of lockup with a fist full of drawn cards and swapped em for stamps. I got the typewriter from an old friend (for a price) and typed up two query letters complete with a sample story "Departure 153" and sent them off with a S.A.S.E. envelope. My choices, after scouring the 2012 Writers Market were, New Libri press and Pocol Press. I have no way of looking these people up on the web but in case your curious I included their web address. I tried to be very professional instead of witty and my usual clown self. After all these people are business people right?

Your experience in the service department of Bud Plant as a professional service department girl? Is that like a secretary? Anyway, I told myself that the first one to write back, from these publishers, and say, "Send what you have" would have got the package I sent you. You *did* get the package or manuscript, right? I only had the one and you offered to make copies, I can be prepared in case they both say, "send it." Now, in the event I do start selling stories and you want to be involved, you should get a percentage of what they offer. If you chooze to be involved you can do so at whatever level you want. (Yeah, I can spell "choose" correctly, I just "chooze" not to) Remember the "idiot" in idiot savant, or is it sevant? No it's savant!) Anyway that "idiot" sometimes, well, you know. *(Note: I've come to realize this "idiot" is really extremely intelligent but being where he is and fighting for his freedom this is his way to "lighten" the situation and that includes spelling, grammar etc)*

So let's talk about this financially. Except for copies or mailing something this is a low cost venture. I will not need any financial backing. We're both in the poor house, well me more than you; I can hustle up stamps and stuff here. Actually I think we have enough material typed and ready to go to attract a publisher. If they're interested they will let us know what they need. They may need a phone number which would be you making decisions based upon what they say. If they, the publishers, tell's you, "Alright, can yer boy write romance?" You can tell em, "He can write anything he sets his mind to!" I need your professional help, aside from that kind of professional help. One day someone is going to notice that I may not be the best speller or my grammar might lack...something, but I can tell a fresh imaginative story that people would like to read. Someone, besides you, that is. So, wha da ya think? Your role in this is pretty much what you've *been* doing. I will succeed in this, as well as getting out of prison. This I must **believe**. I figure I've got a lot of good karma saved up and one day it's going to dump on me all at once. I keep telling myself that anyway.

I worry I'm putting too much on you, that you have better things to do. I'm self conscience about it, so kill me! Please, let me know your thoughts. The publishers will want a way to contact someone (me) that can make a decision concerning the stories and if you send them we have that contact information. You'll be my agent. Able to leap tall buildings in a single bound, able to make any decision concerning these stories and while this may seem like a big responsibility, it truly ain't. Enough said, just let me know. I hope its yes. *(Note: I did say yes and have submitted several stories to different publishers)*

No doubt I'll be back in the dungeon by the time you get back to me. Monday or Tuesday I'll be on the road to Galveston. I value your input and assistance, **but** I value your friendship even more. If nothing else just send me a couple of copies of those stories, and God Bless you up one side and down the other.

Alright already, I'll just shut the fuck up. Your input is important to me. I make light of a lot of stuff but really I'm determined to make this writing thing work.

Okay, I gotta go. My left leg is killin me (arthritis in the knee and hip) but the weather has finally cooled down, thank God, for now anyway. I hope all's well there, take care and all that.

Bye for now,
Walt

****

September 2014 (This letter wasn't dated. It was written on the back of one of two rejection letters.)

Dear Liz;

I may have thought you'd offer. Hopefully Bud will let you copy these stories. Don't send them to me <u>yet.</u> I have to do queery letters for two publishers. If anyone writes back I'll let you know, then you can either send them to their address or back to me. What return address you use is up to you. If you want to send them back to me you'll have to wait til I return from the hospital. I'm leaving early tomorrow morning, that's why I'm writing so fast. When I come back I'm gonna petition my aunt for a deal. She'll send me money if I draw for her. She wants masterpieces but pays garage sale prices. Hey, it's a living. It's sometimes a chore to correspond with her at times. Feel free to send copies to whoever for whatever reason.

I feel you're part responsible for my writing to evolve to this level. Do <u>you</u> think, in your opinion, that these are marketable? You acting as my agent, (lose term but apt.) entitles you to certain liberties. So raise your right hand and repeat after me: "You're an asshole." Not <u>you</u>, **me**! No you don't have to repeat that. What an idiot! Not <u>you</u>, **me**! I'm not suggesting you do anything with em. I think eventually I'll get an, "Alright, send what you got" and they will either like or dislike <u>our</u> stuff.

Do you think a copy of "Angels Inc." should go in there too? Let me know what you really think about what we're doing or trying to do? I really care. Gotta go. Oh I love the redneck pictures you sent, funny!

Your biggest fan
Walt xxx

(Note: He'd hand written three stories and sent them to two publishers. Both rejected them. I don't think it was the story or the fact they were hand written, it was because of where he is. I've since found out, publishers don't like to publish prisoner stories because inmates don't usually stay in one place for long periods and a lot of them cannot accept payment. Plus it's hard for inmates to market their own product. At this time Walter was at a very low place in his thoughts. He has heart problems and along with his legal issues, no one was listening. I was helping in anyway I could but I still felt helpless. It was not a good time for him.

September 26, 2014

See? I'm so freakin smart it's a wonder I got locked up in Texass (I meant to spell it that way) I received a letter from you dated the 21ˢᵗ telling me your going to Ft. Bragg and that you're registered with the phone thing. I will call as soon as I get out of this lockup status and transit. I am looking forward to it. I'll try to watch my filthy fucken mouth too. What an asshole huh?

Thanx, your letter made my whole month and we ain't even got started on October either. I got one of those fill in cross word books to improve my spelling, how's it workin?

You asked which are my favorite story's? My favorite is "Cat Dancer", then "Jragin", then "2ⁿᵈ Chances", then "Departure 153".

Anyway, I need feedback!! It may be a couple of weeks before I can call, but I will, when's the best time?

Bye,
Me

****

October 1, 2014

Dear Liz;

Hi, how's things?

I've been back here since Monday. I had a Chryo ablation done. I was on the table six hours, luckily under anesthesia so I was out. I woke up in recovery with a catheter on or in, boy that was a surprise. I wonder if those two little nurses from last time had something to do with that. I was glad I was out for that maneuver.

Anyways, I haven't heard from you since I dumped all that crap in your lap from the last letter. I hope that's not the reason you haven't wrote. Hopefully I may get a letter tonight, dated two weeks ago. Dealing with the prison mailroom has taught me that you just never know. I think the procedure was a success. My heart hasn't done the whamo-blammo routine since and although I'm pretty bruised and feeling beat up I seem to be okay.

I did get a response from the two publishers I had written (See enclosed one of them) As you can see we ain't movin forward in that direction. At least Pocol Press was straight up with us. I have another idea if you wanna partake. In my "Writers Market" book is a section on screenplays. I picked out three and will send you the address, but only if you wanna send them "Angels Inc" or send me three copies of that and I'll mail em from here. But let's face it, if they wanted to contact me right away...I've already christened you my "mini me". Maybe a simple cover letter from you saying who you are and where or how to contact you with a simple, "What if something fantastic came across your desk from the most unlikely place would you know it? Would you contact the lovely Liz McGuire at the address on this letter? I think the cover letter with that simple question might get them to actually read the script. If they read it I'm sure they'll like it. If not then you probably won't hear from them.

Okay I'm gonna keep this short. I have one stamp and one envelope, but a whole pad of drawing paper and nothing but time. By the time you respond I'll have a fist full of stamps from selling my drawings. Liz, if you simply don't wanna fool with any of this, that's okay, really. I feel I'm taking advantage of your kindness but am hoping that's just paranoia on my part. You're still tops with me, either way.

Oh word is I stand a good chance of making parole in 2015, keep that in yer prayers. *(Note: He didn't in 2014, 2015 or 2016; we're still fighting for his freedom)*

Bye for now,
Walt

****

October 20, 2014

Dear Liz;

Is it me or does it appear that my penmanship is improving? (No pun intended) It's probably me (Pun intended) *(Note: Actually, yes his handwriting and spelling have improved.)*

I gotta tell ya toots, the court reporters text you sent was the funniest thing I've read in a while. I can visualize it going down too. I've had attorneys that seem that stupid too. In fact David Haynes represented me in the evidentiary hearing in 2010, he was pretty stupid. I'd say he was more unprepared and winging it than stupid. Anyway, thanx for sharing, again. My weekend will be better for having received your letter.

I told you I saved $10.00 for the phone, right? Actually, I have $15.00 on my account. $5.00 in case I need something like coffee or cookies. They have imported iced oatmeal cookies and I really like em with my coffee in the morning. Anyway, $10.00 of that is for phone time. I'm told I'll get two–15 minute calls and one seven minute call, for $10.00 that should give us plenty of time to get sick of each other. *(Note: That has not happened and won't)* I'm actually looking forward to hearing your voice and anxious to display my ability to converse like a regular human being even though I ain't.

Alright, the card enclosed is self explanatory and sincere...boy the voices in my head are going off!! No, that's the radio, whew! This card drawing was taken from a local papers comic page, only it was different. I changed it to be this way. I guess I could change the characters and submit it to some card company as an original. Yeah, my drawn card pile is growing. I bought an art pad before coming back here and have a stack ready for my return to general population. I also have one more for you but think I may have sent it years ago. It's a Celtic cross with a rose wrapped around it. I drew it after your comment about Scotland trying to separate themselves from England. It sounded like you were fond of your Scottish neighbors, so I drew it. I'll send it in the next letter. It'll give you something to look forward to.

Oh, about calling, when I get out of lockup I have to wait for our store day, then the next day, the phone time should be activated. Since there is a two hour difference, seven a.m. here is five a.m. there. Are you a morning person? Wait the voices in my head again. Oh yeah, you mentioned dragging yer butt out of bed about 10:30 a.m. I do have a way with words huh.

I really liked this letter you wrote, thanx. Anyway, you will probably have time to consider what might be a good time to call, so write back with that information. Give me your time to call, I'll do the math. Keep in mind the earliest is the best for me because the later we go (noon and beyond... my time) the noisier it gets in the day room. (Where the phones are and the TV.)

My lumps from the surgery are smaller and the bruises are green. Both sides of my belly where I took two weeks of blood thinner shots are green, they used to be purple. I'm still on blood thinners but in pill form. I cut my finger the other day and bled for two hours. I had it wrapped and every time I unwrapped it, it bled. For two friggin hours it bled. I'm careful shaving. I've had a couple of unusual episodes since I've been back, (with my heart) but I don't know if I've just traded symptoms. The rhythm has been the same though, steady which is good. Only time will tell. Last night they came to get me for another trip (checkup) to Galveston, I refused. I think I'm done with that. It's too hard and extremely tiring. Hopefully I get out this coming year and I can take it from there.

I told you about my aunt Carol. She's religious to a fault. She sent me the latest Christian book, it's called "Heaven is for Real" It's a child's account of Heaven after having an out-of-body experience. (Dying on the operating table for three minutes) I read it in a day. While I'm not big on Christian lit (except for the Bible) this being a non fiction, I liked the story and could relate, as a patient, to the father who was the narrator. Would you like to read it Liz McGuire? If so I will send it to you. There's some pretty thought provoking points about what to expect after ye croak. Let me know, I think you would like it. Keep in mind though I'm not being paid to think for a reason.

I have started a Halloween story for Megan. I haven't written anything new for a long time, probably because of this heart business. But I've drawn a series of Halloween cards. Since I haven't done much work on anything and have a whole slew of questions about writing technique's to ask my mentor, I'd be stewpit (my way to spell it, dumb huh) not to take advantage of this. Plus I think Megan is a twisted bitch at heart, said with all due respect, and would enjoy a horror story. She sent me one of her earlier plays, upon my request. I wanted an example of *her* work and to be honest I couldn't follow it, the storyline I mean.

The story I'm working on isn't my normal borderline fairytale where everything seems to be manageable to some degree. This tale is fraught with profanity, violence and a mean evil witch that hurts kids. However, the hero (my stories always seem to have a hero) is so *me* its scary. That's a pun. A scary story yada-yada-yada. This story is more like *work* than any other yet. But that's my point, or one of them. *(Note: It's a wonderful scary story. To me not like Walter at all but it shows his diversity.)* Can I manufacture a story to fit a genre that doesn't just fall out of my head like the others?

That reminds me, I really should write and type up two very short stories, as in "Departure 153", written a while back that are domestic romance type. Did you ever read the one about the women and her husband watching football on a Sunday? Or the one where a woman meets a guy in an elevator and she's late for work? They are written down but back when I was saturating the magazines with hope's of publication. I gave them to Jason (an inmate friend) to hold for me. He, Jason, is a published author. He helped me get started. He was amazed at my ability to just tell a story. "Effortless" he said. Anyway, my odds are that I won't get to any publisher from in here, but instead when I get out. I'll have plenty of material to proceed with, right? Would you like me to write you a story? Got any ideas that plague you? I have story ideas that plague me.

Okay, that's it, I'm babbling. Oh, I wanted to point out that those two rejection letters from the publishing companys, neither one returned the copy of "Departure 153" back even though I sent a stamped return envelope. Bastards!

So, you went to Ft. Bragg. Did I ever tell you I was raised just East of there? Up the hill in Lake County. Clear Lake, Kelseyville, just below Mt. Konocti. Yup, pretty much the same kind of area where you live. I've been through Ft. Bragg but never stopped, yet.

Okay, that's really it. I hope all's well there with you. As soon as I get out of lockup, perhaps within two weeks at the latest, I'm getting that phone time. Just let me know what a good time, your time, is without waking you up. I can call at 5 am, your time, but I don't need to learn any new cuss words. (funny face)

Ummmm, what else? Oh yeah let me know if you'd like that book. I'm gonna keep it till you let me know. You take care.

Always,
Walt.

****

PS: Did ja like the card? *(Note: Yes!)*

****

November 4, 2014 1st letter on this date

Dear Liz;

Just a note. Unless I hear from you tonight, to update you on the phone business. I got out of lockup last week and tried to buy phone time at the inmate commissary but they said, "Yer not even in the system." So I applied to be registered. I registered back in 2006 when they first got the phones for Texas Prison population but somewhere along the way...who knows. Today I, on the off chance, tried the phone and voila! I'm in the system but you ain't. All I could get was "You have no approved numbers to call." Maybe that's why I couldn't buy no phone time. I don't know. But the following is the bonafied number to the site that sets us up. The toll free number is 866-806-7804, or register by going to www.texasprisonphone.com

Before, when I tried and failed, I recited my full name, Walter Gerald Anderson. When I succeeded I just said Walter Anderson so if they say, "Who," maybe it makes a difference. I still did not spend that $ at the store so I'll try again next time and you can double check your registration. Oh they won't accept my prison number unless it has the zero in front of the rest of the numbers.

So, how ya doin? How's Nathan? The dogs and the weather? It finally dropped below 80 here. I'm looking forward to talking to you. Our commissary day is next week. If you can do it soon, perhaps I'll be able to call you before I hear from you. (letter wise)

Okay, unless I hear from you tonight at mail call, this is it. Take care and brace for impact, batten down the hatches, dive, dive, dive!

I remain ever in your service. (proper English?),

Walt xxoo

****

November 4, 2014 2ⁿᵈ letter on this date

Dear Liz;

   I got your letter dated Halloween. I'm sorry I wasn't able to call when you were sulking, your word. I'm good for depression. No, really! Why, once our family doctor prescribed me to a patient… wait, that didn't turn out near as good as it should have. Something to do with a bag of mushrooms, a hula hoop and ten pounds of raw pork. Trust me you don't wanna know, but, hey! They forgot all about being depressed. Only in America, huh?

   When you retype "Departure 153", with the Megan changes in it, can I have a copy? Feel free to add "Liz" changes too if you wanna. Okay, back to the phone thing. There are dorms here at Eastham that have half the people in them. Thirty eight as apposed to eighty. They're called "the outside dorms." They're added on to the back side of the prison in quonset hut type buildings. Three years ago I put in to be placed in one. There are six, I was told "No, you have an escape in 1985 from a Penal facility so…No!" A week ago I was sitting in lockup waiting, hoping to be placed back in Dorm 2 but got moved to Dorm 10, an outside dorm. If there was an honor building to Eastham, it would be the outside dorms. I am furthest away from the infirmary but I can still get there if I need to. It ain't noisy where the phones are.

   My "ticker" seems to be…different. It doesn't go into a-fib as drastically as it used to, but it hurts sometimes when I move around too much and my stamina is down. I've been outside twice and have started working out again, but I'm hindered it seems. I've started to develop a gut and don't like it. Not surprising after being locked up four of the last five months in a small cell 24/7. So I'm gonna start running and lose some weight. Hopefully all I gotta do is work back to what I was doing. My walking pace has always been quick but I can't go as fast as I used to for as long as I used to. I'll work up to it.

   Okay, you asked about nicknames. My nickname used to be "Frog Face" then it was shortened to "Frog" I got that name from an older biker chick when I was 18 years old and living in Fair Oaks, just outside Sacramento. Other than that? Just Walt, Walter, hey you, stupid, Einstein, Helen (as in Keller) or Art. I don't know why but through my life when someone gets my name wrong it's always "Art" Of all the names "Art" seems to be used more often. Oh, that and asshole. You knew that was coming, huh?

   I think 9:30 pm, my time, is the latest I can call, so…I predict one week from today we'll make store or a week from tomorrow, around there. We're on a rotation and we gotta wait our turn. I might get lucky so go to that website and do what you gotta do and I'll do what I gotta do. One day, soon as I can, I'm gonna call you on da tella phone. I'm gonna say, "Hey!, How you doin?"

   I have not sent anymore stories out to any publishers. I doubt we'll get anywhere there, but maybe with that pilot screenplay? I think I stand a real good chance making parole in a few months though. Something to do with this region parole board and their corrupt behavior. They all got fired or resigned due to getting caught doing something they aught not have been doing. Now a fill in board is hearing the overflow cases and paroling everyone that ain't kilt nobody lately. That'd be me, so, then we can start promoting the stories. In the meantime I should write some more, huh?

Going back to nicknames. Of all the nicknames you mentioned people have given you, what's your favorite? You have always signed "Liz" so I'm assuming that's what you want me to call you. I could call you Lucy, but why huh? I like "Liz" anyway, that's how I know you. Would you want me to draw you another card? Have you kept all the cards I've drawn you over the years? *(Note Yes, all of them!)* What happened to the "Cobbler" board? Wasn't that the first? *(Note: Yes it was and it's hanging, framed, on my wall along with all the drawings he's done)* I think I've drawn three boards for you. The reclining Jesus and Santa Claus, right? Do you want another one? I would love another photo of you; I wish I had a current one of me. My hair has turned white but at least I still got it.

Okay, I'm gonna go for now. Till I call or write.

Walt xxoo

****

November 15, 2014

Dear Liz;

Hi you! Alright I've been saving this letter till today, Saturday, nine a.m. when Casey Kasem comes on doing the top 40 for the 70's. Today is 1972, November. Yay! I like the early 70's music as opposed to the latter, too much Disco. Starting off at #40 is Bread with "Surrender." I like Bread but never heard that song. Most of the songs will go unmentioned unless they are significant. "Me and Mrs. Jones" by Billy Paul is #39.

Okay I've got a question for yeeew. What's this? *(Note: He's drawn a picture of a shovel or spade)* If you said "shovel" or "spade" 'cause yer English, you're right! Guess what you won? Well nothing, but the point is... I really enjoyed our phone conversation and the highlight was hearing you laugh. Your laugh fits your picture perfectly. I'm really going to enjoy calling and talking with you. *(Note: We had our first phone conversation and it was as if we'd known each other for a very long time..)*

Oh, #38 is Chicago "We Can make it Happen" I'm not a big Chicago musical fan. After careful consideration, I've come to the conclusion I dug a hole with that "you don't sound like an older women" remark. In fact you don't look or sound like one. I've figured out why, Liz you ain't old! I'm sure you know this and your vanity is well placed. Being a man I have a natural ability to dig holes and drop into them effortlessly making stupid comments. Also, I noticed that you didn't seem to take offense, but in case you did, I'm clarifying what I figured out. At this point I should probably shut the hell up huh. Alright, that did not seem like 30 minutes on the phone with you.

Oh, I talked with my neighbor in this dorm and he said you're going to get a separate bill from the phone place for that collect call. It will probably be around $6,800.00, so what happened to .21 cents a minute? I asked him, "Is it only .21 cents a minute?" He said, "Yes but you get an additional connect fee." Great, why didn't he tell me before I made the call? Probably because he's an asshole. He's a friend of mine who knew I was calling you. I showed him pictures you've sent me and because he's a Texan, bragged about the mountains of California stating, "Yeew ain't got nothing like these here in Texas" After the call I showed him your picture, because he wanted to see who you were. I told him about writing to Bud Plant in '03 and all that. He asked to see your picture so I showed him. He accused me of showing him a picture of my sister and claiming to have a girlfriend that looks as good as you do. I didn't say you were my girlfriend and certainly couldn't let the sister comment go, so I'm planning on torturing him.

This Austin Roberts song, "Something's Wrong" (#29) is a good one. They just don't play these hits. It seems they have 30-50 acceptable hits that dominate the charts or today's play list and that's it! Bastards! Alright, I'm over it, for now.

You'll notice I broke out the lined paper for this letter, it is special treatment after talking to you? Actually, No! A volunteer down at the Chapel for the Catholic Choir sent me this lined tablet because I complained about not having proper paper to copy down songs they want me to learn for the service so...he sent this tablet with a Post-It Note saying, "Shut the hell up about the paper or we'll burn yer heathen ass at the stake!" I believe him too, so...I'm using it to write you. Actually I have plenty of typing paper to write songs. I also have four full page drawings I need to finish before tomorrow night ($3.00 apiece) of Native American Indians. This keeps me supplied with coffee, cookies and soups. I'm in demand around here as an artist. Another reason I wanted to come back to this dorm.

If you come across any Christmas pictures like the Santa one on the board I sent, Norman Rockwell, or cute, just think of me and send them. Christmas is a major card season and I usually do well. But so far I got nothing to draw anymore. I used to have pictures but seem to have tossed old patterns thinking I wasn't gonna need them this or next year, because of parole. I cannot be held responsible for fleeting thoughts, actions or intentions. Hopefully, again, this will be my last Christmas locked up. I'm still waiting on the 5th Circuit Court of Appeals to do something and if that fails? I go to the U.S. Supreme Court. **I have not – will not quit** until some changes have been made.

I told you I wrote Megan a horror story for "Halloween" while I was locked in the dungeon didn't I? Well I haven't heard back from her. It was an attempt at a horror story. I gotta get ahead on these drawings and finish that story about Breast Cancer Awareness "BAM Rally #7" That story can be submitted six months before October. I have a few ideas rattling around in my pea-sized brain to add to "Angels Inc" to make it longer. I should write em down, good idea huh, the writing em down part.

Okay you I'm gonna go for now. Take care and when my Aunt sends the $$ she said she would and I make store, I will call again. Is that time of morning okay with you? You didn't sound groggy or grumpy from being woken up. I hate being woke up in here. So...do you want me to call again? Obviously I wanna, you're addictive. *(Note: He's not stopped and I'm so glad he thinks me addictive.)* I'm gonna get busy on these Indians and listen to the rest of the music count down.

Bye for now.

Always,

Walt xxoo (put em where you want em)

(Note: I will when he comes home.)

****

November 23, 2014

Dearest Liz; (As if you didn't know, seems this phrase has been used before…hmmm..)

Alright, I got your card saying, "call you collect," that it's added into your regular phone bill. This seems too good to be true. However several thoughts want cascading through my head at the same time. First one was, "Yay!" Second one was "Wait, it's a trick, don't fall for it!" And the third thought was, "If you (me) don't call, she'll think ya don't want to." Forth thought "Gasp!!" And the fifth, sixth and seventh thoughts were a variable montage of things to do with Uumpa Loompa's, V.W. cars and wonder what's for lunch?

What were we talking about? Oh yeah, Baseball! (I have to deal with this daily) Alzheimer's and S.T.P (you know, like them say-ance people who can read your mind. Like I can read your mind. Right now its saying, "What in the Wide, Wide World of Sports is this asshole talking about? Right? I knew it. The phone Liz! Jeeze, how am I suppose to keep up with this if you can't.

Okay, Thursday night I called, no one answered. Friday I tried again, early and later, no answer. Then between Friday evening and Saturday morning I came down with Avian Bird Flu, Ebola and throat cancer so my mildly sore throat altered my voice pattern and the electronics lady that recognizes my voice on the phone couldn't / wouldn't recognize it. So voila! I'm writing.

The call process goes like this: After picking up the receiver I hear, "For English press one," so I press one. "For a collect call press one," so I press one. "Please enter your TDCI ID number now", I do it. "Please enter the area code and number you wish to cal,l" I do and wait while the electronic lady verifies that all is in order. "Please state your full name after the beep" (Beep) I say my name. "That is incorrect, please state your name after the beep" (Beep) I try again. "Sorry this call is terminated, goodbye" If it had recognized my name it would say, "I recognize your name. Please hold while I check to see if the party is home to accept this call, this may take a few moments." Then you hear on the other end if you want to accept or decline. If I wanted to be the clown that I am, on the phone instead of just letters, I could use my best Austin Powers voice. You have seen Austin Powers haven't you? The ultimate spoof on British American secret agent movies, you know all that though huh?

I've always admired smart women and prefer them over… stupid ones. Some pretend to be stupid but aren't. Those bare watching, especially if they have big breasts. Okay I just tossed that in to see if you were paying attention. Actually I'm a little loopy from taking this cold medication. I can't call until my voice returns to normal. I could have avoided all that other poppycock by simply saying that in the first place huh? But where's the fun in that? I am a bit on the worried side that for two days no one has answered the phone. Are you okay? I'm supposed to be drawing a card for this guy to send to his grandson. It's a Longhorn card for him. It's a bag of iced oatmeal cookies to me, providing I get it done. I have three bags of cookies in my locker as we speak...or write. Actually commissary wise I'm sitting pretty good. I got coffee, cookies, soups (Top Ramen) and all my hygiene so I'm thankful.

Oh that reminds me, Happy Thanksgiving Liz. It did occur to me that you might be on the road for this holiday, but that's a week away. Are you going to a daughter-in-laws house and let them do the cooking? That's what I'd do. Depending on whether I wanna be invited back next year is how I'd behave. For example, telling the little kids that "That ain't really a turkey, it's a dead possum that was found in the basement." For the record I would never do that. I might con Uncle Bob to do it, but I would never...So Happy Thanksgiving Liz. I hope everything turns up roses for you and your whole family this holiday season, starting with Thanksgiving.

As for me I'm weathering out the first cold of the season in this place. I should be good by next week though. I rarely get sick and when I do I'm either a big baby about it or in complete denial. I really ain't that ill, just enough to alter my voice so I can't call. Take care and I'll call when I can. For now, I'm in the wind.

Always,
Walt.

****

November 27, 2011

Dear Liz;

Hi yourself. Well we were first to chow so we had our Thanksgiving dinner at nine am. That's okay from my perspective, because they didn't run out of anything.

At nine a.m. today the radio station started playing the top 100 songs of 1978. I started listening but soon realized it was not my favorite year for music. Don't get me wrong there's always going to be something I like because I love music, but alas I got too much Disco and / or funk songs that reminded me of some not-so-fond memories, so I changed channels. Here's the best part though, it's a three hour show and hour number three some great idiot at the station screwed up and slapped in the third hour of the top 40 in...I think 1970 – yay! I caught in at number nine, Elvis "The Wonder of You" followed by your homeboys from Liverpool "The Long and Winding Road" and so on and so forth.

I got your letter with the Christmas card material, thank you, obviously. I made the enclosed card and hope it's your first this year. Not sure how seeing it again will effect you but I liked it so... you get it, back. (*Note: The picture is what I sent him. He re-made it into a card*) This probably won't be the only Christmas card I send you, just the first.

If all goes well I should give you a ring next weekend. Now there is a rumor that we may go on lockdown for a unit wide shakedown before Christmas. As I mentioned on the phone we don't get locked down much but when they decide to shake the whole unit down it's a week to 10 days. But I'll write you and let you know.

I'm making headway on a good supply of stamps from my card business. This is good. I'm also close to closing a deal on two illustration boards. Financial independence is almost obtainable, for me. I don't do a whole lot of going without unless I get lazy or it's a time of year where cards are not in demand. Right now I'm set though.

I'm so glad you like talking to me on the phone as much as I like talking to you. I have to admit though when I woke you up the other day after your restless night with Dobby, *(Note: My dog Dobby was not well)* you sounded...I don't want to say grumpy, because that's not the impression I got, would pouty be grumpy in a cute sort of way? Did you think of going out on the balcony with her? I hope she's better by now.

It's in the 70's today but that's gonna change over the next few days. You asked about parole and what happens when you get out. There's a step before they grant parole called "re-entry." It's where they check all the information needed to obtain a Social Security Card, state ID and Birth Certificate prior to your release. But they ain't contacted me that's not a good sign. It's not definitive, but I'm up again in January. I think I'll start pestering the 5th Circuit Court for a response to my petition. It's been my suspicion all along that the 5th Circuit Court will be my salvation, we'll see. Anyways, I'm not as upset over it as one might imagine. It is what it is and that's all it is.

Wow, Tom's wife passing like that so soon after your husband died, provided you both with support in a unique way. He sounds like a great neighbor, an odd blessing but a blessing anyway. 2014 has been a rough year so far, huh? Well that's the thing though, we have another that's got to be better and then we have 2016 and the Presidential Election. I hope I can vote by then, that would mean I won my case in court. Hmmmmm there's something to think about huh?

Okay luv I'm gonna go. I hope all is well and hope to call soon. So far as I know I'm just waiting for our dorm to make commissary some time next week. Till then, take care and thanx again for the card stock pictures.

Happy Thanksgiving.
Always,
Walt

****

December 6, 2014

Dear Liz;

I have your November 29th letter before me and am about to answer it. Your Christmas card is done and sitting next to me waiting for this letter. I will, as you did, take it from the top and work down. Really, as in most things, it's best that way.

First, as you've probably figured out, we're locked down for the end of the year unit shake down. You know, you can call this prison if you ever want to know why I haven't called, and ask em, "Hey! What the fuck is going on?!" Okay the "F" word wasn't exactly the best choice of words but I bet who ever took your call wouldn't notice. I'm actually making a conscience effort to stop cussing as casually as it seems we do in here. It's a common thing in everyday conversation and one doesn't realize how callous we've become in our use of swear words until you stop and listen. Or, someone like you says something. It also diminishes the impact of such words when they become applicable. Though one could argue that such words have no place in the English language and I would disagree. Comedy would suffer. Anyways, where were we? I get off track so easily. Oh yeah, your letter.

I really like this letter, *not* because you're talking about personal things about you, I like most all of your letters. This might be why we're still writing after 10 million years. We *may* be compatible too. This is good. I know that I like you, no, that's not right, well yes it is, but it's not enough, I'm very fond of you? That doesn't seem to do it either. I always agonize over how to sign off your letter. I certainly do not want to overstep any lines you may have drawn in the dirt between us or any man. Do I love you? Absolutely. Am I *in* love with you? How the hell should I know? I'm really a social retard because of all the time I've done over the course of my life. Most times I miss things I should be able to catch, like subtle hints or innuendos between people (men and women) that move them along in the relationship ritual. I know I could not imagine where your head and heart might be in the wake of this year, but I am a practical man and take nothing for granted.

You've said twice that you hoped to see me at your next Thanksgiving dinner. Liz I can't think of any place on God's green Earth that I'd rather be next Thanksgiving and who knows? I might just be sitting across from you at a table filled with food and people who don't understand the spice of life. The moments that keep us guessing and reward us when we guess right. The smarter we are the harder our guesses might be but also, bigger are the rewards. Twice, you told me, "I can't write to you no more," and twice you missed me enough to write anyway. I told you then that I understood and I did and do. It made me want but I'm very cynical in my opinion of the parole board or any Texas Department of Criminal Justice office. I'll get out when I get out.

I'm waiting on the 5th Circuit Court of Appeals to allow me access to their court. If I can get in there, I can win. Oh and for the record, I never once thought of you in the "stupid" women category. However, thank you so much for enlightening me with your medical information. I wasn't sure my stuff still worked until we started talking about certain information. Okay, now we've both opened up, huh? I have no doubt that this might prompt a response from you, or not. (funny face)

I may be locked down for a couple more weeks. I'll surely call when I can. Till then, take care and I hope you like the card, and the letter, as it was written.

With lots of love,
Walt

PS: Hey, you're the onliest one to get a drawn Christmas card this year, cause yer special, Duh!

✱✱✱✱✱✱

December 10, 2014

Dear Liz;

Good morning back! (funny face) It's Wednesday morning and I'm answering your 12/2 letter.

We're still locked down, duh, huh? Our day to get shook down will be tomorrow. At six a.m., actually closer to five thirty the cowboys, the officers that ride the horses and manage the field work, "chain gang" see Cool Hand Luke for reference, will come in yelling to "pack up and git yer asses to the North Chow Hall" There we'll be staged in boxer shorts and shower shoes waiting our turn to drag everything we own to a table and then step back while two bored officers who would rather be doing anything else goes through our stuff. Tossing out what they deem we shouldn't have and then waving us on to wait in a crowded dayroom with 79 other idiots all dragging their property around, until, the search squads get through tossing the dorm. Then and only then, we get to go back to our cubicle, set up our house and wait for them to finish shaking down the rest of the farm. You'll know when that is because I'll call and wake you up.

While we're on that subject when I said you sounded grumpy or pouty previously I wasn't complaining or criticizing, I was actually trying to tell you I was amused. Of course you have every right to have a bad night and be in a different frame of mind, especially with a sick pet. I remember still getting you to laugh and don't ever remember an unsatisfactory phone conversation or letter in all the time we've written or called. So, no reason to apologize to lil ole me. I figure if you didn't want to talk, for whatever reason, you wouldn't accept the call, right? Would I take it personally? ab-so-lute-ly. Actually you could see by caller I.D. who it is and if you didn't have time or for whatever reason, just don't answer it and I'd never know. "Oh she's out" I'd think and try again later.

I'm sending the paper thing they give me at the inmate commissary when I buy phone time. It seems $10.00 into the phone debit thingy would go further than a collect call. This thingy, even after taxes, charges that debit account .21 cents a minute. No hook up charge, so a twenty minute call costs...here we go with the damn math. Son of a gun, you do the math. All I know is I have credit right now for a call and will use it when we get off lockdown. You may be in Bakersfield but I'll try.

Liz, you don't gotta get me nothing for Christmas. I know things are tight and just the fact that I can talk to you through letters and the phone is good enough for me. I'm grateful for your company. If you're set on getting a calendar and they have an angel one left or American Indians I'd like American Indians. #1: You've already done what you're gonna do. And #2: I'll love it, unless it's a puppy calendar, that would bring back bad memories. One Christmas I got a puppy when I was very young and impressionable, 17 I think. This holiday story is better suited on the porch with some hot cider by my chair, my guitar in my lap and playing sad music as a backdrop, can you see it? Well one year I was told if I quit wetting the bed I was promised a puppy for Christmas. (You got your boots on? Because shit's getting deep and thick) Saved by the bell! I gotta go. I'll finish this letter, take care and be good!

Always,
Walt, xxxx

****

December 16, 2014

Dear Liz;

Hi yourself!

I got a letter yesterday evening and one tonight with the computer funnies in it. I feel "spolt" (That's Texican for "Spoiled") It's actually in the Funken Wagnal Dictionary for Texicans or people wanting to understand Texicans.

Thank you Liz. I feel like an asshole for requesting an Angel or Indian calendar, I like your choice much better. Actually I've got too much crap on my "to do" list, I don't need no more. My neighbor has got me drawing for his whole family. That's good for me keeping shit in my food locker but I have very little time for what I feel like I need to get done. For example, you mentioned re-typing "Departure 153", that's not really necessary because I want to rewrite it and turn it into a play. I think a "one-act" play. I have a small book that gives me guide lines to go by and I feel like it would make a great theatrical play. The "Writers Market" book I have has a whole section for play scripts.

I asked Megan for an example of her work. She claims to have written several plays she hopes to get into production. I wanted an example of a *finished* play to tailor mine in the proper format. Keep in mind she teaches creative writing. I've sent a couple of pages of the play. She's…umm… creative! That's for sure.

You asked what I do on lockdowns. Well lately I've been drawing, reading, writing, you mostly, and following the football games on Sunday and Mondays. That's after the part where we spend the day getting searched. It's pretty much confined to the cubicle, with limited movement in the dorm. Depending on the cop working. We have one guard for two dorms. Some are hard assed about the lockdown, some don't care as long as we ain't burning the place down or killing each other. I get up early and do my best work drawing in the quiet of the morning. We eat peanut butter sandwiches, hard boiled eggs and whatever meat sandwich they put in the food sack. Most of the sandwiches are made hours before we get them so, more times than not, it's on stale bread. A Top Ramen soup will soften up a hard bread sandwich. I'm fortunate to have plenty.

I'm also the type of person if I've been paid to do something or say I'm going to do something, it nag's me till it's done. I suppose it's a good work ethic. Speaking of which, if I write that play in its proper format would you want to type that up instead of the story? At least I know it would be spelt (I did that on perpose) right. You know you don't gotta. But if you wanna, that's different. Then we'll decide what to do with it.

Oh by the way, that "I Love Lucy" episode with the chocolates is the most requested episode on this planet, and of course I've seen it, who hasn't? Also the one where Lucy dresses up like Superman and get's stuck out on the ledge of her building is one of my personal favorites. What's not to love about Lucy? I think if I could watch vintage TV, I'd watch the old variety shows like Laugh In, Sonny and Cher, Carol Burnett etc. I'm a big "Family Guy" fan but haven't got to watch an episode since I was in hospital. Oh definitely Benny Hill should be in that group too.

What's a "pastie?" Is it like a meat pie with no meat? I mean like an individual serving type pie? At least that's the mental picture I'm getting. It must be a new thing or at least one that became popular since I got locked up. *(Note: I did tell him that Pasties were the staple food for the miners in Wales and became the same for the gold miners in Northern Calif.)*

I'm glad to hear you and Nathan are almost, perhaps all the way over the "crap cold" I recovered from my sore throat and haven't been sick since. I never was that ill. Just a morning thing...*oh – my – God!!* I'm pregnant! What did you do? Yeah *you!* (smiley face) Who else could be responsible? I only talked to you on the phone. I know right when it happened too. It was when I asked you what you were wearing in your bed and you *told* me! "Why, nothing!" Gasp, what are we gonna tell the kids? Okay, I'll stop, but it was fun huh.

Well, I'm gonna go for now. I hope to be off this weekend so brace for impact! I should be calling. Batten down the hatches. Thanks again for the computer funnies, I enjoyed them and I'll let you know if they won't let me have anything you send. Take care and Hi to Nathan.

Bye for now,

Walt xxoo

PS: I have the rest of this play if you wanna see it. I personally can't make heads or tails of it.

****

December 20, 2014

Dear Liz;

I got the Polar Bear card last night. *(Note: I sent him a card with fuzz for fur on the Polar Bear, like his fuzzy wuzzy bear. He still has it)* In fact they skipped me at mail call and came back later. It is by far the coolest Christmas card in the dorm. (no pun intended) Thank you. Rumor is we'll be off lockdown Monday or Tuesday. It looks like I'll call this coming weekend, Christmas Day at the latest. I'm looking forward to it.

I've been getting up at 4:30 am most mornings. Probably because I haven't been doing anything but reading, drawing or amusing myself conversing with the natives. These guys are something else. It is a scientific study in human behavior sometimes and not too flattering a reflection back on the human race or mankind. We can exclude "race" on this one. Perhaps it's the climate but whatever it is I hope it's not contagious. Here's an example: I live in an 80 man dorm and we, each one of us, are confined to our own cubicle due to the lockdown. No one is allowed out of the dorm unless their dying. We can and do roam around the dorm and talk with each other but no one goes anywhere else. But some of these idiots tell you they know when we're coming off lockdown, when we'll be allowed to go to store, when we will be allowed in the day room, chow hall etc. When asked how they know all this they start making shit up. It's really comical. I keep telling them if they predict the same thing everyday eventually they will be right. I usually get the same response every time, "Wuts eventually mean?" I don't let any of it get me down. It is what it is and that's all that it's ever gonna be. We just gotta roll with the punches and make our way best way we can. Sometimes, when it gets tough, we get a little help from those we surround ourselves with.

I'm lucky and blessed you were insane enough to actually encourage me writing back repeatedly, from Bud Plants Service dept, back in '03. I was happy to have found an outlet for my silly stories and extremely grateful for the art books you sent. And to keep me busy while the Appellate courts jerk me around. What developed to what we have now, in my opinion, is a result of us being who we are because I've never "put" on airs just to impress you. If I've done that at all it was a natural response to who I really am, as is my response to you. What does all that mean? Again, how the hell should I know? But I do know I also find myself thinking about you in my day to day activities and look forward to one day wrapping you up in a great big hug and saying "Thanx for being there" which reminds me, how tall are you? *(Note: I'm 5' 3")* Also the computer photo I sent of me isn't very flattering. My mug shot on my prison I.D. is better that that. You can view that if you haven't already by going to www.texasgov.com they'll give you all my prison information. They have an app that, if you click on it, I think it's "parole" they'll reveal my status as far as parole goes. I haven't ever seen it but my neighbor says his sister or ole lady goes there all the time to get info on him. If you're interested, it don't cost nothing.

I ran across the enclosed article and had to smile, then I had to share it with you, especially since we discussed the use of the "F" word. Regarding the card, I keep meaning to change these characters to something other than "Peanuts" and submit the idea to two or three card places in the "Writers Market book." The concept is original I just used the Schultz characters because they were simple and popular. It's a good idea and maybe I'll submit a few cards. I'll do that after I finish my commissions and "Departure 153" the play already started, "BAM Rally #7" (already started) and it's time to pester the courts again. I should take a hard stand and aside from my many, many fans and their letters (you) which I could not neglect even if I wanted to, and why would I want to?

What the hell were we talking about? Oh yeah Christmas music. No wait!, Don't tell me I'll get it. Ummm…I think it has to do with planets or some…oh the hell with it! Okay, except for writing to you I should take the time to finish all my projects and get them where they're supposed to be.

Do you feel like typing up that play? It really shouldn't be very long and I'll have the exact format already laid out. But first I have to finish it.

Okay you, I gotta go. I hope all is well and I'm pretty sure I'll have already called before you receive this so take care and Hi to everyone.

All my best,
Studly

Yeah, I caught the "young stud" comment. You're very cute and charming when you wanna be.

****

December 26, 2014 (Boxing Day)

Dearest Liz;

I'll start letter today and work on it throughout the weekend. Its five thirty p.m. Friday evening. Three thirty p.m. your time (duh, huh?)

Lately I've been going to bed thinking of you and waking up thinking of you also. No more so than Christmas day. I can't believe you used the word "hokey." Is this the English equivalent for "corny?" I'm good with either. It was your "crush on me" revelation on the phone that instigated the use of the word. It also gave me something's to think about. I don't think our affection for each other blossomed overnight. Certain things, in our lives, have restrained these feelings but I think they were there none the less.

One big one I have is this prison thing. While I *still* believe I will prevail over this conviction, at the moment, I am still incarcerated. When I *do* get parole, they will insist I be in Texas. Later I will be allowed to travel and Grass Valley will be at the top of my list of places to visit. In the meantime, outside of these letters and phone calls, I have little more to offer. I have tangible feelings for you and know you do for me. It makes a difference too. But I'm / we are limited to my situation. Even though we've found a way to overcome this for the time being, we're just going to have to go with the flow. I said all that to say, "If I wasn't hindered by fences, razor wire and umpteen million miles between us, I probably would have kissed you by now." Yeah, I'm sure of it. I'm not sure where that would have led but I would have taken the chance you didn't hit me, kick me or back away horrified. "What in bloody hell do you think you're doing?!" Somehow I don't see that happening. It's not outside the realm of possibilities to insist upon a dance lesson to get ahold of you, dip you and then throw a lip lock on you.

That reminds me with all them dogs you have around, when you do your aerobic type exercises do they ever freak out? I've been alone and tried dancing before only to have the house critter panic and try to bite me. Perhaps it's my technique. The only true dance step I ever learned was the "The Vinny," or better known as the "Saturday Night Fever," John Travolta step in the movie.

It's okay unless there's a ceiling fan or low overhead light fixtures. Experience destroying light fixtures or having my hand caught in the ceiling fan has taught me to scope out the dance floor first.

It's now Saturday the 27th and I should be working on that play. I've come to a place where I have to come up with a way to tell the audience about Harry's cancer and his passing. Every other memory is triggered by objects in the shopping bag. I'll figure it out. I may send the first draft off to Professor Megan to get a definite format for a play. This little book I have from Pen American is very vague on playwriting. But I feel this story, as a play, might be the catalyst to get some attention as a writer. Who knows? I ain't one who gives up easy. Just recently I *finally* gave up trying to learn Spanish. Them bean-eatin-taco-bending-greaseballs that were teaching me were steering me wrong. Quite the comics our little South of the border friends are. I use those words loosely.

Anyways, the sun ain't shined since Christmas. I ain't complaining, I prefer the cooler weather. Especially knowing the alternative, in its extremes, is ugly.

Are you going to put together another garden this year? Oh, Happy New Year. A toast! eh hem, clink, clink, clink, "To long underware, short underware too, and the people who wear em" And my New Years Resolution is, to not make any more resolutions.

Okay I'm gonna go. I look forward to talking with you tomorrow. I'll wait to mail this till then in case there's something else I need to say, just in case. Take care and know someone thinks you're special.

Bye for now, love always,
Walt, xxxooo

PS: Elizabeth Anne, how delightful to have spoken with you this Sunday (12/28) morning. I have my neighbor planning a phone call to get you the website info so you can do some investigating. I will include it at the bottom providing everything goes as planned. What a wonderful difference you make in my life. As stated earlier today on the phone it all seems so natural. Perhaps as Edgar Cayse says, "We knew each other in another life and were a couple." Hmmm, could be. Whatever it is, you bring a certain happiness to me that otherwise wouldn't be there, so as you might say to me, thanx Luv.

****

December 29, 2014

Dearest Liz;

This very well may be the last letter of the year that I write. I'm in the middle of making a ten stamp deal that involves a full page drawing someone wants me to do for his ole lady. I gotta take a picture he has and do the person's likeness as a portrait, and then make her have Angel wings. Okay, first off his ole lady looks like a man, so I know he's seeing this picture differently than me. I don't usually do portraits because my interpretation of a picture and someone else's may be different. However, if I take this commission, I want it understood that if he doesn't like the picture, tough shit. He'll get my best attempt and that's that. This should steer him to one of many other portrait artists that are open for business here about. However, none of them do pen work like me. Pencil seems to be the main medium around here. There are few pen and ink artists and even fewer crosshatch artists. You have some fine examples. Perhaps I'll do you another board when I get caught up. I'm actually not doing bad now.

Today is store day for our dorm. All my drawing over the lockdown and up to today has netted me most of the things I need. Stamps is about all I'm short on. And no you can't send em through the mail either. I got a plan. I also got a little mouse card I'm planning to put in here. This is what you're bringing out in me. I'm turning into a big tough cream puff. I've been called worse.

Alright, lets go over this horoscope you sent. First you, Taurus "the tramp?" I thought it was the bull for stubborn. Really though I'd be more attracted to a tramp than a bull. So aggressive (Not really, your comment) can be annoying at times (Never. Your comment) I haven't found you annoying at all. We just talked about kissing in our last letter so it's nice to know Taurus's are good kissers. At least that's what it says. The one trait not mentioned, in my horoscope, is being skeptical so I would have to see for myself. (he drew lips) That might take some convincing, but I'm willin to sit still for it. Most of the other stuff, the caring, good personality, etc I've figured out already. And, I've always found you attractive. Now my horoscope.

Pisces, the partner for life? I ain't never heard that before. Sensitive, yeah, I suppose, thin skinned, but only if I care about you. If I don't like ya you can't get to me without being physically violent. I am too trusting with certain people. I tend to base my trust issues on risk and reward. (Normally) the bigger the reward (whatever that may be) sometimes the easier it is to trust. But there are risks too.

Thank you for the Maxine cartoons. What's not to like, right?

Okay hot lips, I'm gonna go for now. I have a confession to make. I always liked Christi McVie over Stevie Nicks. I liked her singing and her music. Especially "You Make Lovin Fun" I liked her accent too. Right now I'm listening to Mamma Cass Elliot sing "Dream a Little Dream of Me" On that note I'm going to sign off. Take care and thank you for making mail call special for me lately. I'll call you on Wednesday. Bye for now.

Love, your favorite Texican,
Walt xxoo

PS: And no, I don't always have to have the last word, just this time.

****

CPSIA information can be obtained
at www.ICGtesting.com
Printed in the USA
LVHW060315210721
693278LV00006B/158